SUBMARINE DIARY

D0484782

SUBMARINE DIARY

Rear Adm.
Corwin Mendenhall,
USN (Ret.)

■

with an introduction by
Adm. I. J. Galantin,
USN (Ret.)

BLUEJACKET BOOKS

NAVAL INSTITUTE PRESS / ANNAPOLIS, MARYLAND

To my shipmates on
Sculpin and *Pintado*

Copyright © 1991 by Corwin Mendenhall

All rights reserved. No part of this book may be reproduced without written permission from the publisher.

Originally published by Algonquin Books of Chapel Hill.
First Bluejacket Books printing, 1995

Library of Congress Cataloging-in-Publication Data
Mendenhall, Corwin, 1916–
   Submarine diary / by Corwin Mendenhall; with an
introduction by I. J. Galantin.
      ISBN 1-55750-582-9
      1. Mendenhall, Corwin, 1916–   —Diaries.   2. World
War, 1939–1945—Naval operations—Submarine.
3. World War, 1939–1945—Naval operations, American.
4. World War, 1939–1945—Campaigns—Pacific Area.
5. Pacific Area—History.   6. Seamen—United States—
Diaries.   7. United States. Navy—Biography.   I. Title.
D783.M46   1990
940.54′ 51′ 092—dc20   90-40440
02 01 00 99 98 97 96   9 8 7 6 5 4 3

CONTENTS

ILLUSTRATIONS

INTRODUCTION

by Admiral I. J. Galantin, USN (Ret.)

Most accounts of submarine wartime action are told by or about sub skippers who sank the most ships, were most daring, or endured some particularly dramatic experience. This one is different. "Mendy" Mendenhall, now Rear Admiral, USN, Retired, was an ensign in *Sculpin* on the Asiatic station when the Japanese made their devastating attack on Pearl Harbor and brought the United States into World War II. He had not yet completed the study requirements and demonstrated the practical skills required to earn the designation "qualified in submarines." In seven consecutive war patrols in *Sculpin* he held the important job of torpedo and gunnery officer, then joined the submarine *Pintado,* still under construction in Portsmouth Navy Yard. In her he held the critically important post of navigator and executive officer (second in command) for four more patrols in enemy waters. Aspiring to the most demanding and most rewarding of wartime duties—command of a submarine—he was in reach of that goal when the war ended.

This is the background of experience from which Mendenhall tells the story of two submarines in combat against Japan. These ships were at neither extremity of accomplishment, and therefore more typical of submarine combat in general than were their more renowned or less successful sisters. In the homely words of a low-key, matter-of-fact diary covering almost four years, he tells of tedium and furious action, of elation and frustration, of fear and frolic, of joy and sorrow, all factors submariners learn to live with.

Sculpin and *Seawolf* were the first subs to deploy on war patrol from Manila on 8 December 1941 (7 December in Pearl Harbor). Lucius H. Chappell, a soft-spoken, gracious southern gentleman and thoroughly competent submariner, was skipper of *Sculpin* and would take her on eight consecutive war patrols. In time, four other skippers would exceed Lu's number, but no one would do so all in one ship as he did.

Chappell and *Sculpin* (the names of a sub skipper and his boat can be used interchangeably) are an excellent case study of the first U.S. employment of the submarine in war, its use in World War I having been inconsequential. It was not an auspicious start.

As late as 1939 the Commander in Chief Pacific Fleet considered the best use of his subs to be in direct support of fleet operations. Official doctrine stated: "The primary task of the submarine is to attack enemy heavy ships. A heavy ship is defined as a battleship, battle cruiser, or an aircraft carrier. On occasions, the primary task may, by special order, be made to include heavy cruisers, light cruisers, or other types of ships." This was the concept which guided many years of effort to design and produce a "fleet" submarine, one capable of long-range operations that could meet mission requirements. Fortunately, a submarine designed for operations in support of far-ranging, major fleet units was even better able to carry out independent, distant, commerce-destroying operations.

Sculpin, commissioned in January 1939, was one of a class of six boats in the navy's long, frustrating search for the ideal, all-purpose submarine. Those six boats fell short of that goal in at least two major aspects—they had an operating depth of only 250 feet, and their torpedo tubes were limited to four in the bow, four in the stern. Nevertheless, they fought long and hard despite misdirected prewar training and grossly defective torpedoes.

With the receipt of the Navy Department's message, "Execute unrestricted air and submarine warfare against Japan," our submarine skippers were thrust into the harsh, unforgiving realities of war. Their evaluation in peacetime as capable CO's was based more on administrative skills than on proficient, aggressive torpedo attacks. The cleanliness and material condition of his boat; the smart appearance, disciplinary record, and reenlistment rate of his crew; the timeliness and accuracy of paperwork, these were the factors most apparent to his superiors.

Small wonder that, unlike Lu Chappell, many of the skippers who sailed on the early war patrols were found wanting. Deep within enemy controlled waters on his solitary mission, each CO had to devise his own tactics as he weighed the chances of his ship against real or imagined Japanese capabilities. There was no background of U.S. combat experience from which to assess the worth of specific tactics. Peacetime training, especially as the likelihood of war against Japan loomed larger, had stressed unduly the need to remain undetected. At an average age of thirty-seven, keenly aware of their responsibility for the actions and survival of their crew and ship, they were generally overcautious, too fearful of detection by destroyer sonar or aircraft. Too much time was spent deep, hoping to detect targets by sonar, and even too much time at periscope depth in inefficient visual search. As the war progressed younger officers who had fleeted-up to command, and others who had learned from the painful, pioneering efforts of their predecessors, demonstrated that initiative, boldness, and daring in pressing home attack were often more important than concealment.

Still, we should never forget that the skippers who carried the war to the enemy in the lonely, disheartening, early months of war had, in Admiral Nimitz's words, "held the lines against the enemy while our fleets replaced losses and repaired wounds." They had few of the technologic assets that we who came later could exploit, but they did have the one technical advantage that made everything else possible—good quality diesel engines. After years of failure and trial and error, we had evolved two excellent engines, one produced by General Motors, the other by Fairbanks-Morse. They were marvels of performance and reliability. Pushed time and again beyond design limits, they made it possible to go the great distances of the Pacific, to make high-speed runs to close a target, or to evade counterattack.

However, too often after attacks were made they were frustrated by a grossly imperfect weapon. Our Mk-14 torpedo compared to the Japanese Type 95 as follows:

For the U.S.—a 500 lb. warhead propelled by a smoky, wake-producing turbine to a range of 4,500 yds. at 46 knots, or to 9,000 yds. at 31 knots.
For Japan—a 900 lb. warhead propelled at 49 knots to 6,000 yds. by a wakeless, oxygen-fueled engine.

But the Mk-14 did not perform as advertised. Its story deserves the label of major scandal that went too long uncorrected. It had three defects: running too deep, premature explosion, and a faulty contact exploder. Each of these defects hid the existence of the others.

When Lu Chappell and other frustrated skippers complained of torpedoes running under their targets and the Bureau of Ordnance in Washington took no action, the submarine force commanders took matters into their own hands. Running depth was corrected first, then the Mk VI magnetic exploder was discarded, and finally a more reliable contact exploder was designed and installed. It took almost two years of combat before our submarines went to war with effective torpedoes. In my own war patrols in command of Halibut, in late 1943 I sank a ship simply because two torpedoes punched twenty-one-inch holes in the side of a freighter. On another attack we hit the light cruiser Nachi, and she got home with one of our unexploded fish sticking in her side.

Why didn't we discover these flaws in our peacetime exercises? First of all, we never conducted realistic, "warshot" tests that would culminate in explosion of the warhead. Further, for fear of striking our surface ship targets, we set our exercise fish to run deep under them, and "hits" would be deduced from where the exhaust bubbles crossed the target's track.

The only radar our boats had at the start of the war was the SD, air-defense radar. It was not much good, and never relied upon. The SJ, surface-search radar that became available in some boats in August 1942 was excellent, and when the PPI Scope (Plan, Position Indicator) was later added, it was a marvelous tool for night surface torpedo attacks against Japanese convoys and their escorts.

Through its enormous industrial capacity the United States was able not only to expand our submarine force rapidly, but also to introduce refinements as the war progressed. The major improvement was the increase in operating depth to 400 feet. Next in importance I would put the slow-speed, direct drive main motors, which eliminated the noisy reduction gears.

Some wonder why we didn't adopt the snorkel, like the Germans. We didn't need it. In view of the shortcomings in Japanese antisubmarine warfare, particularly in radar, it would have been a costly, time-consuming mistake to install it.

There were numerous lesser improvements in technology: the bathythermograph, evasion devices, better sonars, small homing torpedoes for use against escorts, depth charge indicators, electric torpedoes, heavier gun armament.

Submarine Diary has special significance for me. I was fortunate in May 1943 to be assigned to *Sculpin* as a Prospective Commanding Officer (PCO) on her seventh war patrol. She lacked the refinements of later technological advancements, but her skipper was a tested, respected veteran, and her patrol area an active one. I had made patrols out of Panama in *S-24*, and had had command of *R-11* in Key West, but policy required that before being given command of his own boat in the war zone an officer without combat experience must make a PCO run with a seasoned skipper.

More than once I would hear Mendy, sweating over the primitive torpedo data computer in the control room, call up to Lu Chappell in the conning tower, "Solution looks good, Captain. We can fire when you are ready."

Then I would feel the same rage and helplessness as Lu and his crew when well-executed attacks brought only the retaliation of depth charges as faulty torpedoes betrayed us. The dangers and hard-won rewards of shared war patrols bind more tightly the bond linking all submariners. The terse, wartime announcement that *Sculpin* was "overdue and presumed lost" brought poignant memories of young officers and crewmen with whom I had stood watches and joined in wardroom or messroom fun. One of them, George Brown, would survive battle and prisoner of war camp. When his captain and exec were killed, he was the young reserve officer who succeeded to the last grim duty of command—scuttle ship. Appendix III, his gripping account of *Sculpin's* final action, evokes both pride and humility.

When Mendy was transferred to *Pintado* after seven patrols in *Sculpin*, it was a submariner's dream come true; he was at last in a "thick skin" (400 foot) boat with all up-to-date equipment. *Pintado's* skipper was my competent, tough-minded friend Chick Clarey, who had shown his mettle in difficult patrols in other boats, and would reach the navy's topmost rank. A quirk of fate would bring us all together once more in the far Pacific.

In November 1944, in *Halibut,* I attacked a Japanese convoy near Luzon, and the ensuing depth charge attack severely damaged my ship. Coming to the surface after dark, we groped blindly to renew contact with the other boats in my wolfpack, *Haddock* and *Tuna.* Instead, we found *Pintado,* who shepherded us some 1,500 miles back to Saipan. There I could compare notes with Chick and Mendy to complete the picture of what had so suddenly and devastatingly wrecked *Halibut.*

Pintado carried on to augment an enviable record of ships sunk or damaged. *Sculpin* lies deep in the South Pacific. *Halibut* ended under the shipbreaker's torch. Remembered here, each did her part in service to our country's need in time of danger.

FOREWORD

This is the account of eleven war patrols made aboard two United States fleet submarines, *Sculpin* and *Pintado,* against Japan during the Second World War. As such it covers the entire extent of the undersea war.

During three and one-half years, in seven war patrols by *Sculpin* and four by *Pintado,* we saw the fortunes of the naval war ebb and flow. *Sculpin* was a part of the U.S. Navy's pitifully small Asiatic Fleet in the all but helpless retreat before the enemy as the Imperial Japanese Forces swept southward through the Philippines and into the Malay Archipelago and Indonesia to threaten invasion of the Australian continent. *Sculpin,* and later *Pintado,* were there as the strengthened Allies took the initiative and proceeded to drive the Japanese navy and merchant marine from the oceans, until by mid-1945 what was left of the Japanese seagoing power was bottled up in the home islands and the Sea of Japan.

Much of the submarines' lack of success during the early part of the war was due to defective torpedoes and misguided peacetime training. Great faith was put in the top-secret Mk-VI magnetic exploder for our torpedoes. Supposedly, when the torpedo ran a few feet below the target's keel, the steel hull's magnetic field would activate the exploder. When hostilities began we promptly learned that the torpedo's depth-control mechanism didn't function properly, the exploder didn't work as advertised, the warheads frequently exploded just after they were launched, and a direct hit on an enemy ship often did not detonate the warhead. Yet so wedded was the navy's Washington Bureau of Ordnance, and some of the Submarine Force high command, to the defective weapons that there was a virtual refusal to accept the evidence as reported by submarine captain after captain, with the result that it wasn't until well into 1943, nearly two years after our entry into the war, that United States submarines began receiving effective torpedoes.

Then the underwater onslaught got into high gear and our subs began making significant inroads against the enemy navy and merchant marine. Long before that happened, submarine skippers had learned on the job to disregard prewar submarine doctrine calling for them to be extremely cautious, keep well offshore, and remain submerged at all times during daylight when patrolling hostile territory. The perceived danger of being detected by aircraft called for patrol at 150 feet, using sound (sonar) information to locate and sink ships. Had our submarine skippers been encouraged from the beginning to move in close to shore and aggressively stay on the surface unless actually threatened, the Japanese sweep to the shores of Australia would have been considerably less easily mounted. As it was, the enemy ships moved along the coastline and landed their troops almost unopposed.

Japan entered the war with six million tons of merchant shipping, and added another four million tons from new construction and captured shipping. By V-J day some 2,117 Japanese navy and merchant marine vessels, totaling over nine million tons, had been sunk by American forces, and much of the fewer than two million tons remaining consisted of numerous small wooden vessels operating in the Inland Sea.

No less than 55 percent of the sinkings—5.3 million tons—had been done by U.S. submarines. Our submarines also accounted for more enemy warships sunk than any other naval arm. The magnitude of this effort can be seen when one realizes that *at no point during the war did the number of men in the submarine force ever total more than 1.6 percent of the total navy personnel*. But the cost of this effort was cruelly high. Fifty-two subs were lost from all causes (including training), and in all, 375 officers and 3,131 enlisted men died, out of the 16,000 who actually made war patrols. Some 22 percent of all those who left on patrol aboard submarines—*more than one in every five men*—failed to return, a percentage far in excess of that suffered by any other branch of the armed forces. Having served in eleven such combat patrols, and being one of the lucky ones who came home safely, I wanted to show a sense of what life aboard a wartime submarine was like by describing the day-by-day activities.

The essence of submarine service was silence and secrecy; long stretches of tedium and waiting, interrupted occasionally by brief periods of excitement, terror, and peril. From the standpoint of public visibility and wartime recognition, the role of the submarine navy was scarcely glamorous. When a submarine left Pearl Harbor, Australia, Majuro, or, later in the war, Saipan and Guam, on patrol, it disappeared from view. Although listening for radio directions from headquarters, submarines were rarely heard from or seen again until the patrol was over and the submarine was out of enemy territory. (Later in the war we began patrolling in two- and three-boat wolfpacks, which reduced somewhat the sense of isolation.)

Even a photographic record of sinkings was seldom available, because once a sub launched its torpedoes it was usually forced to dive deep to escape retaliation from Japanese escort vessels and aircraft. When enemy counterattacks were successful, in most instances nothing more was ever heard from the submarine. Eventually, when the sub failed to return from patrol, it was listed as missing in action and presumed lost, and the next of kin of those aboard were notified.

When a submarine was on patrol, it usually operated submerged during the day, in order to avoid detection by Japanese aircraft or ships, and on the surface during the hours of darkness. Most of the crew—those not assigned to bridge watch—might go for weeks within the cramped quarters of the submarine without ever breathing outside air, for only well outside the combat zone could a skipper allow other crew members to take turns coming up to the bridge for some fresh air and a look at the outside world. (It is well established that several of our submarines were sunk by friendly forces.) At all other times, no matter what the circumstances or how dark the night, a submarine must be prepared to dive instantly, for when on the surface it was always lethally vulnerable to sudden attack.

A patrol might go on for weeks without ever encountering an enemy ship. Compared with the living quarters aboard surface ships, the interior of a submarine was extremely cramped, with only the barest minimum of elbow room.

Yet despite—or perhaps because of—the physical and psychological demands of extended undersea duty, morale in the U.S. submarine service was generally very high. For the seven to ten officers and seventy-five to eighty-five crewmen made to coexist within the limited living and working spaces of a submarine for long weeks and months, with no escape or hiding place possible, the barriers and restrictions of rank and grade that normally characterized military service were less in evidence. Life aboard a submarine was more casual, routines and relationships more informal. Many a submarine officer or crewman, having returned from war patrol and gone ashore, found himself abruptly called to attention and censured for failure to salute or for some uniform discrepancy by higher-ups accustomed to strict enforcement of the spic-and-span regulations on shore. It took a special kind of sailor to wear the dolphins insignia that signified "qualified in submarines"—and all those who did took particular pride in doing so.

The narrative that follows, presented in diary form, is the story of personal experience on eleven combat patrols, beginning with the first wartime foray of the *Sculpin* immediately following the outbreak of the war, and ending with the *Pintado* at a time when there was little left for the American submarine fleet to sink, for the Japanese navy and merchant marine were all but destroyed. The story presented here is of United States sailors doing their duty, as that duty was prescribed for them, in the uncommon circumstances of submarine warfare, thousands of miles away from friends and home.

What we saw and did during those years was much like what thousands of other submariners saw and did. Many of those with whom I served did not survive the war. Those of us who eventually came home—and today, almost fifty years after the outbreak of war, we are a rapidly diminishing band—meet regularly to reminisce about those long-ago times. As we reach our waning years, many of us find our thoughts returning to what we once did, and of those who were our companions then. For although war was and is no way for human beings to live, there are times when there is no choice, for a nation and its citizens, but to fight. This book is about one such time. I wanted to tell how it was, both for my own sake and for that of so many others, living and dead, who took part with me.

Benbrook, Texas   Corwin Mendenhall
February 28, 1990

SUBMARINE DIARY

Prologue: Before Pearl Harbor

My own experience in submarines began almost two years after graduation from the United States Naval Academy at Annapolis on 1 June 1939. I served first on the battleship *Mississippi,* where I was a gunnery officer. Late in 1940 the Navy Department asked for applications for submarine school. Although I had originally planned to ask for aviation training, I sent in my request and was ordered to New London, Connecticut, for the submarine class that began the first week of April 1941. Normally the school would have lasted for six months, but because of the ongoing war in Europe, the tense situation in the Pacific, and the rapid expansion of the peacetime navy as the armed services strove belatedly to prepare for hostilities, the curriculum was condensed into three months.

Upon graduation on 28 June I asked for and was ordered to duty in the USS *Sculpin* (SS-191), one of the new "fleet" boats,* with home port at Pearl Harbor. Originally my orders called for me to travel from San Francisco to Honolulu aboard the cruise ship *Matsonia* in company with a dozen or so sub school classmates, but when I arrived in San Francisco on 17 July, I found that my orders had been changed, and instead I went south to San Diego to join *Sculpin* there on 23 July.

The captain of *Sculpin* was Lieutenant Commander Lucius Chappell, USNA '27.** A soft-spoken, slim, handsome gentleman from Georgia, Lucius Chappell was a highly respected and experienced submariner. Officers and crew alike responded confidently to his cool, relaxed leadership. His smile was a trademark. I never once saw him exhibit any temper or nervousness, nor did I ever hear him raise his voice. He seemed perfectly at ease under all circumstances.

The executive officer and navigator, Lieutenant Charlie Henderson, '34,

---

*In the navy, submarines were customarily called "boats." Several explanations have been given, among which was that it was an adaptation from the German term "U-boat."

**Throughout this book, the numbers following officers' names indicate their year of graduation from the U.S. Naval Academy. Before Pearl Harbor almost 100 percent of the submarine officers were graduates of Annapolis.

could be more volatile than the captain, and on occasion his temper flared, but Lucius's example tended to keep Charlie's emotions from getting out of hand. A native of Louisiana, Charlie had an accent that revealed itself if you listened carefully. Although he had a nervous temperament and smoked incessantly, he was not one to second-guess others or to micro-manage the departments aboard ship, unless a problem became apparent. We were given a very free hand in carrying out our responsibilities. Stern and serious in appearance, he was known as "Cheerful Charlie" by the crew.

Lieutenant (jg) Jack Turner, '36, the engineering officer, was a navy junior (his father was a naval officer). Although he was three years ahead of me, we were in the same battalion at the Naval Academy. Jack knew the boat, and in particular the engineering plant, like the palm of his hand. His quiet good humor served to mask an inner tension that revealed itself only when he was under stress as diving officer during torpedo attacks, or when depth charges were going off around us. At such times he would perspire profusely and his face would become very flushed.

The communications and commissary officer, Ensign Bill (Red) Lennox, had also graduated in the class of '34, but the Depression had caused a cutback in officer personnel and he had not been commissioned. Thus he was still an ensign USNR (U.S. Naval Reserve) while his classmates were lieutenants. Red-haired and Irish, he had a happy-go-lucky temperament and relished telling tales about his years in the Civilian Conservation Corps and later with the Standard Oil Company on Aruba. Holding forth in his native New York brogue, he had no hesitation about giving his views concerning upper-level decisions with which he did or didn't agree.

I was the lowest-ranking officer, or "George," aboard *Sculpin* when we left San Diego for Pearl Harbor, and I settled in to learn my jobs as torpedo-gunnery officer and first lieutenant,* and to qualify as officer of the deck (OOD). I also went to work on the rigorous task of becoming qualified in submarines,** which would give me the right to wear the

*The first lieutenant was responsible for the exterior of the ship: maintenance, painting and repair of the superstructure, main deck, conning tower fairwater, the boat, kingpost-boom and winches, anchor and ground tackle, and the mooring lines.

**For the designation qualified in submarines a person had to be able to operate any piece of equipment from the forward torpedo room to the after torpedo room and explain the function and purpose of that equipment or system. He had to be able to function in any position on the ship, load and fire a torpedo, start and stop an engine, operate the controls in the maneuvering room, and stand watch in any position in the control room. And, he was required to prepare a notebook with sketches and descriptions of the hydraulic system, the fuel system, the high pressure air system, the battery and electrical system, and the golden dolphins, the submarine pin. (Officers wore the gold pin, enlisted men the silver pin.)

In October, Submarine Squadron 2 (SubRon 2), our squadron, got secret orders to leave Pearl Harbor and proceed to the Philippines, where we were to become part of the Asiatic Fleet commanded by Admiral T. C. Hart, '97, father of my classmate Tom Hart. Just as we were leaving the dock, a new officer, Ensign Emmett Mills, USNR, jumped aboard to become George and took on the duties of assistant communications officer. This was welcome help for Red Lennox, for there was a stream of radio messages coming day and night, in code, and the job of deciphering was constant. The rest of us helped when we had time.

SubRon 2 went west as a group, with our tender, *Holland,* like Mother Goose, leading her two divisions of submarines in columns, keeping station and performing destroyerlike fleet maneuvers as we plodded across the western Pacific toward Asiatic waters, conducting Morse code and semaphore signal drills, practice dives and other exercises as we went. Despite the evidence of the German U-boat campaign against England, prewar submarine doctrine still envisioned the function of the submarine principally as an extended arm of the battleship navy, designed primarily to operate against the Japanese battle fleet.

When we arrived in the Philippines we settled in to operate out of the Manila Bay–Cavite Navy Yard complex, continuing training exercises as we had done at Pearl Harbor. The schedule generally called for being at sea for seven to ten days, followed by a similar period of routine upkeep, repairs, and shore liberty. We practiced torpedo firings, gunnery, held qualification runs, and acted as a target ship for antisubmarine exercises. Off duty in Manila I joined the Army-Navy Club, played tennis, swam, went to jai-alai games, and generally enjoyed myself. My Filipino classmate at the Naval Academy, Carlos (Charlie) Albert, lived in Manila and was serving in the Navy Branch of the Philippine Constabulary. We spent much time together. Several times I asked Charlie to meet me at the club for dinner, but he always declined. It wasn't until later that I realized that natives, even Annapolis graduates like Charlie Albert, were ineligible to join the Army-Navy Club or to be there as guests; the ethos of colonialism was very much alive.

On Sunday, 7 December—we were west of the international date line, and it was still Saturday, 6 December back home and in Hawaii—I flew

---

emergency systems, including escape procedures. Having become proficient in the above requirements, he then was subjected to a hands-on walk through the boat to demonstrate that he really knew the practical aspects of the material.

with an Army Air Corps friend, First Lieutenant Karl Lichter, in an executive Beechcraft to the resort town of Baguio, about 130 miles north of Manila, to pick up the Philippine secretary of state, Mr. Vargas, who had been conferring with the Philippine president and the U.S. high commissioner. I piloted the plane from the copilot's seat for much of the way and was able to take a number of photographs of the exceptional scenery. After returning, I left the undeveloped film in my locker at the Army-Navy Club; then we met Charlie Albert and went to dinner and the jai-alai games. As Charlie dropped me off to catch a water taxi back to my ship about midnight, he reminded me once again not to forget his birthday a few days later.

I never got to the party, nor did I ever get back to the club to collect that undeveloped film.

Sculpin's First Patrol

(8 December 1941–22 January 1942)

8 December 1941, Monday   Shouts of "Gunner's mate! Gunner's mate! Where the hell is that gunner?" jolted us awake as the general alarm brought the crew to battle stations at 0345, sleepily pulling on trousers as we answered the call. The source of the abrupt wakeup was the exec, Charlie Henderson, shouting and rushing, in his skivvy shorts, to the control room, then to the forward torpedo room. He was looking for Gunner's Mate 1/c Joe (Gunner) Caserio to have him break out the machine guns, unlock the magazines, get ammunition topside, and man the guns for antiaircraft defense. Thus began a long, frenzied, confusing, uncertain, bewildering day.

That's how *Sculpin* learned that war with Japan had begun. Our Pearl Harbor Day was 8 December because we were west of the international date line, moored to a buoy behind the breakwater in Manila Bay with our tender, *Holland,* moored nearby.

The evening before, the captain, Lucius Chappell, along with Executive Officer Charlie Henderson, Chief Engineer Jack Turner, and Emmett Mills, had gone to a favorite gambling joint hoping to win a fortune. They had arrived back aboard well after midnight and were very sound asleep when the excitement began.

During the late minutes of the midwatch Signalman Striker* Keith Waidelich, the duty signalman on the bridge, read a visual "All Stations Alert!" light from the tower at Cavite and astutely called Quartermaster 3/c Art Jay to back him up in reading the signal. They copied an urgent plain-language message addressed to all ships and stations: JAPAN HAS ATTACKED PEARL HARBOR X GOVERN YOURSELVES ACCORDINGLY.

Jay immediately took the message to Charlie. The exec was notoriously hard to wake. He was too sound asleep to realize what Jay wanted and

---

*A striker was a seaman or fireman who was working toward a rating; thus, a seaman who was working toward the rate of third class signalman was called a signalman striker, or a fireman who aspired to become a third class electrician was termed an electrician striker.

told him several times to go away and come back in the morning. Jay retreated to the control room, puzzling over what to do next, then decided to make another pass at him. This time he told the exec that the message was urgent and proceeded to read it to him in a loud voice. That cleared Charlie's sleepy brain. His first thoughts were of air defense. He alerted the captain, sounded the general alarm, and began looking for Gunner Caserio.

Gunner promptly had ammunition broken out and machine guns manned. My torpedomen commenced readying the "fish" and made preparations to receive eight more from *Holland* to give us a full load of twenty-four Mk-14s. At the same time we also began loading stores; spare parts and other needs were ordered and brought aboard as they arrived, while gun crews were topside at their machine guns in case of an air raid.

To the tune of Manila's wailing air raid warnings, *Sculpin* hurried to an anchorage outside the breakwater, ready to submerge and lie on the bottom if there were a bombing attack.

At 1000 we moved to pier 7 and topped off the tanks with fresh water and diesel fuel from the tanker *Pecos;* then we moved back outside the breakwater. Several men, including two torpedomen, were sent to the Cavite Shipyard for parts and materials. By 1500 *Sculpin* had stripped ship of all secret, confidential, or restricted matter except for the few publications that were absolutely essential, and was loaded with everything that we could get in Manila. I reported to Charlie that my departments were ready for patrol, and shortly thereafter the captain went to *Holland* for instructions.

The captain returned at 1600 with verbal orders from Commander Submarines Asiatic Fleet (CSAF) to get under way immediately and go on patrol. He was directed not to tell anyone the location of the *Sculpin*'s patrol area until we were outside Manila Bay, well into the South China Sea. We saw no air raids before we left Manila. The men who were manning the machine guns spoke boldly of being disappointed at not seeing even one Jap plane to shoot down.*

At 1700 *Sculpin* met *Seawolf*, seaplane tender *Langley*, and tankers *Pecos* and *Trinity* off Sangley Point and stood west toward Corregidor.

---

*Radio messages received on 9 and 10 December told of raids that devastated Cavite Shipyard, mortally wounded *Sealion*, holed sub tender *Canopus*, and wiped out Clark Field. Admiral Hart, anticipating possible hostilities, had already dispersed most of the Asiatic Fleet, but General MacArthur not only failed to heed the warnings but ignored even the 7 December attack on Pearl Harbor and inexplicably allowed the Army Air Corps to be destroyed on the ground at Clark Field.

Ships were darkened and there were no navigation lights on shore. It was an eerie feeling, and it seemed even more threatening and ominous because of the uncertainties, confusion, sudden change of conditions, and our lack of knowledge of what was going on. We passed through the controlled minefields off Corregidor without appropriate charts or piloting instructions, following our leader *Langley*. *Langley* freely used general signals, unaware that we had, in stripping ship, left most of our usual classified publications on the *Holland* and couldn't read them. The captain just ignored the signals, hoping that they weren't important. *Langley*'s captain was probably thinking, "Those stupid submariners! Why don't they answer my signals?" As soon as we were past Corregidor and in the South China Sea, *Langley* dismissed *Sculpin*, fortunately in plain language, to proceed independently.

While we were passing through the area of the minefields a loud thumping was reported on the port side of the after torpedo room, whose crewmen swore that the port propeller guard must have struck one of the mines. They were shaken up.

Safely out of Manila Bay and moving south in the South China Sea, *Sculpin* made her trim dive, one of the first items of business for a submarine on leaving port. The dive was necessary to adjust the weight of the submarine to a condition of neutral buoyancy so the sub could submerge and the diving officer could keep the sub at the desired depth with little or no headway. Technically, the submarine was supposed to weigh exactly the weight of the water it displaced, but while in port, many changes might be made in the weight of the submarine: fuel and water tanks were filled, stores and supplies were taken on, personnel changes were made, torpedoes were loaded or off-loaded, and equipment was removed or installed. Although the chief engineer maintained a record of these changes and compensated for them before getting under way, his compensation needed verification with an actual dive.

The compensation was made through a system consisting basically of a forward trim tank, an after trim tank, and an auxiliary tank located near the center of the boat. By pumping sea water between these tanks and from or to the sea, the diving officer could reach a condition of neutral buoyancy where the boat would stay put, like a balloon, with no need to use speed or control planes to maintain the desired depth.

After an hour below the surface Jack Turner was satisfied with the trim, other checks were completed, and *Sculpin* surfaced. The captain then called the officers to the wardroom to tell us where we were bound: we were to go southeast, by way of Verde Island Passage and San Bernardino

Strait, between the islands of Luzon and Samar, to an area fifty miles square, about fifty miles east of Lamon Bay, Luzon. We were to be submerged from one hour before sunrise until one hour after sunset, remaining undetected and maintaining radio silence in accordance with long-established peacetime submarine patrol doctrine. Once we got to our area it would be unrestricted warfare. No friendly ships would be in our patrol area, so we were cleared to attack any other ships that we saw.

9 December   Being so suddenly immersed in a war patrol routine—under radio silence, submerged all day and on the surface at night—was a very different world for us. *Sculpin*'s air conditioning was not at all efficient, particularly in the humid tropical climate. Showers were closed to conserve water. We depended on the exhaust heat of the diesel engines to distill whatever fresh water was made, and the water was more important for the battery and for cooking than for cleaning people. The boat took on even more of that peculiar submarine smell of diesel fuel, cigarette smoke, cooking odors, paint, and human aroma.

After a few days the captain ordered only limited smoking while submerged. We nonsmokers vigorously agreed with that order, although no smoking at all would have been much better. We were reminded of how thoughtful the limited no smoking was when the boat abruptly filled with smoke after the smoking lamp was lit about fifteen minutes before surfacing each evening. It was a while before we became hardened to our living conditions; and my, did that fresh air smell sweet when *Sculpin* surfaced after a day underwater!

After a particularly oppressive day when we ran submerged, an air suction could be taken through the boat to clear the atmosphere. This was accomplished by opening the forward torpedo room escape hatches and all the compartment doors between the engine rooms and the forward torpedo room. Because our diesel engines required quantities of oxygen, starting one up sucked a hurricane of air through the boat, purging the foul air. Hatches and doors needed to be open for only a few seconds to do the job. Papers, trash, loose clothing, and odds and ends were caught up in the rush of air to the engine rooms.

One aspect of diving procedure that bit the dust early in the war had to do with the use of the main ballast tank flood (kingston) valves, large valves located at the bottom of the main ballast tanks. Cautious peacetime safety procedure was to run on the surface with kingstons closed. Standard diving procedure called for kingstons to be opened as the boat submerged. If the kingstons weren't opened, there was no way for seawater to fill the ballast tanks and allow the submarine to submerge. A submarine on war patrol, however, needed to be able to submerge with the least amount of delay. So right away *Sculpin* ran with the kingstons always open (termed "riding the vents"). There was also the possibility that a malfunction would not allow the kingstons to open, or that they would open too slowly, impeding the dive.*

It was imperative that *Sculpin* make as much headway as possible at night on the surface, because the currents in the straits would be against us in the daytime, and our submerged speed of three knots was so slow that we could easily lose some of our forward progress. When on the surface *Sculpin* ran at full speed on two engines, with the other two charging batteries. As the batteries were charged, engines were shifted to propulsion, so that before long we were running along on all four engines, giving a speed of fifteen to eighteen knots in a moderate sea. The tide tables for San Bernardino Strait predicted an eighteen-hour flood tide against us commencing at 0830 on 10 December. The captain was determined to clear the strait before that time in order to arrive on station as promptly as possible.

We sighted many small craft and fishing boats, day and night, among the many islands and in the passages between the islands. In the daytime several ships' masts and stacks, smoking heavily, were observed through the periscope, but they all passed too far away for identification. I was surprised that most of the ships advertised their presence with so much smoke.

The fathometer (depth finder) quit working, and the electronics technicians concluded that the fathometer head, located on the ship's keel, was flooded. Repairs would have to wait until we got back to port.

The sonar watch kept reporting noises that were diagnosed as coming from the deck superstructure. On the surface after dark the captain stopped the boat, and Gunner Caserio and I went topside to investigate. The gangway gripes had worked loose, and the gangway was vibrating in our flow stream. It took only about fifteen minutes to secure the gripes.

The captain was concerned that the boat might be forced to dive while we were on deck, so we carried survival gear—sidearms, knives, and watertight flashlights—and were prepared to stay afloat in our life jackets until our "home" could come back and pick us up. If it did not, we might have to swim to a nearby island.

---

*The kingston valves were eliminated altogether on the newer submarines. The new boats "rode the vents" all the time.

10 December *Sculpin* made it through San Bernardino Strait ahead of the flood tide and continued, submerged, toward the patrol area. At 1000 I was on watch as diving officer. When I made a sweep with the periscope I saw masts on our port bow, and we went immediately to battle stations. Everyone was keyed up. On closing, the ship proved to be flying the Stars and Stripes, so we secured from battle stations and continued on our way. The object of our attention proceeded into Albay-Legaspi, Luzon.

At 1800 *Sculpin* reached the fifty-mile-square patrol area, and we surfaced after sunset for the night. The weather was miserable, with overcast skies, intermittent rainsqualls, and rough seas.

The first few days under way had been a period of getting accustomed to being submerged all day and on the surface at night. The captain instituted his plan of encouraging everyone not on watch to relax and sleep during the day and do their work at night. That would quiet the ship for the underwater sound equipment, reduce the depletion of oxygen in the air, and cut the rate of air pollution from various sources such as cooking, diesel oil, and tobacco smoke. At nightfall we had our breakfast on the surface. Lunch was at midnight, and dinner was at daybreak, just before we submerged for the day. Snacks and sandwiches were always available in the galley, especially for watch standers. This reversal of activity was called "reversa" by the crew, and we all came to know well what "going into reversa" meant.

A routine problem requiring attention every time a submarine surfaced after a prolonged dive was the buildup of air pressure in the boat caused by leaks from the air banks and from other pneumatic sources such as torpedoes and torpedo tubes, venting negative tank, or just from the rise in temperature inside the boat. Before we surfaced at the end of a long day under, the air compressors would be run to draw down the pressure and charge the air banks. If the excess pressure over atmospheric was not removed before opening the hatch, the abrupt release of the volume of air under pressure would slam the conning tower hatch wide open, and possibly blow a man through the suddenly opened hatch, breaking bones or cracking a skull.

Sculpin's radio setup was such that we couldn't cover both the submarine FOX schedule and get press news as well, so radio copied the submarine traffic. All traffic was in Morse code. When the opportunity presented, John Ludwig, RM2/c, and Bill Logan, RM3/c, who could copy the press stations very well, got whatever news they could. From those messages we attempted to piece together the war and figure out what was going on with our sister submarines, the war in Asiatic waters, and the world in general. Emmett Mills had the job of decoding much of the coded traffic, and his eyes were about to give out from so much close work and strain.

The Japanese wasted no time in jamming the fleet radio broadcasts. *Sculpin* was too far away to pick up NPG Radio San Francisco or NPM Radio Honolulu; our station was NPO Radio Manila. The jamming caused copying errors and made messages difficult to decode. The errors didn't fit the code, so Emmett and Red Lennox did a lot of imaginative guessing.

We eagerly anticipated news of the arrival of the U.S. fleet to defeat and drive back the Japanese. Fragments of Japanese claims of sinking two battleships, ten cruisers, and one aircraft carrier at Pearl Harbor were picked up by the radio gang but were discounted by our wardroom "experts." By now nearly everyone on board was a self-proclaimed master at reading the significance of any nuance that might be perceived in the official radio messages. *Sculpin*'s "war council" reached a consensus that CSAF and General MacArthur expected the Japanese to land on the east coast of Luzon. *Sculpin* was placed in a position to oppose such landings. But why, then, were we stationed so far offshore?

To our dismay, radio messages told of successful Japanese landings on the China Sea side of Luzon at Lingayen Gulf. Our submarines there had not been very effective in opposing the landings. Reports of their torpedo attacks told of misses despite near perfect setups, of fish running hot, straight, and normal but not exploding. Our analysis on board *Sculpin* concluded that the fish must be running too deep, passing so far beneath the target that the super-secret Mk-VI magnetic exploders were not triggered by the magnetic field of the target ship. The captain instructed me to set the depth controls in the fish to a shallower depth than doctrine called for. As more and more reports came in concerning nonexploding torpedoes, the captain kept having me adjust the depth controls shallower and shallower. Finally our fish were set to run essentially on the surface.

11 December Seas were so rough that *Sculpin* didn't come up to periscope depth each hour for a visual check. When we surfaced after sunset, we received orders to proceed to Lamon Bay on the east coast of Luzon, then to go through Polillo Strait and set up a patrol covering both ends of Alabat Island, the two entrances to inner Lamon Bay.

Our exec-navigator, having been unable to get a navigational fix for several days, was far from confident of *Sculpin*'s position. The weather was terrible as we headed west toward the coast, navigating by fleeting glimpses of islands, with inadequate charts and no fathometer. Leadsmen Caserio and Waidelich, taking soundings on the bow, kept reporting "no bottom," which pleased the captain and pilot Charlie Henderson. Land sightings were impossible to identify with any accuracy, and lead-line readings were of little value in the uncertainty of *Sculpin*'s location.

Charlie's nervous temperament came out. He fidgeted as he chain-smoked his cigarettes, letting them hang down from his lower lip as he worked, the ashes falling on his navigation charts and calculations at the control room chart table. His prominent Adam's apple seemed to bounce up and down when he was excited or nervous.

It was a strenuous night as we felt our way to the coast. Finally, at dawn, *Sculpin* submerged, and Charlie, exhausted, hit his bunk, feeling that he had our position well established in Polillo Strait.

I relieved Red Lennox at 0745 for the forenoon watch as diving officer. He advised me that it was still raining hard and pointed out on the chart several prominent spots on nearby land that established our position. I took periscope bearings between the heavy rainstorms and confirmed his fix.

At 1000 I went to the periscope for a routine position check. The weather had cleared some by then, and I saw land on three sides of us—in the wrong places. We were in deep trouble! Ordering "right full rudder" to reverse course, I called the captain, Charlie, and Red. Piecing the new information together, Charlie determined our actual position to be forty miles north of where he had thought we were. We were inside Baler Bay! Luck was surely with us as we proceeded out of the bay and then south toward Alabat Island. That night *Sculpin* reached the real Polillo Strait.

On the surface at night there was always work going on. Maintenance and repair of equipment was a never-ending job. The engine rooms, with their many elements of diesel and supporting equipment, auxiliaries, torpedoes, electrical, radio, sonar, and electronic maintenance, kept everyone busy. Cooks, mess cooks, and stewards would no sooner clean up the galley, crew's mess, and wardroom than it was time to set up for the next meal.

Training periods and submarine qualification sessions were fitted into the schedule. No one had time hanging heavily on his hands. One way or another we were occupied twenty-four hours each day, standing watches, eating, sleeping, working, and learning, with a few minutes sandwiched in for a game of cards, acey-deucey, cribbage, reading, or just talking among ourselves.

12–20 December   These were uneventful days spent watching the entrances to Lamon Bay. Doctrine called for fleet submarines to stay outside the 100-fathom curve. Unfortunately, this prevented us from going in close enough to cover the entrances effectively. *Sculpin* was just too far away, and there was plenty of room for Japanese ships to follow the coastline into the bay, well out of our view. During the daytime, between the rainstorms, we could see the jungles of Luzon and the Alabat Islands through the periscope; and at night some lights on fishing boats and on shore were visible. Although all navigation lights had been ordered extinguished, Tailon Light on Alabat Island was still burning.

The green jungle and palm trees coming down to the water's edge contrasted nicely with the mountains in the background and the blue water foreground. I thought how pleasant it would be to go ashore for a bit of exploring and a bath. No one had had a bath since we left Manila on the eighth.

I practiced a night watch habit first developed when I was officer of the deck (OOD) on the *Mississippi*. To help relieve boredom and to make the time pass faster, I would locate stars and constellations. Each night I would study the star chart before going on watch, then later on the bridge, visibility permitting, I would pick out a particular constellation and at least one star by name in the constellation. By repeating that procedure regularly, adding more and more constellations and stars, with seasonal changes and ship movements to northern and southern latitudes, I was by now familiar with twenty-seven constellations and could locate many more stars than that. Such knowledge of star locations would be invaluable when I became navigator.

One morning Chief Engineer Jack Turner appeared for dinner slicked up with a clean shave and fresh clothing, smelling of scented soap and cologne, with a big smile of self-satisfaction on his face. He was immediately accused of cheating on the closed shower order. His explanation was that while OOD the night before, he had anticipated a rainstorm, took soap and towel to the bridge, and indulged in a refreshing bath. So, a few nights later, not having had a real bath in three weeks, I tried Jack's technique, only to have the rain stop just when I was thoroughly lathered up. The sight of a soap-covered OOD standing his watch in the buff, the binoculars around his neck and a beard his only covering, drew snickers and remarks from the quartermaster and the lookouts. Fortunately another rainstorm soon came along to provide the needed rinse.

Many of us were short of clothes, not having had the opportunity before we left Manila to pick up bundles of laundry that were at the officers' club, or even the dirty clothes in the *Holland* laundry. We fully expected to return, collect our clean laundry, and clean out our club lockers. I had left my watch, class ring, camera, some money, film, and tennis gear in my locker.

On 19 December sonar reported ship's screw noises, but nothing could be seen by periscope. The noises persisted and we followed them for some time. The captain decided that there must be a submarine out there and was considering firing torpedoes. Then the noise suddenly stopped.

Next the air conditioning, inefficient as it was, quit. Auxiliaryman Ernest Baldwin, sweating more profusely than the rest of us, worked feverishly to get it back into operation. Fortunately he had the trouble corrected in a few hours, but the added odor and heat left the boat even more inhospitable.

Baldwin noticed that a great deal of condensation produced by the air conditioning systems was draining into the bilges to be pumped overboard. Why not save that water for use by the crew? He rigged containers under the drain and began collecting twenty or so gallons per day, which was doled out for washing clothes. Some even took sponge baths with the condensate. The water did pick up an odor from the boat's air and was therefore not the most desirable liquid, but, like many of the conditions in the submarine, we learned to accept it.

Leakage of freon gas from the refrigeration and air conditioning systems was excessive. Baldwin's auxiliary team gave the systems a careful inspection, and the many small leaks were repaired by silver soldering. There was, however, a major leak in the number 2 air conditioning unit that would require tender or yard assistance to repair, and number 2 unit was shut down to conserve freon.

Emmett Mills had come aboard with little navy training. He had not gone to sub school, and his lack of training limited the work that he could do. Emmett was still standing assistant OOD watches, working to qualify for top watch. Although Red Lennox was pleased to have him as his assistant for all the decoding that was required, Emmett's lack of training elicited the unkind remark from Red that he was about as helpful as a plebe at Annapolis, and he began calling Emmett "Middie." Others of us picked up the nickname, and it stuck. Before long even the captain was regularly calling him Middie.

The beard-growing competition that Red Lennox and I began when we left Manila was producing some unexpected results in the fuzz on our faces. Red's beard was more brown than red, and mine was more red than blond. Each of us was determined to continue the contest to the bitter end. A number of the crew were also growing beards. Charlie Henderson, Jack Turner, and Middie tried, then gave up the challenge.

21 December   Impatient for action and excitement, *Sculpin* received orders to proceed to the north coast of Luzon and take over the station in the Babuyan Channel just vacated by *Seawolf*. The exec mentally thanked the lightkeeper at Tailon Light, who still hadn't gotten the word to extinguish all navigation aids, for giving him a fine departure point to the new station.

Radio reports indicated that there had been Japanese landings at Aparri, on the extreme north coast of Luzon, and that the Japanese were using an airfield there. We all hoped for some action. The wardroom war council speculated that we were being moved north so that we might be available to go into the China Sea and on to Lingayen Gulf if the five boats on the west side of Luzon needed reinforcements. We were eager to see what developed.

Wardroom discussions centered on the very limited ability of a submarine to cover the large area of water that we were expected to cover. The upper prism of the periscope, raised two feet above the water surface, had a horizon of only 1.6 nautical miles, or about 3,322 yards. Speed submerged was very slow; we could do three knots all day, or ten knots for a half-hour burst. On the surface *Sculpin* was pushed to make eighteen knots in a smooth sea. In an emergency the black gang (navy slang for the engine room crew) could squeeze out about twenty knots for a short time before the plant became too overloaded. We had no radar, the sonar was not that reliable, and, according to the radio messages, torpedoes were not working as expected. With all those limitations, we were doing our best.

22 December   The code books for encoding and decoding messages were constantly in use. A flood of radio traffic would come in during the night when we were on the surface, and every officer not on watch or working with his troops would pitch in to help Red and Middie break them down. That work always extended into the boat's submerged time. When not in use the code books were locked in a safe located under the washbasin in the captain's cabin.

Middie was reluctant to open the safe when the captain was sleeping, so he decided to hide the code books in the wardroom. This worked fine until Charlie Henderson happened to stumble onto Middie's hiding place. Charlie hid the code books in another place without telling Middie.

The books were soon needed, and Middie couldn't find them. He searched the whole of officers' country and asked everyone if we had any idea where the books were before Charlie finally showed him where to find them. A general court martial for Middie was the subject of teasing discussions for several days.

23 December   My twenty-fifth birthday. We spent the day en route to the Babuyan Channel.

As we headed north the weather improved and there was much more phosphorescence in the water than we had seen before. Cruising along at night, stirring up all that light, we felt quite conspicuous. There were frequent masses of light that flashed on and off like a giant underwater searchlight. At times there were smaller flashes all around the boat, which we speculated were stirred up by big schools of fish moving away as we ran through them.

24 December   Christmas Eve. *Sculpin* arrived in the Babuyan Channel and commenced her new patrol assignment. We had been ordered away from Lamon Bay three days too soon. Radio reports said that the Japanese made a strong landing right where we had been watching for so many days.

During breakfast the captain discussed his plan to move in to the coast, to Aparri town, and see what was going on there.

25 December   No significant activity could be seen at Aparri or at the nearby airfield. Fresh water flowing into the sea from the mountains beyond Aparri had a strange impact on *Sculpin*'s submerged trim. One minute the boat was heavy, then the next minute the trim showed too light, keeping the diving officer on his toes. The water itself was chocolate brown.

Jack Turner was the only person in the wardroom who received a Christmas box. Helen had sent him a phonograph and a number of records, which we all enjoyed. Some were current hit tunes and some were classical: "Would that I Could Kiss Your Hand," "Daddy," "Oh Babe," "Siboney," "I Want My Momma," Strauss waltzes, Beethoven's "Moonlight Sonata," and rumbas by Xavier Cugat.

Red Lennox and Chief Stew Burner (cook) Duncan Hughes outdid themselves with Christmas dinner. The choices were ham with pineapple sauce, baked chicken, green peas, steamed rice with giblet gravy, pickles, lemonade, fresh rolls, and both mince and pumpkin pies. Dinner was served at midnight, reversa schedule.

The weather kicked up with high winds, heavy seas, and driving rain, causing uncomfortable surface conditions and difficult depth control, compounded by the fresh water coming from the mountain streams near Aparri.

26 December   The captain surprised us by opening a box that his wife, Marian, sent him for Christmas. He waited until the twenty-sixth, he said, because that was the twenty-fifth at home. There were fun things in the box for all the officers except Middie, who Marian didn't know about when she packed the presents. My present was a baby rattle, since she thought that I was the junior officer on board.

In the morning Red sighted a small merchant ship heading north out of the port of Aparri, but it was too far away for us to close and attack. We saw several large columns of smoke on land east of Aparri.

27 December   The days were flashing by much more rapidly than before. I was becoming hardened to our living conditions and no longer missed bathing. Not knowing what was going on in the outside world was bothersome. We followed the official radio messages with deep interest and tried to guess what was taking place based on the various orders. A newspaper would have been most welcome.

28 December   Floatable trash had been accumulating since leaving Manila, and it had become a storage headache. The captain decided to dump the trash, so we took time to proceed well up toward Calagan Island, counting on the pronounced northwest current either to beach the trash on the islands or to sweep it clear toward Formosa. It was tossed overboard, a welcome riddance.

29 December   Radio traffic told that CSAF had left Manila in *Swordfish* and was heading for Darwin, Australia. The Japanese must have taken over the island of Luzon. But we were still getting messages from NPO radio, Manila. How long would that continue? I worried about my friends Karl Lichter, Spud Sloan, Chuck Osborne, Ole Jensen, Boots Hall, Margie Kiser, and, of course, Charlie Albert. What had become of them?

30 December *Sculpin*'s war council debated what the U.S. submarine war strategy would be. Where would we operate from? How would our operations be conducted? It was a very long distance from Hawaii or Australia to the Philippines or Japan. The torpedomen joked that routine maintenance would wear the fish out before we ever got to fire one.

31 December In the morning five small motorboats, in rough column, were sighted headed north from Aparri. They were not suitable targets for a fish.

During my forenoon diving officer watch I added up the entries in the diving book and found that since leaving Manila we had been underwater for 315 hours and had traveled 828 nautical miles while submerged.

From the radio we learned that a very large force of Japanese ships was at Davao Gulf, Mindanao, in *Skipjack*'s area. *Tarpon* had been badly damaged in a typhoon off Lamon Bay, our old area, and was limping south. We had suffered the force of that storm off Aparri but weathered it better than *Tarpon*.

1 January 1942 *Sculpin*'s war council was suggesting to the captain that he propose to CSAF that *Sculpin* move back to our previous area off Lamon Bay. There seemed to be more going on there, at least from our reading of the radio messages.

The captain's evaluation of the situation, after he discussed things with his officers, was as follows:

1. In ten days of patrol in the Babuyan Channel nothing of consequence had been sighted.

2. Close scrutiny of Aparri had failed to indicate any shipping anchored offshore or any air activity. Although the inner harbor couldn't be investigated from sea, the *Coast Pilot* and charts showed that only minor shipping could be accommodated there.

3. No recent reports indicated any enemy activity at Aparri. On the other hand, there were indications that Lamon Bay might be building into an important enemy base.

4. The enemy had bridgeheads much nearer and more convenient to the scene of hostilities than Aparri, hence it might be assumed that Aparri had decreased in importance.

5. Our information indicated that of all our submarines, *Sculpin* was nearest to Lamon Bay.

Knowing from the earlier radio messages that CSAF was at sea in *Swordfish*, the captain sent a radio message, requiring no answer if approved, stating that unless disapproved, *Sculpin* was proceeding to fill the void left by *Tarpon* and patrol the entrances to Lamon Bay.

2 January   We received no message of disapproval from CSAF, so *Sculpin* said goodbye to Aparri and headed east around Cape Engano, then south for Lamon Bay. The weather remained bad. The heavy seas created by gale-force winds were characterized by the captain as the worst he had ever experienced. Submerged during daylight, *Sculpin* held a depth of 100 feet, listening with the sonar but not attempting to go to periscope depth for visual sweeps. The sea was just too rough for that.

Soundmen reported noises several times, and we hoped that there were Japanese ships nearby, but nothing developed. The noises, the captain, Charlie, and Jack decided, were being generated by something loose in the superstructure.

3 January   Rough weather continued to delay our movement south. Tossing about in the heavy seas, not able to make much headway, and with our submerged speed of three knots, we were getting nowhere very fast.

Work on my submarine qualification notebook was progressing slowly. The sketches took a great deal of time. With watches, work, school, eating, and a little sleeping, there wasn't much time for the notebook.

4 January   The weather finally moderated, *Sculpin* surfaced, and Gunner went on deck to locate the source of the noise. The gangplank had been smashed by the seas and the jack halyard had broken loose and was dangling against the side of the ship. The gangplank was jettisoned and the halyard secured. When we submerged, sonar no longer picked up the noises.

We turned up a box of games that had been given to *Sculpin* by the Coca-Cola Company. It contained several chess sets. A lively competition developed between Charlie, Jack, Middie, and me. Torpedomen from the forward torpedo room saw the games in progress in the wardroom and asked what we were playing. They had no idea how to play chess, so I proceeded to teach them.*

---

*It wasn't long before chess became a favorite of the forward torpedo gang. Then Shadow Alderman took the game to the after torpedo room and competition began back there. I

5 January   *Sculpin* arrived off Polillo Channel and commenced patrol of the entrances to Lamon Bay. We had been on patrol for almost one month without firing a torpedo.

My concept of what a submarine did on war patrol had been arrived at from movies of German U-boat actions in World War I. By those standards, we should be dashing about, sinking ships daily, leading the swashbuckling life portrayed in motion pictures. In actuality, we went for weeks on end without seeing anything to shoot at.

The routine on board a submarine could become monotonous, especially for the crew. Most of them never saw the outside world at all. Only the bridge watch, consisting of the OOD, two or three lookouts, and the quartermaster, regularly made contact with the world outside the boat. The captain, the exec-navigator, and other officers would come to the bridge occasionally to talk and to see what was going on. All others were confined below, scattered through the interior of the boat, performing their work, standing watches, and following the daily plan.

When a sighting was made, word of the contact spread quickly through the boat. Everyone could feel the excitement. The control room telephone came alive with inquiries from various stations trying to find out what was going on. Time permitting, I went to the after torpedo room and the forward torpedo room to talk to the torpedomen and tell them what I knew about the activity.

At battle stations the telephones were manned throughout the boat. The telephone talkers listened to everything that was said and kept people in their areas informed of what was happening.

The prewar fleet doctrine of conducting a sound patrol at 150 feet, then coming to periscope depth for a look once each hour, was discarded. The captain ordered that *Sculpin* remain at periscope depth, searching with the periscope every fifteen minutes except when the seas were too rough.

6 January   The fall of Manila was announced on the radio. This meant that *Sculpin* was now operating behind the Japanese lines. The Japanese were aggressively moving their fleet operations south toward Borneo. I couldn't help thinking of the pitiful Asiatic Fleet: one heavy cruiser (*Houston*), one light cruiser (*Marblehead*), thirteen antiquated destroyers, six old submarines (S-boats), twenty-five "modern" subs, and a couple of

---

was occasionally challenged to a game in the after torpedo room. A chess challenge was the only way that they could get me to go that far aft in the ship, they contended.

river gunboats. That "fleet" was supposed to defend the whole Asiatic area against the overwhelming strength of the Japanese navy.

7 January   While we were submerged, number 7 torpedo tube flooded, although the outer door indicator showed that the door was closed. On the surface in the evening we emptied the tube, but it flooded again in only a few minutes. Attempting to get a better seat on the outer door gasket, we opened the door. Despite repeated attempts to shut it we could close it only partway. We resigned ourselves to having one less fish available for firing and a bothersome after torpedo room situation.

Orders from CSAF directed *Sculpin* to cease patrol and proceed to Darwin, Australia, by way of Molucca Passage, east of Celebes Island. Charlie Henderson estimated that it would take eleven days to reach Darwin. Word of the new orders went through the boat instantly, and there were many questions about Australia.

Since we had seen no ships in Lamon Bay—actually we were too far out to see anything—the captain directed *Sculpin* to proceed through Lamon Bay and exit via the east entrance as we made our way south. That was the most aggressive action for *Sculpin* yet; we were well inside the 100-fathom curve. We saw nothing in Lamon Bay, however.

Doc Miller reported that seven men had come down with minor food poisoning. He recommended light duty for a few days. The poisoning was suspected to be from a salmon sandwich mixture that they ate before going on watch at noon.

8 January   *Sculpin* moved south toward Australia, traveling on the surface at night and submerged in daytime. We would be in range of Philippine-based Japanese aircraft for several more days.

A radio message arrived with the news that Jack Turner was promoted to lieutenant and that Red Lennox and I were promoted to lieutenant (jg), effective 8 January.

9 January   Jack gauged the freshwater tanks and announced that baths were in order for all hands. The subsequent rush to the showers may have resulted in the trampling of some less brawny shipmates. Soaking in that shower under a stream of warm water was a welcome treat.

The weather continued miserable. Through the periscope I saw several rainspouts among the storms. It was so rough on the surface as we moved south, hoping to see action as we passed Davao Gulf, that periodically towering waves completely engulfed the bridge, soaking all those on watch.

10 **January**   I was OOD near midnight as *Sculpin* plowed past Surigao Strait, northeast of Mindanao, when the lookout, Doc Miller, whispered, "Mr. Mendenhall, I think I see a ship ahead, slightly to port," as if they could hear him if he talked louder. I moved across the bridge to see around the radio mast located near the bow. Sure enough, a black shape was looming up out of the rainstorm, developing in seconds into a ship crossing our bow from port to starboard.

Sounding battle stations, calling the captain, making bow torpedo tubes ready, swinging ship to get the best gyro angle, and manually setting torpedo gyros all passed in a flash of time.

The captain arrived on the bridge, panting. He could see nothing. (This was before any appreciation of the importance of night eye adaptation.) He had been in his cabin reading a book. The lookouts and I assured him that there really was a cargo ship out there crossing our bow, bearing moving right, while a similar ship came into view farther away.

The captain said, "Mendy, I don't see a thing. It's all yours. Do your best." He used the angle between my binoculars and *Sculpin*'s bow for our only fire control information. Manually adjusting gyro angles in the fish, we fired a two-fish spread and waited a seemingly interminable time. Thinking that we had missed, the captain directed me to shift the angles and fire two more. Just as the fourth fish left, we saw a gigantic explosion, then a second, as our first two torpedos hit at an estimated range of 800 yards. Two columns of smoke and flames rose several hundred feet above the target, which quickly listed heavily toward us. Pandemonium could be sensed in the pinpoints of flashlights rushing frantically around their deck and bridge.

By that time the captain was able to see the target. He took charge and commenced swinging ship to bring the stern tubes to bear on the second ship. Flashes of gunfire could be seen from the cripple, and as shells splashed around us the captain said, "Let's get out of here." We submerged, missing any chance to fire on the second ship. During the excitement of those last few seconds the captain saw a third explosion in the target, either another torpedo hit or an internal explosion.

Battle stations diving officer Jack Turner settled *Sculpin* down at 100 feet; the time from first sighting until we reached depth was exactly four minutes. Sonar heard breakup noises, providing evidence of the sinking. He went down in the deepest spot in any ocean, the 30,000-foot deep

Philippine Trench. A few distant explosions were quickly pronounced to be depth charges by the wide-eyed, apprehensive control room team. Telephone circuit discipline became lax as the line was filled with inquiries.

After a few minutes *Sculpin* surfaced and continued south to take up her patrol assignment off Davao Gulf. The message from CSAF giving *Sculpin* her assignment had had an urgency that caused us not to tarry in the vicinity of the sinking or to chase after the second ship in the rough, stormy weather.

By a strange quirk of luck, I happened to have been the OOD during night surprise torpedo practice near Kahoolawe, Hawaii, and again in the South China Sea, off Subic Bay, when we scored hits practicing under conditions identical to that night attack.

11 January   *Sculpin* patrolled a position thirty miles east of Cape San Augustin, along the Palau–Davao Gulf traffic lane. Nothing was seen.

12 January   Revised orders came for *Sculpin* to depart station and head for Surabaya, Java, passing south of Palmas Island and through Makassar Strait, between Borneo and Celebes Island. We wondered what caused the change from Darwin to Surabaya. Charlie estimated that submerged in the daytime and making only three or four knots, we would take four to five days to get to Surabaya.

Uncertainties were plentiful. In the crew's conversations the Asiatic Fleet became the RAF, short for "retreating Asiatic Fleet."

A bit of excitement livened up the day when Charlie sighted what appeared to be a big ship and sounded battle stations. Torpedoes were made ready, but my torpedo data computer (TDC) solution did not check out.* Target speed was zero. When we got closer the "ship" was identified as a small island. The captain joked that it was the first time that he had ever seen a ship with such nice greenery growing on the main deck.

13 January   An hour before daylight we spotted the silhouette of a submarine against the moonlight. I was OOD. Calling the captain, I turned to head for the sub, trying to distinguish whether she was friend or enemy. At an estimated 1,000 yards we were in perfect firing position, but then we decided that she was one of our own. Our analysis of the radio orders

---

*At battle stations–torpedo my position was in the control room as operator of the torpedo data computer (TDC). The TDC received inputs of estimated target range, course and speed, plus our own ship's course and speed, with which to calculate gyro angles that were set in the torpedoes to make them steer to hit the target.

and sub movements indicated that it was probably *Pickerel*. There was no indication that they ever saw us as we turned to dive and continue south.

Just before noon Charlie sighted an aircraft carrier screened by four destroyers. They disappointed us by passing too far away, going south at high speed. *Sculpin* had no hope of closing for an attack.

14 January Revised orders came for *Sculpin* to stop at a place called Balik-Papan, Borneo, for fuel. Middie thought that there must be a mistake in decoding, so he repeated his work and got the same translation. Jack tried his hand, with the same result. Charlie finally asked Chief Signalman Weldon Moore to get out the charts and the *Coast Pilot*. Balik-Papan (Balikpapan) was located on the east coast of Borneo off Makassar Strait.

No matter where we were in the western Pacific–Dutch East Indies area, it was the rainy season. Getting soaked several times while on watch at night was not unusual. On occasion the radio antenna would collect a static charge and glow eerily. A ball of light bigger than a basketball might float back and forth along the antenna from the radio mast to the bridge. Once the lookout reported a searchlight dead ahead. I stopped the screws and climbed to the lookout platform for a better look. The captain, in his cabin, sensed that the screws had stopped and came to the bridge to see what was going on. Eventually we realized that the "searchlight" was a static electric charge, Saint Elmo's fire, glowing on top of that pesky radio mast.

15 January Since we expected to cross the equator on the sixteenth, plans were made for the shellbacks to initiate the polliwogs. Weldon Moore would be Davy Jones, Joe LaRose would be Neptunus Rex, and I would be the Royal Prosecutor. The cramped quarters of a submarine dictated much less tomfoolery than I went through when first crossing the equator in the battleship *Mississippi*. Planning the ceremonies was a nice diversion from patrol routine.

I was doing a lot of typing, hoping to finish my submarine qualification notebook before arriving in Surabaya. I was at his typewriter so frequently that Yeoman Bill Langley thought I was striking for his job.

At night we saw a number of immense fires on Celebes Island. Radio reports said that the Japanese had taken Tarakan on Borneo, only 300 miles north of Balik-Papan. Rumors went through the boat that *Sculpin* might not get to Balik-Papan before that refinery town fell.

The *Coast Pilot* informed us that the natives were primitive, cannibalistic tribes who lived in the dense jungles of both Borneo and Celebes. We could see the jungles through the periscope. There were also very high mountains with prominent peaks not far inland. When rainclouds permitted, those peaks made excellent navigation references.

16 January Initiation of the polliwogs went off well. Everyone had a great time. The distraction from routine patrol work was welcome, and my constellation and star identification program during night watches took on new interest as we moved toward the Southern Hemisphere.

17 January *Sculpin* surfaced near the Balik-Papan lightship at sunset to take aboard an English-speaking Dutch lieutenant pilot. We did not have detailed charts of the channel into the port, which was located a few miles upriver. All navigation lights were extinguished. Radio reports had made us aware that there were frequent Japanese bombings of Balik-Papan. Our pilot gave us a running commentary on local activities.

Once *Sculpin* entered the river, those not on watch were allowed on deck. It was the first time since 8 December that many of the crew had the opportunity to get a breath of fresh air and to stretch their legs. While at sea most of them never saw daylight or went outdoors.

It was pitch dark by the time *Sculpin* reached a spot where the pilot assured the captain that the dock was located. The jungle, towering on each bank of the river, gave the feeling of being in a black hole. There were no lights on shore; blackout was enforced. Voice communications were not effective at all between the pilot, our deckhands, and the native linehandlers on the dock, whom we could hardly make out. The biggest problem was of language and terminology. Spring lines and breast lines were unknown to the natives even if they did understand English, and, to compound matters, my mooring lines were rotten and broke readily. The manila had deteriorated from being soaked in seawater for such a long time.

Finally the captain took over. By then he had the feel of the situation, and our electricians had hurriedly rigged portable floodlights on deck. The captain maneuvered *Sculpin*'s bow next to the dock, then directed some of our men to jump to the dock and handle the rotten lines gently. *Sculpin* was moored without further complications.

Word was passed to those on deck and over the ship's loudspeaker system: "No one goes ashore without special permission. There is a danger of being bombed by the Japs, and we may have to get under way at any time."

An official car waited on the dock. The captain was taken to meet the Dutch commandant–port captain. Our crew began fueling ship and making repairs that might be done in the few hours before daylight. Freshwater tanks were filled from the shore connection. Torpedomen got busy moving four fish from the deck storage to the forward torpedo room.

Red Lennox was looking forward to getting a few things for the cooks to add spice to the menu, but quickly learned that he would be allowed only one case of Pet milk and a few pounds of sugar. The Dutch could spare nothing else.

It was a busy night for everyone. Some talked of taking a walk around the port area, but there was no time for that. I didn't even set foot on dry ground, just on the wooden dock. After about an hour the captain came back and told us about his meeting with the commandant. The driver of his car, a Dutch army sergeant, had skirted bomb craters on the way to port headquarters, pointing out that the Japs were careful not to hit the refinery, apparently hoping to take it undamaged. The refinery, however, was mined, ready to be blown up as the Dutch evacuated to jungle hideouts they had prepared and from which they planned to conduct guerrilla warfare. The natives were being armed with guns and knives to assist in the guerrilla activities.

At dawn *Sculpin* was ready for the pilot, with the special sea detail on station and engines running. Daylight and sunrise came, and still no pilot. Shortly after sunrise he came strolling down the dock, calmly smoking his pipe, explaining as he boarded that the Japanese never bombed before noon.

The captain wasted no time once the pilot stepped into the pilot boat near the lightship. We submerged and headed south toward Surabaya. The captain brought us our first real news from the outside world: the disaster at Pearl Harbor, Cavite and Clark Field destroyed, General MacArthur under siege at Corregidor, Luzon taken by the Japanese, Admiral Hart retreated to Surabaya, the Royal Navy ships *Repulse* and *Prince of Wales* sunk by Japanese aircraft off Singapore, the British failure to stop the Japanese landings in Malaysia, British troops retreating to Singapore, Hong Kong under siege, Wake Island overrun. The outlook for victory any time soon was bleak. Our concept of the triumphant Pacific Fleet sailing to our assistance was wishful thinking. We were on our own.

19–21 January   As *Sculpin* moved on south we made plans for the work to be done in Surabaya. We hoped that the Dutch shipyard and submarine base would be able to help with repairs. The preparation of lists of work, spare parts needed, and supplies was evident throughout the boat. Questions were being asked. How long will we be there? What facilities will be available? Will *Holland* be there with our special tools, parts, and repair equipment? The answers would have to wait until we reached port.

On the twentieth we learned by radio that S-36 was aground on a reef and being abandoned not far from our position. The captain didn't want to break radio silence with a transmission to make our position known, but he assumed that CSAF knew about where we were. He expected that *Sculpin* would be sent to help S-36, and we were standing by for such orders when *Sargo,* although farther away, was dispatched to help them.

Odis Taylor, a radioman striker, sheepishly admitted that he and Seaman 2/c Gordon Cox had slipped ashore in the dark to see Borneo. His story went something like this: "Borneo to me meant the land of headhunters, so there was a strong desire to see this strange place. There was a total blackout, so we had to feel our way and cautiously take one step at a time. The low-hanging clouds blocked even the starlight, and there was no moon. We made our way to the gate. There was no guard, so we went out into the street. It was exciting; a liberty in Borneo!

"As our eyes became accustomed to the black night, we could see commercial and residential buildings boarded up. The Dutch were ready to blow up all the facilities, and the oil refinery, to prevent the Japanese from capturing them. Shell Oil signs were everywhere.

"Making a loop onto another street, we looked behind us and it appeared, in the darkness, that a family of baboons was following us. When we would stop, they would stop and look us over very quietly. When we would move on, they would follow forty or fifty feet behind. I threw a stone into the wall of trees and vines along the street. A chorus of chatter and screeching came back when the baboons were disturbed in their jungle.

"We didn't stay out there very long. When we were back on board the boat, we were a little surprised that no one missed us. We turned in to get some sleep. Some time later we were abruptly awakened by a scream: 'Dive! Dive! Dive!' [Red Lennox had been topside when he heard a Dutch seaplane taking off on the river not far from *Sculpin*.] Apparently Mr. Lennox thought it was a Jap plane coming in on a bombing run, so he quickly dropped to the control room and ran aft shouting for the boat to dive."

Cox said that his brain would not believe what his ears were hearing "the night that Mr. Lennox scared the hell out of me."

Sculpin had a bit of excitement on the twenty-first when sonar picked up screw noises and we sighted a ship, but it was too far away to identify. At the same time, through a break in the clouds, the 7,000-foot volcanic peak of Lombok Island came into view, plotting at eighty miles away.

The complete fall of the Philippines was more and more evident. There was a period when we were not sure just where or from whom we would get our radioed instructions, so the radio gang copied messages both from Manila and Java. Then official instructions came to copy Java.

22 January   At 0400 *Sculpin* was at the rendezvous point for the escort to Surabaya, but there was no one there. After searching around for a time, the captain began to talk of spending the day submerged and trying again the next day. Then we sighted, simultaneously, *S-39* and the escort and received "friend" recognition signals. Another Dutch lieutenant-pilot came aboard to show us the way through the lengthy channel, involving the negotiation of Madura Strait and its two minefields. *S-39* followed us during a full day of piloting. At 1700 *Sculpin* tied up at the dock in Surabaya.

Lieutenant Hank Munson, '32, the new skipper of *S-38,* who had just relieved Moon Chapple, '30, was on the dock leading the welcoming party as we tied up. Hank had our schedule in hand. We would be in port for one whole week. Half of the crew would go to a rest camp for three days. (The camp was at the mountain resort town of Malang, about 100 kilometers away.) When the first rest camp group returned, the other half of the crew would take their turn at the camp.

The Dutch submarine base had supervisors on board as soon as we tied up. They offered every assistance, assuring us that they were ready to repair almost anything. *Sculpin* would go into a floating dry dock the next day for underwater inspection, repairs to number 7 torpedo tube and the fathometer head, and to scrape and paint the bottom. Repair and refit work began that night.

Our submarine had come through her first patrol in surprisingly good material condition. The major defects were the problem with number 7 torpedo tube's outer door, the failure of the fathometer, and the freon leak. Repairing these would be most important, along with the usual maintenance that was conducted when in port after a period of operations.

A weak point in the ship's organization was the lack of a means for providing personal items such as soap, toothpaste, shaving cream, razor blades, cigarettes, and sundry items. The exec created a new job, ship's service officer, and gave Middie that responsibility, directing him to lay in a supply of the needed items and to keep books on the enterprise.

The half of the crew that would remain with the boat was taken to a barracks where they were to be quartered while *Sculpin* was being repaired. The officers were taken to the Dutch officers' quarters club, where they were made welcome. Only a skeleton watch would be maintained on the boat.

Among those on the dock to greet *Sculpin* was Chuck Osborne, a shipmate on *Mississippi* who had gone to supply school just before I went to sub school. Chuck had been paymaster on subtender *Canopus,* sunk at Manila. How pleased I was to see him! He informed us that he would return the next morning to make payday. I went with Chuck to the Dutch officers' quarters, arranged for my room, and discovered Moon Chapple in the bar with some Dutch officers who had introduced him to their favorite drink, Bols gin, neat. We talked with Moon for an hour about S-38's experiences at Lingayen Gulf.

Patrol Summary

Number of men on board:
  60 enlisted
  6 officers

Nautical miles covered:
  5,625 on the surface
  1,332 submerged (in 48 dives)

Drinking water:
  12,951 gallons made
  18,795 gallons consumed (6.96 gallons/man/day)

Battery water:
  2,017 gallons made
  2,617 gallons used (58.2 gallons/day)

Fuel used: 64,700 gallons (9.3 gallons/mile)

Duration: 45 days

Torpedoes fired: 4

Sinkings:
  1 *Akita Maru*-class ship, 3,000 tons

Refit in Surabaya

23–30 January 1942   Full-scale refit and repair of *Sculpin* began at day-break. The eagerness, efficiency, and cleanliness of the Dutch were amazing. Pieces of equipment were rapidly disassembled and taken to the shipyard shops. The work tempo was speeded by the fact that Borneo and Celebes were now in Japanese hands, Singapore was expected to fall in a matter of days, and Java was anticipating bomb attacks at any time. Everyone felt intense pressure to get out of Surabaya as quickly as possible. *Sculpin* went into the floating dry dock immediately for repairs to the number 7 torpedo tube and the fathometer.*

Chuck Osborne came aboard and held payday, even though all our records were back on our old tender, *Holland*. Chuck had lugged a paymaster's bag full of greenbacks from Bataan to Corregidor, spent some weeks there, then got to Surabaya by submarine, and he had some unusual stories to tell about his adventures.

As each man came to the head of the pay line he was asked to give his rate, whether he was married or single, and his years of service. Chuck then did a short bit of mental gymnastics (he had no calculator) involving base pay, allowances, time on patrol, sub pay, and his own "fudge factors" and came up with the number of Dutch guilders that he would let the man have. The crewman, in return, signed a pay slip for the dollar conversion. A most unusual payday!

By comparison with quarters aboard a submarine, our rooms at the Dutch officers' quarters were luxurious, and the abundant hot water available for showering was delightful, but there was no air conditioning, and the heat and humidity four degrees south of the equator were oppressive. There was no mail and no way to get any communication out to the United States.

The Dutch-influenced architecture and the tropical greenery and flowers of Java were fascinating. I made the train trip to the rest camp at Malang, 100 kilometers away in the mountains, where I enjoyed a day and two nights of relaxation, eating heartily, swimming, dancing, and going to movies with an attractive young Dutch student who was there for a holiday. I was billeted in quarters with J. D. Fulp, '34, John Hess, '37 (rescued from S-36), and my Annapolis classmate Butch Allen. Among other

---

*A short time after *Sculpin* left Surabaya, the dry dock in which we were repaired was sunk by Japanese bombs, with the U.S. destroyer *Stewart* in the dock. The Japanese salvaged *Stewart* and added her to their fleet.

friends I saw during the Surabaya refit were Condé Raguet, '38, Otto Kolb, '36, Gene Geer, and G. A. Buchanan, '40.

Red Lennox was unceremoniously transferred, on thirty minutes' notice, to *S-38*, and John Hess joined us to take his place. Before he left, Red scrounged a Dutch broadcast radio that was installed in the radio shack, giving us the ability to get better news of what was going on in the world. I spent half a day with Doug Rhymes, '35, and his *Sargo* torpedomen—who had experienced the same frustration with torpedo performance reported by many subs—trying to identify what might be wrong, but we could find nothing.

Captain Chappell was informed that our next mission would be to take supplies and ammunition to General MacArthur's forces at Corregidor and bring back some of those people to safety. The boat was loaded and ready to leave on 29 January, but departure was postponed one day when a convoy of supply ships arrived. We received more food and supplies, cramming them into every conceivable storage space, then carpeting the passageways with boxes that we had to walk on to get from compartment to compartment, but there was no mail and no torpedoes.

At noon on the twenty-ninth CSAF canceled our mission to Corregidor. We were allowed to off-load only the ammunition and were advised to eat our way out of the huge excess of food. With the Japanese moving steadily toward Java, the fewer supplies left to fall into enemy hands the better. In contrast, torpedoes were in short supply; we were permitted to take only sixteen with us.

Sculpin shifted berths several times for various purposes. Once we were alongside *Pickerel*, and I visited classmate Fred Taeusch. Another time we were alongside destroyers that had made a very successful raid on the Japanese transport force in Makassar Strait, a morale builder for the whole Asiatic Fleet. My classmates Ken Hysong, J. V. Wilson, and Jack Michel were on the destroyers, and it was gratifying to be able to talk with them, hearing their accounts of the action and wishing them more such successes.

Not until noon of the thirtieth was *Sculpin* able to get off on her second patrol. Chuck Osborne was there to wish us luck. With Japanese bombing of Surabaya expected and the invasion of Java imminent, we wished him luck, too. He might need all he could get.

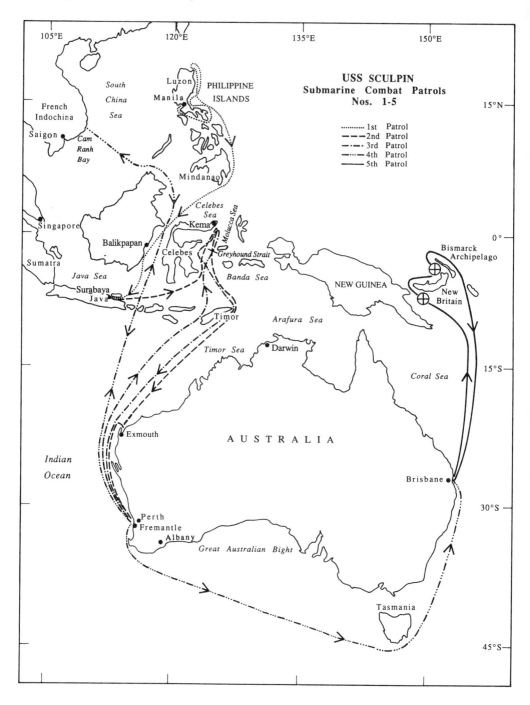

Sculpin's Second Patrol

(30 January–3 March 1942)

30 January Friday at 1305 *Sculpin* cast off all lines and left Surabaya on her second patrol. Orders were to head for a position in the Molucca Sea east of Celebes Island and wait for further instructions.

At the end of the inner channel the captain thanked our pilot and wished him luck in the uncertain future in the East Indies; then the pilot climbed down into the pilot boat and departed. *Sculpin* put on four engines to get out of that vicinity as rapidly as possible, cleared the channel through the outer minefield as the sun went down, and set course for Molucca Strait.

Before we left Manila, the captains of all CSAF submarines were instructed to use their torpedoes sparingly; they might not be plentiful in the future. The marvelous Mk-VI exploder would make it possible to use only one torpedo per enemy ship, according to Washington, but Captain Chappell, after talking with other captains while in Surabaya and having seen so many radio messages about torpedoes *not doing* what they were supposed to do, made it clear to us that he intended to use whatever number of fish he felt was necessary to ensure a sinking. The way he talked, the sixteen Mk-14 fish on board might not last long.

The boat seemed much quieter than usual. After a frantic seven days in port replenishing ship and preparing to get back on patrol, everyone was taking it easy. There had been little real relaxation in Surabaya. During those seven days we must have accomplished the equivalent of six weeks of repair and upkeep.

John Hess, a survivor of *S-36*, had very little with him except the clothes on his back. We welcomed him and shared our wardrobes with him as he settled in as a key shipmate. He also found a niche as a chess enthusiast and acey-deucey fan.

A few other *S-36* crewmen had also come to *Sculpin*. Transfers to and from the boat increased the roster from the sixty on the first patrol to sixty-three on the second. Among the new arrivals from *S-36* was Machinist's Mate 2/c Gus Hollenbach. Other new shipmates were Harold Laman, Pete Surofchek, Junior Shong, Julian Ulmer, Erwin Holland, and

Alvin Shaw. The officers and crew spent the journey back to the patrol area telling of their experiences in Java, Surabaya, and Malang. There were stories of Cavite, Mariveles, Manila, and Singapore; of ships, submarines, aircraft, and guerrilla activities.

When Charlie Henderson laid out our track and projected positions on his chart, it was immediately apparent that someone on the Surabaya staff had goofed. We were sixty miles ahead of the positions they had projected. The captain opened up with the radio to send a correction to CSAF. The proper positions were particularly important so that *Sculpin* would not be mistaken for a Japanese submarine and bombed by our own planes or attacked by our antisubmarine forces.

31 January   At 0500 *Sculpin* submerged for the day and commenced the reversa routine of sleeping during daytime while submerged and working at night while on the surface. The Japanese were only a few miles north of us and were moving south rapidly. Wardroom consensus was that in sending us to the Molucca Sea, the big bosses were anticipating a major Japanese push to consolidate their hold on Celebes and Borneo before taking Java.

Shortly after *Sculpin* submerged, Baldwin reported saltwater contamination in the hydraulic system. All hydraulically powered units were shifted to hand operation. The big concern was that we might have to go back to Surabaya to get help in restoring the hydraulics, which were essential for most normal operations. Going back to Surabaya, under the circumstances of expected Japanese air raids, was not a pleasant thought. Inspections located a leak in the vent and replenishment tank. The auxiliarymen worked all day, and repairs were completed by midevening, the system purged of saltwater, and normal operation restored.

1 February   As we commenced the patrol, shipboard attitudes were quite different from the first patrol. Then, we were all set to fulfill the storybook pictures of submarine warfare, defeating the Japs in short order. After being out for forty-five days and doing so little, and finding in Surabaya that many boats had done even less, we realized that this war was too big for submarines and the pitiful Asiatic Fleet to win alone. News of the retreat of our forces had the effect of stabilizing everyone into a calm, deliberate, and determined team. We might not be winning the war yet, but in time things would begin to swing our way. It would take time—years, maybe.

2 February   Radio orders came for *Sculpin* to patrol the northern entrances to Staring Bay in southeastern Celebes. *Sculpin* would cover the northern entrances, *Sailfish* the southern entrances. Our estimated time of arrival (ETA) was 4 February. Radio traffic was reporting large Japanese convoys moving down the east coast of Celebes, headed for Kendari on Staring Bay.

3 February   At sea again, I realized that we hadn't received one single piece of mail in Surabaya. The Red Lennox–scrounged and newly installed broadcast radio was filling a big gap in keeping us informed of world news, and we would be much better informed than during the first patrol. People came by the radio shack all the time to ask what was going on. The times of shortwave broadcasts and frequencies of BBC, Radio Washington, San Francisco, and other stations in Australia, South Africa, and India were noted so one of the radiomen would be certain to get the news. Broadcasts were also picked up from Tokyo, Berlin, Rome, and Saigon. Enemy "news" was frequently included in the newsletter posted on the bulletin board, just for laughs. The news that our forces had taken some of the Marshall Islands was a boost to morale. We hoped that we were not overly optimistic.

4 February   Just before dawn *Sculpin* moved into position off the northern entrance to Staring Bay, and submerged at 0416 when a patrol boat was sighted. The captain identified the boat as a picket of about 500 tons. Sonar heard pinging, which became fainter and finally could no longer be made out. Two and a half hours later sonar again picked up pinging. It became louder and then faded away. Nothing was seen. *Sculpin* moved in closer to the entrance but still could not see far enough into the bay to sight any ships.

At 1100 sonar again reported pinging. This time the captain saw a destroyer. We tracked him,* went to battle stations, and prepared to fire, but the destroyer, identified as *Asashio*-class, turned away at a range of 5,000 yards and went back on the western leg of his east-west patrol.

During the day we tracked the destroyer on four occasions. Our enemy's sonar was diligently pinging but never detected us. We solved his courses

---

*For clarification, I have used masculine pronouns—*he, his*—throughout when referring to Japanese ships, and feminine pronouns—*she, her*—in reference to U.S. and other Allied ships.

and speeds, but the captain didn't attack, waiting for other ships to move in or out of the bay.

With sunset approaching, *Sculpin* moved closer to his track, waiting for his next appearance. Quietly and methodically, we prepared for him. It was like shooting goldfish in a fishbowl.

Before sundown we fired a three-fish spread at the *Asashio* from the bow tubes, from a range of 700 yards. He was on the eastern leg of his patrol at a speed of twelve knots. The captain watched two fish explode against the destroyer and saw the ship list heavily with his bow well down.* *Sculpin* cleared the area in anticipation of retaliation.

As far as Odis Taylor was concerned, the sinking was his birthday present, since 4 February was his birthday. Stew Burner (Ship's Cook) Bill Zwally surprised Odis with a cake that had one match on it as a candle.

The outer door of number 7 torpedo tube again began to cause trouble. It would not open all the way. To prevent the possibility of an outer door jammed in the open position, as on the first patrol, the captain ordered that the door be kept closed, inactivating the tube.

We were pleasantly surprised that there was no counteraction against us. On the surface after dark a message from CSAF gave daily positions of a large southbound transport due to arrive at Kendari on 5 February, so *Sculpin* moved toward Greyhound Strait, hoping to intercept the transport northwest of Wowoni Island.

5 February   Just after midnight we sighted and avoided a small picket boat. Before daybreak *Sculpin* submerged to commence a sound patrol at 140 feet, to avoid possible detection by aircraft. It was a quiet day until midafternoon, when sonar reported a contact. At periscope depth we identified a large transport of the *Kashin Maru*-class and began maneuvering to attack. The transport was on a southerly course and was escorted by a small destroyer.

We were able to close only to 2,800 yards, but the captain decided that in view of the size and apparent importance of the ship, we should fire torpedoes, even though the range was excessive. After only ten minutes of tracking, *Sculpin* fired a spread of four fish from the bow tubes. My TDC calculated a torpedo run of 3,200 yards.

The target apparently saw the wakes of the fish and promptly turned away, and all missed ahead. The miss could be attributed to a lack of data

---

*Japanese war records later revealed that the destroyer did not sink but was beached, salvaged, and put back in service by the Japanese.

with which to accurately solve the course and speed of the transport. I had only two periscope observations to enter into the TDC, not nearly enough for a good firing solution.

The escort turned to look for *Sculpin* as we went down to 200 feet to evade. For the next three hours the escort searched. Although he made no contact with *Sculpin,* it was a very uncomfortable three hours, with all ventilation shut down, only essential machinery running, and everyone being very quiet. Sonar could hear him charging around, but he finally gave up and left the scene without dropping any depth charges.

After sunset *Sculpin* surfaced for the night.

6 February   Before daylight *Sculpin* went under to conduct a sonar patrol at 140 feet, coming to periscope depth for observations at irregular intervals. At the end of a quiet day we surfaced after sunset.

Just before midnight, southeast of Wowoni Island, I was OOD when the lookouts reported an unusually black shape in the rainstorms. I sounded battle stations and called the captain. This time the skipper's eyes were night adapted. After that previous experience he no longer spent his evenings reading books. The contact was identified as a *Tenryu*-class cruiser. We moved in to attack.

Among the heavy rainstorms we made out an enemy formation, tracked as moving southwestward toward Kendari at an estimated speed of ten knots. Two more big ships were visible to the left of the cruiser, one of them an aircraft carrier. The captain would have preferred to go after the carrier, but we were in a much better position to hit the cruiser, so at 1,500 yards we fired a spread of two fish at the *Tenryu*. I saw one fish explode prematurely between us and the target. The other fish, by its wake, looked as if it would hit, but with escorts appearing out of the rain and headed our way, the captain decided to submerge. At any second a Jap ship might appear out of a rainstorm and slice *Sculpin* in two. The noise of diving prevented our sonar from hearing any explosions, but some compartments in the boat did report explosions.

As we were diving the captain identified one of the larger ships as a *Hosho*-class carrier. *Sculpin* was in the middle of a large formation that was hard to make out because of the heavy weather. Submerged, sonar reported many heavy screws all around us.

7 February   There were too many big ships in the fleet movement, rainstorms to spoil visibility, and just general commotion everywhere for the enemy destroyers to find *Sculpin*. We stayed down for an hour and heard no depth charges. With all quiet and torpedo tubes reloaded, *Sculpin* surfaced just after midnight to find that we were right in the middle of a formation of destroyers.

By this time Jack Turner had relieved me as OOD, and *Sculpin* pulled clear on the surface, taking advantage of the rainstorms and the frequent lightning flashes that illuminated the enemy. We were still apparently undetected.

At 0100 we sent an urgent message to CSAF concerning the ships we had seen. A primary mission of this patrol was to inform CSAF promptly of any significant ship movements. The captain believed that this took priority over attacking the destroyers, because the Allied high command needed information on Japanese fleet movements to direct the actions on Java.

The night was far from over. At 0215 Jack sighted another formation, and *Sculpin* went to battle stations to begin a surface approach. This time one of the six destroyers saw us and forced us to dive.

He closed in as we were going down, and a string of eight depth charges exploded around us as we passed 225 feet, shaking the boat severely, breaking light bulbs, and causing numerous leaks and much other damage.

Sculpin plunged alarmingly down to a depth of 345 feet. The control room crew was dead silent, and all eyes were glued on the depth gauge. The rudder and the stern planes were jammed, making depth control very difficult. Sweating profusely, Jack managed to stabilize at 345 feet, far below the test depth of 250 feet, by holding a ten-degree up angle on the boat at two-thirds speed. Too much noise would be created if he pumped ballast to adjust the trim.

Painfully Jack worked *Sculpin* upward. When we finally reached test depth the rudder and planes worked normally. The sea pressure at 345 feet must have bound the shafts, causing the rudder and planes to be difficult to operate.

Jack was pleased to have the two-thirds speed to keep *Sculpin* from going any deeper and to help move up to a safer depth, but he knew that at that speed we were making much too much noise. The commotion might draw the enemy to us, with disastrous results, so it was imperative that *Sculpin* slow down as soon as possible. Some discreet pumping was done to adjust ballast.

While Jack was fighting to control the boat, an electrical fire broke out in the control room behind the interior communications (IC) switchboard, filling the control room with harsh black smoke that burned the eyes and made breathing difficult. The fire was quickly snuffed out with a CO_2 fire extinguisher, but the charred-rubber odor permeated the air. Investigation established that the fire was due to seawater coming down the multiple conductor cable to the port annunciator from a ruptured box on the bridge, allowing water to flow inside the cable to the IC board. That leak was quickly stopped.

The after engine room reported that their hatch had momentarily lifted and a small amount of water had come in there. Reports were coming in from throughout the boat of grounded circuits, broken gauges, and other damage. Charlie kept a list of the items as they were reported. I was at the TDC, ready to go where I might be needed.

Once ballast and trim were adjusted, Jack signaled the maneuvering room to slow to one-third speed. Maneuvering telephoned that they were unable to answer his order—the electrical controllers were jammed at two-thirds and couldn't be shifted to any other position. Tension mounted. Everyone in the control room realized that the propellers had to be slowed in order to cut down noise and permit *Sculpin* to escape.

The captain, exec, Jack, and "plank-owner"* Chief Electrician's Mate John Pepersack conferred over the dilemma; then John ran aft to the maneuvering room to assess the situation. After a few minutes he returned to report that someone would have to enter the main electrical cubicle, a locked cage with DANGER signs posted all around it. Inside it were the bus bars that carried the ship's electric power, and through which power was transmitted to the main motors. No one was allowed to go inside without the captain's permission, and then only when the electric circuits were not energized.

After more discussion, Pepersack, insisting that he could safely remedy the controller problem, was given permission to go into the cubicle. The exec relieved Jack as diving officer, and Jack went with Pepersack to the maneuvering room.

They unlocked the cage door and, with Jack aiming a battle lantern and ready to assist as best he could, Pepersack entered. He found that the depth charging had loosened a nut, which had fallen into the controller linkage and was jamming the controllers in the two-thirds speed position. His primary concern was to get to the dislodged nut without being electrocuted. With extreme caution he gingerly wriggled into position, removed the guilty nut, and restored the ability to vary the ship's speed.**

---

*Plank-owner is the navy term for someone who was a member of the crew of the boat when she was commissioned.

**John had calmly run the risk of electrocution to save his ship and shipmates from

A faint cheer and deep sighs of relief broke the tension in the control room when Jack telephoned to say that maneuvering could answer all bells. Smiles erased the distressed frowns, and eyes quickly turned from the depth gauges where they had been glued for an eternity. Jack returned to the control room and resumed his duty as diving officer.

During Jack's struggle with depth, speed, and damage control, the soundmen were busy following what they estimated to be at least eight destroyers, which were industriously charging around, pinging furiously, as *Sculpin* crept away. Through the noise, the soundmen could distinguish many heavy ships going south. Forty ships were counted moving out of Staring Bay. A major operation was in progress. The presence of that large force, with the water noise they generated, was of major assistance to *Sculpin*'s getaway. After things settled down, an inventory was made of damages. Not only were there broken light bulbs, shattered gauge glasses, and grounded circuits, but the entire torpedo firing system and the battle order transmitter were out of commission, and would be until we reached port. The transmitter cable had been pushed through the hull stuffing box, allowing water to enter the conning tower until the hole was plugged.

At sunrise all was quiet. The ocean was empty when *Sculpin* came to periscope depth. The captain ordered 140 feet for the day to make repairs and to recover from the night's activities. By sunset most of the damage was repaired, except that the torpedo firing circuits and the TBL radio would be out of service for the remainder of the patrol. The TBL radio transmitter itself had been bashed in when the vertical antenna clutch slipped and sea pressure drove the antenna into the boat. Torpedoes could now only be fired manually, at the torpedo tube, when ordered by telephone from the conning tower or the bridge.

Surfacing at sunset, *Sculpin* put on her best speed toward Buton Passage in an attempt to regain contact with the enemy fleet, and tried to send a report of the fleet movement to CSAF. The primary radio transmitter was slightly damaged in the depth charging and would not put out full power, but a contact message was sent anyway, in hope that the weak signal would be picked up by someone, but no one acknowledged the message. The radio gang worked frenziedly to bring the transmitter up to full power.

---

disaster. For his heroism, Chief Pepersack was later promoted to chief warrant electrician. Quiet and unassuming, John grudgingly accepted the accolades with a "gee, that can't be me" attitude.

8 February   After midnight, with no station sending a receipt for the contact message, we broadcast blind with the best possible antenna loading: ADDITIONAL DOPE X ACTION CSAF X LARGE SORTIE LAST NIGHT X LIGHT AND HEAVY FORCES COURSE SOUTHERLY SLOW SPEED X DETECTED BADLY DEPTH CHARGED LOST CONTACT X MOVING SOUTH TO REGAIN X SCORE TO DATE ONE SUNK ONE MISSED ONE DOUBTFUL X SEVEN FISH LEFT.

Sculpin searched an area as far south as the north entrance to Buton Passage and east to Anamo Island without regaining contact with the enemy, then headed northeast at high speed to clear the position where the radio transmissions had been made.

Before daylight we submerged to conduct a sound patrol at 100 feet, making periscope observations at irregular intervals. No contacts were made. *Sculpin* surfaced after sunset.

In the evening a CSAF message to *Sailfish* ordered her to return to port. That left *Sculpin* as the only submarine covering Staring Bay. A contact report from *Sturgeon*, located farther south, confirmed the very large Japanese force that *Sculpin* had reported.

9–11 February   CSAF ordered *Sculpin* to move north of Greyhound Strait to Kema. At 0430 on the ninth we submerged to conduct a sound patrol at 100 feet until sunrise, then moved up to periscope depth for daylight patrol. No contacts were made, and we surfaced after sundown. By midevening our passage through Greyhound Strait was complete, and we continued north toward Kema.

We saw many small patrol boats over the next several days, but we were seeking bigger game. From the experience of the previous week we knew that we were behind the Japanese lines and that most of their combat ships were south of us.

Our Surabaya-installed broadcast receiver was able to pick up news only from Tokyo. We were too far away, and poor atmospheric conditions prevented getting anything directly from the United States or any other friendly source. Tokyo was broadcasting absurd claims of having sunk twenty-nine of our submarines. The official navy command radio reported the first Japanese air raids taking place on Surabaya.

Continuing north toward Kema, we submerged each day before sunrise to conduct a sound patrol at 100 feet. After the sun was up we moved to periscope depth. Charlie Henderson projected that we would arrive off Kema on the twelfth.

At that point I was hooked rereading Farwell's *Rules of the Road*, along with working regularly on the diagrams and sketches for my submarine qualification notebook, which was a never-ending project.

On the eleventh a radio message informed us that Admiral Hart had asked to be relieved as commander-in-chief of the Asiatic Fleet. *Sculpin's* wardroom strategists reached the conclusion that our admiral was leaving because of the lack of support out here in the far western Pacific. We hoped that he would go back to the United States and campaign for more help for our RAF (retreating Asiatic Fleet). The navy high command, according to our between-the-lines reading of the radio messages, had retreated across the island of Java to Tjilatjap, on the south coast. *Holland* would soon be there.

We made no worthwhile contacts during the move north to Kema.

12 February   *Sculpin* submerged off Kema at daybreak and continued the practice of conducting a sound patrol until sunrise, thereafter at periscope depth.

Everything was quiet until early afternoon, when we sighted a ship coming out of the port of Kema. We began tracking, went to battle stations, and were ready to fire. At a range of 2,000 yards the contact was better identified as a small patrol boat. He was not pinging but seemed to be searching, and was not a torpedo target. While tracking the patrol boat, we moved in a northerly direction. The movement was unfortunate, because as we broke off from tracking the patrol, a large destroyer and a tanker were seen slipping into Kema from the south. They had hugged the coast of Celebes. The captain planned to wait outside for the tanker as we surfaced after sundown.

13 February   *Sculpin* submerged at 0426 to patrol at 100 feet until sunrise, then waited at periscope depth for the destroyer and tanker that had entered Kema the day before, but we didn't see them again. Another quiet day ended with surfacing after sundown.

We could see many bright lights along the shore and in the hills south of Kema. The Japanese appeared to be working on a large construction project, perhaps an airfield or a base. The weather cleared and visibility was better than usual, but there was a bright moon, and the captain didn't want to go too close to the coast for fear of being sighted, so we stayed well offshore.

News came in confirming U.S. raids in the Marshall Islands. Everyone enjoyed hearing something favorable instead of the gloomy things being heard from Tokyo and our official channels.

14–16 February   Each day *Sculpin* submerged before sunrise, conducted a sound patrol until sunrise, then moved up for a periscope patrol, surfacing after sunset. The conditions under which we lived were uncommon: up all night working, sleeping all day while submerged, without water for baths, growing beards. The foul-smelling atmosphere seemed normal.

I tried to interest Charlie and the captain into moving close inshore at night to lob a few shells into the activities there and perhaps generate some excitement, but they didn't like my suggestion.

Nearing midnight on the sixteenth, CSAF ordered *Sculpin* to move south and cover the northern entrances to Kendari, particularly those from Greyhound Strait, so we headed south.

17 February   At 0302, with clear skies and bright moonlight, smoke was sighted to the southwest and tracked as moving southwestward toward Greyhound. *Sculpin* went to flank speed to run around, gain position ahead of the smoke, and make a submerged attack after daylight. Since we were short of fish forward, the captain wanted to get into position for a stern tube shot.

We submerged at 0432, and half an hour later the target could be identified as a 3,500-ton merchantman. We went to battle stations and continued maneuvering for attack. At 0551 the captain fired two fish from the after tubes at a range of 2,200 yards. His original plan was to fire three, but he held the third fish. At the last second, on pure intuition, he directed me to override the TDC solution of target speed at nine knots and enter a target speed of six knots; and he watched the two fish miss astern of the target.

Later analysis showed that we should have used nine knots. Even then, if the original plan to fire three fish had been carried out, the third fish would probably have hit. The captain was crestfallen. He took full responsibility for the miss, and knowing how rotten I felt about it, urged me not to feel bad over his mistake. There were no other contacts, and *Sculpin* surfaced at dusk. Two and a half hours later we were through Greyhound Strait and headed south toward Kendari.

Jack was OOD near midnight, in conditions of poor visibility, when he sighted what he first thought was a cruiser of the *Yubari* class accompanied by a destroyer, on a southeasterly course. Later, the "cruiser" was identified as a large destroyer. Going to battle stations while remaining on the surface, there was no time for me to get a TDC solution. The captain set gyros and fired two fish from the bow tubes at the big destroyer from a range of 800 yards, using an estimated course of 125 degrees t (true) and a speed of twelve knots. The destroyer must have seen *Sculpin,* because he backed emergency. Our bridge watch could see white water at his stern for a few seconds, then he turned toward us. *Sculpin* went down fast.

A string of five depth charges went off very close as we passed 150 feet. Ten minutes later a string of three more charges went off well astern of us while we stole quietly away at a depth of 230 feet. The Japanese searched energetically but never gained contact.

Two major concerns followed the depth charges: the starboard main motor controller was partially disabled and could only be moved to the slow position; and the starboard shaft developed a loud squeal, which mysteriously stopped in a few minutes.

18 February   All sound contact with our antagonist was lost a few minutes after midnight, but *Sculpin* remained submerged to correct the controller problem. Three hours later the controllers were operating properly. Another nut had worked loose in the control mechanism, preventing a full shift. Fortunately, this time the nut was not inside the bus bar cubicle. When it was removed, the controller could be shifted, if handled gently. We surfaced at 0310 and continued toward Kendari.

Before sunrise *Sculpin* submerged for the day, conducting the usual sound patrol at 100 feet until sunrise, then we patrolled at periscope depth. The day was quiet. The crew rested from the previous busy night. The controller was fully repaired and back to normal as we surfaced after sunset.

19 February   Shortly after midnight a message from CSAF directed *Sculpin* to go east of Timor and Wetar islands, then south to Australia. Charlie set a southeasterly course, and we made what headway we could while running submerged during daylight and on the surface at best speed after dark.

Reading between the lines of the latest messages, we decided that Surabaya and Tjilatjap were being evacuated. Headquarters, repair facilities, and base activities were moving south. *Holland* was on her way to Australia. The RAF continued its retreat.

This meant that Allied forces were losing still more ground, ground that would be much harder to retake. The talk in the boat always centered on why something wasn't being done to help us. I kept insisting that we were just too close to the fight and that actions were undoubtedly being taken that we didn't know about. The wardroom analysts came to the conclusion that we would eventually find ourselves in Fremantle, particularly after study of the navigator's charts and the *Coast Pilot*.

20 February A few seconds after midnight John Hess saw lights ahead and what appeared to be the vague forms of ships among the black rainclouds on the horizon, so he made an emergency dive. Sonar heard nothing, though, so *Sculpin* surfaced and continued on toward Australia.

Duplicate orders came to go east of Timor-Wetar, then a cancelation of those orders was received. The captain was perplexed. He decided to keep on going as we were, thinking that what with packing and moving so precipitously, there must be plenty of confusion at headquarters.

From the radio intelligence traffic we could see that *Sculpin* was crossing a number of ship traffic lanes with potential for sighting Jap shipping, but we saw no ships. I wanted to use our last three fish.

During the day several distant explosions were heard, but we saw nothing.

To remove any doubt about the confusing messages concerning *Sculpin*'s orders, the captain sent a message to CSAF telling him that we were proceeding east of Timor and Wetar as previously directed.

21 February *Sculpin* passed east of Timor during the night. The weather was clearer. We could see the volcanic peaks on Timor, and in the southern sky the Southern Cross was rising higher and higher each night as we moved south.

Philosophizing with the torpedomen in the forward torpedo room, we agreed that our war consisted of days of dull, monotonous training, preparation, and vigilance, with infrequent periods of intense activity and excitement. The talk of the ship, however, was centered on *Sculpin*'s destination. Speculation was rampant.

22 February My star-constellation study project was moving along beautifully in the cloudless weather. The constellations, and at least one star in each, were becoming old friends. And they relieved the boredom of the hours standing on the bridge at night. More and more of the stars of the southern hemisphere were coming into view.

Through the periscope I could see the volcanic peaks of Timor fifty miles to the north. The weather was increasingly kind, the seas calm, and the air much cooler. Bridge watches were something we looked forward to eagerly. Torpedomen, engineers, electricians, seamen, and firemen kept asking for permission to come to the bridge for a breath of that delicious fresh air and to see the stars. Three at a time were allowed up. It was the first time for such a luxury since leaving Surabaya.

Sculpin was now in the Indian Ocean, headed south.

23 February   Bored with working on my submarine qualification, I selected books to read. *Lorna Doone* and Lin Yutang's *My Country and My People* were a strange combination, but they were relaxing and a welcome diversion.

I looked through my Navy Mutual Aid Association booklet and followed the recommendation that I write a will. It would be sent home when we reached port. I also wrote a letter to the Farmer's National Bank in Annapolis, asking them to send a signature card to my father so that he could sign on my account there.

Among the food items crammed into *Sculpin* at Surabaya were cases of Dutch canned fruit, which wasn't bad, and hash and sauerkraut with sausage, both of which soon got tiresome, primarily because they were not the type of food to which the crew was accustomed. The cases of food that we had to walk over in the passageways at the beginning of the patrol had all been consumed now, and we had eaten the better part of the canned food from U.S. sources. Chief Cook Duncan Hughes was down to working the Dutch items into the menu. A few people became downright nasty at seeing Dutch hash or sauerkraut on the mess table, and the displeasure was not particularly soothed by assurances that better things would soon be available. As substitutes for the Dutch items, Duncan brought out Spam and powdered eggs, which stirred up a hornet's nest.

24 February   A message in the radio traffic directed *Holland* to go to Exmouth Gulf, and from that we knew that we would certainly be ordered to Exmouth. Charlie got out the charts and the *Coast Pilot*. Located on the west coast of Australia, Exmouth Gulf was in one of the most unsettled, wildest parts of the continent. The bay was not charted, and the nearest town, Onslow, with 400 people, was fifty miles away. Would CSAF attempt to set up a base there? Across the entrance to Exmouth was a dotted line marked "unexplored." That would be interesting.

This was the longest period of calm, beautiful weather I had ever experienced in a submarine at sea. The stars were brilliant and the water was very phosphorescent, so that at night the bridge watch would be startled into believing that a torpedo was heading our way.

When submerged we sometimes saw fish through the portholes in the conning tower.* One small, bright yellow fish with black stripes played around the rail for about twenty minutes during my forenoon watch.

25 February   We submerged for the day. Middie was looking through the periscope during midafternoon and sighted a Jap *I-61*-class submarine on a southerly course at an estimated speed of twelve knots. We did our best to close, but with our slow submerged speed our closest approach presented a torpedo run of 2,700 yards, and we had only one fish in the forward torpedo room. The captain decided to give it a try. With luck we just might hit him.

The *I-61* saw the torpedo wake, made an emergency turn, and then submerged. The fish missed by a few yards. It was too bad that we didn't have more fish in the forward room. A spread pattern would have given us a better chance of a hit.

26 February   The expected orders came in; *Sculpin* was to join *Holland* in Exmouth Gulf. On my afternoon diving officer watch I saw a Consolidated flying boat go by headed for Australia. A long message came in concerning submarine results so far. The boss was obviously trying to bolster the spirits of the RAF. I penciled in my guesses for the Navy Cross awards: C. C. Smith, *Swordfish,* for greatest tonnage sunk; Bull Wright, *Sturgeon,* for sinking a carrier; Ken Hurd, *Seal,* for valuable intelligence and one sinking; Mort Mumma, *Sailfish,* for first Jap warship sunk, first depth charging, and first nervous breakdown; Gene McKinney, *Salmon,* for most ships sunk; Moon Chapple, *S-38,* for the beating he took in Lingayen Gulf; and J. C. Dempsey, *S-37,* for valuable scouting and sinking ships in Makassar Strait.

27 February   Chief Engineer Jack Turner reported that the battery showed signs of sluggishness from being operated continuously at the top of the cycle. A deep discharge to the low-voltage limit was prescribed to manage the system properly, so *Sculpin* ran at 100 feet for twelve hours, but the speed produced too much vibration to allow the periscope to be raised. The heat generated by all those amperes being drawn from the battery made the atmosphere in the boat very uncomfortable. Everyone was glad to get the discharge over and be back on the surface for the cool night air.

---

*Sculpin had small portholes in the conning tower, with heavy glass to withstand the pressure when submerged. They were permanently closed with heavy steel blanks welded over them during the refit following the second patrol.

Many of us were looking forward to meeting *Holland*. There was the possibility that their laundry still had our clothes, which had not been ready in Manila. There also might be mail, and even Christmas packages. *Sculpin* needed torpedoes. High on the list of reasons that we wanted to be near *Holland* was our need for parts to repair the air conditioning. It was not working very well; it needed freon and one unit was shut down.

28 February *Sculpin* was off Exmouth Gulf just before daylight. *Holland*, anchored inside the gulf, picked us up by radar and challenged, using the signal searchlight. With recognition formalities over, *Sculpin* was directed to proceed into the gulf and moor alongside *Holland*.

Our entry into the gulf was cautious and very slow, without charts, feeling our way, and with a leadsman on the bow taking soundings as fast as he could. Charlie was understandably anxious, while the captain, his usual calm self, was in control. *Stingray* and *Snapper* were already alongside *Holland* as *Sculpin* joined the nest after sunrise. Destroyer tender *Black Hawk* was anchored a short distance away with several of her destroyers.

We quickly reached the conclusion that our stay would be short. Exmouth Gulf was wide open to the weather as well as to surface or submarine attack, with nothing to break the Indian Ocean waves. It was no place for refit, recreation, or relaxation.

The captain went to *Holland* for instructions and returned in a short time with the announcement that we should be prepared to leave in a few hours. Our destination was Fremantle, the port of Perth, a few miles up the Swan River from Fremantle. *Snapper* and *Sculpin* would act as escorts for *Holland* en route. It was a rapid change of mission: from submarine combat patrol to escort duty!

We loaded six torpedoes and provisions for the few days' run to Fremantle. Those laundered clothes that I had been worrying about were ready for pickup. While we were busily doing as much as we could alongside *Holland*, seaplane tenders *Childs* and *Preston* came in from Darwin, Australia, to be repaired alongside *Black Hawk*. *Preston* tied up briefly alongside *Holland* to discharge several refugees, and I had the opportunity to talk with my classmate Herb Kriloff. The ship had suffered a bomb hit to the after deckhouse during a Jap bombing raid. The superstructure was riddled by bomb fragments, and thirteen men had been killed. Herb was philosophical; things could have been much worse. *Preston*'s planes were all shot down or otherwise destroyed.

Holland was crowded with passengers: a mixture of Dutch, British,

Australian, New Zealand, Philippine, and other nationalities, picked up in various places or evacuated from Tjilatjap. There were several high-ranking officers, including some whose commands had been sunk, ranking from admiral on down.

At noon *Sculpin* left the nest and anchored a short distance away; and at 1700 *Holland, Sculpin,* and *Snapper* left Exmouth Gulf for the two-day run to Fremantle. *Sculpin* and *Snapper* were stationed on each bow of *Holland* as an antisubmarine screen, zigzagging while the soundmen pinged away. We were very apprehensive, feeling that our activity was frivolous. If we did locate anything, what could we do? No doubt those on board *Holland* felt better for our presence, but we definitely did not share their feelings.

1 March, Sunday This was a day of badly needed rest. By the time we left Exmouth everyone had been active for almost twenty-four hours, and the exposure to so much sunshine had left many tender skins badly burned. Those on the bridge had to cover up and be especially cautious.

Here in the Indian Ocean, on the other side of the world from home, there was nothing but cold saltwater between *Sculpin* and the South Pole. The fine, cool weather brought out windbreakers and watch caps. The sunshine and calm seas were appreciated. A continuous stream of crewmen asked for permission to come to the bridge to relish the fresh air, and the chief of the watch in the control room had to ration the time that any one man could spend on the bridge. The cigarette deck was a favorite spot.*

2 March As was customary during the last few days on patrol, planning went full speed for the repairs and maintenance to be done in Fremantle. Lists of jobs, supplies, and parts were put together. One very encouraging factor was that we would be alongside *Holland,* our mother tender. On board *Holland* were our records, special tools, spare parts, and specialists to help with repairs. We had been away from our home tender for too many months.

Each day on my morning watch I found several flying fish on deck that had landed there during the night. I couldn't pass up such a treat. Steward's Mate Cleo Boyd picked up the fish and prepared them for my breakfast: poached flying fish, soft-boiled eggs, strips of bacon, and grits! I offered some of my treat to the other officers but none accepted. Were

*"Cigarette deck" was the name submariners gave to the small portion of deck located at the after end of the bridge, aft of the periscope shears. When out of the war zone, sailors might get permission to go to the cigarette deck to talk, smoke, and get fresh air. Some boats even had a bench there on which two or three people could sit while relaxing.

they just being polite? As for me, I had no hesitation in eating Boyd's breakfast to the last bite. One morning there were squid on deck. I showed Boyd how to prepare them and relished them for lunch.

3 March Just before dawn, the light on Rottnest Island* was sighted. With Rottnest Light to help fix the position of our formation, it was a straight shot to leave the Indian Ocean, negotiate the channel, and have *Sculpin* tied up at the dock at 0900 sharp. A general sense of relief was evident in *Sculpin*. We were no longer sitting ducks for an enemy submarine.

Patrol Summary

Number of men on board:
  63 enlisted
  6 officers

Nautical miles covered:
  4,050 on the surface
    925 submerged (in 30 dives)

Fuel used: 43,882 gallons (8.7 gallons/mile)

Drinking water:
  13,984 gallons made
  13,302 gallons consumed (6.03 gallons/man/day)

Battery water:
    735 gallons made
  1,453 gallons used (48.4 gallons/day)

Duration: 30 days

Propulsion:
  Engines used: 289 hours
  Battery propulsion: 402 hours

Torpedoes fired: 14

Sinkings:
  1 *Asashio*-class destroyer
  1 unidentified cruiser damaged**

---

*I was later told that the island was first discovered by a Dutch explorer who, on going ashore, found one of the animal inhabitants to be a small kangaroo about the size of a large rat; so the name of the island, in Dutch, became Rottnest (Rat Nest) Island. Rottnest is just offshore from the Swan River, the channel leading to the port of Fremantle.
**Later, intelligence confirmed that the unidentified warship was a *Tenryu*-class cruiser, verified in Japanese radio messages as badly damaged and listing heavily.

Refit in Fremantle

3–13 March 1942 *Sculpin* was scheduled to be in port for only a week, so the work pace was hectic. Just after we moored, Chuck Osborne came aboard and held payday. He had managed to get from Surabaya to Tjil-tajap, Java, by leasing a train to haul stragglers out before the Japanese began bombing heavily, and from there he was evacuated to Fremantle by *Holland,* again with stories to tell. We were glad to see him safe and sound.

Sculpin was showing signs of wear and tear. During the refit, in addition to the needed repair work, an aircraft-detecting radar (SD) was installed, the conning tower fairwater was cut down to change our silhouette, and the forward radio mast was removed and its antennas rerouted. Before going on patrol *Sculpin* would load a full complement of twenty-four torpedoes.

An Australian cruiser, HMAS *Adelaide,* was moored near us and we exchanged visits with them, getting to know the officers well. I also struck up friendships with several Australian civilians. One in particular, Bob Watson, was especially hospitable and invited me to his home several times. I reciprocated with meals in the *Sculpin* wardroom. We were in-trigued by the Aussie accent, slang, and terminology. Soon *Sculpin* sailors began to adopt the Aussie speech.

Sargo came in on 6 March, having been bombed and badly damaged by an Allied bomber as a result of a mixup in communications. They were understandably shaken up. Condé Raguet, my sub school classmate and good friend, filled me in on the details.

It became obvious that difficulties with the SD radar installation would not permit us to leave for patrol on the eleventh, and our departure was put off from day to day. During the delay several supply ships from the United States came in, carrying the first mail that we had received since last November. There was much anxiety in the letters from home over our safety.

The war news was dismal. We watched the few remaining Asiatic Fleet destroyers limp into Fremantle from the Java Sea engagements. Losses mounted up. *Houston* was lost with Hal Hamlin, '38, my classmates Ken Kollmyer and Frank Weiler, and Johnny Nelson, '40; *Edsall* was lost, with classmates Russ Dell and Chick Gilmore; *Asheville* was lost, with Louis Gulliver, '36, one of my Naval Academy first classmen; *De Ruyter,* a Dutch cruiser, was lost, with Otto Kolb. What a tragedy!

The local people, who expected to be subjected to Japanese attack at any time, heaped praise on our Asiatic Fleet forces, considering us saviors. They couldn't do enough for us.

By midday of the twelfth a firm departure time was announced for 0900, 13 March. Chuck Osborne was there to wish us luck, and Bob Watson arrived with a crate of hams, bacon, sausages, cheeses, and a suckling pig from his packing house and creamery. The crew loitered on deck, enjoying their last few hours of fresh air and sunshine, and reading and rereading those welcome letters from home.

Sculpin's Third Patrol

(13 March–27 April 1942)

13 March This was my duty day, and I was looking forward to getting the boat under way. Maneuvering *Sculpin* out the channel was one OOD responsibility that I really enjoyed. Commander Joe Connolly, '21, our SubDiv 22 commodore, looked anxious and somewhat forlorn as he bid us good-bye, waving from the dock as we pulled away at 0900. He was always such a fine friend, and so understanding.

We were headed for the west coast of Mindanao, Philippines, south of Surigao Strait. Our orders were to roam the area all along that coast, performing the function that subs were meant for instead of trying to stop an invasion. *Sculpin*'s crew numbered sixty-three this run, just as on the second patrol, and the officers were the same ones that had made the second patrol.

It would take at least one week to reach our patrol area. Since there was no date or time set for our arrival, the captain decided to save fuel by cruising on the surface at night at economical speed, on only two engines. The Japs were bombing northern Australia, and we didn't know how much antisubmarine activity they might throw at us. We would commence submerging to 125 feet for daytime cruising, sound patrol only, on the fourteenth.

Australia and the Aussies had captured our affection. Their friendliness and hospitality were heartwarming. They felt that we were saving them from a Japanese invasion and had gone out of their way to do things for us, although there was really very little that submarines alone could do to stop the Japs.

A few men expressed the intention to marry Australian women when we got back. Based on letters that I censored, those marriages seemed more than probable.* Aussie accents and slang expressions popped into everyday conversations.

---

*All outgoing mail was read by officers for possible breaches of security, initialed and stamped CENSORED, or returned to the writer for correction.

The "new" magazines and letters from the United States gave one more than just an impression that back there they considered the war against Japan a side issue, to be dealt with after the war in Europe was won. We in the Asiatic Fleet were expendable.

14–17 March   Official mail from Washington contained instructions from the Bureau of Ordnance concerning modifications to be made to the TDC. Some changes were so involved that I didn't see how they could be done without approximations that would not be proven until fish were actually fired and targets hit. Time would tell.

The exhaust from the main engines was a black color that was not at all normal. It should have been almost invisible. The black gang scratched their heads and went through a series of adjustments to correct the problem, but they were unsuccessful. By the sixteenth, Jack Turner had reached the conclusion that he had gotten dirty fuel from *Holland*. Our centrifuges (filters) had to be cleaned every fifteen minutes instead of the usual once each watch. Jack reserved two tanks of oil that he knew was clean, saving them for use when we might be in close contact with the enemy.

While in Fremantle I needed several uniform items that were not available from *Holland*, so Bob Watson took me to the Royal Navy supply store. There I got khaki that approximated U.S. khaki, a Royal Navy white cap cover (ribbed), and half-Wellington boots. The boots were a real find. I was continually asked where in the world I had found such handsome boots, and obtaining another pair became an objective for my next visit to Fremantle.

I passed around two boxes of cigars in celebration of my promotion to lieutenant (jg). I could not find appropriate collar marks, but Auxiliary-man Earnest Baldwin helped me clean the gold plating off the ensign marks, converting them to silver.

A rumor was going through the boat that hazardous duty pay for submarines had been increased. No one saw an official statement; that would wait until we got back to port.

Following our short, busy days in port, with all the intense activity, everyone concentrated on resting, reading mail, and getting settled into the seagoing routine. The boat was very quiet for the first few days.

17 March   CSAF radio orders changed *Sculpin*'s destination, directing us to go to the Staring Bay area of Celebes Island, our old stomping ground. We were specifically ordered to be there before the twenty-fourth, and we wondered why. We joked that CSAF felt that we knew the place better than most others and had staked a claim there. The captain ordered early nighttime cruising on two engines with two engines on the battery charge, working up to four engines on propulsion as the charge was completed. The speed was needed to be on station as ordered.

18 March   *Sculpin* received a message announcing the award of the Navy Cross to our captain. Everyone felt that Lucius Chappell was the best submarine commander and leader in the submarine force. Doubtless almost every other submarine crew felt the same way about their skipper.

A CSAF message told of a Japanese carrier due to arrive at Kendari on 24 March. That answered the question of the importance of the 24 March date.

Spirits in the boat were boosted by still another message reporting a raid by RAAF (Royal Australian Air Force) and U.S. planes on a Jap ship concentration at Port Morseby, New Guinea. Twenty-four ships were reported sunk or damaged. That was more to our liking.

Other messages told of MacArthur's plans to set up headquarters as Supreme Allied Commander in Australia.

19 March   While heading for the passage west of Timor Island we encountered a troublesome cross sea that caused the boat to labor and the bridge to be unusually wet. *Sculpin* hadn't seen anything like that for some time. During midevening a giant wave sent so much water over the bridge that tons went through the conning tower hatch, then on into the control room. As a result, the torpedo air compressor, the low-pressure air blower, and the hydraulic motor controller panel were all grounded. The captain ordered a course change and slowed to ten knots until sea conditions improved. Technicians went right to work making repairs.

Reading and rereading letters from home, I decided that the folks back there totally misunderstood the facts of this submarine war in the Far East. They expected to hear from me frequently, even though I had repeatedly warned them that such would definitely not be the case. They could not understand why they had heard nothing from me since November.

Just before the war began I subscribed to the Dollar-a-Month Book Club, and now I enjoyed the selections, along with the magazines that had arrived with the mail in Fremantle. When I finished reading a book, it was promptly caught up in the ship's library, and when next seen, weeks later, it would be tattered if not completely worn out. *Whistle Stop*, by Martha Wolff, was the latest book club offering.

20 March   Another quiet day, just as the past week had been as far as sighting anything of the enemy. Several times sonar reported hearing what was thought to be submarine noise, but we were never able to develop anything to shoot at. The noise would intensify, then fade away and leave us wondering. Repairs to the water damages of the nineteenth were completed, and all systems were go again.

I kept remembering a night at the Lido Club, on the ocean near Fremantle, when a Dutch aviator sang "Song of the Fatherland." How moved the crowd was; they continued to stand after he finished, and his solo was followed by a cheer that almost lifted the roof off.

21–22 March   Surface conditions changed to mirror calm with very clear water. The captain ordered listening patrol at 100 feet to avoid the possibility of being sighted by air patrols.

The captain was quoted as observing that he was always glad when Mendy was relieved on night watches because "Mendy always finds ships at night." Some reputation!

The twenty-second was livened up only by the seizure of a piston in number 4 engine. This was the first such problem with *Sculpin*'s engines. The diesel mechanics had an around-the-clock job to get the engine back on line; they laid the blame on the dirty fuel received from *Holland*. *Sculpin* was slowed to a point where we were not certain of making it to Staring Bay in time to welcome the Jap carrier on the twenty-fourth.

23 March   This day there was another problem: number 2 periscope cable was damaged as a result of a kink over the hoist drum. Fortunately the kink was near the bitter end. The periscope was made operable by shortening the cable and resweating the lug. It could not be fully housed, however, and about nine feet of periscope stuck above the shears, a fact to be considered when we were submerged near a surface ship.

The weather again changed dramatically—to rough seas, rainsqualls, and hazy visibility. A CSAF message reported major enemy units in the Staring Bay area.

Most of the new literature aboard had been devoured by now, and a wardroom chess tournament was under way. John Hess started me off with a loss right off the bat.

24 March   *Sculpin* completed the passage through Ombai Strait, west of Timor, before daylight. The rainstorms were so heavy that we submerged twice because of poor visibility. The old saw about not being able to see your hand in front of your face took on real meaning. Surface cruising was uncomfortable; the safest place to be was underwater, where you could at least listen with sonar. The moon was up earlier in the night, casting dark shadows from behind the black clouds of the threatening rainstorms. Unexpected temperature layers in the water and strange currents made depth control tricky.

A CSAF message reported that the Jap carrier would not arrive at Staring Bay until 26 March. That was good news; we would be there on time to greet him.

25 March   A violent rainstorm forced *Sculpin* to submerge shortly after midnight and conduct a listening patrol. By 0338 visibility had improved enough that we could surface and take position off the southeast approaches to Staring Bay. We saw nothing all day.

On the surface after sunset I was in the control room waiting to hear the radio news from London when the whole ship gave a shudder. I knew that a torpedo had been fired. The leading torpedoman, TM1/c Bill Dowell, earlier had gotten permission to conduct routine maintenance and tests in the forward torpedo room. They planned to fire inboard slugs to test the air impulse system. What we felt, however, was no inboard slug.

I raced forward, knowing that something had gone terribly wrong, and found that in the process of firing water slugs, a 2/c torpedoman became confused, manually disconnected the safety interlocks on the wrong tube, number 4, and then manually fired number 4 tube, which was loaded with a torpedo. The outer door of number 4 was closed, so the torpedo battered the door open and went out. It was anybody's guess where that fish went.

Just before the untimely firing, Dowell, who was in charge, had gone to the after part of the torpedo room looking for a tool. He had not had an opportunity to double-check the procedure, as was his responsibility, nor had he given permission for the manual firing, which he was required to do before any firing could take place. The junior torpedoman had committed a grievous, possibly even a disastrous, error.

Number 4 torpedo tube was functioning properly as far as the gyro spindle engaging and disengaging were concerned. The stop bolt lifted properly, but attempts to operate the outer door were fruitless. Our inboard analysis of the situation was frightening. The torpedo might be wedged partway out of the tube, possibly armed and ready to explode if jolted.

The only way to find out was to go over the side and make an underwater inspection, and I was the logical one for that job. Gunner Caserio and two other men would accompany me to tend a safety line. With *Sculpin* stopped dead in the water, I went over the side with a watertight lantern and face mask and swam down to the outer door for a firsthand look.

The torpedo had forced the shutter and door, stripping gears and playing havoc, but it had gone away from the boat, so any fear of a wedged-in, armed torpedo was eliminated. Stew Burner Bill Zwally, one of those tending the safety line, was reported to have remarked that he had a perfect opportunity to get rid of Mr. Mendenhall if he wasn't such a good shipmate. My ego soared when I was told of that remark.

Sculpin's Torpedo Department was in hack. We would have those broken and loose exterior parts knocking around, making noises, until we got to port for repairs. As an added precaution, the inner door to number 4 tube was shored up with steel angle irons and wire straps pulled taut with chain falls.

Disciplinary action for the 2/c torpedoman was postponed until the next refit period.

Sculpin continued on patrol but saw nothing of the enemy.

26 March   Daylight submerged hours were uneventful. Back on the surface at sundown, *Sculpin* received a CSAF message to patrol the approaches to Staring Bay south of Greyhound Strait. The captain immediately put on all four engines and headed north.

I was OOD, anticipating my relief near midnight, when we sighted dense black smoke to the northwest. The captain came to the bridge and directed maneuvers as we worked our way around an unescorted ship to a good firing position. Our potential target was moving to the southwest at about ten knots. Everything was going well until the captain went below for a short time. During his absence the exec changed course toward the target, causing *Sculpin* to lose her advantage.

By the time the captain got back to the bridge we could see the target plainly. It was a cargo ship of about 4,000 tons, but we had lost position. By maneuvering on the surface we could still have reached a good firing spot. Instead, because of the bright moonlight, the captain followed the exec's advice: submerge for a periscope attack.

We were too far off the target track, and missed with a three-fish spread from the bow tubes, at an estimated range of 3,700 yards. The captain's judgment was far better than the exec's; he would have kept us on the surface, in a much better maneuvering posture, for a more promising attack at short range.

27 March   The target, unalerted, continued on south toward Staring. We reloaded fish, then surfaced in an attempt to run around for another shot. At daylight, still 5,000 yards off the track and with no hope of getting closer, *Sculpin* submerged and gave up the chase. It was a bitter disappointment after all the problems of the past few days.

The Jap carrier had not put in an appearance as scheduled.

28 March   Just after midnight, Middie, newly qualified as OOD, saw a dark shape ahead. It disappeared. The soundmen reported screw noises, so *Sculpin* submerged for an hour to avoid the possibility of being the target of an enemy submarine.

Before daybreak, south of Greyhound Strait, *Sculpin* submerged for the day to conduct a periscope patrol.

We sighted the upper works of a large cargo ship at 0630. The ship tracked as going northerly, toward Greyhound, and was estimated to be about 8,000 tons. *Sculpin* could close only to a range of 14,000 yards, much too far for our fish.

In midafternoon, another large cargo ship, about 7,500 tons, and one escort were sighted heading north. At battle stations we tracked the ship, maneuvering for forty-five minutes to reach an excellent firing position at a range of 1,350 yards. My TDC solution looked good, and we fired a three-fish spread from the bow tubes. All fish ran hot, straight, and normal, but there were no hits.

The captain saw agitation and excitement among the target ship's crew and bridge personnel. From their actions he concluded that they could see the torpedo wakes running under them. He watched the escort moving rapidly in our direction, so we went deep to evade. The escort never did establish contact. Distant explosions were heard.

After a short time *Sculpin* came up to periscope depth, where the captain could see the superstructure of the escort, now miles away. By sundown our torpedo tubes were reloaded; and at dark we surfaced for the night.

29 March   This was a quiet Sunday spent patrolling the northeast approaches to Staring Bay. Nothing was sighted.

Having used seven fish from the forward torpedo room, we made plans to move south about forty miles to be near a small island named Runduma, away from the traffic lanes, so the torpedomen could move the four fish from the deck storage to the forward torpedo room. We needed calm weather to make the transfer. The moon would be bright. The captain wanted to be near land so that those working on deck could swim to safety should they be left in the water if *Sculpin* had to dive to avoid a Japanese ship or airplane.

Transferring the fish would require opening a section of the topside decking. A king post and boom would be rigged, with chain hoists to help jockey the fish out of storage and lift them up to deck level. The angled torpedo loading hatch to the forward torpedo room would be opened, and the fish, one by one, would be gently snaked along the deck to a position where they could be further skidded down to the torpedo room.

I had never moved torpedoes at sea. Under these conditions it would be tricky, and we made careful preparations to do the job. Gear was assembled: life vests, matches in watertight containers, survival equipment, guns, knives, waterproof flashlights, and minimum compact rations. Each man had his own bundle of clothes with a white hat, a white uniform, dungarees, extra shoes, and anything else that he thought he might need if left on a jungle island. We were rank amateurs at contemplating such eventualities.

Gunner and I memorized the recognition signals for the next several nights, just in case we needed to signal with our flashlights to contact *Sculpin* from the island.

30 March   During daylight *Sculpin* was on periscope patrol of the northeast approaches to Staring Bay but sighted nothing. At sunset we surfaced to move to Runduma for the torpedo transfer.

By midevening, in a calm sea, under cloudless skies and bright moonlight, *Sculpin* was in position and ready. The torpedo-moving team went on deck to perform their job. Everything came off like clockwork. We had guessed that it would take us four hours. Actually, with ten men plus Gunner and me, the work was wrapped up and all was secure in only two hours. The captain and the exec were pleased with the performance, and we all breathed a sigh of relief when our men were safely back inside the boat. For several days the main topic of conversation would be stories about that night's work.

Added to the many barnacle scratches that I had picked up during my dives to inspect the torpedo tube outer door, I sustained a mashed finger, additional bruises, and greaselike blotches all over me from torpedo preservative. Doc Miller helped the healing process with his superior cures, after first removing the stains with medical alcohol.

A CSAF message projected major movement of Jap ships in the next few days from Kendari toward Darwin in northern Australia. *Sculpin* moved to cover the southern entrances to Staring Bay.

The exec informed me that as soon as I got my submarine qualification notebook finished, the captain would recommend to the Bureau of Personnel in Washington that I be designated qualified in submarines, adding to my incentive to finish that job. The notebook was essentially complete, anyway.

31 March We patrolled the southeast entrances to Staring Bay, near Wowoni Island, uneventfully until close to midnight, when, again in bright moonlight, heavy black smoke was sighted. The smoke tracked as moving south toward Staring at about ten knots. We continued tracking while the captain maneuvered for a favorable position to attack. As we closed the range we saw a cargo ship, estimated at about 5,000 tons. There was no escort.

1 April At 0310 *Sculpin* was in excellent position. We submerged and then fired a three-fish spread from the bow tubes at a range of 1,000 yards. The setup was perfect. The captain watched the wakes of the fish as they ran under the target. There were no explosions. We had missed again. The target continued on as if nothing had happened.

The captain was furious and expressed his disgust at the way the torpedoes performed. He talked of going back to base and not risking his ship and crew with such unreliable weapons until the torpedo deficiencies were corrected.*

Shortly before midnight I was again OOD; the moon was high and thinly covered with clouds. We saw light flashing under the clouds near the horizon, seeming to be distant gunfire. After much discussion we concluded that the source of the flashes of "gunfire" was moonlight reflecting from small ripples on the glassy surface of the sea.

2–10 April The next eight days were spent patrolling the various entrances to Staring Bay: north of Wowoni, east of Wowoni Strait, and the northern approaches to Buton Passage. All was quiet.

A detailed check of every fish in the tubes and of all ready fish found nothing out of specification. However, we found that two of the fish that had been transferred from deck storage had serious problems with their

---

*I spent much of the next two days minutely going over the data, recomputing everything, and could find no reason for the misses except a torpedo depth control failure or a malfunction of the detonators in the warheads.

warheads. While they were in the airtight storage air pressure had leaked from the torpedo high-pressure air flasks into the storage, and on into the warheads. As the storage doors were opened on the night of transfer, we heard the air hiss out of the storage. When pressure was released from the storage, the pressure that was trapped inside two of the warheads had no way to equalize quickly with the outside air except to push out, like a balloon, the soft copper lining of the detonator cavity. The detonators themselves were stored safely inside the boat.

I reported the damaged warheads to the exec and the captain, explaining what had happened. With their permission, we believed we could make repairs that would permit us to use the two fish if they should be needed. Permission was granted, and we began work on one torpedo, expecting to learn from any problems on the first warhead so repairs would be easier on the second.

We rotated the torpedo upside down to bring the detonator cavity up where we could get at it. Then we carefully cut out the soft copper cavity lining. The high explosive in the warheads was known to be insensitive, so we were not hesitant to do this work. Some of the explosive had shattered, and there was a small amount of chunks and powdered particles in the bottom of the cavity. The loose explosive was spooned out and dropped into a bucket of water, then taken to the bridge to be given the deep six.

Most of us had never seen high explosive that closely. Explosives were always packaged in one way or another, invisible inside a warhead or other ammunition component. Actually seeing and feeling the live explosive was a new experience.

While the cavity was being attended to, the copper lining was carefully hammered into the proper shape over a wooden mandrel that Auxiliary-man Baldwin had made in duplication of the real detonator. We used an assortment of nonsteel tools in the process of reshaping the liner: jacks, wooden plugs, wedges, and hammers. It was painstaking, tedious work, taking more than six hours for the first warhead. We were so engrossed in the work that it was not until later, as we thought over what we had been doing and what might have happened, that the possibility of danger dawned on us.

Periodically the captain came to the forward room, watched for a few seconds, shook his head, and went back to the after areas of the boat. The first repair was completed on 3 April, and we began work on the second warhead. At the end of the workday on 4 April the second fish was ready to fire.

Easter Sunday was on 5 April. No enemy activity was seen in the Staring Bay area. The Japanese surely were aware of *Sculpin*'s presence because of the attacks we had made. That may have caused them to be especially alert and to tailor their movements to avoid us. Staring Bay had so many entrances, and *Sculpin,* following doctrine, stayed too far away from any one of the entrances to be effective.

Radio messages concerning Corregidor and Bataan on the seventh were ominous. MacArthur had gotten away just in time. I wondered what had happened to my friends in Manila. There were cheering messages concerning the British shooting down or damaging fifty-seven Japanese planes at Colombo.

By the ninth *Sculpin* had patrolled every conceivable entrance to Staring Bay. Inactivity was becoming tedious. Then, shortly after submerging at daylight, Middie reported a ship sighted. We began tracking. The "ship" turned out to be an island, and the exec, getting a better point at last to fix his position after the hazy, stormy weather, found *Sculpin* to be thirty miles south of where his DR (dead reckoning) said we were. Shades of Baler Bay!

Number 4 engine suffered another piston seizure: the dirty oil from *Holland.* Jack and his black gang had their work cut out for them to get that engine back on line quickly.

Disappointed at having made no sightings for ten days, the captain decided at last to go in closer and take a look inside Staring Bay. The wardroom junior officers had been regularly hinting that we ought to do so, particularly since radio messages indicated a concentration of ships in the bay.

The Dutch broadcast radio from Surabaya was a godsend. From that radio, however, we learned the discouraging news of the loss of two British cruisers and an aircraft carrier in the Bay of Bengal. Encouraging reports concerned Allied planes from Australia bombing Japanese positions on Timor and New Guinea.

11 April   We went into Staring Bay, but not far enough. The nearest *Sculpin* got to the middle of the bay was about twelve miles. The captain said he was satisfied that there were no ships there; then in the same breath he said he thought he saw masts of at least one ship. We were still five miles outside the 100-fathom curve when the last observation was made and we turned and headed out to deeper water. If there were masts of one ship, there probably were others. We could have gone in another 10,000 yards and barely reached the 100-fathom curve. We were just too far away to be effective. Prewar caution was too persuasive for the captain.

After sunset *Sculpin* surfaced and headed for Greyhound Strait, following instructions from CSAF.

The education program for my men was at the point where I had ten men ready for their final "qualified in submarines" examination by either Charlie Henderson or Jack Turner. The men had to be taken through the boat to answer questions about the functions of the various systems and to show that they could perform any operations that might be asked of them. Several had been ready for weeks, but both Charlie and Jack kept putting me off because they were too busy. Now they both agreed that they could actually schedule and complete the examinations by the end of the week. Great!

12–13 April   More quiet days off the southern end of Greyhound Strait.

I assembled general information about torpedoes not found in the training manuals for my torpedomen strikers (seamen working toward the rating of third class torpedoman), and began using that in our school. We were as far as we could go on advancement and qualification until Charlie and Jack did their part.

14 April   *Sculpin* moved to patrol the Salabanka Strait–Peleng Strait line. Again, there were no sightings.

For some days I had observed our leading torpedoman, Torpedoman 1/c Bill Dowell, becoming more and more nervous. He had lost weight and looked bad. On the thirteenth he complained to Doc Miller that he had a splitting headache; then he proceeded to pass out right on the spot. I had been urging him to take it easy, stay in his bunk, and let the "youngsters" do the work, but he was too active in temperament to follow my suggestion. Doc and I realized that we were going to have to be very careful with him because he appeared to be on the verge of a nervous breakdown.

I took Dowell off all duty and ordered him to stay in his bunk. He still complained of splitting headaches. It was pitiful to see the normally vigorous man so thin, trembling, and faltering in speech. The prospect of losing Dowell when we got back to port was one thing I hated to think of, but I knew that it was a near certainty. He was badly in need of rest and relaxation from the stress of submarine patrol.

15 April   The area west of Peleng produced no sightings.

My concentrated educational program for the torpedomen strikers was good therapy for Dowell. He had a special assignment to that project, and it kept his mind busy so he wouldn't feel completely left out of things. After school the strikers wanted to know if apples for the teacher were in order, which reminded me of how good it would be to eat some fresh fruit and vegetables. Canned food was tiresome. We hadn't seen anything fresh for a long time.

The captain sent CSAF a summary of *Sculpin*'s patrol activity and included the gratuitous information that we could remain on station for one more week. I hoped to see some action and get rid of more torpedoes.

16 April On the Nederburgh–Thames Reef Line; we spent another uneventful day. During midevening CSAF orders told *Sculpin* to proceed to Fremantle, going east of Timor Island. Charlie's projected route would take us by the southern entrances to Staring Bay on the seventeenth.

Dowell was looking better every day, but he was still weak and nervous. The striker's school kept his mind on things to teach the younger men.

Radio news told of the loss of *Perch* in the Java Sea. My classmate Jake Vandergriff was a member of her company.* *Perch* had followed *Sculpin* to the Staring Bay area after our second patrol.

17 April Submerged, an hour after sunrise, moving across the southern approaches to Staring Bay, Jack, then diving officer, sighted masts to the northwest. We began closing. At 0831 the masts were identified as those of a large tanker and one escort. We were unable to get closer than 8,000–10,000 yards, not nearly close enough to fire our fish. The tanker appeared to be heading for Ambon. If we had delayed for only a few minutes the night before, we would have been in good position for an attack.

At sunset *Sculpin* surfaced and sent a message to CSAF concerning the tanker. According to our information, *Swordfish* might be in position to use that intelligence off Ambon.

The captain ordered four engines on the line to make best speed toward Fremantle. We continued submerged in the daytime because we were still well within Japanese antisubmarine territory.

Encouraging news reports told of our airmen bombing Cebu, Davao, and points on Luzon.

18 April *Sculpin* rounded the corner east of Timor, then headed southwest toward the Indian Ocean.

---

*Surviving the sinking of *Perch,* Jake was imprisoned by the Japanese and was repatriated at the end of the war.

As we rounded the Timor corner there were rough seas to negotiate. On one occasion the boat took an unusual down angle. Bilge water entered the casing of number 2 generator, grounding the wiring. The casing was drained, then flushed out with battery water. Heaters and fans directed on the generator helped to dry the dampness. The fields still showed zero resistance, so repair work was discontinued until we reached Fremantle.

Good news came in by radio concerning the Doolittle bombing raid on Yokohama, Tokyo, and Kobe. We could feel the enthusiasm throughout the boat. Those planes bombing Japan could only have been launched from aircraft carriers. Then there was news of Royal Air Force bombing raids in Germany, almost around the clock for one week, as well as the RAAF and U.S. aircraft increasing pressure on the Japs north of Australia and in Borneo. Smiles lit up through the length of the boat. Any shred of encouragement was appreciated.

19 April   I finally finished my submarine qualification notebook. Charlie drafted a letter recommending me for the designation "qualified in submarines."

We had been wearing shorts and sandals for so long that I began to anticipate the cool weather of Fremantle. As we were leaving on this patrol, the pilot informed us that temperatures of sixty degrees were average for May.

Churchill's *Blood, Sweat, and Tears* was my spare-time reading at this point in the patrol.

20–23 April   *Sculpin* continued to spend days submerged and nights on the surface. Nighttime speed was "best on 3 engines," as there was no urgency to get to port a few hours earlier.

On 20 April, just before daybreak, flares were sighted to northwest at an estimated 15,000–20,000 yards. No gunfire was heard, so the source was ruled to be aircraft. There was no action against *Sculpin*. We neither heard nor saw any planes.

By this point in the patrol I had written eight letters to be mailed when we got in, besides completing the qualification notebook and the regular school program for my troops, and had done so much reading that my eyes were very tired. Quentin Reynolds's *London Diary* was the current book on my bunk.

On 23 April the captain ordered that *Sculpin* stay on the surface continually. The fact that the air conditioning quit was a strong incentive for the decision. That last day submerged, with no air conditioning, was a killer.

It seemed strange to be on the surface during all twenty-four hours of a day. The cool, fresh air and beautiful days gave everyone a shot in the arm. CSAF was notified of our ETA off Fremantle as 27 April, two hours before dawn, by long-standing navy custom. Job orders, work requests, supply lists, spare parts lists, and addenda to the captain's patrol report were ready.

A bridge game fad hit the wardroom. Maybe it was the cooler weather. I had extra time now that my qualification notebook was finished. With four officers standing deck watches, there was more time for diversions. Charlie Henderson and I teamed up against Jack Turner and John Hess each night for a few hands of bridge. Release of tensions was evident throughout the boat as everyone anticipated getting to port.

More reading time brought out LaBoyteaux's *The Rules of the Road at Sea* for review, and I was even wishing for some correspondence course work in strategy and tactics and international law. Those courses had been discontinued for the duration of the war, dropping me out of the navy's formal education program.

24–26 April   These were more uneventful days spent moving down the west coast of Australia. As I had hoped, the flying fish and squid were again plentiful, providing great breakfasts when poached, with bacon and grits. The air was cool enough for us to sleep under a sheet, which in itself was unusual. The crew was regularly cautioned to be very careful about getting too much sun; we had been out of the sun for a long time. As was customary, at any one time a few of the crew were allowed to come on the cigarette deck for fresh air and sunshine. The chief on watch in the control room kept score and timed their visits to the bridge. Even in the middle of the night someone would pop up through the hatch to ask for permission to come up and breathe that fine air and admire the stars. I took the opportunity to point out stars and constellations in the Southern Hemisphere's sky. The Southern Cross and Scorpio shone like diamonds.

The exec, Doc, and I counseled Torpedoman Dowell about his health and nervous condition. He realized that he shouldn't go out on another patrol and raised no objection to being transferred when we got to port.

By the twenty-sixth I had written fourteen personal letters to mail on arrival, in answer to those I had received just before we left on patrol.

The stack of the crew's mail mounted in the wardroom waiting to be censored, a task that none of the officers looked forward to.

The poker game in the crew's mess got to be too high-stakes an affair. Officers' Steward A. L. Newton, on his base pay of $21 per month, was reputed to be something like $500 ahead. That could have meant trouble, so Charlie stepped in and stopped the game.

At almost midnight on the twenty-sixth a cheer went through the boat when the announcement was made over the loudspeaker that Rottnest Island Light was in sight.

27 April   I was OOD on that cold, rainy, wintry predawn. Wearing our heaviest sweaters, windbreakers, and watch caps, we met our escort, USS *Isabel*, at 0330. My Royal Navy half-Wellingtons were welcome ankle warmers. Recognition signals exchanged, we followed her around for some time in a puzzling series of maneuvers. (The purpose, we found out later, was to kill time because the antisubmarine boom across the river entrance, installed while we were away, would not open until 0700.)

The boom was only partially open at 0710 when *Sculpin* impatiently squeezed past and headed for the navy base. The captain had his patrol report in hand as Admiral Lockwood and his greeting party waited on the dock for our lines to be secured. The admiral, with typical enthusiasm, jumped from the dock to *Sculpin*'s deck even before the brow was over.

The homecoming was not a happy one. I overheard the captain forcefully giving the admiral his thoughts about our torpedoes.

The patrol report stressed problems with torpedoes, saying, ". . . I was completely disheartened and demoralized. I had little heart for further action until analysis and reasons for the misses could be established. What were the deficiencies? What corrective action was necessary?" The report continued with recommendations for the tender experts' attention:

1. Closely examine the remaining torpedoes. Check all adjustments, particularly depth control and exploders.
2. Have the torpedo repair officer check our routines, preparation, and maintenance.
3. Examine all torpedo tubes for possible problems.
4. Fire dummy torpedoes in port to check out the torpedo tubes.

Further recommendations were:

5. Remove the decking over the boat storage to make it easier to remove torpedoes from their deck storage.

6. Remove the boat stored in the superstructure. (That was one piece of equipment we could easily do without. The engine in the boat never ran properly, launching the boat was a pain in the neck, and the boat wasn't seaworthy because of its very low freeboard.)

7. The mattresses on all bunks had become unsatisfactory. The submarine navy must provide better mattresses.

8. Remove the distant tracker from the conning tower.

In regard to the physical condition of the crew, the captain wrote as follows:

> There was a deteriorating physical and psychological well-being that was cause for concern. Sleeplessness, headaches, lassitude, loss of appetite, decreased mental alertness, emotional instability, and increased nervousness were noticeable. Any change of course or speed, particularly on the surface, caused noticeable tension. A competent, experienced helmsman would get far off course trying to move the compass card to the lubber's line. The slightest physical ailment would affect all out of proportion, and it was necessary to make free use of sedatives.

Patrol Summary

Number of men on board:
   63 enlisted
   6 officers

Nautical miles covered:
   6,747 on the surface
   1,118 submerged

Fuel used: 69,160 gallons (8.76 gallons/mile)

Drinking water:
   15,578 gallons made
   15,469 gallons consumed (6.94 gallons/man/day)

Battery water:
   2,402 gallons made
   2,566 gallons used (57 gallons/day)

Duration: 45 days

Torpedoes fired: 9

Sinkings: none; no damage done

Refit in Fremantle and Albany

27 April–29 May   The feeling of homecoming at Fremantle was promptly cut short when the welcoming party informed us that *Sculpin* was to leave the next day to go farther south for refit at a place called Albany, about 200 miles away on Australia's south coast. The possibility of Japanese air raids on Fremantle, of great concern at the time, caused the shift. My *Mississippi* shipmate Chuck Osborne came by to say good-bye. He expected orders to duty in the States.

Sculpin left in late afternoon for the two-day trip, encountering very rough weather with cold, rain, and heavy seas. There were many seasick seamen and officers. At Albany refit commenced early on the morning of 30 April alongside *Holland,* with three other submarines in the nest. The damaged number 4 torpedo tube was top priority. There were no spare parts on board *Holland,* so a machine shop in Perth was contracted to manufacture them. Chief Torpedoman Arthur P. (Doggie) Dawes reported for duty to replace the ailing Bill Dowell. The torpedoman who caused the accident to the torpedo tube was tried by summary court-martial and sentenced to reduction in rating, a fine, and a bad-conduct discharge.

The citizens of Albany—a small, remote town—turned out in force to make us feel at home. We frequently saw the mayor, councilmen, and others at the Freemason Hotel, where we were quartered; the Albany Club, where we were made honorary members; and at parties given by the city, the tender, or by individual submarines. An Australian destroyer, HMAS *Voyager,* was in Albany and we entertained her officers, exchanging visits and meeting them at the hotel, club, and parties. Bob Watson in Perth had given me a letter of introduction to his friends Bill and Elsa Anderson. They invited me to their home and we saw each other at social functions.

The captain sent my submarine qualification letter off to be favorably endorsed by the commodore on its way to Washington. Each day we kept expecting the torpedo tube parts to come in, but they didn't, so on 14 May Charlie Henderson and I went by train to Perth for four days' leave. There we saw friends and spent enjoyable days and nights sightseeing and at parties and dances.

The parts for the torpedo tube arrived in Albany on the same train with Charlie and me on the nineteenth and were immediately installed. Everyone's work had been completed for several days, with fuel and stores loaded and twenty Mk-14 fish on board, waiting for my department to finish the tube work.

Well after dark on 21 May the tube repair was wrapped up. The next day *Holland* divers completed underwater inspections and we fired dummy torpedoes to make certain that everything functioned properly. Finally, on 23 May, under-way tests were completed in Albany Bay and *Sculpin* headed directly for Fremantle. With good weather this trip, we arrived there early in the morning of 25 May.

Final preparations for patrol were made during a four-day stay while we again enjoyed the hospitality of Aussie friends. Ensign Frank Alvis, USNR, reported for duty from sub school, taking over the duties of first lieutenant and becoming assistant communications officer to help Middie with his load of decoding. John Hess left us to be exec of *Searaven*. His experience, friendship, and steady hand would be sorely missed.

Sculpin's Fourth Patrol

(29 May–17 July 1942)

29 May *Sculpin* was under way from Fremantle at 1500, accompanied by Australian destroyers HMAS *Stuart* and HMAS *Voyager*. On this patrol the number of men in the crew increased to sixty-seven; the officers numbered the usual six, with Frank Alvis in place of John Hess. We were carrying only twenty fish because they were still in short supply in the western Pacific.

During the refit two new instruments had been installed: a tank compass and a bathythermograph. The compass, the magnetic type used in Army tanks, was located near the gyro compass, to be used as a backup for the gyro. The bathythermograph was an instrument that created a graph showing water temperature at various depths below the surface of the water. The purpose of the graph was to provide the Diving Officer with knowledge as to where rapid exchanges in water temperature occurred, thus aiding in evasion of antisubmarine attacks. Routinely, on first submerging for the day, a sub would go deep to get the bathythermograph trace, to be prepared for contact with the enemy.

At a gathering of officers in the wardroom, the captain went over the planned route of the patrol, which was to be in the South China Sea off the coast of French Indo-China. The route to the area was circuitous and involved. We were going by way of Lombok Strait (between Lombok and Bali), Makassar Strait (between Borneo and Celebes), Sibutu Passage (between Tawi-Tawi and Sibutu, the Sulu Archipelago), through the Sulu Sea, between Pearl Bank and Doc Can Island, north of Bancoran Island; thence through Balabac Strait (between Balabac Island and Bangii Island), into the South China Sea, continuing west to the coast of Indo-China near Camranh Bay.

Commodore Connolly had warned the captain that *Sculpin* would probably be required to transfer at least one officer and a number of enlisted ratings when we got back from patrol. This meant that we must get as many men trained as possible in their specialties, as well as qualified in submarines, in anticipation of transfers. My school programs went into high gear.

Sculpin submerged for a trim dive after we passed the 100-fathom curve, also giving the sonar operators on *Voyager* and *Stuart* the opportunity to practice on a real submarine. An hour later they signaled *Sculpin* to surface and we all headed north, but they made much greater speed than we could. As *Sculpin* fell behind, we exchanged flashing light messages of bon voyage with our *Voyager* friends before they disappeared over the horizon.

During our refit the Asiatic Fleet designation was abolished, so there was no longer a CSAF. The new name was a mouthful: Commander Submarines Southwest Pacific Force (CSSWP).

The long period in port had given *Sculpin*'s men the much-needed rest that the captain, in his patrol report, said was so essential. Throughout the ship one could feel the excitement and eagerness at getting back to the war as we moved north through calm seas under clear, sunny skies.

30–31 May, 1 June   Everyone enjoyed the fine weather with near full moon at night. It seemed just like a pleasure cruise. My constellation and star identification pastime received renewed attention. Venus came up like a lighthouse in the east, over the distant Australian mainland. Canopus was more brilliant than I had ever seen it, changing color from white to red to green.

Sculpin's circuitous route to the South China Sea would cross many shipping lanes and, we hoped, present us with opportunities to sink ships even before reaching the patrol area.

The navigator was pushing to get *Sculpin* through Lombok Strait at night, on the surface, because the currents could be quite difficult to buck when submerged. As we got back into patrol routine, there was a stack of new *Time, Life,* and *New Yorker* magazines waiting to be read. Few of us had taken time to do much reading during the refit.

Middie settled in as communications and commissary officer. With John Hess no longer aboard, Jack Turner, Middie, and I were standing all the OOD watches while Frank Alvis was learning the ropes and working to qualify as OOD. With only three of us on top duty, the watches came up too regularly, and we urged Frank to qualify as soon as possible. I had moved up in the hierarchy to number 4 and turned the job of first lieutenant over to Frank.

Jack promptly gave Frank the nickname "Meatball," because his fair skin burned so easily in the intense sunlight of OOD watches. He was always red faced, even after only a short time in the sun.

2 June *Sculpin* went to the reversa routine. As we submerged, it was evident that something was not right with the operating linkage to the flood valve of negative tank. (Negative tank was normally empty, but it was routinely filled on diving in order to give the submarine added negative buoyancy and thus assist the boat to submerge more rapidly. Negative was blown dry with air pressure once the boat was settled down underwater.)

Jack suggested that we could keep negative tank full all the time until our return, when repairs could be made. The captain agreed, and we continued on our way. That modified the normal diving procedure; now *Sculpin* would be sluggish in getting underwater, adding another factor that needed to be kept in mind by the watch making the dive.

3–4 June These were routine days spent approaching Lombok Strait. The names of three new submarines were showing up in the radio messages, indicating that *Gar, Grampus,* and *Tautog* were under the command of CSSWP.

Those of us who did the decoding wished there were some way for those boats to get their standing instructions without burdening us with so much decoding. To be absolutely certain that *Sculpin* did not miss any important orders, radio copied all the messages, not just those with a heading indicating *Sculpin* as the addressee. We then had to decode all those messages. Some instructions and orders to the new boats were voluminous.

My submarine qualification school got under way with twenty-five students.

On 4 June we spent the day at 125 feet, approaching Lombok, and commenced passage through the strait just after dark, on the surface, as Charlie had planned.

5–7 June An hour past midnight on the fifth, *Sculpin* was through Lombok without incident. There were a number of expected riptides, causing the navigator concern over his position. One time we stopped to let him get a better fix. Many lights were seen on shore and on numerous small craft in the area. The captain talked with the bridge watch, suggesting that we ask the Japs to let us stop on Bali for shore liberty. He also speculated about Dutch friends in Surabaya, telling about a New Year's dinner date with friends there. Would we make it? The broadcast radio reported thousand-plane raids on Germany. That was encouraging.

Shortly after midnight I was OOD when a ship was sighted, then another. We began our approach to look them over and found that they were just big sailboats. Those sails were deceiving.

Sculpin continued heading north through Makassar Strait. Small sailing boats were frequently in sight, as well as lights at night on Celebes, as we favored that side of the strait.

The lack of enemy contacts allowed me to stay busy during working hours supervising the torpedo gang, catching up on paperwork, and reading the numerous bulletins that had come in from Washington, particularly from the Bureau of Ordnance concerning torpedoes and gunnery. Then there was my school for submarine qualification and trying to help as many men as I could qualify for their dolphins. I took a great deal of satisfaction in reorganizing the torpedo and gunnery files, reducing them from ten to only three, slashing red tape, shredding and burning superfluous dictates.

In the mail were a number of unexpected personal letters from friends at home, telling me how much they were thinking of me. Some were in response to letters I had mailed when we got in from the last patrol. That was a mighty fast turnaround.

On 7 June the radio was reporting news of the Battle of Midway. The reports said that two Jap carriers were sunk, maybe three, and battleships and cruisers were badly damaged. My *Mississippi* skipper, Admiral Spruance, was in command. There were high spirits on board *Sculpin*.

8 June On the 12–16 (1200 to 1600) watch as diving officer, off Tg. Mangkalihat, I sighted smoke to the north and called the captain, and we began tracking as we attempted to close in while submerged. The contact was moving southwest at ten knots. After three hours we surfaced and put three engines on propulsion, full speed, with the fourth engine on the battery charge. *Sculpin* circled around the smoke to gain a favorable attack position.

Before midnight the bridge team could make out the upper structure of a cargo ship of an estimated 5,000 tons and the tops of an escorting *Mutsiki* destroyer. Twenty minutes later, realizing that *Sculpin* was as close to the ships as she would get, the captain fired a spread of three fish from the bow tubes at the destroyer, and one fish at the cargo ship, but from the long range of 2,500 yards. We were much too far away. All missed.

Just before we fired, the lookouts saw an exchange of flashing light signals between the destroyer and the cargo ship. The destroyer made a radical course change in our direction, and the soundmen reported that he speeded up. The water was quite phosphorescent, so the wakes of the torpedoes made a distinct trail. The two ships not only sighted us but saw the wakes of the fish and turned in time to avoid being hit.

The destroyer continued toward *Sculpin* at high speed, so we promptly submerged, rigging for a depth charge attack as we went down.

Jack found a deep layer in the water, indicated on the bathythermograph trace, where he could balance the boat at 250 feet, needing no headway for depth control. Air conditioning, fans, and anything not necessary for ship control was shut down. It was very uncomfortable. Standing at the TDC in the control room in my khaki shorts and sandals, I looked down and saw a pool of sweat on the deck around my feet.

9 June   After about an hour, hearing nothing of the destroyer, the captain gave me permission to reload torpedoes. The enemy speeded up as soon as we used air pressure to blow the water out of the torpedo tubes. Sound reported that he had been idling almost directly over us.

Six depth charges exploded well astern in the first attack. We slipped away. Two more explosions of a second attack were farther away. The soundmen thought that the destroyer was locked onto a school of fish, which he proceeded to follow and attack repeatedly, as sonar heard more explosions in the distance.

Sculpin stayed down for more than four hours. Before dawn, when the captain saw nothing by periscope, we surfaced for thirty minutes to pull a suction through the boat, getting a load of fresh air before submerging for the day.

Still in Makassar Strait, moving toward Sibutu Passage, *Sculpin* spent the day at 150 feet in anticipation of Jap antisubmarine action. They had to be well aware of our presence, but nothing happened.

In midafternoon we sighted the upper structure of a warship to the west, much too far away to close for an attack. *Sculpin*'s battery was depleted from the actions of the previous day and night, so at sunset we surfaced for a welcome night on the surface and a badly needed battery charge.

10 June   The day was uneventful as we approached Sibutu submerged. In midafternoon a destroyer was sighted going westward at high speed, too far away for *Sculpin* to close. We surfaced after sunset and shortly thereafter entered Sibutu Passage. We completed our transit of Sibutu in an hour, then set course to pass between Pearl Bank and Doc Can Island. After we cleared Pearl Bank, we set course in the Sulu Sea to pass north of Bancoran Island.

As luck would have it, after all the fine weather we had been experiencing, the bad weather commenced when least needed, as we left Sibutu and entered the Sulu Sea. Those were dangerous waters—shallow and with many shoals—to negotiate by DR and with limited visibility.

11 June   *Sculpin* spent another uneventful day submerged in the Sulu Sea, moving northwestward toward Bancoran.

My letter writing tallied ten letters, replying to those that I had received in Albany from friends and relatives. The Ordnance Department orders, paperwork, and files were nearly complete. Typewriting skills came in handy, as I didn't want to load up the new 3/c yeoman, Arnold Stafford, too heavily. He had just come on board, relieving Bill Langley, and was still learning the ropes.

North of Bancoran we set course to enter Balabac Strait. Charlie projected that *Sculpin* would clear Balabac about three hours after midnight on 13 June.

12 June   Twice during midday we came to the surface for a few seconds so Charlie could get a quick sun line and better establish *Sculpin*'s position. The deeper water of Balabac would be welcome, even though it was not all that deep. Near midnight *Sculpin* commenced passage through the northern Balabac channel, continuing westward.

13 June   Ahead of Charlie's projection, *Sculpin* completed passage through Balabac Strait at 0207 and moved into the South China Sea, heading for the coast of Indochina. The water was finally deep enough for us to submerge comfortably.

How times had changed! On the first few patrols I remembered complaining about needing a bath, a shave, and clean clothes. Not having those luxuries was taken for granted now, and I didn't even notice the submarine's smell.

In midafternoon, crossing the south end of Palawan Passage submerged, smoke was sighted to the northeast, tracked as moving to the southwest. Forty minutes of closing maneuvers brought *Sculpin* into a position to see the ship making the smoke: a cargo ship of about 4,000 tons making an estimated speed of ten knots. After another forty minutes of tracking we saw two additional columns of smoke, following about five miles astern of the original ship. The new smoke columns were soon identified as coming from two tankers. We pressed in to attack the cargo ship.

The captain maneuvered *Sculpin* so he could fire from the after torpedo room. At 1619 he fired a spread of three fish, using a target speed of ten knots and range of 750 yards. He saw one hit. Two separate and distinct explosions were plainly heard throughout the boat. The target listed to port and a cloud of smoke rose from his well deck. His speed slowed noticeably.

We turned our attention to the two tankers following him, also on a southwesterly course. Thirty minutes of maneuvering brought *Sculpin* to a good firing position; then one tanker turned directly toward us, attempting to ram, while the other turned away. They both began firing deck guns at our periscope. The captain decided to withhold firing and maneuver during the night, on the surface, for a better attack position. Occasionally he turned his periscope to the burning cargo ship and reported that it was lower and lower in the water.

Keeping the black funnel smoke of the tankers in sight, *Sculpin* surfaced just before sunset and commenced an end around run, circling to get ahead of them. They were continuing in a southwesterly direction but had increased speed to twelve knots. I had the watch as we closed in on the surface, after dark, maneuvering for a good position to fire.

When we got closer we realized that the smoke we were stalking was from a previously unseen cargo chip, not from the two tankers. Multiple smoking ships and darkness were confusing. At about 1,000 yards the cargo ship opened fire with deck guns and turned radically toward *Sculpin*, attempting to ram us. Splashes were popping up all around, so we submerged.

We went down in a hurried dive, but the forward torpedo room didn't have enough advance warning to close the tube outer doors, so two fish were flooded. Those two fish would require servicing before they could be used.* We stayed down only long enough to replace the flooded torpedoes, then surfaced just before midnight to give chase.

Ten minutes after surfacing, the two tankers were again sighted ahead of *Sculpin*, and we began another stalking gambit. Middie relieved me as OOD for the midwatch, and I manned the TDC in the control room. The

---

*The torpedoes were removed from the torpedo tubes, drained of any sea water that might have gotten into the workings, valving, and combustion pots, and checked. Customary maintenance and routines were performed, and they were made ready for firing.

captain and the exec were up and down from the bridge to the TDC like a couple of yo-yos, checking the computer solution.

14 June   At 0150, south of Dangerous Ground, again in excellent position and at 1,000 yards' range, *Sculpin* fired a spread of four fish from the bow tubes at the 8,000-ton trailing tanker. The bridge watch saw two massive explosions as we turned for another end around run to get ahead of the other tanker for a submerged attack after daylight.

The cargo ship seen earlier, which we had confused with the tankers, was lost in the darkness. Smoke and flames from the burning ship we had hit were no longer visible, and we concluded that he had sunk. Heavy smoke and flames poured from the damaged tanker while *Sculpin* put on four engines to run around the remaining tanker. During all these maneuvers the forward torpedo room gang was checking out the flooded fish, making them ready for firing.

Before daybreak *Sculpin* submerged and continued maneuvering to gain a firing position. Battle stations sounded at 0721. The damaged tanker was listing and smoking heavily, with lifeboats lowered to the rail, but attempting to keep up with the undamaged tanker.

At 0755 *Sculpin* fired a spread of three fish from the bow tubes at the undamaged tanker from the long range of 2,150 yards. He was then on a more westerly course, slowed to ten knots. The target zigged radically to head directly for *Sculpin,* and all our torpedoes missed. Then he began firing guns at our periscope, which their lookouts had spotted in the glassy sea.

The captain put on more speed to cross the target's track and fire from the stern tubes. While this tactic was under way and stern tubes were being readied, a poppet valve gasket in the after torpedo room carried away, allowing nearly seven tons of seawater to enter the bilges.

Jack momentarily lost depth control. Going to two-thirds speed, he brought *Sculpin* back to periscope depth, but the captain decided to forgo firing. There was just too much uncertainty about range, speed, and enemy course to expect a hit, other than by pure luck. *Sculpin* went to full speed to try to gain position for another attack, but that was a losing game.

By 0800 it was evident that we could no longer engage that convoy. Our submerged speed was no match for their surface speed. We would also probably be the object of an antisubmarine search by both air and surface forces. The captain ordered 125 feet for the day as *Sculpin* continued west across the South China Sea.

15 June Sea conditions had worsened, and waves and riptides in the vicinity of Rifleman Bank made depth control impossible at periscope depth. Daylight hours were spent at 125 feet, listening. That was everybody's opportunity to get some rest after the previous strenuous days.

We had only six fish left—five in the after torpedo room and one in the forward torpedo room—and we hadn't even reached our patrol area.

Studying our location on the chart of the South China Sea, I was intrigued by the red dotted lines around the very large area labeled "Dangerous Ground" and the notation concerning the area: "The large area west of Palawan is known to abound with dangers. No systematic surveys have been carried out and the existence of uncharted patches of coral and shoals is likely; the positions of the charted banks and shoals cannot be relied upon. Vessels are warned not to attempt to pass through this area."*

16 June *Sculpin* skirted south of Dangerous Ground, submerged off Ladd Reef in the daytime, and continued west toward Indochina. The weather was overcast, with frequent rain and rough seas. When my turn at watch came around, I could hardly tell whether the periscope was above water or not.

On the surface after dark, the broadcast radio came in with reports of Coral Sea, Midway, and Aleutian islands actions. We hoped that the U.S. claims were correct; Tokyo Rose was telling a different story. More classmates and friends went down, on *Lexington* in particular.

My paperwork and letter writing were ahead of schedule. I was reading *Wild Geese Calling,* by S. E. White, and *This Above All,* by Eric Knight.

17 June As we approached the coast of Indochina we were cutting across the Saigon–Bangkok–Camranh Bay shipping lanes, so the captain selected stations off Pulo Cecir de Mer and Cape Varella. CSSWP intelligence messages indicated that the Japanese were routing their ships close to the coast to avoid submarines.

---

*Later in the war, *Darter* (Dave McClintock, '35), on her fourth war patrol, was with *Dace* (B. D. Claggett, '35) in south Palawan Passage between Dangerous Ground and Palawan Island on 23 October 1944. Early in the morning they sank the heavy cruisers *Atago* and *Maya* and severely damaged the heavy cruiser *Takao*. *Darter*, maneuvering to finish off *Takao* in a high-speed end around, grounded on Bombay Shoal in Dangerous Ground at midnight at a speed of seventeen knots and rode up to a depth of nine feet forward. Efforts to get off the reef were fruitless. *Dace* closed *Darter* and, after confidential gear had been smashed and classified matter burned, safely transferred everyone from *Darter* to *Dace* before daybreak.

The weather continued bad; my right wisdom tooth was acting up, and my disposition suffered. Doc prescribed aspirin, and the discomfort soon went away.

CSSWP advised *Sculpin* to take a look at Spratley Island, east of Indochina on the edge of Dangerous Ground. Later instructions would detail what was expected of us. The island was only about 500 yards by 300 yards. CSSWP thought the Japs might have an airfield there.

18 June   *Sculpin* was off Cape Varella, about 100 miles north of Camranh Bay—the same Camranh Bay we learned of when studying the Russo-Japanese War. In 1905 the Russian fleet, moving from European waters to engage the Japanese fleet, stopped for a long time in Camranh Bay to coal ship and make extensive repairs before going on north to defeat at Tsushima.

At this stage of our training program there were four men ready for the next step in submarine qualification: taking a trip through the boat with either Charlie Henderson or Jack Turner.

Just before midnight we sighted smoke to the north, and *Sculpin* began closing maneuvers. A major consideration in the captain's plan of attack was that we had only one fish forward and five aft.

The smoking ship was identified as a 7,000-ton cargo ship, heading south, and *Sculpin* moved in for a stern tube shot. While the captain was focusing his attention on the smoking ship, another, lighted, smaller ship came up from the south and ran between *Sculpin* and her target. The captain considered firing at the second ship. He had lights on, but they were not in the international code. He just might be a diplomatic or hospital ship, so we waited for the lighted ship to move clear. Curiously, the lights went out as soon as the ships passed each other. We thought it possible the Japs had a wartime rule of the road under which their ships turned on lights under certain conditions to help in passing situations and to avoid collisions.

19 June   The captain and the exec were again up and down many times from the bridge to the TDC, checking the computer solution. Just after midnight, with target course 180 t, speed thirteen knots, and solution checking beautifully, the captain decided to use only the one fish from forward, at a range of 2,000 yards. Because of the clear night and bright moonlight, he did not want to move in closer. The very shallow water nearer shore also entered the equation.

After the lone fish left the tube, we waited what seemed an interminable time and were ready to concede a miss when an explosion was heard throughout the boat. I hurried to the bridge to see an impressive cloud of smoke and flames.

A few seconds later a second explosion shook *Sculpin*. The target stopped, showed many lights, and another tremendous cloud erupted from his forward hatch. Our telephone circuit filled with inquiries. Some thought *Sculpin* had collided with something or run aground.

After the explosion Chief Torpedoman Doggie Dawes got permission to go to the bridge to see what the burning, sinking ship looked like. It was the first time he had come up to see something like that, and his eyes were not accustomed to the dark. He stood next to someone he thought was one of the lookouts, slapped the man on the back, and demanded, "Gimmie them ga-dam glasses so I kin see." He later told us how embarrassed he was when the exec answered, saying, "Sure, sure; here, take a look," as he handed Doggie his binoculars.

Our target headed for the beach as a patrol boat headed out from shore, so *Sculpin* pulled clear toward deeper water.

The hit with only one fish fired made us feel much better about the performance of the torpedoes. At least they worked right some of the time. With good course, speed, and range information, and a good TDC solution, the torpedoes might perform as advertised. Some did, at least.

We basked in the good feeling of success during our day submerged. By nightfall the weather was bad again. I had the evening watch and was being soaked by the driving rain when Charlie called up news of a message from Washington: I was promoted to lieutenant as of 19 June. Congratulations on the promotion seemed strange, because I was not yet accustomed to being a jg and had hardly worn that insignia. My bar was homemade, although Jack Turner had given me a spare when he made lieutenant. No one on board had an extra set of lieutenant's insignia, and I was unsure of being able to get any in Australia. So with Ernest Baldwin's help I set out to manufacture a pair in his shop. For raw material I used the Australian florin coin, which was silver and exactly the right size. Using a saw, files, and chisels, we managed to hack them out, leaving the coin's engraving as a special flourish. Baldwin silver-soldered clasps on the back. Polished, the bars looked distinctive and neat, I thought.*

---

*From that time on, those bars drew attention. I was frequently asked where in the world I got the great insignia. I wore them for many months until, after the sixth patrol, ending in Pearl Harbor, I was stopped by Captain G. C. (Turkey Neck) Crawford, '21, who ordered me to get regulation insignia. I was proud of those special bars and had worn them as a badge of distinction. In the "civilization" of Pearl Harbor, however, Commodore Crawford had hard-nosed, regulation ideas.

20 June   *Sculpin* spent a quiet day off Cape Padaran. My qualification school was paying off. Charlie passed four students with flying colors, and "qualified in submarines" would be entered in their personnel records. More students were knocking on my door, wanting to be next for examination by Charlie or Jack, giving me a comfortable feeling of self-satisfaction.

With five fish aft and none forward, the captain wanted to move three to the forward torpedo room. Gunner Caserio allowed that by now we were masters at moving fish around the deck at sea in the dark of night. We still had to be careful, though. It would be humiliating, to say the least, if a Jap plane or destroyer caught us on the surface, with men and fish on deck and hatches open, in the process of moving those fish.

21 June   Another quiet day off Cape Padaran. The weather turned calm. *Sculpin* moved offshore to be away from the ship traffic lane, and we began the torpedo-moving project in midevening. Three fish were moved forward, with everything wrapped up in two hours: Captain's congratulations to the fish wranglers on their record time.

Sculpin then moved to patrol submerged off Pulo Cecir de Mer.

22 June   The shift of torpedoes was made just in time. Immediately after we came to the surface at dark off Pulo Cecir de Mer, the bridge watch sighted smoke to the north. In bright moonlight *Sculpin* closed to see three ships in column: two cargo vessels followed by a tanker, heading toward Saigon. As we maneuvered to gain position in bright moonlight, *Sculpin* was illuminated by an aircraft flare close aboard to starboard.

The captain ordered "dive," and we went down to evade the expected air attack, but none occurred. A few minutes later another flare was seen through the periscope. After a short wait *Sculpin* surfaced to chase the ships, but by that time they had moved close inshore where the water was too shallow for us to follow.

23 June   Still off Pulo Cecir de Mer Island. All was quiet until, again on the surface, just after dark, an aircraft flare was seen to the northwest. The bridge was cleared in preparation for a dive, but nothing developed, so the watch went back to the bridge.

24 June   Seeing the flares led the wardroom strategists to decide that something must be going on in the Pulo Cecir de Mer area, so the captain decided to spend more time there. The weather was cloudy but generally clear in the daytime. At night there was a tendency toward heavy showers, sometimes in bucketfuls. I wanted to locate a number of constellations and stars in that phase of the sky, but the weather interfered.

Training, school, torpedo maintenance, and ship's work were in good shape. Reading, recreation, bridge, chess, acey-deucey, and letter writing were fitted into the schedule. I counted sixteen letters ready for mailing, with only two more correspondents left on my list.

25 June   All was quiet off Pulo Cecir de Mer, but the weather worsened. Control was difficult at periscope depth. Strong winds whipped spray, making periscope observation unreliable. On the surface, the bridge was drenched. CSSWP intelligence messages made the captain decide to move to Cape Padaran.

26 June   Just after midnight, off the south entrance to Camranh Bay, Jack found a ship close inshore and moving to the southwest. *Sculpin* began tracking, maneuvering to gain position for attack. The target was estimated to be making a speed of ten knots. In bright moonlight *Sculpin* submerged with scarcely twenty minutes of tracking, and the captain fired a two-fish spread from the stern tubes, with a TDC-calculated range of 1,325 yards. They missed. Our time for tracking was too short, and there was too much uncertainty as to range and speed. The captain gave me only two observations on which to reach a solution. Moonlight periscope attacks were not my preference.

Second-guessing the captain and exec, I felt that we were too impulsive and should have spent more time shadowing the ship. The moon was due to set at 0400, by which time we could have had a good speed and course solution. After moonset, on the surface, and closing in to a shorter range, we would have had a much better chance for hits.

Sculpin surfaced fifteen minutes after firing to give chase. The target headed toward Cape Padaran and shallow water. A few minutes later a patrol boat, possibly a submarine chaser, came out from Fanrang Bay, then a similar boat appeared from the direction of Cape Padaran.

Those movements, along with the shallow water, discouraged the captain from any further pursuit of that target, so we pulled clear and at dawn submerged for the day in the Cape Padaran–Pulo Cecir de Mer traffic lane.

We saw no more ships, and after sunset *Sculpin* surfaced and set course for Cape Varella.

27 June Submerged off Cape Varella, we had a number of small craft and fishing boats continually in sight.

My qualification students were doing so well that it appeared that all except the six boots would be qualified before we finished the patrol. During free moments I was reading *To Sing With Angels,* by Maurice Hindus.

Sculpin moved up the coast toward Xuandai Bay, dodging small craft all the way. Dogging the watch rotated me to the afternoon stint, noon until 1600, and midnight until 0400 for the next week.* That schedule was a killer. With four hours taken out of the very core of the "night," I never got enough sleep.

28 June During my midwatch I sighted a fishing boat to starboard and turned away, only to find that we were heading directly toward two more, so I veered back to go between them. All was going well until another boat was seen to starboard, headed directly for us, close aboard. With the weather conditions as they were, they were very hard to see. We finally got clear of the fishermen by moving a few miles offshore.

29 June Off Cape Varella, during my diving officer watch, I read in the *Coast Pilot* that "there are wild and dangerous animals in the jungles at Cape Varella," but it didn't specify what the animals were. The mountains and jungles were interesting to see through the periscope. The lighthouse, quite a large structure, appeared to be very new.

The day submerged was quiet and uneventful. At night CSSWP directed *Sculpin* to remain east of longitude 110° E from 30 June until 3 July but gave no indication why. This presented the opportunity to investigate Spratley Island. Charlie set course to carry out that errand.

30 June A monsoon wind kicked up heavy seas, and many of the crew were seasick. No one could work when the boat was on the surface, and holding periscope depth was impossible. *Sculpin* spent the day about 100 miles east of Pulo Cecir de Mer, moving toward Spratley at a depth of 125 feet, listening. No contacts were made.

Seas were so rough that I spent the night in my bunk, reading *What*

---

*Periodically the 16 to 20 (1600 to 2000) watch was split into two watches, 16 to 18 and 18 to 20; this was called "dogging the watch." This would make a person's watch duty rotate so that he wouldn't have the same watch continually (including the midnight to 0400 watch, which was not anyone's favorite).

Makes Sammy Run and hoping that we would find something on Spratley as a target for the deck gun. The gun crew was eager to go topside for a little excitement and a change from the routine of being cooped up in the submarine.

1 July   Off Spratley the seas continued rough, with rain most of the day so hard that we couldn't see the island. When we came up occasionally for a look, the periscope appeared to be still underwater. By midafternoon the rain let up and the sea calmed enough for us to stay at periscope depth. We moved closer to see what was on the island. The answer was, quite simply, nothing. There was no sign of human activity. According to the *Coast Pilot* the island was small, flat, and sandy with a dozen or so palm trees on the south end. That was all.

To break the monotony, although the waves were still moderate, the captain decided to fire a few 3-inch rounds at the island. We surfaced an hour before sundown, manned the gun, and prepared to fire, but the firing was promptly called off after three rounds were lost overboard, with our sub tossing about in the moderate seas. We certainly didn't want any of our gun crew to get hurt just for a diversion. Although no shots were fired, the gun crew had something to talk, brag, and kid each other about for days afterward.

2 July   CSSWP ordered *Sculpin* to be clear of the South China Sea by midnight, 3 July, so Charlie set course to pass west of Rifleman Bank, then south of Dangerous Ground to retrace our outbound route back to Australia.

Bad news on the broadcast radio told of the British retreating to Egypt. The Russians were being pressed hard at Sevastopol. The Australians were being pulled out of Libya and brought home to Australia to defend against the Japanese advance toward their homeland.

3 July   Submerged, *Sculpin* passed west of Rifleman Bank with no contacts. On the surface at midmorning we received orders to return to Fremantle. The earlier orders hadn't told us what our destination was, just that we were to be out of the South China Sea by midnight.

During dinner the captain told us that before we left Fremantle he had been informed that *Sculpin* might be in the Mare Island Navy Yard, California, for a major overhaul by the end of the year. That meant probably two more patrols before reaching the United States. Our ship was in real need of a major overhaul, all agreed.

4 July   *Sculpin* crossed the southern end of Palawan Passage. The lack of contact with the enemy had become tedious. My records showed that so far in the war we had fired forty-five torpedoes and had damaged or sunk seven ships. A rough cost estimate for all those torpedoes, based on fragments of information, was $45,000.

5 July   Near midnight *Sculpin* entered Balabac Strait, completed the passage, and proceeded northeastward into the Sulu Sea, to go north and east around Bancoran Island.

Radio messages from the Bureau of Ordnance contained instructions, corrections, and other orders concerning maintenance, calibration, and firing procedures for torpedoes, causing me even more concern that someone had been asleep at the switch back there for years. Reliable knowledge of the depth performance, tactical characteristics, and exploder functioning of our fish still was hazy. No wonder we were not hitting the targets. Throw in operator error, plus inaccurate ranges, and you have few hits and fewer ships sunk.

6 July   We were submerged when we passed close by Bancoran near noon. Those of the crew who wished to were given the opportunity to look through the periscope at the huts and fishing boats and see a few people on the western end of the island, unaware that we were watching them, go about their daily chores.

7 July   *Sculpin* completed transit of the Pearl Bank–Doc Can Channel shortly after midnight, and submerged at dawn to continue southeastward toward Sibutu Passage.

At 1240 Jack sighted smoke to the south and called the captain, and *Sculpin* maneuvered to close for attack. Twenty minutes later we could see that the smoke was created by a cargo ship and a tanker, escorted by one destroyer, headed in a northerly direction.

My TDC computed their speed at ten knots. Sonar reported that the destroyer was pinging only occasionally, unaware that we were closing in on them. The tanker was estimated to be of about 8,000 tons.

We were too far off their track, so we used high speed to get closer. The best position that we could reach was 2,500 yards from the tanker. One hour after they were sighted, we fired a spread of our last three fish at the tanker, two from aft and one from forward.

The captain saw a plume of steam from the destroyer's whistle as he sounded the alarm and turned toward us with a bone in his teeth. *Sculpin* went deep to evade, rigging for depth charge.

A loud explosion resounded throughout the boat when one torpedo hit. Sonar followed the cargo ship as he continued north into the Sulu Sea. The destroyer didn't make an aggressive search for *Sculpin*. Back at periscope depth the captain watched as the destroyer followed the listing and burning tanker toward Tawi-Tawi Island.

When *Sculpin* surfaced at dark, we could see an immense fire in the direction where the tanker and the destroyer were last headed. Those of the crew who wished were permitted to go to the bridge to look with satisfaction at the fire as *Sculpin* continued eastward, leaving the Sulu Sea to pass through Sibutu Passage.

We regretted that the shortage of torpedoes in Western Australia had denied us a full load of twenty-four when we left on patrol.

8–11 July   *Sculpin* cruised daytime at 125 feet, nights on the surface at best speed on four engines after the battery was charged, as we went south through Makassar Strait. With no torpedoes, the captain's standing orders were to avoid any ships that we might sight and get to the relative safety of the Indian Ocean as rapidly as possible.

Reviewing my torpedo records for the captain's patrol report, summing up from the beginning of the war, we had made seventeen attacks, with seven resulting in sinking or damage. That was a pretty sorry record. Torpedoes, torpedoes, torpedoes. A few misses were due to poor information into the TDC, but most were torpedo problems: premature explosions, failure to explode, erratic torpedoes.

Reading Somerset Maugham's *Ashenden,* I was intrigued that he went to some length to show that a secret agent's life was usually not very adventurous. He did this in a subtle, interesting way. The same might be said of a submarine's war patrol work.

At night the various OODs had a difficult time dodging the sailboats, which were more numerous than when we went north. I almost ran one down as it popped into view out of the black night with no lights. When I made an emergency turn, the captain felt the sudden change of direction and came running to the bridge. We were cruising along at eighteen knots with four engines on the line in calm seas. Standing orders were never to challenge anyone, but if we were correctly challenged to answer promptly.

On Saturday, the eleventh, *Sculpin* approached Lombok Strait submerged, surfaced at dark, and was through the strait at midnight. I was OOD and saw many lights along the shores of Bali and Lombok. Some of the lights were on the water. We watched their motion carefully to be certain that they were not antisubmarine boats.

The mountains of the islands stood out sharply among the stars, serving as excellent navigation aids. There were riptides, as expected, that pushed *Sculpin* around and splashed water over the deck. Strong currents ran through the strait.

12–13 July Dogging the watch on the twelfth gave me the 4–8 watches for the remainder of the patrol. I would be OOD going into the channel and mooring at Fremantle.

An aircraft flare or Very rocket startled us during the morning watch on the twelfth, causing concern, but the flare was some distance away and we did not see an airplane or ship.

Sculpin continued south at 125 feet during daylight. On the thirteenth the captain didn't order the dive until 0800, well after sunup, saying that he was sorely tempted to stay up all day. That sunrise was spectacular and the fresh air invigorating.

A noticeable change in activity took place. Laundry was washed, blues were pressed, and other preparations were made for arrival in Fremantle. My torpedomen didn't have any fish to maintain, so they were taking advantage of the opportunity to get the torpedo rooms in top shape, equipment overhauled, and the torpedo tubes in good order. All my job orders were ready, my supply lists were complete, and I was ready for port.

Our training programs had worked exceptionally well. As predicted, all the students qualified except for the six boots, and congratulations were in order. Advancement in rating was far ahead of expectation. Our torpedomen were a great team.

Reading *Morale and Its Elements* by Ernest Hocking didn't add one bit of knowledge that we were not already familiar with. Captain's orders were to remain on the surface commencing the fourteenth. Anticipation was high at the prospect. The shipboard change in attitude was apparent, going from the tensions of being a potential target for enemy attack to a much more relaxed attitude.

14–15 July The surface-running days were enjoyed by everyone. On the morning watches we were seeing beautiful sunrises as we proceeded down the west coast of Australia. There were just enough cirrus clouds to reflect the light perfectly, and for an hour before the sun peeped over the horizon there was a gorgeous display of color, first blue-gray, then slowly changing to burgundy and on to red, then to pink, and finally all the clouds were a beautiful golden color; and then the sun came up, turning the clouds a fleecy white.

After hearing me brag about how good the flying fish were, especially with ham, eggs, grits, and gravy, the captain finally succumbed and joined me in eating them poached for breakfast. He knew grits and gravy; he was from Georgia.

In the bright sunshine the weather was warm enough at midday to take off our shirts and carefully expose the skin that had been away from such luxury for so many days. I made a round of pictures, concentrating on all those who had grown beards.

16 July   The weather had turned downright wintry. Some rain fell, and I was reminded of Bremerton, Washington. Jack conducted a battery equalizer, putting the propulsion totally on the batteries for a six-hour discharge to low voltage. The engines got a rest for those few hours, and the engineers took advantage of the opportunity to do work that was impossible to perform when the engines were running.

Excitement built higher and higher in anticipation of reaching Fremantle, especially among the newly married men. Three or four others declared their intention to get married. That seemed foolish to me. To an Australian woman, marrying an American might be glamorous, but there could be a lot of hurdles ahead. The pay of a U.S. sailor was great in Australia, but there were major differences between living in Australia and in the United States. My advice to the crewmen was to wait a while.

17 July   At 0330 *Sculpin* answered the challenge of an escort and followed her into the Fremantle channel. The antisub boom was no longer in service. As we negotiated the channel we received a signal from our *Voyager* friends, welcoming us and inviting us for a drink before lunch. A crowd greeted us as we tied up at the dock. Admiral Charles Lockwood, '12, and Commander Connolly came aboard, as customary jumping to *Sculpin*'s deck before the brow was put over. They welcomed us with broad smiles, handshakes, congratulations, and much back slapping. Crates of fresh fruit and containers of ice cream were passed aboard. We were starved for fresh things and wasted no time in devouring the treats as we talked to our welcomers, who understood and urged us on.

As the captain handed Commodore Connolly his report of the fourth war patrol, the commodore informed him that we would go on south to Albany for refit on the following Tuesday, 21 July.

Sculpin was showing the wear and tear of extended operations. The list of items needing repair or replacement included

1. Negative tank: control linkage inoperative.

2. Port main ballast tank group: a five-degree list developed in twenty minutes while riding the vents. LP (low pressure) blowers had to be run frequently. Finally, the flood valves (kingstons) had to be closed on number 2 and 3 tanks.

3. Number 1 air compressor was out of commission; ship's force could not repair.

4. Number 3 main engine governor failed; unable to repair.

5. Number 2 main engine had a cracked liner; ship's force might be able to repair.

Patrol Summary

Number of men on board:
  67 enlisted
  6 officers

Nautical miles covered:
  8,058 on the surface
  1,292 submerged

Fuel used: 81,870 gallons (8.7 gallons/mile)

Drinking water:
  19,042 gallons made
  26,086 gallons consumed

Battery water:
  3,126 gallons made
  3,126 gallons used

Duration: 49 days

Torpedoes fired: 20

Sinkings: 2 cargo ships and 2 tankers, totaling 27,000 tons

Refit in Fremantle, Albany, and Brisbane

17 July–1 September A musical chairs routine of tenders and submarines shifting around had *Sculpin* scheduled to go to Albany for refit, which suited me just fine. I liked that area and the local residents. We did stay the weekend in Fremantle, allowing me to see my friends in Perth. I made plans to take the train back in a few days. The married men got to see their wives and make plans for them to go to Albany or to return to Fremantle on liberty. While we were away Chuck Osborne had departed for duty in the United States, and we missed him.

Admiral Lockwood came aboard the morning of the twentieth for the two-day ride to Albany, where he planned to greet the arriving tender *Pelias*. Accompanying the admiral was Lieutenant Colonel Duffy of the Australian Imperial Forces.* The admiral and the colonel were fine shipmates, and everyone enjoyed having them with us. *Pelias* was one day late in arriving, so the admiral waited with us at the Freemason Hotel. We continued to enjoy his company while the relief crew worked on the boat and our crew was sent to the rest camp. The admiral's driver was an accomplished pianist and they enthusiastically joined singalongs in the hotel lounge. Australian songs were in vogue, but "Deep in the Heart of Texas" was never left out since the admiral was from Texas. When *Pelias* finally arrived I was pleasantly surprised to find that my classmate Ben Fischer, a Supply Corps officer, was paymaster aboard ship.

With no pressing problems in my particular areas of responsibility, I rode the train back to Perth on the twenty-fourth with a six-day pass. While I was there, Bob Watson took me on a three-day kangaroo hunt at a ranch sixty miles north of Perth.

Back in Albany, away from ship's work, I enjoyed tennis with Chester Nimitz, Jr., '36, Bob Carroll, and Middie, as well as hiking the hills and making the social whirl at parties hosted by our Aussie friends.

With refit complete, on 10 August *Sculpin* conducted under-way tests in the bay and headed for Fremantle in very heavy weather. We were one day late getting there, arriving on the twelfth with exterior storm damage that needed repair. We were immediately asked to submit lists of all supplies and spare parts that we might need if we were away from *Holland* for six months. The rumor mill ground away. Why would they ask for lists like that?

During those few days I had time to see my Aussie friends and visit with navy friends in port, including Condé Raguet, Doug Rhymes, and Larry Julihn, '37. In last-minute personnel changes, Yeoman Aaron Reese reported aboard to take over the ship's office duties from Arnold Stafford.

---

*The colonel was just back from North Africa. The Australians had been brought home to defend their country against the expected Japanese invasion. His unit had gone to Africa with 1,000 men and 40 officers; they had returned with 12 men and 3 officers. Colonel Duffy was on the staff of General Gordon Bennett.

Just after *Sculpin* exited the channel on the sixteenth, the captain read orders that had *Sculpin* going to Brisbane, on Australia's east coast, south by way of the Antarctic Ocean, a 3,000-mile voyage. Now we knew the reason behind the request for those lists.

It was winter in that part of the world, and cold, but fortunately the sea was relatively calm, providing a much smoother passage than promised by the *Coast Pilot*.

On 22 August, while routine maintenance was being performed on torpedoes in the after torpedo room, the starting lever on one fish was accidentally tripped. The engine started but was quickly stopped by Guy Boos, the alert lead torpedoman. Fumes and smoke drifted throughout the boat. At first Charlie Henderson was furious, threatening to demote Boos, but my persuasive arguments convinced him otherwise, and ultimately he even suggested a promotion for Boos's smart action.

We arrived in Brisbane on 27 August, and tender *Griffin* went right to work on the very low resistance that had developed in both main motors during our trip around Australia. At the submarine base at New Farm Wharf, we began final preparations for patrol under a new boss, Commander Task Force 42 (CTF 42).

At the customary arrival conference, one of the Supply Corps officers was Ensign Hollis Cooley, USNR, one of my first classmen at the Naval Academy, and a classmate of Jack Turner's. When he graduated in 1936 he hadn't received a commission because he couldn't pass the eye examination. Now, in wartime, he had been given a commission. Hollis didn't recognize me with my red beard and didn't catch my name when we were introduced. As the conference went along, several times he answered my questions with a snappy navy "Yes, Sir," or "No, Sir," or "Aye, Aye, Sir." It was an amusing turn of events; not too long ago I had been the one standing at attention for him and giving him the "Yes, Sir" replies. When the meeting was over I took him aside to make myself known, and we both got a kick out of the episode. Thereafter *Sculpin* received top-notch treatment from the *Griffin* supply organization.

The supply department had several special periscope cameras that were being issued to see how they performed. Hollis tipped me off, and *Sculpin* was issued one of them.

While in Brisbane those few days we met a number of Aussies who outdid themselves with hospitality. Tennis and picnics were much in vogue. There were also many navy friends: not only Hollis Cooley but Grumpy Carlson, '38, Bill Lennox, and classmates Max Kerns and Monk Hendrix.

On 31 August Lieutenant (jg) George Brown, USNR, reported aboard from sub school to become assistant engineering officer in anticipation of Jack Turner's upcoming departure. George was a Yale man and had served in the cruiser *Chester* for two years before asking for sub duty. Once given his job assignment, he promptly put on dungarees and joined the black gang performing an engine overhaul.

On 1 September *Sculpin* was ready for patrol, and departure was scheduled for the next day.

Practice torpedo crosses ahead of target destroyer, September 1941. Aircraft photo made from 1,700 feet.
—*U.S. Navy*

USS *Sculpin,* San Francisco, 1943.
—*U.S. Navy*

Sculpin skinheads after crossing Equator: *left to right,* Louis E. Woodin, William H. Partin, Gordon Johnson, Ernest M. Olson, George Rocek.

Author in foul-weather gear, aboard *Sculpin.*

Author, San Francisco, 1943.
—*U.S. Navy*

Members of *Sculpin*'s torpedo gang.

Sculpin in rough weather, southwest Pacific.

Officers of *Sculpin*, fourth patrol: *left to right*, Frank Alvis, Jack Turner, Charles Henderson, Emmett Mills, author, Lucius Chappell.

Sculpin's engineers, San Francisco, 1943: *left to right,* Frank J. Dyboski, George Brown, Paul A. Bachofer, Richard E. Hemphill. Lieutenant Brown was the sole surviving officer when *Sculpin* was sunk on its ninth patrol.

Left: Gus Hollenbach and *Sculpin*'s chief cook, Duncan Hughes.
Right: Author aboard *Sculpin,* Brisbane, Australia, 1943.

Lucius Chappell with *Sculpin*'s flag, San Francisco, 1943.

Aboard *Sculpin* at San Francisco, 1943: *standing, left to right,* John J. Pepersack, Alvin W. Coulter, Keith E. Waidelich, John B. Swift, Gus Hollenbach, Ralph S. Austin, Frank J. Dyboski, Chesley A. DeArmond; *kneeling,* Carlos Tulao, author, Weldon E. Moore (who made the flag), and Jack Turner.

Launching of USS *Pintado*, Portsmouth, New Hampshire, 15 September 1943. The author is standing second from left on bow.
—*U.S. Navy*

Submarine operations off Portsmouth in January ice.

Lieutenant Commander Chick Clarey reads the orders of taking command of *Pintado*, January 1944.
—*U.S. Navy*

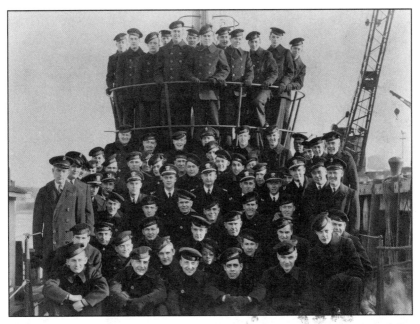

Officers and crew of *Pintado* after commissioning, Portsmouth, New Hampshire, January 1944.
—*U.S. Navy*

Pintado in rough weather.

Pintado crewmen receiving awards, Saipan, 1944: *standing, left to right,* author, Edwin W. Frese, Gerry E. Pettibone, John R. Hill, George C. Morris, Ben Sisti; *kneeling,* Emiel L. Sullivan, Aubrey J. Sanders, Frederick W. Powers, Eric P. Bailey.

Bridge of *Pintado*, looking for enemy aircraft off Saipan.

Left: Ben Sisti trying his hand with a .45-caliber pistol.
Right: Ed Frese with submachine gun.

Japanese hospital ship, photographed through periscope of *Pintado,* March 1945.

Center and right: Pintado crewmen enjoying rest camp, Majuro Atoll, 1944.

Admiral J. H. Hoover presenting
Navy Cross to Chick Clarey,
Saipan.
—*U.S. Navy*

Admiral Charles A. Lockwood,
Jr., pinning Silver Star on Doug
Morse, Pearl Harbor, Hawaii.
—*U.S. Navy*

Pintado enters Pearl Harbor, September 1944. Note the cluster of tiny Japanese
flags for ships sunk, made by Ray Emerson.
—*U.S. Navy*

Walter Regiec, William R. Thompson, and James A. Foley with
Japanese man-of-war flag.

Left: Author receiving Silver Star from Captain E. M. Eller, Brisbane.
—*U.S. Navy*
Right: Author receiving Bronze Star from Secretary of the Navy James V. Forrestal
at Annapolis in late 1945.
—*U.S. Navy*

Sculpin's Fifth Patrol

(2 September–26 October 1942)

2 September *Sculpin* cast off all lines at 0800 and headed downriver into Moreton Bay. Nearly seven weeks had passed since the fourth patrol, and everyone felt better to be heading back out to the action.

Our pilot came aboard just before we left New Farm Wharf. The river made a number of bends and sharp turns, and the pilot, an older man, took great pains to explain to me, as OOD, the fine points of negotiating the channel. He had an aviator son in the RAAF in Egypt, and he gave the bridge watch a full account of his son's activities.

The first order of business was a test-trim dive in Moreton Bay. That showed no problems. Our pilot particularly enjoyed the dive. He had been out with S-boats, but never in *Sculpin*'s type, and he commented about the differences in our capabilities, which were noticeable even to a civilian. Then Charlie swung ship to compensate the magnetic compass, the first time that had been done since I reported aboard.

As darkness set in we proceeded out the channel, dropping the pilot off at his waiting pilot boat. *Sculpin* then headed northeast, to pass east of the Great Barrier Reef. Orders from CTF 42 were to go to an area north of New Britain. The route to the area was through Vitiaz Strait, between New Britain Island and Cape Cretin, New Guinea. We were to pass close to Normandy and Kiriwina islands and look for any Japanese activities there. Returning to Brisbane at the end of the patrol we were to go through Saint George's Channel between New Britain and New Ireland. Charlie immediately began worrying about navigating the confined waters of Saint George's Channel, where radio reports told of the presence of many Jap warships.

On this patrol *Sculpin* enjoyed the luxury of sixty-five crewmen and seven officers. A great spirit of enthusiasm was noticeable throughout the boat. We were on a mission again, with a load of twenty Mk-14 fish. One of the cargo ships that crowded Brisbane harbor had brought a load of Mk-14s, so we didn't, after all, find ourselves loaded with the ancient

Mk-10s. (We had been told at the arrival conference to be prepared to take the Mk-10s because of a shortage of Mk-14s in the western Pacific.)

3 September   At 0210 *Sculpin* stopped a merchant ship and identified her as a friend. At 0457 recognition signals were exchanged with a friendly formation of warships. At 0957 *Sculpin* submerged to conduct drills and to work a battle problem. During the dive Jack became aware that the stern planes were not functioning properly. Technicians began work to find and correct the trouble.

4 September, Friday   This turned out to be a bleak Friday for *Sculpin*. As work was going on to correct the difficulty with the stern planes, another problem developed. Number 4 main motor threw a binding strip on its commutator, causing a zero ground and putting that motor out of service. The commutator could only be repaired by the tender at Brisbane.

Reluctantly the captain radioed CTF 42 that we were returning to port for help, limping along on only one propeller.

Radio intelligence messages reported a Japanese buildup north of the Solomons, possibly aimed at Guadalcanal. We had hoped to get there and engage in the action, but now that was not possible. Two S-boats were ordered to cover the station where we had expected to be.

5 September   With only one propeller to shove *Sculpin* along, we couldn't make much headway back to Brisbane. The weather was sunny and hot. Four-hour watches on the bridge produced red noses and a pink glow. Warnings were repeated to everyone to guard against sunburn. The heat even induced me to shave my beard, then four months old.

George Brown was a bridge player, so Charlie, Jack, and I joined him in sessions after dinner. Middie and Frank Alvis were fully occupied decoding the many messages that continued to come in concerning actions in the Solomons area.

Sturgeon passed us, going north to patrol. We exchanged recognition signals and other information by flashing light.

6 September, Sunday   At 0900 *Sculpin* moored at the naval base alongside the gunboat *Tulsa*. Tender repairmen began work immediately on number 4 main motor. George was in his element down in the bilges with the electricians, in greasy dungarees and other snipelike attire (snipe was a term used to denote people in the Engineering Department, particularly the lower ratings).

No liberty was granted. Strangely, the stern planes were working just fine, thank you. Several theories were offered, but no conclusive explanation was found for the transient problem. The motor was forecast to be fixed in time for *Sculpin* to leave the next day. My classmate Jack Cameron was serving in *Tulsa*. He invited me to lunch in their wardroom, and we enjoyed an hour of swapping stories.

Another flood of mail arrived. Everyone was writing letters home, which meant that all the officers except the captain and the exec were censoring mail so it could be sent off before we left port.

As a result of one letter from home, I paid a call on the pay department on *Griffin* to complain that since May my pay had been reduced by allotment for a $100 war bond each month, but somehow the word hadn't gotten to the right people, and none of the bonds had reached my home in Anahuac, Texas. Hollis Cooley promised to see that things were made right. It took him a moment to place the "new officer," this time minus beard.

7 September The repair force had difficulty getting number 4 motor back in working order, so *Sculpin*'s departure was put off another day. Except for Jack, George, and the electricians, the crew was loafing, waiting to leave on patrol. With no liberty, there was chafing at the bit to get going.

Sailfish came in with classmate Ben Jarvis. Ben had just finished sub school and was torpedo and gunnery officer. We visited for an hour or so while I helped him with some of his questions and offered solutions we had reached in *Sculpin*.

8 September The main motor problem was solved just after midnight, but other minor engineering problems delayed our departure until mid-afternoon, when all was finally well in the Engineering Department. The captain didn't want to leave port until everything was working fine.

The few extra hours in port meant still more letters to be censored. Additional mail came aboard—personal letters, magazines, packages, and official mail—so there was more than enough reading material for everyone.

As *Sculpin* went out the channel she was buzzed repeatedly by the RAAF fighter plane, the pilot waving as he flew low over us. We also saw a flight of American P-38s, the first time I had seen that type of aircraft except in photographs.

George Brown's earlier navy experience worked to good advantage. His attitude, actions, bearing, and questions were impressing everyone as he promptly started work on qualification. From the day he reported for duty he pulled his weight and more. I hoped that Middie and Frank would get the message and move ahead on their qualifications as well.

Sculpin's orders were modified by a message telling us to omit the Normanby-Kiriwina portion of our route and go directly to latitude 7°30′ S, longitude 151°45′ E, staying within a thirty-mile radius of that point until directed to comply with the balance of the original orders. The circle was within easy striking distance of the Jap bases at Lae, Rabaul, and Bougainville.

8–11 September   En route to our position, we were catching up with reading the official mail and keeping an eye on the radio traffic to find out what was happening around our assigned patrol area.

The *ONI Weekly* (Office of Naval Intelligence), which came in the official mail, featured *Sculpin*'s third patrol. No boat was named, but the circumstances and events fitted that patrol perfectly.

Radio reports showed many Jap ships—carriers, cruisers, destroyers, and transports—moving near the patrol area that we eventually expected to be in.

On the eleventh, *Sculpin* spent the first half of the day submerged while the engineers installed a new cylinder liner in number 2 main engine, but Jack Turner was not satisfied with its performance when we used it on the surface. They would try again the next day.

12 September   The first full day submerged, and the beginning of reversa. I slept as much as I could during daylight in order to force myself to stay awake all night and get into the reversed routine. I was successful, but Charlie Henderson, as always, had his troubles, storming around, fulminating over not being able to make the shift. He received plenty of ribbing in the wardroom.

Sure enough, George's performance shamed Frank and Middie into getting busy on their qualified in submarines work. With George working so diligently, they had to get busy. Although Middie had been on board a full year, he still had a long way to go to qualify.

The OOD watch list was leisurely, with five of us taking our turns at it, quite a change from the first patrol when there had been only Red Lennox, Jack Turner, and myself.

13 September   The cutback on watch-standing chores gave me more time for my school programs. Again we had twenty-four men needing attention. Since I was over my personal submarine qualification hurdle, Charlie designated me schoolmaster for enlisted qualification. He also gave me permission to institute the rule that no one would be considered for advancement in rating who was not qualified in submarines. That got their attention in a hurry.

The captain had never been entirely happy with the officers' stewards on the first four patrols and had convinced the personnel office in Albany to swap them for two Filipino stewards who had been stewards for flag officers in the Philippines. Eugenio Apostol was an officers' cook 1/c, and Carlos Tulao a steward 1/c. Both were excellent cooks, adding little touches to the mess fare that dressed up our meals most favorably. They were always good-natured and smiling, rattling dishes, silver, and pans in the pantry, chatting away happily in their native Tagalog. Any small compliment, comment, or praise spurred them to even greater effort.

14–19 September *Sculpin* arrived in the specified latitude-longitude holding position on the fourteenth. The next five days were uneventful. The weather was generally bad, with rain showers and overcast skies.

I found a sunlamp that Doc had inexplicably hidden in a box behind the TDC and told no one about. I unpacked it, rigged it over my bunk, and tried it out. Soon other officers wanted to try it, too. The thing was deceiving. Only a few minutes' exposure would give a real burn.

Tired of reading the magazines that arrived in Brisbane, I commenced *The Giant Joshua,* by Maurine Whipple. It was not very interesting reading, and the captain agreed with my assessment.

Our holding circle was out in the middle of nowhere. *Sculpin*'s wardroom strategists hoped that we would be sent to a more promising location, and soon. We were bored. When we moved from Fremantle to Brisbane, having read all the radio traffic about these waters being filled with Jap ships, we had thought that surely we would not stay on station for more than a few days before running out of fish. Radio messages told of Jap cruisers along the New Guinea coast shelling Allied positions at Milne Bay. We hoped the boss would send us to try for a shot at them.

On the seventeenth the last of the torpedomen finished his qualification. That meant that advancement in rating would be pushed next. My students were eager to be promoted and were urging me to get busy with that schooling.

Two more books attracted my notice: *Out of the Night,* by Jan Valtin, and *The Captain from Connecticut,* by C. S. Forester. Forester's seagoing tales held my attention. His skill in weaving a story, with his knowledge of the sea, ships, honors, traditions, and the romance of the days of iron men in wooden ships, was outstanding.

At dusk on the nineteenth, during a slight clearing in the clouds, Charlie got a reasonable fix, the first in fifty hours. *Sculpin* was slightly to the east of her circle. Radio orders came from CTF 42 telling us to check Milne Bay, New Guinea, from a position north of Kiriwina Island. At last we were doing something.

20–21 September   We could see nothing moving in or out of Milne Bay. The patrol was getting to be monotonous. *Sculpin* spent the two days watching the entrance to the bay.

At sunset on the twenty-first *Sculpin* surfaced and received orders to proceed to the coast of New Britain, about 100 miles away, and reconnoiter Thilenius and Montagu harbors, but to be back in our circle in the middle of nowhere by 25 September.

The skies had been overcast. Charlie hadn't gotten a good fix in several days, and his DR was suspect. He hoped not to repeat the Baler Bay episode.

I overheard Middie and Frank giving George a bad time for doing so much work on his qualification and shaming them to get busy on theirs.

22 September   At daybreak *Sculpin* submerged five miles south of the southernmost of the ring of islands surrounding the harbor of Thilenius, a neatly sheltered anchorage of several square miles behind a fringe of reefs and tiny islands. The *Coast Pilot* said that all the deep-water entrances were from the east, so we concentrated on those channels.

It was difficult to get a good look into the harbor from seaward. The principal fringe islands were fairly lofty, upward of 100 feet high, and numerous islets not shown on the chart cluttered the view. A heavy mist prevailed. No shipping or shore facilities were seen. It was entirely possible that both were present but concealed from seaward observation. *Sculpin*'s sketchy charts made it prudent not to approach too closely because of the possibility of uncharted reefs.

I was OOD as we submerged. As I was going down the ladder from the bridge to the conning tower I followed the last lookout a little too closely. He grabbed the step instead of the ladder rail, and I stepped on his hand, which he instantly jerked away. My foot was on the lookout's hand, unsupported, leaving me clawing the air. I finished the trip down the ladder on my knees, peeling a chunk of skin off the left knee. The injury made walking difficult, climbing ladders painful, and would take pampering and time to heal. Doc Miller came to my rescue with his usual thoughtfulness to anyone needing medical attention.

We sighted the masts of a ship in midafternoon. *Sculpin* commenced maneuvering to close, but the nearest we got was 13,000 yards. The ship was identified as a *Hibiki*-class destroyer exiting the harbor at high speed through a western channel. According to the *Coast Pilot* there was no such exit. Apparently the Japs knew more than we did.

23 September   The day was spent submerged near the western channel that the destroyer had used. We observed no more in the harbor than on the previous day. From that location a number of buildings could be seen on the southern island, with a flagpole flying a Japanese flag. Lack of action was discouraging. Three weeks after leaving Brisbane, and we hadn't seen anything worthy of a torpedo.

At night, as *Sculpin* moved on the surface to take a look at Montagu, a message from CTF 42 directed us to leave that vicinity in the evening of the twenty-fourth and carry out the balance of the patrol orders.

24 September   We saw no ships when submerged off Montagu during daylight hours. There were buildings on one island similar to those on Thilenius. The captain asked me if I wanted to take a periscope picture. I told him that we were too far away to get anything meaningful. We were fully twenty miles away, when we could easily have gone fifteen miles closer.

At sunset *Sculpin* surfaced and headed for Vitiaz Strait, from where we would go north, then east, to our area north of New Britain. We were glad to try another location.

25 September   On the surface after dark the exec found his landfall on New Guinea's Teliata Point to help him negotiate Vitiaz. He wanted to go close inshore where the water was deep and avoid the shallower areas offshore. Surprisingly, we could actually smell the dank odor of the tropical jungle long before we could make out Teliata Point. A strong current pushed us through the strait, past Tolokiwa Island.

26 September   Completing transit of Vitiaz at 0145, *Sculpin* proceeded toward her next station north of New Britain, anxious as ever for action. A couple of false alarms did enliven the night. On two separate occasions the bridge watch sighted dark spots on the horizon. We manned the TDC and attempted to track the contacts, but they turned out to be nothing more than small, inoffensive islands, minding their own business.

Frank and Middie began taking lessons in running the TDC but had difficulty understanding what the instrument was doing. I was never convinced that either of them could remember from one day to the next just what I was trying to teach them.

Middie was a bell tapper; he regularly followed me on watch and was habitually late. No matter what I did in the way of hints, sending messages to remind him, or waking him up early, he dawdled around and was always overdue getting to the bridge to relieve me. Persistence would pay off, I kept telling myself.

27 September   *Sculpin* was heading right into the strait between New Britain and New Ireland, intent on setting up patrol off Rabaul. The Japanese were reported to have established a major base there. Radio intelligence reports told of as many as fifty ships in the harbor and of much ship traffic in and out. The night was unusually clear and bright. We could see the mountains of New Ireland about fifty miles away, and to the south the mountains of New Britain. They were excellent aids for the navigator.

28 September   At eight minutes past midnight Cape Lambert, New Britain, was sighted, and before dawn *Sculpin* submerged for the day in the northern approaches to Rabaul. Right at sunrise a seaplane tender of the *Chiyoda* class was sighted, moving north. *Sculpin* tried to close but got no nearer than 20,000 yards.

An hour later masts were sighted to the west, and *Sculpin* commenced closing. The possibility of an attack was evident after twenty minutes of tracking, so we went to battle stations. The target was a large tanker of the *Omurosan* class, with only one small escort visible. They were zig-zagging wildly on an easterly base course at a speed of eleven knots. After an hour of maneuvering to gain firing position, we fired a spread of four fish at the tanker from the stern tubes at a range of 1,860 yards.

The captain saw two hits, and three explosions were heard throughout the boat. After watching for only a few seconds longer, the captain took *Sculpin* to deep submergence as the escort headed for us with a bone in his teeth. Sonar reported hearing the screws of two escorts.

Long before reaching *Sculpin* he commenced dropping depth charges. We knew that he was way off target. All was quiet for about twenty minutes. The crew was released from battle stations, and I went to my bunk for some rest.

No sooner had I gotten in the bunk than I was almost knocked out of it by a string of four very close depth charges, seemingly right over me. I could hear water spewing into the compartment. I ran to the control room to report that water was coming into officers' country in the vicinity of the head (toilet), and then went back to find the leak.

A gauge line to sea, located in the officers' head, was broken. Water was building up on the splash-tight deck over the forward battery. We dared not let that saltwater get into the battery below, because deadly chlorine gas would be formed when the saltwater reacted with the sulphuric acid in the battery.

Calling for damage controlmen to come quickly, I went into the head and, by draping myself over the commode with my head back of it, I was able to use my hands to hold the gauge tubing and cut off the flow of water. The position was very awkward, and the pain of holding the water back with my hands was too much for me to stop the flow for more than a few seconds. It was incredible how much water could come in through a quarter-inch tube at a depth of 275 feet.

Baldwin arrived with plugs, turnbuckles, and other equipment to plug the leak. With him and a helper working on that job, I went to the after end of the compartment to help remove the water.

A bucket brigade was hurriedly formed. Jack trimmed the boat with a ten-degree up angle so the water would accumulate at the after end of the deck, in officers' country. He had to maintain two-thirds speed to keep *Sculpin* from going deeper. *Sculpin* was tons too heavy, having taken on water from a number of leaks throughout the boat.

I took on the job of dipping up buckets of water, handing them through the compartment door for the bucket brigade to pass on aft and dump. The most comfortable position I could find was in the yeoman's chair in the ship's office, facing aft, filling buckets to be passed aft. The brigade was dumping the water into a bilge and into the canned-goods storeroom just aft of the control room.

We were able to keep the water level below twelve inches at our bailing location for the half hour that it took Baldwin to stop the leak. Then we bailed out the residual water and dried the deck. Fortunately, no water got into the battery.

Others throughout the boat were also making repairs, stopping leaks, and getting back to normal, while the captain directed evasive action over a period of about two hours. When we went back to periscope depth, nothing was in sight.

I went to the control room to cool off and talk to the captain, the exec and Jack. We were all wringing wet with sweat. As I walked in, the captain looked at me quizzically and asked what I had been sitting in. The seat of my khaki shorts was a dark color. I put my hand to the seat of my pants to feel squishy cloth, and the hand came back bloody.

Retracing my steps, I found pieces of glass in the chair where I had been sitting for a tense two hours. The light bulb above the yeoman's chair, shattered by the depth charges, had fallen on the chair, and during the whole time we were bailing I was sitting on the broken glass. I had been so keyed up that I didn't realize that my rear was being shredded.

Every compartment in the boat suffered damage of one category or another. Individually the damages were not that serious, but collectively the crew would be working for days to make everything right. Numerous light bulbs, gauge glasses, and steam-tight light fixtures were broken, and many valves were opened slightly. Motors were shorted by leaked water, as was number 2 periscope control switch. The conning tower door gasket was cut and leaking, and the object prism in number 2 periscope was chipped. Repairs to some of the damages could not be made until we got back to Brisbane.

When we dumped the water into the canned-goods storeroom, partially filling it, the paper labels were washed off many of the remaining cans of the Dutch sauerkraut, sausage, and stew concoctions that we had loaded in Surabaya. For some weeks afterward the crew insisted that Chief Cook Duncan Hughes would send a mess cook for an armload of cans, open them, and thus determine the menu for the meal. They didn't care for the Navy-supplied Spam, either.

By a little after noon the leaked water was all pumped out and the most critical damage repaired. Torpedo tubes were reloaded and ready for more action. I had the 16–20 watch, after which I finally found time to clean up and go to bed for some badly needed rest. I had been up for nearly thirty hours.

29 September   We spent a quiet day with no contacts in Steffen Strait. Some damage repairs were still in progress. After the tense activities of the day before, anyone not on watch was resting. It was without doubt the worst depth charging that *Sculpin* had experienced. There was much superficial damage. It appeared that we might not have any air conditioning until a seldom-used motor in the after engine room was moved to work the air conditioner. The conning tower door could not be opened, but the leak around its gasket was stopped. Frank Alvis, then commissary officer, lost sugar, coffee, and dried beans to the saltwater; and about 500 pounds of boned beef spoiled after the freezer motor shorted out. The ice machine motor was flooded.

30 September   We were submerged on the Rabaul–Portland Island shipping lane but saw nothing. Lack of contacts permitted more attention to damage repair. In my case, sitting down had to be negotiated with care. Doc was a big help with his medical miracles. It occurred to me that in later years it could be embarrassing to be asked to show my war scars.

1–2 October   Those were quiet days on the Cape Stephens–Cape Queen Charlotte line until sonar picked up screw noises near sunrise on 2 October. *Sculpin* maneuvered to close and went to battle stations. A transport of the *Nittu Maru* class escorted by a *Hatsuharu* destroyer was in sight. After thirty minutes of tracking, the TDC solution looked very good and we were anticipating another sinking. *Sculpin* was still too far away to fire torpedoes when the destroyer apparently made contact with a school of fish and at once commenced attacking, while the transport made a seventy-five-degree course change away from *Sculpin*. The captain watched the destroyer, along with some aircraft, conduct a determined depth-charge attack on a spot 5,000 yards away from *Sculpin*. They got away.

3 October   On the Cape Stephens–Portland Island line: we sighted smoke at midmorning and began closing maneuvers. The movement of the smoke was such that we had to use high speed, depleting the battery significantly. An hour later the masts and upper works of a transport were in sight, but we were unable to get closer than 20,000 yards. Identification of the transport was not possible. The chase was abandoned.

Shortly after dark the bridge watch was treated to an impressive pyrotechnic display and decided that a Fourth of July celebration was in progress in the waters between New Ireland and New Hanover.

During the past several days sonar had picked up fast screws and pinging that would come in strong and then fade away. Nothing was seen, but sonar kept picking up the noises. We concluded that the noises came from small antisubmarine craft patrolling waters where there was heavy Japanese ship traffic.

Periodically we observed aircraft flares at night to the south, always in the distance. There was evening radio news of Allied air attacks on Rabaul, which may have been the source of the flares. We also saw flashes of bomb explosions and tracer shells in the direction of Rabaul.

4–6 October   No contacts were made except for more of the intermittent screw noises reported by the soundmen. On the evening of the fifth, through persistent rainstorms, the bridge watch saw a small destroyer passing at high speed in the direction that sonar had reported the screw noises.

The quartermasters began to refer familiarly to this patrol location as "in the slot," since we were in the restricted waters between New Britain and New Ireland. We were beginning to think we had seen our last action of the patrol.

We were unable to open the conning tower door as a result of the depth charge damage, and garbage had to be carried up to the bridge to be thrown over the side. The weather had been bad—rainy and overcast—so garbage accumulated in the crew's mess. The captain was hesitant to get rid of it because we could be surprised by a destroyer popping out of the gloom. Finally he stopped dead in the water to allow the soundmen to listen carefully for any hint of enemy presence. When nothing was heard, the smelly task of carrying the garbage to the bridge for the deep six was accomplished.

The best radio programs from the United States were coming to us by way of the BBC. We were enjoying the World Series baseball games between the Yanks and the Cards, and a number of bets were made on the outcome. Another radio favorite was the "Hit Parade" of songs that were the vogue in the States. No one was familiar with the list of favorites on the selection of the year; we were very much out of date.

I went to the maneuvering room for a few days to operate the engineering plant controls to sharpen my proficiency at diving and surfacing.

George and I made a wager under which I would pay him one Aussie pound for each fish fired at a contact that he made on his watch, and he would pay me the same for each one fired as a result of a contact made on my watch.

7 October   At 1145 George was diving officer and sighted smoke to the north. Tracking and closing maneuvers began, and I routinely manned the TDC. Forty-five minutes later a *Hatsuharu*-class destroyer was identified leading a column consisting of a 5,000-ton transport followed by a 10,000-ton transport believed to be a *Fuji Maru* (later determined to be

Naminoue Maru). They were holding a steady easterly course at fourteen knots.

Half an hour later *Sculpin* was at battle stations with the captain remarking that he was tempted to go after the destroyer. Another twenty minutes of maneuvering and tracking brought *Sculpin* to a position 1,200 yards from the 10,000-ton transport, where the captain fired a spread of four fish from the bow tubes.

Jack momentarily lost depth control, so the periscope was underwater and the captain couldn't observe hits, but three explosions were plainly heard. The screws of the transport stopped, and sonar reported break-up noises. A few minutes later, back at periscope depth, he was able to see the badly damaged, burning, and sinking transport, and also saw the destroyer heading toward us.

Sculpin went deep, rigging for depth charge, but no concerted antisub attack developed. The destroyer halfheartedly dropped a few depth charges several hundred yards away, while our sonar followed the remaining ships as they moved on. Before the destroyer left, he went right over *Sculpin* without making contact. The swish, swish of his propellers could be plainly heard by everyone as we braced for the shock of depth charges. None came.

I must have sweated off fourteen pounds during the hours of silent running, with everything shut down except propulsion. The boat was very hot, and the substitute air conditioning motor had still not been fully activated.

Since we fired four fish as a result of a sighting by George, I owed him four Aussie pounds.

8 October   Early in the morning we sighted smoke to the north, but *Sculpin* could close only to an estimated 20,000 yards. The source of the smoke was two big transports, escorted by a destroyer, on an easterly course. We could not get near enough to identify the classes of the ships, which were following the same route as the ship we sank the day before.

Right after sunset a destroyer and two smaller patrol boats passed to east at high speed on a southerly course. *Sculpin*'s sinking of the ship the day before had them stirred up.

9 October   A quiet day. Sonar heard fast screw noises at intervals, but nothing was seen by periscope. Night visibility was terrible. *Sculpin* stopped periodically to permit sonar to listen for contacts; the captain didn't want to suddenly find himself nose to nose with a destroyer.

We hadn't used the new periscope camera yet. Each time we fired fish there were destroyers around and the captain could not allow me time to get set up for pictures.

10 October   At 0950 George sighted smoke. We tracked the smoke but could not develop the contact. We could hear distant explosions that might have been depth charges on a false contact. Those ships were going north, probably empty, and so would not have been as valuable to sink as ships heading south.

By midmorning *Sculpin* was in the location given by CTF 42 as the date and time position on the track of a convoy that would pass through our area, but we saw nothing. Just after dark, aircraft flares were observed in the distance to the north. We heard explosions and supposed that they were from Allied bombs at Kavieng.

A period of poor night visibility set in, so the captain's night orders were to stop once in a while to permit sonar to listen all around for a few minutes for enemy ship noises. Radio traffic told us that *Greyback* and *Trout* were in patrol areas adjacent to ours.

11 October   Several sightings of faraway smoke were made but could not be developed. When I relieved George he claimed to have smoke in sight. His smoke looked like clouds to me. I contended that he was trying to take credit for sightings that were about to occur on my watch.

My paperwork, reports, and other projects that I had planned for the patrol were all complete ahead of schedule. All that was left was to supervise my troops and conduct the schools I was involved with. That left more time for bridge, chess, acey-deucey, and reading. We were enjoying the BBC broadcasts, especially "Command Performance," with Cary Grant as MC. The bookworm was reading Louis Bromfield's *Wild Is the River*.

12 October   Watches were dogged, giving me the forenoon watches, when most of the sightings had been made thus far. I hoped this would give me the opportunity to even up the score in my bet with George. Wardroom strategist analysis of the sightings and of our successes was that we were too far offshore. Jap traffic was to the east of our location. The captain and exec still wanted to stay in deep water, far offshore.

A message from CTF 42 told *Sculpin* to stay out of Saint George's Channel when departing the area on the seventeenth. Charlie was pleased at the change. He had been worrying, dreading the earlier orders to go through Saint George's. The new orders were to go north around New Hanover and check the east coast of New Ireland on our way back to Brisbane.

13 October   Starting at midnight, for an hour and a half, *Sculpin* played hide-and-seek with several patrol boats. There was no indication that we were ever spotted. At 0433 a number of brilliant flashes, followed much later by rumbles of explosions, came from the direction of Rabaul.

We had seen at least fifteen ships going in and out of Saint George's Channel. Why did Charlie choose daily patrol spots so far away from those solid evidences of the enemy shipping lane?

This was another wasted day. I missed having Red Lennox to kibitz with about the tactics of where we should be in order to find Jap ships. We didn't go into the traffic lanes where we saw so many ships moving in and out. Our nearest approach was actually forty-five miles away. I was disappointed. It was an extremely cautious attitude. By this time we should have had at least five sinkings, be out of fish, and on the way back to Brisbane.

14 October   CTF 42's orders not to go through Saint George's Channel forced *Sculpin* to move across the traffic lanes, leading to the action I wanted.

On the surface at daybreak, west of New Hanover, *Sculpin* was surprised during a rainstorm by one large and one small transport, escorted by only one destroyer. George was OOD. We barely had time to go to battle stations. I had no TDC solution when the captain fired a spread of four fish from the bow tubes at the large transport, using an estimated target speed of eleven knots. Range was estimated at 1,900 yards. The fish all missed ahead of the target, indicating that the captain had over-estimated the target speed. The spread was not enough to compensate for the speed error. The destroyer immediately came charging in our direction.

We stayed on the surface for thirty minutes and avoided the destroyer by running into a rainstorm before submerging. We could hear depth charges going off in the direction where the destroyer was last seen. He was locked onto something other than *Sculpin*.

The day was quiet until midafternoon, when Frank sighted the smoke of what appeared to be three different groups of ships moving toward Saint George's from the north. I manned the TDC and we began to track the contacts.

Surfacing at dark, still west of New Hanover, *Sculpin* went after the nearest convoy. We saw three large ships between rainstorms, with no visible escorts. On the surface we ran around the convoy for two and a half hours and were in position and ready to fire. It was midevening, and we had been tracking ships since about 0530. I felt as if I had been operating the TDC continually for days.

The captain selected a large tanker, the last ship in the column, and fired a spread of four fish from the bow tubes, using a speed of ten knots, at 1,500 yards. He watched two of them hit and we heard three explosions. My TDC projected three hits. The bridge watch could see lights of much activity on the tanker as he listed heavily and began to sink.

Two destroyers appeared out of another rainstorm astern of the sinking tanker, along with several other ships that were intermittently hidden by storm clouds. The destroyers came searching toward *Sculpin,* one firing his guns. *Sculpin* ducked into a convenient rainstorm and evaded on the surface. The consensus of those on the bridge was that there were five or six ships in the convoy. Not having radar, we couldn't tell just how many were there. The destroyers apparently did not see *Sculpin* and made no attack. We lost them in another rainstorm.

With only four fish remaining (in the after torpedo room) and with rainstorms all over the area, the captain was of no mind to attempt to run around and attack that convoy again, especially with the destroyers alerted.

15 October A few minutes after midnight, feeling that we had shaken the destroyers, *Sculpin* slowed from flank speed, put two engines on battery charge, and began charging the high-pressure air banks to full capacity. The torpedomen gave the four remaining fish a thorough checkout.

An added deterrent to stalking the convoy was that Charlie had not gotten a fix in over thirty-six hours. With all of *Sculpin*'s convoy chasing over two days on DR, the unknown currents just might have pushed us too close to the shallow water near the islands.

Using his DR position, Charlie laid out a route for *Sculpin* to the north around the tip of New Hanover. It was a quiet day, and the captain expressed the thought that maybe we should move some fish from aft to forward. I was ready, but Charlie was negative. He had become more and more nervous as the patrol progressed. Anyway, the weather was not favorable for torpedo moving, so that settled that.

I was hoping to be the OOD when we sighted some ships to fire at so I could cut back my debt to George. Several of us had been reading the book *What Makes Sammy Run,* whose main character was called Sammy Glick. Jack dubbed George "Sammy," and soon we all began calling him that.

16 October   The day was spent passing the Japanese base at Kavieng on the north point of New Ireland. My hopes of getting some of my bet back from George rose on two occasions when I sighted smoke in the direction of Kavieng, but nothing developed. We did hear a number of explosions.

The radio messages indicated that the Japanese were mobilizing forces to attempt to push the marines off Guadalcanal. Wardroom strategists thought there was a high probability of seeing a carrier. With only four fish left, and those in the after torpedo room, any attack could be difficult.

CTF 42 sent a new routing for *Sculpin* to get to Brisbane: north of Bougainville and Ysabel Islands, then south past Guadalcanal and directly to Brisbane.

17 October   Another quiet day. At 0908 *Sculpin* left the patrol area while submerged and headed for Brisbane. More messages told of Jap landings on Guadalcanal. Many Jap ships were in the Solomon Islands area.

A nasty boil on the inside of my right kneecap had been developing for several days, and Doc didn't have anything that would slow it down. The soreness was so painful that he told the exec and the captain that I should stay in my bunk, so the exec took me off OOD watches. Reading and helping Middie decode messages kept me occupied but not active enough to use much energy.

18 October   At 1235 Middie sighted smoke to the east. I managed to limp to the control room to man the TDC and commence tracking the smoke. One and a half hours later the captain described a strange-looking ship of about 4,000 tons: a gun on the forecastle, another gun on the forward well deck, two guns on the after well deck, a small seaplane on the well deck aft, and many depth charges in stern racks. He was pinging and zigzagging wildly. Conclusion: we had an antisubmarine ship (Q-ship) in our sights.

At battle stations thirty minutes later, we fired three fish from aft at 1,900 yards' range. The captain saw one fish explode in his wake, close to his stern, and one hit just forward of his bridge. A large cloud of smoke and flames billowed up from the forward well deck. He began firing guns at our periscope and turned toward *Sculpin.*

Eight minutes later the captain fired our last fish at him from a range of 1,300 yards and ordered deep submergence to evade his expected attack. A minute later a very heavy explosion was heard and felt throughout the boat. Sonar heard break-up noises, and no further screw noises were heard.

Promptly coming up to periscope depth, we watched him all afternoon as *Sculpin* moved on south. I finally got to use the new periscope camera. He was listing heavily, very low in the water, apparently sinking and without propulsion. As darkness fell a great column of smoke appeared and we pulled away.

The captain broke radio silence. On the clipboard was a message to CTF 42 briefing the results of the patrol, indicating that we had expended all our fish, and, of all things, that the torpedo officer was confined to his bunk with a serious boil. So the whole submarine force now knew of my boil. It was very embarrassing. Later, Middie confessed that the clipboard copy was a fake; the wardroom made up a special message for my benefit.

CTF 42 directed *Sculpin* to return directly to Brisbane, north of Buka Island and east of New Guinea. With no torpedoes, the captain ordered us to run at 125 feet in the daytime and at four-engine speed on the surface at night. He wanted to get back to friendly waters as quickly as possible. Charlie projected that *Sculpin* would be off the entrance to Brisbane on 26 October.

19–20 October   After the excitement of sinking the Q-ship, my boil began to clear up. The credit went to Doc's medication and the hot water bottles that Tulao kept supplying. I was fed up with staying in that bunk.

Chief Signalman Weldon Moore had designed a ship's flag and was well along in making it. It had a navy blue background and was three by five feet in dimension, with a sculpin fish riding a torpedo in the center surrounded by tiny Jap flags, one for each ship hit; warships were indicated by the rising sun emblem, and other ships by the merchant flag. Near the top edge was a replica of the ribbon of the Navy Cross that our captain had been awarded. It was very handsome. I helped Weldon with the sewing and picked up pointers on using the sewing machine which I put to good use in my own wardrobe repair.

21 October   During the early evening *Sculpin* encountered a destroyer, fortunately in time to avoid detection. On the surface, running at flank speed, we got away after a tense hour.

Radio messages from *Sturgeon* to CTF 42 reported that she had had a rough time with Jap destroyers off Guadalcanal. She suffered a persistent fuel leak, causing a permanent oil slick. She was ordered to return to Brisbane and would arrive there two days ahead of us.

The names of more submarines that had joined our sub fleet were appearing frequently in radio traffic: *Trout, Gudgeon, Grampus,* and *Greyback. Saury* and *Salmon* were moving from Fremantle to Brisbane, stopping in Sydney for torpedoes.

Still unable to get around easily or climb ladders, I was helping Middie with decoding. My wagering score with George took a decidedly favorable turn. We bet the full eight pounds that I owed him on the Navy-Yale football game. Navy won the game, so we were even.

22 October   The captain decreed that the twenty-second was our last day to submerge. We had permission from CTF 42 to run on the surface continually when south of latitude 12° S. The weather was noticeably cooler. We were in the southeast trade winds, and living aboard our submarine was much more comfortable. After learning from the radio messages of all the new submarine arrivals, we began to give more and more credence to the captain's forecast that *Sculpin* would soon go to the United States for navy yard overhaul.

The trouble with the prediction was that the Jap buildup for a major push on Guadalcanal could easily change the picture. We hoped that Dugout Doug's air boys would keep pasting them with bombs and ensure *Sculpin*'s trip to the navy yard. (Dugout Doug was an unflattering reference to General MacArthur.)

23–25 October   On the twenty-third, *Sculpin* commenced running on the surface night and day. My knee was almost well, and I resumed standing OOD watches. The weather was better, but the sea was rough enough to make a number of the crew seasick after so long in calmer waters. We were tense, knowing that Jap submarines had been active off the east coast of Australia.

Jack took over navigation of the ship, in anticipation that Charlie might be transferred after this patrol. I did a twenty-four-hour turn at navigation to sharpen my eyes and brush up on procedures.

George and I got into another football bet. (He always wanted to wager on something.) We made one-pound bets on the Navy and Yale games to be played on the twenty-fourth. Yale lost and Navy won, so I was now two pounds ahead.

Sleeping with the cool fresh air was much more restful than in the stale, humid, warm air that we suffered while submerged every day. I noticed that there weren't any flying fish on deck in the mornings as there had been off the west coast of Australia. Maybe it wasn't the right time of year.

We were ahead of schedule, so on Sunday, 25 October, *Sculpin* submerged and conducted a three-hour battery discharge. We needed to kill some time before our ETA on the twenty-sixth.

Up to this point the captain had required the use of zigzagging. *Sculpin*'s wardroom strategy group convinced him that zigzagging was a waste of time, so he discontinued the practice. Our argument was that zigzagging kept the OOD alert, exercised the helmsman and the quartermaster, but might not really be of much protection to a submarine. After that it was fifteen knots during daylight and twelve knots at night, holding a steady course.

26 October I was the midwatch OOD just after midnight when we sighted Moreton Light twenty-six miles to the southwest. It reminded me of Rottnest Island Light off Fremantle. I had heard Perth and Brisbane referred to in Australia as the twin cities.

Moving toward the channel, we came upon a group of Allied destroyers and cruisers. They were apparently unaware that *Sculpin* would be approaching Brisbane, and when we flashed our recognition signal they turned wildly and scattered. In a short time, after they decoded the signal and realized who we were, they regrouped. At 0430 *Sculpin* exchanged recognition signals with the Colundra Head signal station and received permission to enter port.

Captain Christie, '15, CSSWP, along with a crowd of other officers, welcomed us as we moored at New Farm Wharf, astern of sub tender *Griffin*. As he submitted his patrol report the captain was informed that he had been recommended for another Navy Cross.

The concluding remarks of the patrol report were as follows:

> Morale, as always, was excellent. I consider myself fortunate beyond my deserts in commanding a ship's company, officers and men, whose spirit is so uniformly and uncompromisingly aggressive. In this connection the following anecdote is worth repeating. On 28 September, when the ship was barely under control following a severe depth charging, as soon as the principal leak was very precariously plugged, a Filipino mess attendant, who had been engaged for an hour or more in bailing to protect the forward battery, in all seriousness asked the executive officer, "Now we go up and shoot the destroyer, maybe?"

Finally, the commanding officer wishes to place on record his conviction that every officer and man attached to the *Sculpin* has performed his duty in an exemplary and highly commendable manner. The following singled out by name as deserving of special recognition by higher authority are simply instances which stand out above an exceptionally high level:

Lieutenant C. M. HENDERSON—For the continuous excellence of his performance of his duties as executive officer and navigator and specifically for the initiative, ingenuity, and determination with which he attacked, localized, and finally corrected the damage resulting from a severe depth charge attack on 28 September. He undoubtedly saved the ship from serious injury which would have necessitated her return to base, and possibly from destruction.

Lieutenant John H. TURNER—For the continuous excellence of his performance of his duties as engineer officer and specifically for the skill and determination he displayed in maintaining depth control, without discharging ballast by either pumping or blowing and without resorting to high speeds to attain dynamic lift, while the ship was approximately ten tons heavy as a result of injuries received in a depth charge attack and was being actively hunted by the enemy. He undoubtedly made it possible for the ship to escape further and concentrated punishment which might well have proved disastrous.

Lieutenant C. G. MENDENHALL, Jr.—For the uniform excellence of his performance of duty as torpedo officer. Since the commencement of hostilities, this ship has fired sixty-seven torpedoes in twenty-one attacks. It is entirely due to Lieutenant Mendenhall's industry and devotion to duty that there is no reason to believe that any of the torpedoes ran other than hot, straight, and normal, and largely due to his skill as TDC operator that twelve of the attacks resulted in destruction of or injury to enemy ships.

Ernest S. BALDWIN, 393 06 41, CMM(AA), USN—For the skill, ingenuity, and determination which he displayed, under the direction of Lieutenant HENDERSON, in successfully plugging a serious leak through the pressure hull of the ship which was then at approximately 275 feet keel depth and being actively hunted by the enemy.

Although normal maintenance and minor repair work were needed, the boat was in relatively good material condition. A squeal had developed in the starboard propeller shaft which required attention. My torpedo tubes, for once, had no major problems.

Patrol Summary

Number of men on board:
  65 enlisted
  7 officers

Nautical miles covered:
  7,459 on the surface
  1,136 submerged

Fuel used: 72,230 gallons (8.4 gallons/mile)

Drinking water: 20,782 gallons consumed

Battery water: 3,400 gallons used

Duration: 48 days (42 submerged)

Torpedoes fired: 20

Sinkings: 2 tankers, 1 transport, 1 Q-ship

Refit in Brisbane

26 October–17 November   Refit activities took on a more leisurely pace in Brisbane. There was no rest camp setup as in Fremantle-Perth and Albany, and we continued living on board while the repair and refit work went on. George and I rented a car to have more freedom of movement, but driving a U.S. car with the steering wheel on the wrong side for Australian left-of-road driving made for a strange feeling.

The refit schedule called for *Sculpin* to leave on patrol on 18 November. Our first destination would be Sub Base Pearl, then we would go to a U.S. shipyard. We would carry the old Mk-10 fish, since the patrol would end in Pearl Harbor and the more modern Mk-14s were needed in the western Pacific. All of this was secret, but it was generally known all over the sub base and even among civilians in Brisbane.

Sculpin was dry-docked for six days to remedy the squeal in the starboard propeller shaft, scrape and paint the ship's bottom, check the fathometer and sound heads, and perform other routine maintenance. The traditional old navy routine of all hands going over the side to scrape and clean the ship's sides and bottom was new to quite a few of the recently arrived officers and crewmen. They required prodding, and even a few threats of disciplinary action, to get the work done. After all, from their standpoint they were just in from the war zone and rated better treatment. A radioman, torpedoman, or cook couldn't see why he should be scraping barnacles and wire-brushing rust off the ship's bottom. Perseverance paid off, however, while the combined forces of dry dock, tender, and ship worked around the clock to prepare *Sculpin* for sea.

By 4 November all the torpedo gang's work was done: exchanging Mk-14 fish for Mk-10s, converting the fire control system and TDC to the Mk-10 tactical characteristics, and conducting planned maintenance. Charlie gave me permission to grant liberty at noon until departure.

Ashore, classmate Bill Ruhe introduced me to friends with a fine tennis court, which we used regularly. One acquaintance led to another, so in the end I had a wide selection of diversions: tennis, picnics, and swimming excursions to the seacoast, with Bill, the captain, Charlie, Condé Raguet, Harry Hull, '32, Doc Mainwaring, Monk Hendrix, and Franz Hoskins, along with their Australian dates.

Electrician's Mate Elmer Zimmerman honored me with an invitation to his wedding. The bride came across Australia from Perth for the ceremony at the Episcopal church, and there was a beautiful reception afterward. Meanwhile, Doggie Dawes was feeling low at having to leave Betty, his bride of a few months.

Charlie puzzled over his next duty choice: he was told that he could stay in the Pacific and get a command as soon as one was available, or he could go to new construction in the States after our sixth patrol. He needed to make up his mind soon.

Everyone enjoyed a very relaxing time. We might never get back to Brisbane again, but there was much anticipation of going home to the United States after such a long time away.

Sculpin's Sixth Patrol

(18 November 1942–8 January 1943)

18 November Division Commodore Connolly came aboard before lunch for a short talk to the crew at quarters and to make presentations of enlisted men's promotions. In his talk the commodore expressed his appreciation for *Sculpin*'s work and confirmed that we would end the patrol in Pearl Harbor, then go on to the West Coast for a major overhaul. The high spirits that those announcements created were evident with most of the crew, although there were a few who had wives and prospective wives in Australia, and they were feeling low.

While we were at quarters a truck from Peters Ice Cream Company delivered twenty gallons of ice cream to the ship. Our friends the Christophersons wanted us to have a remembrance of their friendship.

During lunch the commodore told us that he had asked for Silver Star medals for Charlie, Jack, and me, but Captain Christie had turned him down.*

Other navy and civilian friends came by to express best wishes for a successful patrol. At 1400 *Sculpin* cast off all lines and headed downriver on her sixth war patrol. As we pulled away, the well-wishers on the dock waved good-bye, and they were still waving as we lost sight around the first bend in the river.

Our departure to patrol so soon after the fifth patrol was nothing less than a miracle. During the twenty-two days in port, work on the boat was handled by three different tenders, we were committed for six days in dry-dock-related work, and we shifted berths nine times. Dry-docking and shifting berths so many times cut significantly into the time for refit work.

Two hours after getting under way we made a test-trim dive in Moreton Bay. With everything checking satisfactorily and trim confirmed, *Sculpin* surfaced to begin negotiating Hamilton Patches to reach the South Pacific

*Under later awards criteria those honors would have been automatic.

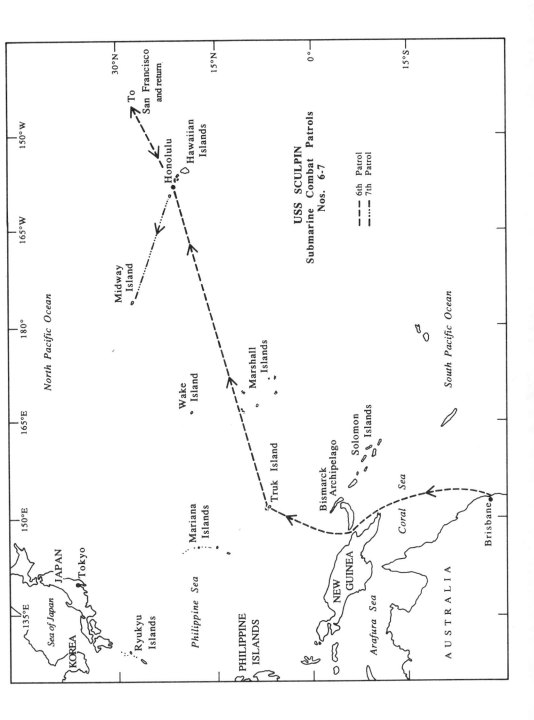

USS SCULPIN
Submarine Combat Patrols
Nos. 6-7

----- 6th Patrol
········· 7th Patrol

Ocean. Nearing sunset, finally outside the channel entrance, the pilot got into his waiting boat and *Sculpin* headed north.

Our route to the patrol area off Truk Island would take us through Vitiaz Strait, then north to our station south of Truk. *Sculpin* was to remain on station until 27 December. When on station, operational control of *Sculpin* would shift from CSSWP to Commander Task Force 7 (CTF 7) at Pearl Harbor.

Because of the long duration of the patrol and the long distance that we would travel, the captain ordered the use of the most economical speeds to conserve fuel. We might need our highest speed to chase Jap ships at Truk, and he certainly didn't want to run out of fuel before we reached Pearl. That would be most embarrassing.

19–21 November   These were surface-cruising days; but each day we submerged for a short time to check trim, conduct drills, and run off a battle problem. When we surfaced, a battle surface drill was conducted to give the gun crews practice at manning the guns and experience in handling the weapons.

On the twentieth and twenty-first we fired the 3-inch gun for the first time since the war began. *Sculpin* had ten rounds of 3-inch ammunition for practice. Gunner Caserio created targets of packing crates that were nailed and lashed together, which gave the gun crews something to aim and fire at. A few men in the gun crews had never fired a 3-inch gun, so that was their initiation. I was a bit apprehensive at first, but everything went off smoothly, and they even scored a few hits at 1,000 yards. Gunner was proud of his work at constructing targets and the way the gun crews performed.

Contrary to the predictions of the commodore before our fifth patrol, we were heading for the United States with very few changes in personnel. The personnel office explained that the crew deserved time in the United States because, by that time, many would have made six successive patrols and been overseas for well over one year.

Sculpin's crew consisted of sixty-eight men, with only six newcomers, and only one of the new men was not qualified. A few holdovers from previous patrols had also not yet qualified. My schools would be less intensive than on previous patrols, with concentration on advancement in rating.

Charlie's decision on his prospective command assignment was to go to the United States for new construction. I would have made the same decision.

The weather continued good, with light seas and sunshiny days. We were all getting back into the swing of patrol routine, reading mail and magazines that had accumulated in port and telling stories about the great times in Brisbane. There was more talk of marrying Australian women.

22 November As we neared New Guinea, *Sculpin* went into reversa while staying submerged all day. The captain was reluctant to submerge, he said, and stayed up until the sun was well above the horizon before he ordered the dive.

23 November A CTF 42 intelligence message gave *Sculpin* the route of a Japanese convoy that was expected to go from New Guinea to Rabaul. *Sculpin* was directed to stop and patrol the route until released to go on north to Truk.

South of New Britain we saw nothing except a few aircraft flares at night. My hope was to attack a lot of enemy ships so we would use as many of the old Mk-10 fish as possible. A quip circulating the torpedo rooms was that those fish were older than the men working on them and deserved to be treated with the respect due to the elderly. The Mk-10 torpedo, we were told, was developed during World War I.

24 November With the south coast of New Britain in sight through the periscope, I saw a big bomber fly by about ten miles astern of us and decided that it was one of ours, en route from bombing Bougainville to a base in northern Australia.

BBC news from Africa did not sound good. Hitler had sent reinforcements to his North African forces, which slowed the Allies considerably.

25 November A false alarm. Before noon Charlie was making a sweep with the periscope and was positive that he had an aircraft carrier in sight. We went to battle stations and began tracking. The captain secured all from their stations when he realized that the contact was another of those deceptive small islands.

In Vitiaz Strait we saw many aircraft flares over Lae, New Guinea. We speculated that our bombers were working over the Jap installations.

26 November, Thanksgiving The traditional Thanksgiving feed was served: turkey with all the fixin's, and my favorite, cherry pie.

My thoughts went back to Thanksgiving 1941, when Hal Hamlin, Boots Hall, Margie Kyser, and I had spent an enjoyable evening together at the Army-Navy Club in Manila. What had become of them, and of Charlie Albert? Hal was rumored to have survived the sinking of the cruiser *Houston* and to be a prisoner of the Japs. An article in *Life* magazine noted that Margie was reported as being held in Manila. No word about Boots.

27 November   *Sculpin* was watching the convoy route given in the intelligence report of 23 November. We were about fifteen miles north of Tolokiwa Island. From that distance we could see interesting jungle—all green, with high interior hills. I would have liked to go ashore and explore.

The area of our last patrol north of Rabaul was now being covered by three submarines. It should be a good spot, because the shipping route is restricted by the islands of New Britain and New Ireland, forming a funnel toward Rabaul.

28 November   This was another day spent waiting for the convoy, but we saw nothing. On the surface after dark, *Sculpin* was ordered to head for Truk. Our route passed through Jap shipping lanes, and we should have opportunities to attack. I was curious to see how the Mk-10 performed.

There was much speculation and rumor through the boat about how much leave we might get when we reached the repair yard on the West Coast.

29 November   *Sculpin* passed the Vitu Islands submerged. One island was an ancient volcano with one wall of the crater broken away, creating a sheltered bay, like Koko Head on the island of Oahu. It seemed an ideal place for a hideaway. The entrance to the crater was deep water, as was the bay inside the crater. We passed very close and got a good look at the cultivated hillsides and the smoke rising from clearings. The green hills and jungle against the blue water made a great scene for a shot with the periscope camera. We would see the results in Hawaii.

War news continued good, and I hoped for something better as we looked for ships to sink. U.S. radio stations were coming in more clearly as we proceeded north, but reception of the BBC from London was still best. "Command Performance," from San Francisco, was a favorite program when the static permitted.

30 November   School for qualification and advancement really took off when we left Brisbane. Going home was a great incentive for qualifying and advancing before reaching the States. The thought of wearing dolphins to show the folks at home, and the extra prestige and pay of a rating, were foremost in our minds.

There were still stacks of magazines: *New Yorker, Time, Life, Newsweek,* and others to check through. I was also enjoying reading *Mrs. Miniver.* The humanness of those intimate word pictures were what made the book so appealing. I could see, feel, and imagine myself in every one of the episodes.

1 December   Only twenty-one more days till Christmas, which, if all went well, would be spent in the vicinity of Truk.

Sculpin crossed the equator. I had lost count of the number of times we had done that. To fill out the day, I was a member of a summary court-martial for an apprentice seaman who deliberately left the ship on his duty day in Brisbane and stayed away until we sailed. He received a sentence of twenty days' solitary confinement and loss of $108 in pay.*

2 December   We almost saw action when a convoy was sighted in bright moonlight at 0130. We attempted to run around it during the nearly four hours before daylight, but they apparently detected us and turned away, well out of range. Daybreak was on us, so we submerged and watched the smoke disappear over the horizon.

At noon a destroyer and three scouting planes appeared, looking for *Sculpin.* The earlier ships must have reported our presence. We watched them search for several hours, but they never came closer than four miles. The sea was dead calm and clear, and visibility was unlimited. *Sculpin* couldn't hope to get near enough to the alerted destroyer for a shot.

3–4 December   Still en route to Truk. Radio reports kept feeding information to *Sculpin* about much enemy traffic in and out of there. We were eager to see for ourselves.

Steward Apostol gave me a short haircut. We debated whether I should keep my beard until we got to the mainland, and I decided to keep it.

"Command Performance" came in loud and clear on the fourth, with a Charlie McCarthy–Betty Grable show that was a hit with the crowd gathered around the loudspeaker in the forward torpedo room.

Something was amiss in *Sculpin*'s radio shift from CTF 42 to Pearl

---

*The captain's review reduced the sentence to ten days' solitary and no loss of pay. The sentence would not be carried out until we reached San Francisco.

Harbor (CTF 7). Middie's keys wouldn't break the code. Radio copied messages addressed to *Sculpin,* but he couldn't crack them. Then, on a detailed check of the radio logs, Middie found that one message from CTF 42 was actually missing.

The captain opened up with the radio and asked NPM Radio Pearl to repeat that specific message. NPM didn't answer *Sculpin*'s call, apparently not hearing us. Finally Brisbane came in and offered to relay the message, which they did. At last the missing message was retransmitted, and it specified the key to be used. Middie got the proper key out of the safe and then was able to bring us up to date.

5 December   *Sculpin* was off a southwest entrance to Truk for the first day of patrol. The problem with Truk, we soon realized, was that there were too many channels for enemy ships to use. The immense lagoon was surrounded by islands and coral reefs, with numerous deep passages between them. The captain elected to patrol too far out from any channel for *Sculpin* to be effective.

6 December   When I shoved the periscope up at daylight I was excited to see a Jap cruiser of the *Natori* class to the west on a northeasterly course. A closer look disclosed another of the same type ahead of the first. *Sculpin* was too far away and had no chance to get into firing position.

While watching the cruisers the captain sighted smoke to the southwest, and we commenced tracking that contact. After thirty minutes of tracking he described two ships, a small tanker and a medium-sized transport, on a northeasterly course toward Truk. A few minutes later a *Minekaze*-class destroyer came south from Truk at high speed and joined the two ships to escort them northward. Things were looking favorable for a shot until the escort came out, after which they changed course radically. *Sculpin* could get no closer than 8,000 yards. Reluctantly we secured from battle stations.

While on watch as diving officer, I added up the figures from the diving book showing that *Sculpin*'s first year of the war had seen us underwater for 2,918 hours, traveling 7,318 miles while submerged.

7 December   A message from CTF 7 told *Sculpin* that several ships were due out of the south entrance, so we spent the day there, but really too far out—fully twenty miles from the entrance. We saw a transport and a submarine come out, but they were too far away for us to get close enough for a shot. At our distance from the lagoon, ships coming and going had too much freedom to change direction and avoid us.

A couple of fishing boats were around us most of the day. We were concerned that they would snag *Sculpin* in some of their fishing gear.

8 December   I was OOD at 0330 when the starboard lookout sighted a very large, dark shape in the direction of Truk. We attempted to close, but he was moving too fast and was too far away for us to catch. I thought it was a battleship or very heavy cruiser, escorted by a destroyer. They were really pouring on the speed.

Hoping that the place where I had sighted the cruisers on the 6th was a regular rendezvous point, we moved to spend the daylight hours there. The weather was against us, with heavy clouds, rain, and poor visibility most of the time. We saw no signs of ships.

9 December   Another quiet day, this one spent off the approaches to Otta Pass. There were the usual clouds and poor visibility. The lack of action was becoming tedious. During spare time I was engaged in a chess tournament with the torpedomen in the after torpedo room. It was the room against me. They won one match, I won five.

Before leaving Brisbane, Doc had swapped the old sunlamp for a new one. My suntan was on a maintenance routine so I wouldn't look too anemic when we reached Pearl and the West Coast.

10 December   George got a big surprise when he was making a regular periscope sweep and a plane sighted the scope and dropped a bomb. The bomb fell some distance away, but George, seeing the geysers with periscope magnification, thought it was right on top of *Sculpin*. He certainly looked startled as I saw him on my way to the after torpedo room—eyes unusually wide open, hair actually standing on end. I went to the after torpedo room to calm those fellows. The explosion shook them up, and they telephoned the control room in an agitated state, needing reassurance that all was well.

Sculpin was still too far from the lagoon entrances—at least twenty miles away. Fishing boats worked around us regularly. One of them fooled the captain. He thought it was a much larger craft and was ready to call us to battle stations until he saw a giant of a crewman go up to the wheelhouse. That gave him a reference by which to judge the size of the boat, which was only a few hundred feet away, and he changed his mind.

When we surfaced at dark we saw searchlights playing around the south entrances to the lagoon.

11 December   This was an unusually bad weather day. The sea was rough and there was continuous rain. *Sculpin* was offshore at the location where a radio message had indicated a tanker was due to pass. We saw nothing, possibly because our position was doubtful. The weather was so unfavorable that Charlie had been unable to get a fix for several days.

12 December   Bad weather continued. Just after surfacing for the night we found a small vessel in the rain and began to close. The contact was a fishing boat. The boat turned, apparently confused, and headed right for *Sculpin,* at which time we submerged to avoid him. Charlie, still relying on DR, was worried about the possibility of our being in too close to the coral reefs near the atoll. Stars or sun lines would have been welcome.

13 December   CTF 7 sent *Sculpin* to meet a Jap sub that was to pass near Truk, but nothing was seen. At dawn, just before submerging, Charlie finally got a good position and found that we were thirty-five miles from his DR position. No wonder we didn't see the sub.

14 December   During a quiet day submerged the weather broke. The sea was not as rough when we surfaced, and we actually saw the moon at intervals. So far this was turning out to be a hard luck patrol. The torpedomen talked about how embarrassing it would be if *Sturgeon,* on station north of Truk, racked up a better record than *Sculpin.* There was quite a rivalry between boats over who had the best patrol record.

15–16 December   The weather was even better than the day before. Except for Frank's sighting of an airplane on the fifteenth, these were both quiet days. The plane was not on patrol but heading in to land at Truk. The commonplace statement after sighting smoke, a plane, or other possible activity became, "Well, we got away again." I continued to believe that we were not close enough to the islands. There was just too much searoom for the Japs to run around, in and out of Truk, with *Sculpin* too far away from any channel entrance.

17 December   Just before noon a large aircraft carrier, not shown on our recognition aids, was sighted to the east, moving on a southwesterly course. *Sculpin* had no hope of attacking him. The nearest we got was about 18,000 yards. The captain called me to the periscope to look at and photograph the unidentified carrier.

Shortly after the carrier passed I thought I saw masts sticking up over the horizon; but they turned out to be a string of buoys to which fishermen had tied lines or nets. Each buoy was marked by a bamboo pole with a small flag on it. From a distance, they gave the illusion of being masts of ships. We turned so that we would not become entangled in their fishing gear.

18 December   An exciting day, but no torpedoes were fired. Shortly after midnight I sighted a dark shape to the south, turned *Sculpin* for a better look, and called the captain. The dark shape loomed up in a hurry as an aircraft carrier. Then, ahead of the carrier, we saw a light cruiser preceded by a destroyer. *Sculpin* was in a bad spot, on the full-moon side, with conditions almost like daylight. The captain put on four engines for emergency speed and turned to get into attack position by circling around them, but they were making too much speed for us to hope to come within firing range. I noted that the captain may have been reading in his cabin again, because he had trouble seeing them and kept asking me to tell him what I saw.

The lead destroyer disappeared behind the carrier, and another destroyer appeared from behind the carrier, where he had been hidden from our view. A few seconds later we saw both of them headed directly for *Sculpin* with bones in teeth. At 5,000 yards both opened fire, using searchlights to illuminate us. *Sculpin* submerged to evade. We heard a few depth charges in the distance as they searched for us. Sonar listened to the pinging and screw noises while they kept us down for three hours and then left.

19 December   When I went to the bridge for the midwatch *Sculpin* was circling a large tanker in bright moonlight, maneuvering to get into position ahead, dive, and fire while submerged. Instead of relieving Jack Turner as OOD, I manned the TDC.

With *Sculpin* ahead of the tanker and almost in place to dive, a destroyer was sighted coming from Truk to escort him to port. Sighting the destroyer caused the captain to dive before he planned to, but we were not sighted, and we expected to find ourselves in a very good firing position, although at a much longer range than we preferred. Our solution of his course, speed, and range tracked well in the TDC. Everything looked good.

At 0121 the captain fired a spread of four fish from the bow tubes, with a 3,000-yard run. He saw two hit, and two heavy explosions were heard and felt in the boat.

The fourth fish failed to clear the torpedo tube, and the torpedo room reported that the fish was still in the tube with its engine running. A second impulse of air finally got the torpedo out. Sonar didn't hear the fish running, so we considered it no longer a problem, probably headed for the bottom.

Sonar reported breakup noises from the tanker. His screws stopped and were not heard again. Then the target burst into flames, and the captain turned his attention to the destroyer that had earlier caused us to dive prematurely.

Confusion must have reigned on the surface, because it was some time before the destroyer came to look for *Sculpin*. We evaded, and he didn't come close with his eight token depth charges. He searched for a short time, then went to pick up survivors from the tanker.

Although the moon was bright, there was a tropical haze over the surface of the ocean, so the captain could never see the tanker clearly, but he thought it was at least 10,000 tons. *Sculpin* spent the remainder of the day at 135 feet conducting a listening patrol, sure there would be ships and planes out looking for us. That was a long time underwater. The air in the boat was mighty thin when we surfaced after sunset.

We made an analysis of the failure of that fish to leave the tube and came up with three possibilities: (1) the impulse pressure was too low; (2) the firing key had not been held down long enough; and (3) the tube was vented too soon, allowing sea pressure to push the fish back into the tube. Torpedo firing procedures were tightened up to prevent another such problem.

20 December   Another uneventful day, spent recovering from the excitement of last night. On night watches, when the sky was clear, I had a good feeling at being able to see the northern constellations again, especially the North Star and the Big Dipper. Christmas was only a few days away, the third that I had spent away from Anahuac.

21 December   Another disappointing day. Just before being relieved at noon I sighted masts and a ship's funnel. We commenced tracking until the captain identified the ship as the hospital ship *Takasago Maru*. He was painted with the international colors of a hospital ship: white, a broad green horizontal stripe around the hull, with giant red crosses on bow, quarter, and stacks. I took a roll of pictures through the periscope. Except for the paint job, he looked like one of the big cruise ships that we saw in Honolulu.

22–24 December   The twenty-second was a bad day at chess. Both George and Charlie beat me, and the weather was gathering for another rough spell.

On my birthday, the twenty-third, a message from Admiral Nimitz addressed to all ships arrived:

> TO ALL FIGHTING MEN IN THE PACIFIC X ON THIS HOLIEST OF DAYS
> I EXTEND MY GREETINGS WITH ADMIRATION OF YOUR BRAVE DEEDS
> OF THE PAST YEAR X THE VICTORIES YOU HAVE WON THE SACRIFICES
> YOU HAVE MADE THE ORDEALS YOU HAVE ENDURED ARE AN INSPI-
> RATION TO THE CHRISTIAN WORLD X AS YOU MEET THE JAP ALONG
> THE VAST BATTLE LINE FROM THE ALEUTIANS TO THE SOLOMONS
> LIBERTY IS IN EVERY BLOW YOU STRIKE X NIMITZ

The cooks were busy on the twenty-fourth preparing a special feast of turkey and fixin's, cranberry sauce, mashed sweet potatoes, asparagus, peas, and fruitcake. Middie brought out decorations he had squirreled away to make the wardroom and the crew's mess as festive as possible. Christmas dinner was served at midnight on the twenty-fourth.

25 December, Christmas   It appeared that even Tojo was giving *Sculpin* a present when a small transport escorted by a destroyer came in from the east in midafternoon. Everything was developing well during an hour of tracking, then they made a radical zig toward us, heading directly for *Sculpin*. The captain put on speed as he tried for a stern tube shot, but the torpedo gyros, those old Mk-10s, weren't following the gyro setter. As we strained to set gyros manually, the ships moved beyond range.

Everyone said that I had a hangdog look about me, and I was sure that I did. There was just no way for us to have known that would happen, and, after it did happen, no way to fire in time.

Sculpin surfaced at dusk and ran west at flank speed for four hours in search of the transport but never could sight him in the dark and rough weather. While we were attempting to regain contact, a message from CTF 7 placed a Jap submarine at latitude 10°45′ N, longitude 159°30′ E. For information, we guessed, since no one was told to go there and wait. CTF 7 certainly didn't expect us to do so. It was much too far away, way out of our area.

26–27 December   The weather was so rough on the twenty-sixth that waves washing over the periscope made seeing anything very difficult. My chess score for the day was good. I beat Torpedoman Boos three games, and George Brown two out of three. We were at last hearing some good old Christmas music from the United States. Up to now we could only get that music from Tokyo and Berlin.

Jack opened the showers on the twenty-seventh, with prospects of heading for Hawaii at midnight. Those baths were welcome after almost six weeks of making do with condensate from the air conditioners. The condensate picked up an unpleasant odor and was really no substitute for water from the freshwater tanks.

Amateur poets in the after engine room frequently made up poems about whatever *Sculpin* and crew were doing. Their work decorated the bulletin board and was passed through the ship for everyone to enjoy. The current output (condensed) began, "Dear Mr. President of the U.S.A.," then went on as a letter telling all about leaving home, going to Manila, fighting in the Dutch East Indies, and so on, until *Sculpin* got her orders home, and ended:

> But we don't want no medals
> Nor parading through the crowd.
> The thing that we want most of all,
> Why it would be ecstasy,
> Give us thirty days leave with travel time
> In the good old U.S.A.

My current reading was *Hill of Doves,* by Stuart Cloete. I couldn't say a lot for the book; it was too long-winded with no action. This patrol could be similarly characterized.

28–29 December   *Sculpin* didn't leave her area to head for Hawaii until late on the twenty-eighth. The chase to reestablish contact with that transport on the twenty-fifth had sent us far to the west of our area.

On the twenty-ninth the captain talked of staying on the surface commencing the thirtieth. We were far enough from Truk or any other Jap base to be free of antisubmarine forces. When we got near to Wake and the Marshalls we might need to spend a day or so submerged.

Helen MacInnes's book *Above Suspicion* turned out to be a good one. I was tempted not to read it because of the title, which for some reason didn't appeal to me.

30–31 December   Staying on the surface continually was the always welcome treat. The fresh air and sunshine were appreciated by those few who had the opportunity to get to the bridge, and the interior of the boat was much cooler and more comfortable. The odor of diesel fuel, cooking, and cigarette smoke was flushed away by the continuous fresh air. The exec passed the word that two sightseers could go to the bridge at a time. That created a waiting line.

The captain radioed Pearl Harbor that our ETA was 8 January and informed them that after that date our call signs and recognition signals would be out of date.

1 January 1943   We spent the day submerged about 200 miles from Wake Island. The electricians wanted to work on the main motors, and it was a fine opportunity to get that done. Resistances were low and needed to be brought up.

Jack and Charlie spent hours giving Middie, Frank, and George quizzes on qualification subjects. The captain wanted them to be qualified before we reached the West Coast, so they were getting the cram treatment.

Radio copied an NPO message which gave the call signs and recognition signals for the period following 8 January. Middie was pleased because he had been worrying over his lack of proper call signs.

2–8 January   We experienced cool weather and rough seas most of the way to Pearl, and we knew that the voyage to the West Coast would be even cooler and probably rougher, since we would be bucking trade winds all the way.

We crossed the international date line on the fourth, so *Sculpin* had two January fourths in 1943. Starting on the fifth, U.S. patrol planes were sighted each day. They seemed to be expecting us, and we exchanged recognition signals with them.

The exec appointed Frank Alvis and me to make an audit of Middie's books as ship's service officer. Middie had started the endeavor in Java, with payment in Dutch guilders. Most of the crew also had Philippine pesos at that time, so he accepted those as well as guilders. Later, the books were converted to Australian pounds, and still later, in Hawaii, would be converted to dollars before dissolving the enterprise. Our audit came out four cents short. We had no U.S. money to make the pot right. Rather than have Yeoman Aaron Reese retype the whole thing, we simply added a footnote blaming the lack of balance on the exchange rate. Another general court martial in prospect!

Jack was suggesting to the captain that we stay in Pearl long enough for him to overhaul two engines. Those thoughts were not received kindly by any of us, although I did hope to be there long enough to see a few of my friends.

By 7 January we were seeing Hawaiian weather—smooth seas, lots of sunshine, and cottony clouds. There was a feeling of unusual excitement through the boat. Uniforms and caps were cleaned, shoes shined, neckerchiefs pressed, and clothes washed. Anticipation ran high.

Entrance instructions told *Sculpin* to meet our escort, *Litchfield*, about sixty miles from Oahu. A check of our navy directory showed classmate Jack Wallingford serving in *Litchfield*. I looked forward to seeing him.

8 January   I relieved Jack Turner as OOD at 0400 and just had time to get settled down when the lookouts sighted *Litchfield*. We closed in and challenged twice before they replied. It made me realize anew how difficult it is to see a submarine in the dark of night. I notified the captain that we were following our escort to Pearl, and we continued toward the channel entrance. I again enjoyed the fun of navigating to the channel, piloting the channel to the submarine base, and mooring the boat at the dock.

Admiral R. H. English, '11, Commander Submarines Pacific Fleet (ComSubPac) and a large group of officers and enlisted friends, along with a band, were on the dock to greet us. There were a number of friends I had not seen in a long time: Pete Madley, '37; Judd Yoho, '36, one of my first classmen; Mac McGrath, '40; and Jack Wallingford. They crowded aboard to talk and to have coffee in the wardroom. We were overwhelmed with visitors.

Most of the day was spent digesting the details of our stay in Pearl and absorbing what little information was available about the West Coast overhaul. The torpedo gang was overjoyed to learn that all the Mk-10 fish would be taken off the boat and left at Sub Base Pearl. We would leave for the West Coast on Monday, 11 January.

After lunch a relief crew came aboard, and *Sculpin*'s crew spent time with them to acquaint them with the boat. Concurrently all the crew and officers prepared to go to the Royal Hawaiian Hotel to spend the weekend. I had never in my life expected to be staying at the Royal, and it was all courtesy of the U.S. Submarine Force.

Anyone going outside of Pearl Harbor was required to carry a gas mask, so the sub base sent masks aboard for us. We were warned that the military police would arrest anyone without a mask. When the boxes of gas masks were opened, there were only thirty-five masks for seventy-five people. Base working hours were over by the time the shortage was discovered. The sub base and staff had closed shop and gone home. The exec had to make a number of telephone calls, right up to the admiral, he claimed, to get the situation rectified. All our crew were eventually outfitted with masks and bused to Waikiki.

During that busy day the captain submitted his report of *Sculpin*'s sixth war patrol. The patrol had lasted for fifty-two days, forty of them submerged. He said little about the material condition of the boat, knowing that we had prepared long lists of navy yard work for our arrival in San Francisco.

An immediate problem for the torpedo fire control experts at Sub Base Pearl was that *Sculpin*'s gyro angle setters were not able to follow the orders of the TDC and set the Mk-10 gyros when the boat was swinging rapidly. We made tests to try to determine the problem but failed to find any reason, except that the setting motors might be too small to carry the load. Other submarines carrying those torpedoes needed to know of that problem.

Accommodations for the crew had been unsatisfactory in that *Sculpin* had sixty-eight men on board and only forty-six bunks. A system was worked out for some of the junior men in which three men were assigned

Patrol Summary

Number of men on board:
  68 enlisted
  7 officers

Nautical miles covered:
  8,706 on the surface
  832 submerged

Fuel used: 82,880 gallons (8.7 gallons/mile)

Drinking water: 21,784 gallons consumed

Battery water: 4,100 gallons used (78.8 gallons/day)

Duration: 52 days (40 submerged)

Torpedoes fired: 4 Mk-10

Sinkings: 1 tanker, 10,000 tons

to two bunks. This hot-bunk arrangement worked in conjunction with the watch bill, so the three men never needed to sleep at the same time.

Overhaul, Pearl Harbor and San Francisco

8 January–23 May 1943   Information at Pearl was sketchy concerning *Sculpin*'s overhaul in San Francisco. We did learn that we were going to an activity contracted by Bethlehem Steel Company at their new submarine repair facility at the Sixteenth Street Piers in South San Francisco. Beth Steel used the navy dry docks at Hunter's Point in their repair work. *Sculpin* would be the first boat they worked on, so we knew there would be a learning period both for Beth Steel and for *Sculpin*.

I touched base quickly with many of my friends in Honolulu. Classmate Red Balch and I had dinner with Kak Hamlin (Lowrey). She had no direct news of Hal, who was on the cruiser *Houston* when it went down in the Java Sea, but she also knew of the rumors that he was a Jap prisoner being held in the jungles of Southeast Asia.

Sculpin was under way at noon on Monday for the seven-day run to San Francisco. I tried my hand at navigation on that leg of our journey. Bushels of mail and Christmas packages had come aboard over the weekend in Pearl, keeping everybody busy reading and rereading messages from home. I counted sixty-four letters in my stack.

Sargo was following us one day later, also going into overhaul at Beth Steel. I looked forward to being with Condé Raguet in San Francisco. Our two subs were sister ships in the same division, so we were together frequently, and Condé was a Naval Academy friend and sub school classmate.

Commander Kraut Dettmann, '20, a submarine construction specialist, was waiting on the dock as we tied up at Beth Steel on 18 January, prepared to oversee our overhaul. A large barracks barge was moored alongside *Sculpin* with living accommodations, a galley, storerooms, offices, and workshops for our crew and officers. Everyone moved aboard for the duration of the overhaul.

On 21 January the radio and newspapers were full of the tragic news that ComSubPac, Admiral English, and members of his staff were missing on a flight from Hawaii to San Francisco. Then followed confirmation that all had perished in a crash during bad weather in the mountains north of San Francisco.

On the twenty-first Charlie Henderson was detached to take command of *Bluefish,* being built in Portsmouth, New Hampshire. On the twenty-ninth Al Bontier, '35, reported as Charlie's replacement as exec, and Jack Turner learned that he would soon leave to be executive officer of *Ray.*

Besides general repair and overhaul work, major alterations would be made:

1. Installation of high-capacity battery cells and provision for better ventilation and access
2. Moving the 3-inch gun from aft to forward of the conning tower
3. Modification of the cigarette deck space and installation of a 20-mm gun mount aft of the bridge
4. Installation of an SJ (surface search) radar unit
5. Replacement of the sonar with new, more efficient, equipment
6. Replacement of the main engine mufflers
7. Installation of electric vapor compression water stills
8. Removal of the boat and boat storage facility
9. Removal of the torpedo storage under the weather deck

All this was to be accomplished by mid-April.

I followed a busy schedule, working on the boat at Beth Steel and commuting to Alameda to spend nights with my cousins the Richardsons, who insisted that I occupy their guest room. In 1939 they had introduced me to Ann Weedin when I was in San Francisco with the battleship *Mississippi.* After that I always stopped there and dated Ann. They kept me involved in a continuous round of social activities—dinners, picnics on weekends, movies, or just visiting friends and relations. Everyone wanted to do something for me.

Ann and I had been seeing each other constantly and getting along famously, so we decided that we would get married. The sensible thing would be to wait until the war was over. But then, to be practical, why wait? I wanted to go home to Anahuac first, then when I got back we would set a date.

We had all wondered who would be our new ComSubPac. Our speculation ended when the navy announced that our old friend from Perth, Admiral Charles Lockwood, was moving from Australia to Pearl Harbor. He would put new life into the effort to correct our torpedo problems.

On 26 February Middie and I began a thirty-day leave by hitching rides on military planes. Twenty days in Texas were filled with seeing family and friends, making talks at schools and civic organizations, and enjoying just being at home. Then I went to Corpus Christi to hitch rides back to the West Coast. The plane that I was on went to Seattle, so I saw friends there before returning to Alameda.

While I was on leave Ensign Joe Defrees, '42, reported from sub school. His mother, Mrs. Joseph R. Defrees, had been the sponsor at *Sculpin*'s launching in July 1938. Admiral Defrees was at that time Director of Shore Establishments, Navy Department. Meanwhile, Middie Mills was notified that he would be transferred before *Sculpin* left San Francisco. The faces aboard our warhorse *Sculpin* were rapidly changing.

Ann Weedin and I were married on 7 April, with Condé Raguet as best man, and went to Lake Tahoe for a few days' honeymoon. Back in San Francisco, Beth Steel was having difficulty putting *Sculpin* back together. The completion date was postponed repeatedly, with frantic twenty-four-hour-a-day work to make the ship operational. Two days of sea trials were finally under way at noon, 25 April. With that hurdle successfully negotiated, the captain vowed that *Sculpin* was going to leave San Francisco on 1 May regardless of the number of minor things that needed attention. Our crew would turn to and make things right on the way to Hawaii. We were all irritable over one delay after another.

A restless crowd of friends and relatives, wives and children, a number crying and near hysteria, waited on the dock until near noon to wave good-bye when cleanup work was completed and all hoses, electrical connections, and lines were cast off. Middie was a teary-eyed, forlorn sight, as was Kraut Dettman, as *Sculpin* rounded the turn to go west, under the Golden Gate Bridge, and headed back to war. *Sargo* would follow us the next day.

About three quarters of the way to Hawaii *Sculpin* and *Sargo* spent two days looking for possible survivors of an army bomber that had gone down on a flight to Hawaii. Nothing was found.

From 8 May until 22 May *Sculpin* was in refresher training, working from Sub Base Pearl, getting ready for her seventh war patrol. A full load of twenty Mk-14 torpedoes was loaded.

While busily getting ready to go out I was very pleased to see classmate Paul Schratz, and I listened sympathetically to his problems in adjusting to the realities of the submarine war. About a year late getting to sub school, he had missed the first disheartening, frustrating years of retreat from Manila with the RAF and the troubles with torpedoes that didn't work.

During the refresher training a prospective commanding officer (PCO), Lieutenant Commander Pete Galantin, '33, reported aboard for his practice patrol. He had just completed PCO School at New London, Connecticut. The submarine force was sending officers who hadn't had combat experience to make a patrol with a seasoned captain before they were given their own ship. And, Pete Summers, '36, confided that he saw my name at the top of the list of those to go to new construction as executive officer. That news boosted my spirits sky high.

Sculpin's Seventh Patrol

(24 May–4 July 1943)

24 May, Monday All morning a parade of enlisted men and officers, a number of them the captain's and Executive Officer Al Bontier's classmates, came aboard to talk, drink coffee, and wish us much success and a safe return. Admiral Lockwood stopped by and chatted about how much he enjoyed cruising with us down the Australian coast from Fremantle to Albany, and the stay in Albany. The crew lounged on deck, talking to visitors while waiting for the call to maneuvering watch. Condé Raguet came aboard for a cup of coffee and to wish us well. His *Sargo* would be following us on patrol in a few days. Classmates Joe Vasey and Benny Goodman also came to say bon voyage and good luck.

Near noon, just before we took in the lines to leave on patrol, the promised SJ (surface search) radar officer expert reported for duty. He was perspiring and obviously rushed to get on board. Another George, he was Lieutenant (jg) George Embury, USNR. His late arrival was the cause of our delay in getting under way. We needed expert help with the new radar.

Once out of the Pearl Harbor channel, the captain called all officers to the wardroom for a briefing on *Sculpin*'s orders:

First of all, magnetic exploders were to be used on all torpedoes—to our disgust. Our patrol area was to be off the east coast of Honshu Island, Japan, north of Tokyo. Our route would take us north of the Hawaiian chain to Midway, where we would stop long enough to get fuel and make any voyage repairs that might be needed. From Midway *Sculpin* would go directly to Honshu. The path was far from possible detection by Japanese antisubmarine planes, so we wouldn't need to submerge during daytime until about 7 June, when we neared the Japanese coast.

George Embury was not a sub school graduate. His training was all in the field of electrical and electronic engineering. The exec gave me the job of teaching him to be a submarine officer; he would stand watches with me. George was eager to learn, bright, and attentive, and he seemed potentially to be a very capable officer.

25–27 May The 1,200-mile run to Midway was made on the surface at fifteen knots except for frequent drills and battle problems—practice dives and exercises to shake down the boat, train the crew, and, particularly, to get the new hands broken in, while we learned to use the new equipment installed in San Francisco.

Sculpin's crew numbered sixty-nine men, more than on any previous patrol; the new radar added electronics technicians. Twenty-three men who had made all six previous patrols were still with us; the captain and I were the only officers in that category. With eight officers on board we would have more time to oversee our departments and spend less time standing watches.

Officer duties were the same for me as on the previous patrol. George Brown had the job of chief engineer, Frank Alvis was first lieutenant, Joe Defrees was communications and commissary officer, and George Embury was assistant communications and radar officer.

In spite of the beautiful weather, Embury was seasick. He would get his sea legs in a few days, we hoped.

The captain told me that at headquarters he had seen my name at the top of the list of execs for newly constructed boats. He had been advised that I would leave after this patrol. I didn't tell him that I already knew about the list. I dreaded the thought of leaving *Sculpin*; she had been home for so long, there had been so many great shipmates to serve with, and we had gone through rough times together.

The captain asked me my thoughts about Frank Alvis taking over the torpedo-gunnery job. My reply was positive, so I was delegated to break him in at operating the TDC and managing the Ordnance Department, and have him ready before the end of the patrol.

Most of the crew, including myself, had never been to Midway. We were looking forward to seeing the birds that were reported to be the main attraction of the islands; I had seen them featured in articles in the *National Geographic Magazine*.

28 May At 0605 *Sculpin* met surface and air escorts off Midway and proceeded in to moor alongside *Snook* at the pier. The fuel and water hoses were immediately attached to shore connections to top off the tanks. Two voyage repairs began, one to the follow-up system on the main gyro, which was not working properly, and the other to the top bearing of number 2 periscope, which was binding. *Sculpin* had no technician trained in gyro systems, so repair experts from a tender or base were needed.

During our few hours at Midway I went ashore to tour the island with a few crewmen who were not involved in the work on board ship. There wasn't much to see. Two islands, Sand and Midway, were little more than deposits of coral sand a few feet above sea level with a few scrubby salt-cedar-like trees on Midway. There were a few buildings, formerly the headquarters of Pan American Airways, that housed the navy establishment. At the PanAm Hotel I saw Don Scheu, '40, for a few minutes. I would have stayed longer, but I wasn't sure how long I could be away from the boat.

The most interesting sight was the birds: frigate birds, terns, seagulls, and albatrosses (gooney birds). They had no fear of humans and were underfoot almost everywhere. It was the time of the year when half-grown gooneys, the size of young turkeys, numbered in the thousands. They were awkward and gawky, with blackish down; thus the name.

By 1400 all was ready for *Sculpin* to depart. When noses were counted, Gunner's Mate Bob Wyatt was missing. (Gunner Caserio was now chief of the boat, and Wyatt had succeeded Caserio in charge of the Gunnery Department.) Gunner Wyatt (all gunner's mates seemed to be "Gunner") had taken two ammunition ready locker parts to a shop on shore for minor alterations. One of the torpedomen knew where to find him and went in a jeep to bring him back. Later, a sheepish Wyatt hurried down the pier carrying his parts, while the crew, at maneuvering stations with engines running, snickered and made sarcastic remarks.

While we were waiting for Wyatt, *Flying Fish* came in to moor nearby, and I was very pleased to have the opportunity to exchange greetings with classmate Bob Gurnee. Then, with Gunner Wyatt aboard, *Sculpin* departed to pay a call on Japan.

29 May   As we cruised west we conducted daily training exercises and ran through every maneuver in the book to get the crew thoroughly familiar with any circumstance that might arise. The drills included a battle surface and the firing of the last of our allowance of practice ammunition. The 3-inch, 20-mm, and .50-caliber machine-gun crews profited by the training.

Sculpin went into the reversa routine and also crossed the international date line on the twenty-ninth, so we skipped 30 May. The next day was the thirty-first. Al Bontier didn't have the trouble that Charlie Henderson had in getting into the reversa routine.

The new vapor compression stills produced enough water to permit showers to open regularly. Old-time *Sculpin* sailors thought they were living easy.

31 May–7 June Moving west on the surface, *Sculpin* conducted daily drills and training. The weather was unusually calm, cloudless, and sunny, perfect for watches on the bridge and for Al's celestial navigation. We saw a number of large Japanese glass fishing-net floats, which I wished we could pick up for collectors' items. There were plenty of very large sharks and a few whales. Watch standing, paperwork, administrative tasks, reading the mail from Washington, and then plowing through the stack of *Time, Life,* and *Reader's Digest* magazines that had been delivered before we left Pearl kept everyone fully occupied.

On 5 June a storm came through, causing some seasickness. Embury was one of those affected. Temperatures were noticeably cooler. Foul-weather jackets were comfortable on the bridge, especially at night.

Pete Galantin familiarized himself with the ship, stood OOD watches, and was in the conning tower with the captain at battle stations. He also helped Joe Defrees with the decoding tasks. The nightly deluge of coded radio messages needed to be translated as rapidly as possible. Pete was two years senior to Al, but he wasn't in the chain of command, so Al's responsibilities didn't change. There was never any conflict. We all respected the logic of the situation and appreciated having another experienced officer with us.

7 June *Sculpin* was in her patrol area. The *Coast Pilot* predicted frequent fog in that locality at that time of the year. There were indeed fog banks floating by, and after avoiding three fishing or patrol boats, the captain ordered "dive" at 1000. We expected to be submerged in the daytime until we were on the way back to Midway. On the surface at dark, *Sculpin* was told by ComSubPac to go to latitude 31°30′ N, longitude 142°10′ E, where a Jap carrier force would pass on the ninth, near midnight.

The captain immediately headed south at full power. We had about 400 miles to go to contact the enemy force. If everything went just right, we would make it.

8 June Frequent patches of fog gave cover from airplanes, but it was off and on, and we had to dodge a number of fishing or patrol boats. The SJ radar was proving its worth in helping to spot the boats and avoid them in the fog. Embury, who now had his sea legs, was getting a workout manning the radar and training operators.

9 June   *Sculpin* was in position just after midnight, and right on schedule a force of two carriers, escorted by a cruiser, was sighted to the southwest. Radar gave a range of 11,500 yards. Tracking showed them moving on a northwesterly course at 20 knots. We were just forward of their starboard beam. *Sculpin* did her best to close, with the four diesels straining at emergency flank speed, but our nearest approach was 7,000 yards, with a TDC-calculated torpedo run of 7,800 yards. Even then they would be pulling away from us. The captain fired four fish from the forward tubes at the last carrier in column and immediately swung ship in an attempt to bring the stern tubes into play, hoping to get off four more fish. The fish were set to run at slow speed (31.5 knots) for 9,000 yards. We listened anxiously for explosions as we worked at the TDC, calculating the setup for a stern tube shot.

One fish exploded prematurely at about 300 yards. The enemy ships were going too fast for *Sculpin* to fire the stern tubes. About eight minutes after firing, we heard three explosions. We hoped that they were hits, but no indication was seen as radar tracked the carrier force out to 14,300 yards. The bridge watch saw much signaling by lights between the ships immediately after the explosions.

Sculpin next made a futile attempt to run around the task force, but they had increased speed. We then went to the position of the target but found nothing.*

At daybreak *Sculpin* submerged, expecting air and surface antisubmarine searches, but none were seen. At 2015 we surfaced and headed back to our area. The return would be more leisurely, submerged in the daytime, conserving fuel on the surface at night.

10–13 June   The cold, damp, foggy weather resulted from a warm water current from the south meeting a cold current from the north, right in *Sculpin*'s patrol area. The bathythermograph traced some weird temperature pictures. Temperatures would plunge at periscope depth, then rise as we went deeper, and plunge again at 150 feet, but the depths where temperatures changed weren't consistent. Ocean currents were mixing hot

---

*After the war, Japanese records showed that their light carrier *Hiyo* was damaged by torpedoes in that location on 9 June 1943.

and cold water in unpredictable patterns. Sonar conditions were very unsatisfactory.

A message from ComSubPac on the eleventh reported that *Trigger* hit one of the carriers when they passed through her area.

At daybreak on the twelfth *Sculpin* submerged close inshore at Shioya Saki. Through breaks in the fog we could see the mainland of Japan for the first time. No ships were spotted; but patrol boats were frequently in view. They were too small for our torpedoes and the captain thought them too heavily armed for us to take on with our guns.

During the early morning hours of the thirteenth we heard explosions, in groups: seven at 0426, eight at 0435, and finally five single explosions between 0522 and 0545.

One day blended into another, each like the previous. We lost track of time. My department's paperwork was squared away. I was preparing Frank to take over my job and helping Embury to become a submarine sailor. Routine maintenance and troubleshooting, plus training, occupied the working hours, and then there were watches to stand. Recreation time was devoted to games of cards, acey deucey, or chess. At this point in the patrol my recreational reading was *Brittany*, by Helen MacInnes.

14 June   Another quiet day close to the coast, near Kinkasan Island, until Joe Defrees sighted smoke to the north shortly before sunset. *Sculpin* commenced tracking, and thirty minutes later the captain described four ships with a small escort: a medium transport (4,500 tons), one small oiler, and two small cargo ships. They were on a steady course at a speed of ten knots. He selected the transport as a target and fired a spread of four fish from the forward tubes at a range of 2,000 yards.

The captain saw one premature explosion, and it shook the boat. We knew unmistakably that it was premature because it detonated much too soon after firing, rattling dishes in the pantry. Some thought *Sculpin* had run aground. The captain described frantic activity on the deck of the transport as the Jap swung away from us. While he had the periscope turned to watch the other ships, another explosion was plainly heard throughout the boat. Quickly turning back to the target, the captain described a gaping hole in the transport from below the waterline up to the main deck, just forward of midship. Sonar reported that the transport's screws had stopped; they were not heard again.

Looking back at the escort, the captain saw him following the torpedo wakes toward *Sculpin*. At 500 yards, with a zero angle on the bow, we went to 250 feet while rigging for depth charge. The escort dropped five charges, none close, searched for a short time, and left the scene. Back at periscope depth nothing was in sight or heard on sonar, so *Sculpin* surfaced for the night.

15–18 June   These were quiet days off Kinkasan Island. Visibility was restricted by the continuous heavy fog. On the seventeenth *Sculpin* stayed on the surface, under heavy fog cover, to use the SJ radar to track the small boats that we frequently sighted in clearings but could not pick up visually when hidden in the fog. The radar operators got some valuable tracking practice.

Periodically radar reported that they were picking up interference from the direction of the land to west. That was our first indication that the Japs were using radar, too.

During the night of the eighteenth *Sculpin* moved east, fifty miles from the coast, to give ComSubPac a report of the premature explosions and the results of our attacks to date. Repeated efforts by the radiomen failed to reach anyone.

19 June   At 0128 radar reported a contact to the southwest at 8,000 yards. During thirty minutes of tracking *Sculpin* closed to a range of 6,700 yards. From the bridge we could see that the contact was quite small. (In that latitude, at that time of year, there was never complete darkness during the night.) The radar operators were learning the technique of estimating a target's size from the pip characteristic on the radar screen. After an additional thirty minutes of tracking *Sculpin* submerged to continue closing. At 0314, with a range of 1,000 yards, the captain decided to use guns against the fishing-patrol boat.

Gun crews were called to stations, and at 0325 *Sculpin* surfaced to begin the attack. The 3-inch gun commenced firing at a range of 500 yards. Continuing to close, the 20-mm gun opened fire, then at 50 yards the .50-caliber machine guns. In thirty minutes the target was on fire and sinking, and *Sculpin* broke off the action and retired to the east at best speed. We submerged at daybreak for daylight patrol along the Kiska traffic lane.

Another fishing-patrol boat came into sight to the southwest in mid-afternoon. This one was similar to the boat sunk earlier in the day and had an impressive array of unusual radio antennae. After watching the boat for almost an hour, the captain decided to hit this one with guns just as we had done earlier in the day. So with a fog bank for concealment,

Sculpin surfaced, closed to 400 yards on radar information, and commenced firing the 3-inch gun as we pulled out of a fog bank.

After forty minutes of 3-inch and 20-mm pounding, the target was awash and on fire. The name on the stern of the boat was *Miyashiyo Maru*. We ceased fire and the captain moved *Sculpin* closer until her bow almost touched the target. A boarding party led by George Brown, with Joe Defrees and three crewmen, looking like pirates with knives tucked in their belts and .45 caliber pistols in their hands, waited on *Sculpin*'s bow, ready to board the Jap and take the guns mounted on the bow, stern, and on top of the wheelhouse.

A long swell was running, making it difficult to step directly across the space to the deck of the wallowing Japanese boat. Each man timed his jump over the gap that opened and closed with the swells. Joe Defrees was the last to jump, and, being a short individual and overanxious to get on board the Jap, he mistimed his jump, making a grand splash as he hit the water.

There were some Japs in the water, too, clutching pieces of timber, some hiding behind the hull of their boat. Our men on the bow were shooting at them. I went forward to stop them from taking any more potshots at the Japs.

Our other concern was that Joe might be crushed between *Sculpin* and the other boat. But Joe was more concerned that someone might shoot him, and yelling, "Don't shoot me!, Don't shoot me!" he made record time swimming to *Sculpin*'s stern, to be hoisted aboard by helping shipmates. He was still clutching his .45 automatic, with his Bowie knife in his belt, as he ran, thoroughly soaked, back to the bow, intent on getting aboard the Japanese boat. By that time the boarding party had returned, so Joe missed being able to brag about boarding a Jap ship.

The boarding party brought back one wooden dummy gun from the bow, two rifles that they found near the wheelhouse, and a piece of radio equipment from the radio room. The fire raging in the interior of the boat made it impossible to get to the real machine gun on top of the wheelhouse.

With the boarding party safely aboard, *Sculpin* pulled clear to patrol the Kiska traffic lane.

20–21 June   These were more quiet days. Fog was a constant problem. We tried again to get that radio message off to ComSubPac but were unsuccessful. Finally the message was sent blind, with the hope that someone would copy it and see that it reached the proper destination.

The longest day of the year was spent off Kinkasan. Wags in the crew composed humorous citations and made medals for George and Joe for their part in boarding and sinking the *Miyashiyo Maru*. The presentation ceremony was held in the crew's mess, with an audience of everyone not on watch. It produced much laughter and was a welcome tension reliever. The bulletin board reported the ceremony thus:

UNIQUE ACTION AND DECORATION 6-19-43

For the second time in as many issues, the *S-Periscope* presents to its readers the account of singular action, which was rewarded by an original citation and decoration. A complete survey of Navy files indicates that this was the first award of its kind ever given. This unusual citation is listed below:

Special award of the Leather Heart to Lieutenant G. Estabrook Samuel Glickstein Brown, Jr., USNR: Wounded in Action.

On June 19, 1943, Lieutenant Brown was scratched behind the left ear when he gallantly attacked, single-handed, and captured one Japanese superfine Wooden Machine Gun from the bow of the *Miyashiyo Maru*. Lieutenant Brown was conspicuous in his dauntless attack and easily overcame the resistance of no less than ten enemy fishing lines. During the fray he stumbled and fell. One of the bamboo poles, seeing the opening, treacherously attacked, wounding him behind the left ear. He calmly continued his mission in spite of blinding pain and unceasing agony.

For such outstanding and courageous action Lieutenant Brown is awarded the Leather Heart. This medal is authorized to be worn while in the head, the ribbon of golden (baby) brown to be worn on sleeping attire.

22 June   Shortly after midnight radar again picked up interference from the direction of Kinkasan. At daybreak *Sculpin* submerged for the day. The fog had dissipated, the weather was crystal clear, and the Japanese mainland was plainly in sight through the periscope. We could see farmers working in their fields.

At midmorning Frank sighted smoke to the west and we began tracking. Forty-five minutes later the captain saw three small cargo ships in column on a northerly course. The TDC calculated their speed at eight knots. Even using our highest sustained speed submerged we couldn't close to the desired short range for firing, but at 1100 sharp the captain fired a spread of four fish from the bow tubes at the last ship in column. The range was a long 4,000 yards.

As the captain watched, one fish exploded prematurely at about 300 yards, giving the target all the warning he needed. With the long torpedo run, he had plenty of time to turn and evade the remaining fish. The other ships turned radically, scattering in different directions. The target ship commenced firing his guns at *Sculpin*'s periscope.

The captain was dejected. Three firings and three premature explosions. After a day of head scratching, inspections, and analysis, we could only conclude that the magnetic exploder was the source of the trouble.

In midafternoon our sonar heard echo ranging to the west for forty-five minutes. Antisubmarine folks were looking for *Sculpin*. The patrol boats must have been small, for nothing was sighted by periscope.

At dusk we surfaced and headed east for breathing room and to send a message to ComSubPac asking for permission to deactivate the magnetic exploder. Radio couldn't contact a station to take the message. They tried on three occasions during the night to get someone to forward it, but no one answered our radio call.

23 June   *Sculpin*'s position was certainly compromised, so we moved to patrol an area off Shioya Saki. There we were, eighteen months into the war, with thousands of torpedoes fired, and despite its poor performance and hundreds of premature explosions, we were still required to use the magnetic feature.

The captain, on his own initiative since we could not get through by radio, ordered me to deactivate the magnetic influence exploders. The fish would then explode only on contact against a solid object; there would be no more depending on high-technology magnetic impulses.

24 June   All was quiet off Shioya Saki, with only small fishing boats in sight and farmers working in their fields on shore.

Infrequently the vapor compression stills were shut down for repair or for cleaning. That meant closing the showers, and there was griping and grumbling among those who were new to submarine patrols. The old hands from the S-boats and early fleet submarines knew how fortunate we were.

25 June   Still off Shioya Saki, *Sculpin* submerged at daybreak. Two hours later smoke was sighted to the northwest and we commenced tracking. During thirty minutes of tracking, the contact was identified as three small freighters moving south, very close to the shore. Our chart showed a depth of ten fathoms. We were only able to close the range to 7,000 yards, too far to fire fish; the captain was hesitant to go into such shallow water, so we abandoned the chase.

Around midafternoon, one large and three small cargo ships were sighted to the southwest, moving north. They also were very close to shore, so close the captain at first thought they were aground. We tracked them for a time but broke off at 5,500 yards when it appeared that further pursuit would be fruitless.

Nearing sunset the masts and smoke of three more transports, in column, were sighted to southwest. Tracking showed them to be on a northerly course but zigzagging wildly, at ten knots. Sound conditions were typically unfavorable.

Following an hour and a half of closing maneuvers, at 1931 we fired a spread of four fish at the 2,500-ton center ship in the column from a range of 1,500 yards. Sonar couldn't hear the fish running or the two explosions the captain saw as he was busily turning *Sculpin* to bring the stern tubes to bear, lining up for a shot at another ship. The damaged ship turned toward the shore, showing a badly mangled stern.

The leading ship speeded up and continued north. The last ship in column turned directly toward *Sculpin,* so at 800 yards we went deep for a short time to avoid a possible collision. Any chance for another shot was gone. Sonar didn't hear the ship's screws until he was almost over us.

Back at periscope depth the captain reported that the damaged ship was still heading toward shore and smoking heavily, as if a fire raged in the area that was hit.

We surfaced after sundown to commence a run around the two remaining ships, hoping to contact them off Kinkasan.

26 June   At 0315 Kinkasan was sighted. Intermittent fog made visibility difficult. Seventeen minutes later radar made a contact to the northeast, but it did not develop. At daybreak *Sculpin* submerged off Kinkasan.

Two and a half hours later sonar heard screws to the northeast. While making a sound approach through a rift in the fog, the captain saw a destroyer headed directly for *Sculpin* at 2,300 yards, so we went to 100 feet to let him pass over. There was no indication that he ever had contact with us, so we immediately came back to periscope depth and moved to the southwest.

Another forty-five minutes went by, and then sonar reported screw noises, two heavy and one light. *Sculpin* commenced a sound approach; then the captain sighted a ship coming out of the fog, very close aboard, so the sound approach was broken off and we went deep to avoid a collision. Normally unflappable, the captain was obviously excited, and said, "Those rivets looked like dinner plates."

Sound conditions continued poor. The soundmen lost contact when the ship was only 200 yards away. Back at periscope depth a few minutes later, the captain shoved the radar mast above water to see what help that might be. Apparently the radar signal attracted antisub activity, because for forty-five minutes in midmorning the captain watched a destroyer and two patrol boats as they ran in and out of fog banks, searching. At 1015 sonar reported that they believed that the destroyer was getting an echo from *Sculpin*. Watching the searchers, the captain became convinced that they were intermittently picking us up, so we went down and rigged for depth charge. At 120 feet George Brown found a beautiful temperature inversion under which to hide, while sonar listened to the destroyer and patrol boats as they conducted an industrious search.

The captain turned *Sculpin*'s stern toward the searchers, presenting a small target for their echo ranging, while creeping away at very slow speed. After an hour of evasion no more echo ranging was heard, so *Sculpin* came up to periscope depth. Nothing was in sight, so the crew was released from depth charge quarters.

We were only two miles off Kinkasan. Our radar signals must have alerted that station, and by radio they had coached the antisub team to our location.

On my 12–16 diving officer watch, a few minutes after noon, I sighted smoke to the northwest. We commenced tracking the smoke. The fog had lifted. Two hours later the captain saw two medium-sized transports and one small transport with a destroyer escort. They were close inshore, moving south. He watched the escort guide his convoy around the spot where *Sculpin* had been, going behind the Yenoshima Retto Islands, close to Oshikahanto. The water was very shallow, and they knew that they were safe from attack there.

At sunset *Sculpin* surfaced and moved offshore for the day to allow the crew some rest.

27 June, Sunday A quiet day, submerged, about eighty miles east of Honshu. The captain and the fire control party had been at it almost continually for twenty-four hours. We needed rest.

On my afternoon watch I sighted a fishing-patrol boat. The captain was tempted to hit him with the guns, but then decided that with the skies as clear as they were, we might be on the surface too long and give an antisub aircraft the opportunity to attack us.

28 June Before sunrise *Sculpin* was again submerged off Kinkasan. For the first four hours of the morning numerous fishing boats were working in our vicinity.

At 0940 we sighted smoke to the southeast. We commenced tracking and maneuvering for a firing position. Thirty minutes later the captain could see a loose convoy of two large and three small transport ships, with one small escort, zigzagging on a northerly base course.

Sculpin maneuvered for nearly two hours to reach an excellent firing position. Then, with everything ready to go, the convoy made a radical zig, causing drastic changes in the data to the TDC and resulting in large gyro angles in the fish and too long a torpedo run.

Having invested so much effort in the approach, and disgusted with the performance of the fish, the captain was determined to fire; so he sent a spread of four fish from the stern tubes at the leading large transport. Those were our last torpedoes, and they all missed.

Sonar reported that the target reversed his screws for a short time, then all ships speeded up, stopped zigzagging, and continued their northerly course. The captain swore that the torpedo tracks passed under the target.

The escort circled back, searching for *Sculpin*. Sonar didn't hear any pinging as the escort dropped a few depth charges several hundred yards away and then went back to his convoy.

At noon sonar reported echo ranging to the west. An antisub patrol boat came out from shore and searched for the next two hours. We kept him in sight as we moved east, and finally lost sight of him.

At dusk *Sculpin* surfaced and set course for Midway Island. After the battery was charged, four engines were on the line delivering full speed to get us as far away from Honshu as possible during the night.

A message went to ComSubPac saying that we were heading for Midway, along with the disappointing results of our attacks.

29 June We spent the day heading east, course 090 t, submerged because of the possibility of enemy antisubmarine activity. At night, after batteries were charged, four engines were back on the line for full speed. The captain's expressed intention was to stay on the surface day and night until *Sculpin* reached Midway.

30 June–4 July The weather was cool, with a moderately rough sea and mostly overcast skies all the way to Midway. We would all welcome warmer weather and clear skies, but that wouldn't happen until we got there. The fresh air was invigorating, as usual, following many days underwater.

I took on the navigator's duties on the return trip. Paperwork, reports, work lists for the repair crews, and lists of spare parts were ready to turn in when we reached Midway. A number of the crew were ready for their final submarine qualification activities, which involved more of my time. George Embury had to spend so much of his time troubleshooting the radar that he had little time to learn submarining. He was trying diligently but needed much more coaching to be ready even to attempt the details of qualification for submarines.

Wardroom talk invariably came around to speculation as to where Mendy would go for his job as executive officer of a new submarine. Al knew that he would leave to command a new boat, so there was also speculation about a new exec for *Sculpin*.

We crossed the international date line on the Fourth of July, so we had two Fourths of July in 1943. The cooks prepared a big turkey dinner to celebrate the first one. Apostol and Tulao proved that they hadn't lost their touch in the galley. We would be entering Midway on the second Fourth of July.

My first good star fix came on the night before we were due to meet our escort to Midway. With the SJ radar to fall back on, I was not concerned over meeting the escort, as I would have been on previous navigation duties.

4 July At 0810 *Sculpin* was met by an air escort, exchanged recognition signals, and proceeded to port. I had the forenoon, channel-mooring, watch. That was my last OOD watch at sea with *Sculpin*.

At 1124 we were moored in the nest alongside *Sperry* at Naval Base Midway. Arriving at Midway was routine, not the local event that it had been in Java, Australia, and Pearl Harbor. We might have come in from Hawaii or from the States, instead of from a patrol along the coast of Japan that had lasted forty days, twenty-two days in our area off Honshu.

The captain's patrol report spelled out, in no uncertain terms, his distrust of the magnetic impulse exploder and urged that remedial measures be stepped up, since there was abundant evidence, extending back more than eighteen months, that the exploder was not performing properly.

Sculpin's material condition was excellent. The alterations performed in San Francisco were extremely beneficial to the overall operation and habitability of the ship.

SJ radar was revolutionary, whether for fire control, for ship detection at night or in limited visibility, or for navigation. With no deck torpedo storage, the job of moving fish around at sea was, to our great relief, eliminated. The freshwater stills allowed everyone to bathe more frequently and thus added to cleanliness, reduced skin problems, and improved morale.

Patrol Summary

Number of men on board:
   69 enlisted
    8 officers
Nautical miles steamed:
   3,250 from Pearl Harbor to patrol area
   2,950 in patrol area
   2,000 from patrol area to Midway
      Total: 8,200 miles
Fuel used: 85,450 gallons (10.4 gallons/mile)
Duration: 40 days
Torpedoes fired: 20 Mk-14
Sinkings:
   2 transport-cargo ships
   2 fishing-patrol boats (sunk with 103 rounds of 3-inch ammunition)

Refit in Midway

More 4 July   A relief crew came aboard, and everyone moved off the boat—the crew to newly erected barracks, and the officers to the Gooney Bird Hotel. *Sculpin* would be in refit for only ten days. The short seventh patrol had left the boat in very good condition, and little repair work was needed.

There was no city life available on Midway, just eating, sleeping, swimming, shell hunting, diving, playing tennis, relaxing, games, and movies at night. Beer and liquor were strictly rationed.

The first few days at Midway were, as expected, long and busy with arrival conferences, lining up repair work, and, after the day's grind, staggering to the Gooney Bird Hotel for supper and a bunk for the night.

That first night Pete Galantin, the captain, Al Bontier, Frank Alvis, and I went to see the movie *Black Swan*.

The Gooney Bird Hotel had once been Pan American Airways Hotel, built in 1935 as a stopover and resting place for passengers and crews of transpacific clipper planes. The hotel was a simple wooden one-story structure located in a grove of ironwood, or salt-cedar trees. It was austere but seemed luxurious to men who had been cramped into bunkrooms on the boat.

Pete Galantin checked off the ship. Everyone had enjoyed having Pete make his PCO patrol in *Sculpin*. He fit well into our shipboard activities. We particularly appreciated his help standing OOD watches and decoding the volume of radio messages that came in. I knew he benefited from the experience of the patrol. One thing for sure, he knew how miserably those torpedoes performed.

Al Bontier learned that he was going to command a new-construction boat, the *Razorback,* with my good friend Johnny Haines, '38, as his exec, so he would be leaving very soon. Al's relief would be my classmate Butch Allen. We were last together in Java, at the Malang rest camp and as seatmates on the train from Malang to Surabaya. As for me, I was very pleased to have things turn out as they did. Soon I would experience new construction and be on a submarine with the latest equipment.

Mail was waiting by the ton. I had a stack of welcome letters from Ann to work my way through. With so much going on, Joe Defrees didn't have the time to sort through the bags of official mail, but I was pushing him to find my orders.

5 July   Joe found my orders. I was going to be exec of the *Pintado* (SS 387), building in Portsmouth, New Hampshire, and was to report there on 14 August. I promptly sent cables to Ann and to Anahuac to let them know what was happening.

A check of the dictionary showed that *Pintado* was named for a large, mackerel-like fish common around Florida and the West Indies. From Spanish, the word *pintado* might be interpreted as "painted," probably due to the colorful appearance of the Spanish mackerel when wet, just out of the water. I remembered catching Spanish mackerel in the Gulf of Mexico offshore from Sabine Pass, Texas.

The Midway transportation officer advised me that the first available flight to Pearl Harbor would be on Saturday, 10 July, but that I should stay in touch for possible changes, so I resigned myself to waiting and went for a swim. The water was cool and clean, and the sandy bottom was visible out into the deeps, giving the water an emerald green color. Everyone swam nude, reminding me of childhood days in Winnie, Texas, when we shucked off our clothes to swim in the rice canal. That muddy water, however, could never compare with the crystal clear water at Midway.

We were pleased to see that our Royal Navy submariner friend, Commander Tony Miers, V.C., D.S.O., was at Midway for a few days, on a mission for Admiral Lockwood. He had been so easy to know and like when we first met in San Francisco during *Sculpin*'s major overhaul, and later in Pearl Harbor, and he hadn't changed one iota since then.

6 July Frank and I got up at 0530 for tennis and a swim before breakfast. Then I sauntered leisurely to the boat for my last watch and packed two boxes of personal gear for shipment to Portsmouth. *Sculpin* was moored alongside the sub tender *Sperry* at the dock.

Sperry left the dock in the afternoon to let a tanker take her place and pump fuel into the tanks ashore, and I spent two hours maneuvering *Sculpin* around the lagoon. There was no time to call the captain; I was on my own, so I sent a messenger to tell him and the exec what was going on.

The tanker pulled clear when she was through pumping fuel, allowing *Sperry* to go back to the dock. Then, when *Sperry* was ready to receive *Sculpin,* I brought the boat alongside in a one-bell landing. Feeling proud of my team, with all secured, I looked up to the deck of *Sperry,* towering over us, to see Commodore Karl Hensel, '23, formerly one of the no-nonsense, all-business instructors at the sub school, watching me. He called down, "Well done, son!" giving me a real shot in the arm. I had always thought that no one could possibly do anything exactly right in his eyes.

The captain sent a fantastic letter to the navy personnel office in Washington telling them that he considered me fully qualified to command a submarine.

Frank Alvis took over my Ordnance Department job and I was ready to head for Portsmouth, so I was coasting toward being detached.

7 July George Brown was quite late getting to the boat to relieve me. There had been a big celebration at the Gooney Bird, although I never did find out just what was being celebrated. When I arrived at the Gooney Bird I found a note saying that I should get in touch with the transportation office. I did, and was told that an unscheduled PBY (flying boat) was going to Oahu at 0630 the next morning.

I spent the rest of the day checking out and saying good-bye to my *Sculpin* shipmates. There were still nineteen men on board, plus the captain, with whom I had made all seven patrols. I tried to see each one and wish them the best of luck. The last item of personal effects that I had to dispose of, since I was afraid the glass might break during transportation in my baggage, was my ration of one unopened bottle of White Label scotch. As I left the ship I presented the bottle to Yeoman Aaron Reese and asked him to share it with the crew.

Interlude: Midway to Portsmouth to Pearl Harbor

(8 July 1943–15 May 1944)

8 July–14 August 1943 On the eighth I rode the PBY to Oahu, checked into the sub base BOQ, and began another wait for transportation to the United States. While there I saw navy and civilian friends. Butch Allen came through the sub base on his way to *Sculpin*. We had a short visit because he had only a brief time between planes for Midway.

At 0900 on the thirteenth I reported aboard army transport USAT *Brazil*, a converted luxury liner, for the cruise to Oakland, California. There were only twenty passengers on a ship that had just discharged 4,500 troops in Honolulu.

My roommate was Swampy Lajaunie, '37, another submariner on his way to new construction, home state Louisiana, as evidenced by his accent. *Brazil* was scheduled to reach Oakland on the nineteenth, so we settled in to read, play bridge, talk, and relax. A main turbine breakdown slowed the ship down, so our arrival was delayed until the twentieth.

Ann and I rode trains to Texas to visit my family. Arriving near midnight at the small whistle-stop town of Devers, where there was no passenger station, we were let off the sleeper car onto the loose gravel of the railbed, looking into the dark of the deep ditch along the railroad right-of-way, wondering if anyone was meeting us. I suggested, as a last resort, that we might telephone my cousin Theresa Boyt, who lived nearby, if we could find a telephone. Clouds of mosquitos were buzzing around us. Ann, wanting to look her best for her first meeting with my family, had insisted on wearing a dark wool suit and black hat. I tried to prepare her, but she was accustomed to California weather and couldn't believe my warnings of the sultry, humid August heat of the Texas Gulf of Mexico. I was in my navy blue dress uniform, and the heat and humidity hit like a sledgehammer. Both of us were promptly soaked with perspiration.

We could hear voices on the other side of the noisy train but had to wait until it pulled away before a joyful reunion with Dad and Mother. The time was one o'clock in the morning, and we had another eighteen miles to drive south to Anahuac.

After a few days with my family, I reclaimed my car and we drove a zigzag course across country, visiting more relatives and finally arriving in Portsmouth, New Hampshire, on 10 August.

The search for living space ended with a second-floor apartment in a big, old, uninsulated New England frame house, formerly a summer home, in York Harbor, Maine. Even in August the house was cold.

The next few days were spent getting our bearings and settling in, and then, on 14 August, I reported for duty in connection with fitting out and commissioning *Pintado*.

14 August 1943–1 January 1944   I met the captain, Lt. Cmdr. Bernard A. (Chick) Clarey, '34, for the first time and found that there was plenty of work waiting for me. Precommissioning meant receiving the crew and officers as they arrived, setting up the ship's office, the ship's organization, and the personnel records, and sending crewmen and officers to various training activities and manufacturing plants where machinery and equipment were being built and tested before being shipped to Portsmouth for installation in *Pintado*. I was involved in organizing, overseeing, and documenting all those activities.

Pintado's keel had been laid on 7 May 1943, before any of her complement arrived. Launching was on 15 September, and by that time many of the crew were on hand. They didn't all arrive at once but were phased in over a period of time, giving us the opportunity to see that officers and men were sent to appropriate schools. Some went for special training before actually reporting in Portsmouth and were prepared to take over responsibilities on *Pintado* right away. Commissioning was scheduled for the first of January, 1944.

While the shipbuilding was progressing, the navy yard provided a specially fitted out barracks barge similar to the one we used when *Sculpin* was overhauling at Bethlehem Steel, from which we could work. The barge was always moored close to *Pintado* for our convenience. Some of our crew were New Englanders, and they were soon dropping lobster pots into the river, providing welcome seafood to our menu.

Several other submarines were under construction at Portsmouth, and we swapped stories with their officers and discussed and helped each other with solutions to problems. Freeland Carde and Oliver Bagby, both '38, and Harry Higgs and Link Marcy, both '39, were there as execs to commission new boats.

In no time we became aware that our sister submarines had acquired slot machines, which they installed in the public area of their barracks barges; the income went into their welfare and recreation funds, and those execs highly recommended the venture. So *Pintado* invested in a machine, and our fund grew just as we were assured it would. In addition to our own crew, many navy yard workmen were clients, regularly dropping by to plug nickels into the one-armed bandit.

An "attack teacher" at the navy yard allowed us to train the torpedo fire control team in simulated problems. This trainer might be compared to a Link trainer for aviators. The torpedo fire control team took stations similar to those on board ship, and the captain made observations of a phantom target through a periscope, which were transmitted to a TDC, and maneuvered his make-believe ship to attack. The TDC received information from a simulated radar to help solve the torpedo firing problem, just as would be done on board ship.

After a month in York Harbor, Ann found an apartment in Kittery, Maine, conveniently located on the waterfront near the bridge that crossed the Piscataqua River to the navy yard. I could walk to work now and not leave her stranded in York Harbor without an automobile.

In October, with the splendid colors showing in the autumn leaves, we made a weekend trip to Cannon Mountain with Harry and Mickey Higgs. The trip to Cannon Mountain convinced us to trade our Chevy coupe for a Buick two-door sedan. On another weekend we went to Cape Cod.

A puzzling aspect of my relationship with the skipper manifested itself almost immediately after we met. He somehow learned that I had been regimental commander at the Naval Academy and proceeded to make some cutting remarks to me about my position at the school. He kept saying, "You're the five-striper, you ought to know that." At first I thought the remarks were a rather crude attempt at humor, but when they continued I decided that he was being childishly serious. I tried to ignore the remarks, be tough-skinned and do my job. Ann sensed my occasional bruised feelings and never did really warm up to him. She pretended to, but I knew it was an act.

As time went on, when a *Pintado* problem came up like one we had solved in *Sculpin*, I would offer the *Sculpin* solution. Chick would summarily dismiss the suggestion with disparaging remarks about *Sculpin* and her captain and exec. This was very unkind treatment, particularly in the presence of others, so thereafter I tried to keep *Sculpin* out of my vocabulary.

Chick also had the problem of graduating from being executive officer of *Amberjack* to being the captain of *Pintado*. Simultaneously I was working as executive officer, and we were both determined to meet the commissioning date of 1 January.

1–17 January   *Pintado* was up to a complement of sixty-five men when commissioning day arrived on 1 January, and she was ready to complete inspections, make test dives, and be accepted by the navy. Immediately after acceptance the schedule called for shakedown and training exercises out of Portsmouth, then torpedo trials at Newport, Rhode Island, and more training from the sub base at New London, Connecticut, before heading for the Panama Canal and on to the Pacific.

We carried eight officers on board, which was quite an increase over the meager five on *Sculpin* when I first reported there. Besides the skipper and myself, there was Lieutenant (jg) Doug Morse as first lieutenant; Lieutenant (jg) Ed Bower, '41, as chief engineer; Lieutenant (jg) Ed Frese, USNR, as torpedo-gunnery officer; Lieutenant (jg) George Murray, USNR, as commissary officer; Ensign Gerry Pettibone, USNR, as communications officer; and Machinist Harold (Brant) Brantner as assistant engineer. (See Appendix 2 for *Pintado*'s full roster.) A number of the officers and crew were reserves, sub school graduates who had never been to sea before. Many were not qualified in submarines, so intensive training was the order of the day.

The day after *Pintado*'s commissioning ceremony, followed by parties at the officers' club and a ship's party at the Kittery Grange Hall, team training continued alongside the dock as we made ready to get under way and go to sea for trials and more training. At the dock the crew walked through exercises in rigging for sea, rigging for dive, clearing the bridge, dry dives alongside the dock, battle stations, making ready the torpedo tubes, manning the guns, fire drill, collision drill, operating the many systems in the boat, starting and stopping the engines, and turning the propellers over slowly while moored at the dock.

Early January was a mighty cold time for getting under way and proceeding to sea for those first few dives. There were ice patches on the water, and ice formed on exposed surfaces above the surface. When we submerged, the ice melted, but it formed again soon after we surfaced. When the sea was rough, the spray coming over the bridge would freeze before it hit, as if someone were throwing gravel at us. After a few minutes on the bridge we would have a coating of ice.

As we prepared to make one of the early practice dives off Portsmouth,

I was carefully checking the bridge and bridge personnel to be sure they had all gotten down the hatch. We were ready to submerge and everyone was below when I took one last look aft. To my astonishment, on the main deck, as far aft as one could go, was someone diligently peering through binoculars. My shout brought Fireman Vic Kazma back to the bridge.

Drenched and shivering from the icy spray, he explained that the chief of the watch told him to take the lookout aft. He had certainly done that. A few seconds more and he would have been swimming, though not for long, for a swimmer would not survive for more than a few minutes in that cold water.

On another occasion Boatswain's Mate Eric (Boats) Griffin received permission to go on deck to check on a problem; he was not expecting us to dive for some minutes, which would allow him plenty of time to get back inside the boat. Just as the diving signal sounded, the control room reported that Boats was still on deck. Under the pressures of the situation, the OOD had forgotten Griffin. A quick blowing of the ballast tanks brought our partially submerged submarine back to the surface. Boats was atop the periscope shears, still mostly dry, but after his reprieve he couldn't talk for at least ten minutes. When he finally regained the power of speech, in his heavy Louisiana accent, his words were not repeatable.

As soon as *Pintado* began to head to sea for operations, it became evident that George Murray had a problem with motion sickness. We would have to see whether he could overcome it. Doc Denningham, the chief pharmacist's mate, fed him seasickness pills, but George still had difficulties.

With *Pintado*'s departure from Portsmouth imminent, and the boat's schedule filled with training and other busywork for the exec, I knew that I would be extremely busy both in Newport and afterward in New London. I didn't need the distraction of a wife, so we planned for Ann to drive to California as soon as *Pintado* left Portsmouth. Her mother came east by train to accompany her on the drive. Mom, as we both called her, had never been in the cold of a New England winter, so we were apprehensive over how she would react to the weather.

The Buick needed a tuneup, new tires, and other adjustments before the drive. There was also insurance with USAA in San Antonio, wills to be witnessed, and license plates. I had to turn all these details over to Ann, who had never before shouldered such responsibilities. But she took them on in fine style as she learned to be a navy wife.

18 January–4 March   Loading, testing, inspections, and training exercises were performed until 17 February. During that time the skipper officially accepted the ship for the U.S. Navy. Then *Pintado* was off to Newport for two days of torpedo trials. When those were successfully completed, we moved on to begin intensive training from the sub base at New London.

Several of the crews' and officers' families followed us to New London to be together as long as possible. Most of the officers' wives stayed at the Lighthouse Inn, where we could gather in the evening from time to time for a relaxing hour away from work.

Pintado went to sea daily for training exercises, making submerged approaches on target ships, firing practice torpedoes, and generally sharpening the team's skills. There were times when I wished there were thirty-six hours in the day so I could get all my work done. I was spending almost all day, every day, on the bridge, in the control room, or in the conning tower, so busy that I sometimes forgot to eat, and regularly had only four hours' sleep at night.

During this training period the torpedo fire control team had the opportunity to work together and smooth out operating procedures. My battle station in *Pintado* was in the conning tower, as assistant to the captain, reading the bearings from the periscope, watching the conduct of the attack, and monitoring the performance of the fire control team. The fact that the TDC was in the conning tower where the captain could readily see it, talk to the TDC operator, and be more intimately involved in that aspect of the fire control problem was a significant improvement over *Sculpin*.

While we were operating from the sub base it became evident that the skipper could not, for reasons that were never fully clear to me, tolerate Ed Bower as chief engineer. They clashed at times, due, I thought, primarily to personality differences. Chick could be volatile, while Ed was more laid-back.

At New London the boat was degaussed, a procedure whereby the boat's magnetic signature, created during the pounding, welding, and shaping of her construction, was measured, and then heavy electrical cables were draped around the hull and energized to neutralize or minimize the boat's natural magnetic field.

Ed Bower, who had the OOD watch, was conning the ship when *Pintado* went into the degaussing slip. There was a fierce flood tide running, forcing the boat's stern out, which was very difficult for anyone, even someone familiar with the Thames River, to anticipate. The degaussing pier was splintered, but the boat received only superficial damage. Chick was furious; his shiny new command lost some paint, and Ed received the brunt of his temper.

Chick abruptly made arrangements with the personnel office at the sub base to have Lieutenant (jg) S. J. (Robbie) Robinson, '42, relieve Ed Bower. I didn't know that Chick was even contemplating the action until it took place. Suddenly Ed was no longer with us, and Robbie was there in his place. We then had a new chief engineer to break in.

My own problem was that Chick continuously conducted the ship's business as if he were the exec as well as the captain. At regular meetings of officers, with Chick presiding, we would arrive at a course of action—for example, for Engineering Department work—then a day or so later I would see that Robbie was not following the agreed-on program. When I questioned him, his answer was, "The Old Man changed things and told me to do it this way." (In the navy the captain is always the "old man," no matter what his age.) Chick could not break away from being the exec of *Amberjack;* he kept giving orders and directions without realizing that he was cutting his exec out of the chain of command. I was constantly discovering that changes had been made without my knowledge and having to ask him about the revised directions.

In early March *Pintado* was certified by the sub base experts as ready to go to the Pacific. We were to stop en route at Key West for special operations.

5–31 March   *Pintado* headed south on 5 March. At Key West we were to provide services to a group that was developing a new torpedo for the Bureau of Ordnance. The fact that we were stopping there, and what we would be doing, were very sensitive information. We didn't know how long we would be there, but we assumed it would be for only a few days.

The voyage to Key West was uneventfully routine. The weather was excellent: calm seas and no seasickness. We continued training with drills and battle problems along the way.

When we arrived on the tenth, however, we were told that our stay would last for three weeks. The weapon being developed was a small electrically driven antidestroyer torpedo (Mk-32, nicknamed "cutie"), which would home in on the noise of the propellers of a ship. It was not as big in diameter as the after torpedo tubes, out of which it would propel itself when activated from inside the boat. *Pintado*'s job was to take the torpedo to sea for a few hours daily so the scientists and engineers could launch it from our tubes in order to chase a destroyer target and gather data on the tests.

I immediately called Ann, who by then was in Missouri with her grandmother, and prevailed on her to drive to Key West. She was then three months pregnant. Mom Weedin took a train from Sedalia on to California. Several other wives also came to Key West, and we found quarters for them at the La Concha Hotel. Everyone thought that the warm climate and vacationlike setting would be a welcome change from the cold of New England, and it certainly was. Our esprit soared. George Murray even made arrangements to marry his fiancée, Beth, in the chapel at the navy base. Chick gave the bride away.

On the way south from New London Motor Machinist's Mate (MoMM) Don Davis had been under Doc Denningham's care for a chronic cold and lung congestion complaint, so when we arrived at Key West he was sent to the local navy dispensary, where his problem was diagnosed as pneumonia. A replacement was necessary. One of the prospective MoMM replacements sent for interview was John Maguire. As John went through the control room he couldn't pass our ship's slot machine* without plugging in at least one nickel. He hit the jackpot, and nickels scattered all over the steel deck, making quite a clatter. I heard the racket as Robbie Robinson and I waited in the wardroom, and when he told us what had happened, I replied that he had the job because we couldn't let that money get away from the ship's welfare and recreation fund.

The day after we arrived in Key West, as we were coming back to the dock from operations offshore, I spotted two familiar faces in navy officer uniform watching *Pintado* tie up. Lieutenants (jg) Ed Green, from Beaumont, and Brad Pickett, from Liberty, Texas, were watching the strange submarine moor. I knew both of them from my teen years in Texas. They had no idea I was on board until I called out to them. After that we saw each other frequently during *Pintado*'s stay, and I arranged to take them to sea with us for one day. Both Ed and Brad were in Key West at the destroyer sonar school.

Civilian radio and newspaper stories brought devastating news: *Sculpin* was lost. The boat that had been my home for seven patrols was lost on her ninth patrol. Although I knew that Lu Chappell was transferred after the eighth patrol, classmate Butch Allen, on his second patrol as exec, and George Brown, on board for five patrols, were gone. So was Joe

---

*Routinely, the slot machine was locked in a storeroom when the boat was under way. It was on the navigator's chart table in the control room when in port.

Defrees, on his third patrol. (Ironically, Joe's mother christened *Sculpin* when she was launched.) Nine of the crewmen had been on board for all nine patrols: Phil Gabrunas, James Harper, Richard Hemphill, Weldon Moore, Arny Moreton, George "Moon" Rocek, John Swift, Ellis Warren, and Gunner Wyatt. There were so many friends we would not see again in this life. (See Appendix III for details of the loss of *Sculpin*.)

Our busy ship's schedule helped to block out the loss of *Sculpin*. However, at night, in the quiet of our room, Ann frequently broke down in tears as she remembered the losses and contemplated my return to the undersea war.

Ensign Gerry Pettibone received his promotion to lieutenant (jg). In anticipation of the traditional navy over-the-side accorded the newly promoted, our new jg went topside in old wash khakis, prepared for his dunking. Seeing that he came prepared, the crewmen ignored him, and he assumed that he had escaped his initiation. Later that day, when Gerry changed into dress khakis and went topside to go on liberty, he didn't make it to the gangway. My own promotion to lieutenant commander came through on 15 March, although I couldn't pin on the gold leaves until I passed the physical exam. That I put off until we got to Pearl Harbor. Meanwhile George Murray continued to have his problem with seasickness.

31 March–7 April, Panama   On 31 March *Pintado* departed Key West for the Panama Canal, and the wives scattered to their various homes. Ann stopped off for a visit with my family in Texas. When she was in Beaumont my Grandmother Gripon decided to accompany her for the balance of the drive west so she could visit her son, my Uncle Walter, and his family in Alameda.

Pintado's contribution to the Mk-32 torpedo development project must have been worthwhile, because a short time after our stay in Key West that torpedo was introduced into the submarine fleet. When we arrived at the sub base in Panama on 5 April for a four-day layover, my work was so pressing that I got off the boat only twice. The crew's first efforts were concentrated on field day, cleaning the ship in preparation for captain's inspection, which we scheduled for the morning of 7 April. The inspection went off well. Afterward we held a ship's picnic, beach party, and softball game against Freeland Carde's *Pilotfish* team at the navy recreation park. We lost the game, which qualified us to pay for their beer.

When *Pintado* had arrived in Key West there were already a few sailors in our crew who had pierced their left ears and were wearing gold rings, pirate style, wanting to make the point that they were a different breed of navy men. During our few days in Panama a spate of additional pierced ears became evident. Remembering my experience with Commodore Crawford, I wondered what the official reaction might be when *Pintado* reached Pearl Harbor.

8 April–23 April   *Pintado* departed Sub Base Panama the morning of 8 April, destination Pearl Harbor. The trip through the canal had been an adventure never to be forgotten. Words could not describe the scenery, the engineering marvel of that canal, and the thrill that I felt piloting a ship through it (with the assistance of the required civilian pilot).

A few days into our trip west we pulled the old mail buoy trick. Announcements were made over the loudspeakers that we were approaching a mail buoy and would pick up mail. Anticipation was talked up among conspiring crewmen and officers, and the ETA for reaching the buoy was announced.

George Murray was the consensus goat for the deception. He took the bait, with only minor prodding to overcome his skepticism, and volunteered to be the lookout for the buoy and to get the mail when we reached it. After spending considerable time standing on the bridge and diligently searching with binoculars, George finally realized that he was the butt of an old snipe hunt–type trick. He took the joke very good-naturedly, as one might expect from the divinity student that he had been.

Halfway to Hawaii, cruising through that clear, cool, blue water, I suggested to the skipper that we stop for swim call. He had never stopped a sub to allow swimming before and was understandably cautious. Most of the crew had never enjoyed that pleasant experience, either. *Pintado* came to a stop, flooded down just enough for the deck to serve as a swim platform, and many of us had the pleasure of an hour's dip in the deep Pacific, far from any land. The swim provided a nice break from routine and something to talk about for days.

The executive officer–navigator's job ran on a twenty-four-hour schedule. From reveille to taps there was the usual ship's routine: drills, paperwork, and management-administrative things. Schools, education, and departmental training were the responsibility of each department head, but I stayed right on top of what was being done, urging them on. The navigation part of my job I had to fit in as best I could, with star sights at dawn and dusk, sun sights during the day, and time to study charts, tide tables, and the *Coast Pilot*. Then there were nightly random walks through the boat to talk with crewmen. I made it a part of my routine to walk through the boat every night after midnight to see how things were going. From time to time emergencies popped up that had to be dealt with. All this made for full days.

Even though the sea was generally calm and the weather good, George experienced chronic queasiness. We talked it over with Chick and Doc, and a consensus was reached that he would be left at Sub Base Pearl to see what the doctors could do for him, and *Pintado* would have a place for him at a later date.

My previous experience with navigators had been that they were almost always slightly apprehensive of the first landfall, particularly after being at sea for some days. Now it was my turn to navigate, and certainly I was a bit anxious about arriving at Pearl as forecast. But after cloudless days and nights offering perfect sextant conditions, with the SJ radar to aid in fixing the ship's position using the distant islands of the Hawaiian group and peaks of Mauna Loa and Haleakala, we hit the entrance grid to Pearl Harbor right on the nose.

We made contact with our escort at daybreak on Sunday, 23 April, exchanged recognition signals, and proceeded in to the sub base.

23 April–15 May   Admiral Lockwood, with members of his staff, watched *Pintado* moor at the base and came aboard as soon as the brow was on the pier. We were given the typical warm Lockwood welcome to SubPac and handed a schedule of activities that would end on 15 May. *Pintado*'s first war patrol would commence on 16 May.

The days were busy with loading food, supplies, and spare parts and making preparations for patrol. Fourteen days of under-way training were scheduled. Personnel changes also needed to be arranged. And I hoped to find the time to see my friends on shore.

Arrangements were made to transfer George Murray to a shore job so the doctors could solve his seasickness problem. His replacement was Ensign Jerry Mitchell, USNR, who took on the job of commissary officer. Yeoman 2/c John J. Flynn came aboard to man the ship's office, Chief Torpedoman Red Hill joined us as chief of the boat, and Quartermaster 3/c Alex Dings reported to beef up the quartermaster group, since my mainstay for navigation, Chief Quartermaster Ray Emerson, was fully occupied with that.

On 25 April I finally escaped *Pintado* and caught a bus to Kailua to spend the night with Jimmy and Julieanne Montague. It was a relaxing evening. Jimmy had to go on duty very early in the morning, before anyone else was awake, so Julieanne and I had breakfast before I caught my bus to the sub base.

On the twenty-eighth I was invited to have dinner and spend the night with the Lowreys. Kak Lowrey Hamlin had received a postcard from Hal, from a Jap prison camp in Burma, confirming that he had been captured when the cruiser *Houston* was sunk off Java.* In the morning Mr. Lowrey dropped me off at the bus station when he went to work.

Royal Navy Commander Tony Miers came aboard to introduce his countryman Lieutenant Commander Larkin, who would be going out to operate with us on some of our training days. He had commanded two British subs and wore a chestful of ribbons.

On 2 May I passed my physical examination for promotion and pinned on the gold leaves of a lieutenant commander. After supper a messenger came to the wardroom and told me that someone wanted to see me topside. Completely unsuspecting, I went to see who my visitor was and was immediately tossed overboard by the gathering of shipmates who were gleefully waiting for me.

By 5 May I made the mental entry that everything on *Pintado* was running much better. The crew and officers were learning fast. Now that they were away from the States, they didn't rush ashore as soon as we were moored and leave jobs hanging. Chick was acting more like a captain, and not an exec. Doug Morse, Ed Frese, Robbie Robinson, and Brant Brantner were keeping the pressure on their people, getting things done. Yeoman Flynn was a real worker who did his job right the first time. Ray Emerson had the quartermaster situation well in hand. Red Hill, the new chief of the boat, was a big redheaded fellow who took no foolishness from anyone. We had received no remarks or orders from headquarters concerning the earrings that *Pintado*'s crew were wearing; it seemed that by now there were many other sailors from other boats with pierced ears. And, despite what I considered very free spending of welfare and recreation funds on ship's parties, athletic gear, and flowers to wives delivering babies, we still had a balance of almost $2,000, thanks mainly to the one-armed bandit.

During the training period the boat was twice put in a floating dry dock to repair leaky outer door gaskets on torpedo tubes. New VHF (very high frequency) voice radio and IFF (identification friend or foe) were installed. Fourteen days of under-way training involved the firing of eleven

*Hal and Johnny Nelson, '40, from Orange, Texas, both from cruiser *Houston*, survived the Japanese prisoner-of-war camp in Burma and were repatriated at the end of the war.

exercise torpedoes: six Mk-23s (improved Mk-14) and five Mk-18s (the new electric torpedo). Sound tests showed no abnormal noises from *Pintado*. There was also a three-day convoy exercise with *Shark* and *Pilotfish* in preparation for operation as a "wolfpack." Captain Leon N. Blair, '23, made the wolfpack training runs; he would be the pack commander aboard *Pintado,* which would be his flagship.

Unexpectedly my cousin Major Norman Kopke from Beaumont came to the boat to see me. One of Norman's responsibilities was overseeing the officers' club at Hickam Field, right next door to Pearl Harbor. He had received a letter from home telling him that I might be at the sub base. He took me to dinner at his club, where another Beaumonter, Troy Cousins, joined us for dinner. They had many questions about submarine operations, and we also talked much about the people we all knew in Beaumont.

A letter from Ann informed me that she was going back to work as office manager for the Blankenship Trucking Company in Alameda. She also told me of Marian Chappell's unexpected death. Tragedies seemed to strike everywhere. I wondered where my ex-skipper Lu Chappell and the children were.

On 15 May I again went to dine and spend the night at the Lowrey home. In the morning Mr. Lowrey performed his usual courtesy of delivering me to my sub base bus as he went to work, unaware that he would not see me again for many months.

Pintado's First Patrol

(16 May–1 July 1944)

16 May   Having completed all preparations for patrol, *Pintado* was under way right after lunch, headed for Midway in company with *Shark* (Ed Blakely) and *Pilotfish* (Boney Close), with a PC (patrol craft) boat as escort for the group. (The captains of all three subs were classmates, USNA '34.) After dark, her escort duty over, the PC returned to Pearl Harbor.

All three boats were making their first patrols. The commodore of the group, Captain Blair, was in *Pintado*. He was making his first war patrol. The official designation of the wolfpack was Coordinated Task Group 17.12 (TG 17.12), and the name given to the wolfpack was Blair's Blasters.

We were seen off by a small group of friends, among them George Murray. He was sad and misty-eyed, bidding us good-bye while he remained behind for treatment of his chronic seasickness.

We were scheduled to reach our patrol area just west of Saipan Island on 29 May. Allied landings were due to take place there in early June, and the objective of the wolfpack was to prevent Jap reinforcements from reaching Saipan before the Allied troops went ashore. On 8 June the Blasters were to move farther west, toward Luzon, in order to be clear when the landings took place.

In midafternoon the Blasters made trim dives to 400 feet in the submarine operating area. Just before the dive we discovered a broken bell crank in the stern plane indicator in *Pintado*'s after torpedo room, so the dive was made without the use of the stern planes. The bell crank was repaired soon after surfacing.

On the surface two hours after the dive, the Blasters formed a scouting line at five-mile intervals and proceeded toward Midway at three-engine speed, zigzagging day and night.

While at the sub base I had become aware that several of my sub school classmates were moving into command positions. I began to anticipate orders to command my own submarine.

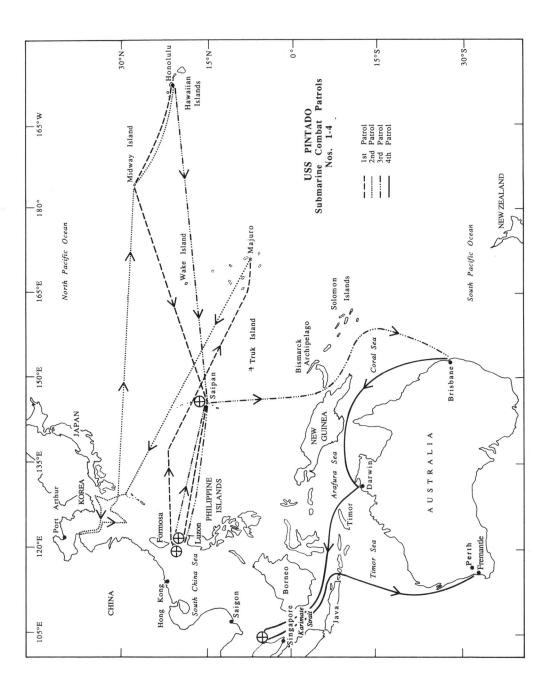

USS PINTADO
Submarine Combat Patrols
Nos. 1-4

- - - - 1st Patrol
· · · · · · 2nd Patrol
– – – – 3rd Patrol
——— 4th Patrol

17–19 May   En route to Midway we conducted daily drills in wolfpack communications, training dives, tracking drills, fire control problems, and school of the boat. A very important goal was to train and qualify as many men as we could. Of the seventy-two men on board, only twenty-eight were qualified in submarines, and forty-three men were on their first war patrol. On the nineteenth a battle surface drill was held during which five rounds were fired from the 4-inch gun and one pan of ammunition from each 20-mm gun. A few rounds were also fired from the .50-caliber and the .30-caliber machine guns.

Commodore Blair proved to be a colorful and interesting shipmate. I already knew, from having heard Lucius Chappell of *Sculpin* speak of him, that his nickname was Chief. I remembered Lu saying that he was part American Indian. Of course, no one in *Pintado* called him Chief in his presence, but we used the name out of his hearing. His husky voice was resonant and he spoke in a volume that could be heard throughout officers' country. Sometimes his hearty laugh reverberated all through to the control room and the forward torpedo room. He liked nothing better than to have an audience listen to his stories, which seemed to be in endless supply. He also played acey-deucey, and struck up a game with anyone who tarried in the wardroom. We enjoyed having Chief as a shipmate.

An amusing eccentricity of Chief's was his coffee-drinking habit. When he asked the steward for coffee, of which he drank numerous cups every day, the steward had standing instructions to bring a cup of steaming hot coffee along with a glass containing a few ice cubes. Chief would dip ice cubes out of the glass with his fingers and drop them into the coffee, then talk and tell stories until the coffee was stone cold before he got around to drinking it.

After watching Chief's treatment of his coffee a few times, Steward John Singleton brought a cup of cold coffee along with the glass of ice cubes. He was promptly sent back to the pantry for hot coffee, with a stern rebuke never to bring anything but steaming hot coffee to the commodore.

Chief took up residence in the wardroom and made that his task group headquarters. He made no effort to interfere in any way, and I never heard him voice any comments about the way we ran the ship; he only ventured to walk through the boat infrequently, talking to shipmates, and occasionally came to the control room to look at my charts and to the conning tower and bridge to see how things were going.

20 May At 0800 Blair's Blasters entered Midway Lagoon. *Pintado* moored alongside *Bang* in the nest at the side of tender *Proteus* and topped off with fuel and water. *Proteus* assisted in minor repairs to the antenna trunk; then we were ready to depart. Freeland Carde, exec of *Pilotfish,* and I spent time together on wolfpack communications procedures.

Ensign E. F. (Bonny) Bonjour, USNR, reported for duty as an addition to our officer group, taking on the duties of assistant first lieutenant. That brought the number of officers on board to ten, seven of whom would stand watches.

Chief Blair held conferences of the commanding, executive, and communications officers to go over the operating and communications procedures for the wolfpack. Of particular interest was a procedure for keying the SJ radar to challenge, exchange recognition signals, and communicate between the boats in the wolfpack.

Most of the crew had never been to Midway. Early liberty was granted to allow as many as possible to see the island and the birds, take a swim, and partake of a few beers at the recreation center.

21 May At 0700 the Blasters were under way for patrol. Jerry Mitchell and I promptly started a beard-growing contest. I felt that I had an advantage because of my previous proven record during *Sculpin*'s seven patrols, but he just wouldn't take my word for it.

Pintado was carrying a mixed load of twenty-four torpedoes: Mk-14, Mk-23 (improved Mk-14), and Mk-18 (electric). Where *Sculpin* had four torpedo tubes forward, we had six tubes. The torpedoes were all carried inside the boat, as contrasted with *Sculpin*'s early patrols when four fish were stored in the superstructure. Use of the infamous magnetic exploder was no longer required, and our skipper planned to routinely set fish to run at a depth of six feet.

22–28 May The Blasters were proceeding at two-engine speed to conserve fuel while conducting daily training exercises and schools. Messages were passed to *Shark* and *Pilotfish* by having them come close aboard, then throwing a messenger line across with a line-throwing gun, and finally passing a watertight container across with the messenger line.

Captain Blair continued to display an interesting personality. He brought a chief steward, a Filipino, with him who was a welcome addition to our pantry team. He also kept Chief's uniforms in immaculate condition. Chief wore regulation khaki short-sleeve shirts and short trousers, always clean and neatly pressed by his steward, and we working submariners in rumpled, frequently soiled, clothes couldn't compare with his polish. Outside the wardroom Chief wore a baseball cap of a type we had not seen before. At sea *Pintado* sailors didn't wear any head cover except when on bridge watch. Chief also wore shined brown shoes with knee-length khaki socks, while *Pintado* people wore sandals with no socks. The finishing touch for Chief was a pair of brown leather gloves, which he put on when he left the wardroom to make a tour of the boat or to visit the control room, the conning tower, or the bridge. (The crew speculated that he was a professional gambler and needed to protect his touch.) To complete the picture, he frequently had a big cigar in his mouth.

That Filipino steward was a wonder. He could do anything from cut hair to patch and mend clothes, as well as being a fine chef. I got a weekly haircut and beard trim from him. One morning I asked him to put some pecans in my waffles. They were excellent. Others tried them with the same reaction. From then on we regularly enjoyed pecan waffles. He also made great desserts. We savored his special ice cream many times, and also some great strawberry shortcake. From a culinary standpoint the outlook for the wolfpack was a decided success, and he set a fine example for our *Pintado* stewards.

On 22 May we moved the calendar ahead to 23 May as we crossed the international date line.

On 27 May a single "Betty" Jap patrol plane was sighted by the lookouts, once in midmorning and again in midafternoon. The planes were not picked up by the SD radar. At each sighting *Pintado* submerged for thirty minutes, apparently undetected by the planes, then surfaced to continue west.

When the first Betty was sighted I was on the bridge with the quartermaster, Frank Earnest, as signalman, getting a visual message from *Pilotfish,* who was heading directly for us in order to read our signals. I had my binoculars on them, helping Earnest, when all of a sudden I was jolted by Ed Frese, the OOD, exclaiming, "Holy Crock!"—this was one of his favorite expressions—"There's an airplane!" I turned, saying, "Where?" and aimed my glasses in the direction he was looking. There it was. So I shouted, "Let's get out of here!" and we submerged.

I could imagine the disbelief on the *Pilotfish* bridge at seeing us dive right under their nose, in the middle of exchanging messages. Then they sighted the plane and submerged as we watched them by periscope. The plane didn't drop any depth bombs. This was a very different war from the one I had left in July 1943.

Anticipating seeing more Japanese patrol planes, the skipper agreed to a system of paying prize money to lookouts for sighting them as well as for sighting Jap ships. A lookout would get $5 for each sighting. We thought that the bonuses for sightings would create additional interest and give the lookouts incentive to be exceptionally alert. The money would come from the welfare and recreation fund, which I managed.

Up to this point I had been regularly suggesting that the smoking lamp be out when we were submerged. The skipper was a smoker, so he resisted, but he finally agreed to try such a rule to see how it worked. I felt that he agreed with me just to shut me up, thinking that the smoking lamp being out would be very unpopular. But it worked the other way, and after a few days of a more comfortable atmosphere, the non-smoking-while-submerged rule became permanent. Even then, sometimes toward the end of a day the odor of cigarette smoke could be detected behind the closed door of the skipper's cabin. Ed Frese was not the least bit reluctant to comment, looking Chick straight in the eye, "Someone around here is sneaking a smoke," as Chick looked embarrassed. We kidded him, accusing him of being a nicotine addict.

My attempts to convince Chick to try the *Sculpin* reversa practice weren't successful. He wasn't impressed.

29 May   At 0500 the Blasters submerged for the day only thirty-seven miles from the patrol area. Our hope was to enter it undetected. In mid-morning we sighted another Betty through the periscope. The Japs were looking for us. At dusk we surfaced, and two hours later we were in our area west of Saipan.

Patrolling submerged during the day and on the surface at night, all three boats were exposing their vertical radio antenna for the first five minutes of each hour to maintain group contact and control by radio. The distance between boats was fifteen miles.

30–31 May   The thirtieth was a quiet day with no contacts. But at 0758 on 31 May the Blasters surfaced to check a contact report from *Silversides* of a convoy located to the southwest of Saipan, headed for that island. The message came to us as a rebroadcast by ComSubPac. The Blasters moved to the southwest on a scouting line, fifteen miles apart, to intercept the convoy. After searching all day on the surface, near sunset *Shark* reported seeing smoke to her south about twenty-five miles from *Pintado*. The commodore instructed *Shark* to take a position on the port side of the convoy, *Pintado* the starboard side, and *Pilotfish* to take a trailing position. The moon was bright, with good visibility.

Ten minutes after *Shark*'s report we sighted three columns of smoke to the southwest about twenty miles away, drawing right, so we changed course and increased speed to intercept.

In the fast approaching darkness, after closing for ten minutes, we could see the dim outlines of ships on the horizon but couldn't identify or count them. Continuing to close, a few minutes later we made radar contact with an escort at 8,500 yards on the starboard bow of the convoy. We couldn't see him until coached on by radar. *Pintado* went to a full speed and turned to put the escort astern and open the range, track the convoy, and gain a better attack position.

The convoy was tracked as headed due north at a speed of eight knots during the next two hours of stalking. Then we sighted *Shark* 6,500 yards to our west, exchanged SJ recognition signals, and with visual signals by shielded searchlight compared notes on the composition of the convoy and its course and speed. *Shark* had counted three cargo ships and three escorts. At that time their base course was still north; the zigzag leg was course 310, still at eight knots.

Both subs continued to stalk the convoy. By then we believed that at least one of the ships had radar because our radar was picking up persistent interference from the direction of the convoy. We were being very careful with our radar, using it only intermittently in order to reduce the chance that they would detect it.

1 June   Continuing our maneuvers to gain position ahead, right at midnight *Pintado* submerged 24,000 yards ahead of the projected track of the convoy and waited, tracking the smoke that was plainly visible in the bright moonlight.

At 0122 the bearing of the smoke began to change radically, drifting to the east, indicating that our convoy had made a major course change. The zig caused *Pintado* to lose contact, so we surfaced and ran at full speed to the northeast to reestablish it. At 0233 we picked up SJ radar interference to our port that was evaluated as being one of the Blasters near the convoy, so we headed that way. The moon set at 0256. The night became quite dark, making conditions excellent for a surface attack.

Thirty-five minutes later we reestablished radar contact with the convoy at 18,000 yards. They tracked as back on course 310, still at speed eight knots. As we closed to 10,000 yards, the outlines of ships were visible even in the inky darkness, and *Pintado* continued toward a position to attack.

At 0342 we heard three explosions that we believed to be *Shark* hitting a ship in the convoy. The convoy made another course change, which placed *Pintado* in a favorable position on the port side of the formation.

We promptly went to battle stations, commenced our approach, and prepared for a surface torpedo attack. There were then two 5,000–6,000-ton freighters in column on the starboard side of the convoy, and one identified as a big *Tarayasu*-type freighter (10,254 tons), alone and heavily loaded, in the port column, with the columns about 800 yards apart. Escorts were on the bow and quarter of the *Tarayasu*.

At 0415 the range to the *Tarayasu* was 4,700 yards, torpedo run about 3,900 yards. Then a lookout reported gunfire from the convoy, so the skipper rashly turned *Pintado,* at flank speed, to open the range, thinking we had been detected. That was a mistake; no one else saw any gunfire. I told him that I thought we should have more evidence than what the lookout "thought" was gunfire. The movements of the convoy and the escorts gave no evidence that they had sniffed us out, but by turning away and going to flank speed we lost our attack position.

Again *Pintado* maneuvered at full speed to regain position for attack. At 0430 we made our second move in, on the port side of target *Tarayasu.* Ships in the starboard column were in the line of fire beyond our target. Slipping undetected between the two escorts just before daybreak, the skipper fired a spread of six fish from the bow tubes, set to run at six-foot depth and explode on impact. The setup was near perfect: a 1,200-yard torpedo run, near zero gyro angle, ninety-five-degree port track.

Five torpedoes hit the *Tarayasu.* He disintegrated and sank. Other explosions were heard as *Pintado* turned to bring the stern tubes to bear on the remaining freighters, passing only 700 yards from one of the escorts. Both escorts turned toward us, so we went to emergency flank speed, running directly away from them, reaching a speed of twenty-one knots. (The order of speeds, from low to high, was: one-third, two-thirds, standard, full, and flank. "Emergency" flank meant for the engineers to "pour on everything including the galley range," but that speed could not be maintained for very long and could damage the engineering plant.) Surprisingly the escorts didn't press a counterattack, and we pulled clear to regroup and attack the remaining ships.

Several unidentified explosions were heard during the excitement of evading the escorts. Ed Frese, operating the TDC, predicted that our sixth fish should have hit the leading unidentified freighter in the starboard column. That ship turned on two green lights in a vertical line on the port wing of his bridge, and we wondered what the significance of the lights could be.

That first torpedo attack impressed me as solid proof of the value of having the TDC with the fire control team in the conning tower, where all aspects of the problem were easily watched and controlled. Further, with the fish set to run at a depth of six feet and to explode on impact, we had a real winner. Everyone was elated.

With daylight near, *Pintado* pulled clear on the surface, reloaded torpedo tubes, and prepared to attack the remainder of the convoy. At 0500, in daylight, there were several more explosions, and we saw a second ship in trouble. From our bridge the flashes of the blasts were vivid. The ship broke in two, and the bow and stern sank separately. The tops of one remaining ship were visible at the scene, with escorts milling around, apparently picking up survivors.

Chief Blair, who somehow managed to stay in the wardroom during the action, listening on the telephone, finally came to the bridge to be filled in on what had taken place and to give his suggestions for further action. My urging that we move in closer on the surface, then submerge to attack the remaining ship, was countered with fears that the escorts, some of which we couldn't see at our distance, would detect us, lock on with sonar, and depth charge us. Finally, at 0651, *Pintado* submerged to move in. We should have gone much farther on the surface.

While we closed in on the one-freighter remnant of the convoy at standard speed, with bearings steady, he put on speed at 0745 and pulled away to the northwest. We had no chance of catching him while submerged, and the possibility of aircraft attack was enough to keep us from going to the surface to chase him.

All morning we could hear distant explosions that we thought were depth charges. Every time we came to periscope depth to size up the situation, we were hampered by seeing the tops of escorts in the distance or aircraft patrols searching for us.

Finally, as things quieted down in midafternoon, we planed up to thirty feet for a good look with both SJ and SD radar. No contacts were made, so we surfaced and searched to the northwest at full speed.

Near sundown a radio report from *Pilotfish* advised that she was in contact with another convoy of at least five ships on a northerly course. The commodore directed her to follow her contact, report positions, course, and speed, and wait for *Shark* and *Pintado* to join her before attacking.

During midevening *Shark* reported that she had lost contact with the one remaining ship of the first convoy, so *Pintado* and *Shark* turned south to look for *Pilotfish* and convoy number 2.

At midnight the skipper and I realized that with all the excitement and activity of the day, we hadn't eaten for twelve hours, so we asked the pantry to send sandwiches and coffee to the conning tower.

2 June   The little that remained of 1 June and all of 2 June were spent searching for *Pilotfish* and convoy number 2. Several times we submerged when SJ radar contact was made on low-flying night-patrol aircraft. Each time we stayed down until all was clear, then surfaced to continue searching for *Pilotfish*. We didn't use the SD radar because previous experience indicated that Japanese aircraft could home in on its signal.

Gerry Pettibone's foot was broken on one of our quick dives to escape from aircraft. In the pitch dark, Doug Morse slammed the conning tower hatch down as Gerry was scrambling in behind him. They hurriedly cleared the bridge, submerging to avoid what one lookout reported as an airplane on the horizon, coming in fast. Doug could see the exhaust flames from the plane's engines, but the plane didn't drop any bombs or depth charges.

Doc Denningham bandaged Gerry and made him as comfortable as possible, but he continued to hobble around. Doc suggested that arrangements be made to transfer Gerry to a sub that was returning to base; but Gerry put up strong resistance and would have none of it. So he was taken off OOD watch and worked only on communications in the wardroom with Chief Blair.

Pintado's activities over the preceding two days were a shot in the arm to the crew. All of that boring training and drilling was proved to have been well worthwhile. Their attitude and enthusiasm improved 1,000 percent.

Our search for *Pilotfish* generated a giant circle, during which time the skipper and I took a nap, until finally, late in the afternoon, another radio message placed *Pilotfish* west of us, so *Shark* and *Pintado* turned in that direction at flank speed. We had really been burning up fuel for several days, running at flank speed a great deal of the time.

Near sunset *Shark* reported seeing smoke to the southwest. *Shark* closed *Pintado* to sight contact, then we both headed for the smoke, tracking the movement as we closed in. One and a half hours later radar made contact on something ahead of the smoke, 9,500 yards from us, showing strong SJ interference. We asked over the wolfpack radio circuit whether the interference was from *Shark* or *Pilotfish*. There was no answer, so we concluded that the enemy had a radar-equipped escort leading the formation.

Fifteen minutes later both radar and visual contact were made with a large convoy at 26,000 yards. As we closed in, sixteen ships, including escorts, were counted on the radar screen. In the bright moonlight we sensed that the escorts leading the convoy may have made visual or radar contact with *Pintado*. One escort headed our way. We saw a puff of smoke from his stack, and as we tracked him the radar range decreased from 15,000 yards to 9,700 yards.

We went to emergency flank speed and turned to run directly away from him. The TDC showed that he was doing twenty-four knots to our maximum of twenty-one knots. That was a losing game. At a range of 6,800 yards, decreasing steadily, we went down to 400 feet, rigging for the expected depth charge attack.

Sonar listened to the escort move in; and then he dropped forty-eight depth charges. None were very close. His sonar was probably confused by our high-speed wake, which must have persisted for a considerable time, and a nice temperature gradient at 175 feet was no help to him either. Some of the explosions were so far away that we came to believe that they were not intended for us at all. Either *Shark* or *Pilotfish* must have gotten in for a shot at the convoy. By unintentionally drawing off at least one of the escorts, we hoped that *Pintado* contributed to their success.*

While submerged I took advantage of the opportunity to eat a sandwich before turning in for a short nap. Wolfpack activities and convoy chasing left little time for regular meals and sleep. I kept going on nervous energy.

3 June   At 0055, after carefully checking out the above-water situation with both SD and SJ radar, *Pintado* surfaced and immediately made radar contact at 9,500 yards. Sight contact came a few seconds later. It was an escort. We turned our stern to him and went to flank speed, losing him at 13,000 yards, then slowed to full speed to commence an end around the convoy on northerly courses.

While we were running as fast as we could to get ahead of convoy number 2, we sighted the smoke of the convoy on the horizon to the north at 0512, and shortly thereafter the masts of a large ship were seen. Raising the periscope while running at high speed on the surface, with dead calm seas, we could make out the tops of other ships. *Pintado* spent most of the day continuing her efforts to circle around convoy number 2, diving for short intervals to avoid aircraft and running away to open the range

---

*Later, we learned that *Shark* was the one. She got in to sink a tanker and probably a freighter.

when escorts threatened. Tracking showed that they were zigzagging radically.

Through the day of high-speed running, still circling to get ahead of the convoy, we thought we had their course solved on several occasions only to find that they had changed base course again. By late afternoon we were again ahead of the convoy. They were south of us, and we sighted *Shark* on our starboard beam, having completed her end around simultaneously with *Pintado*. Both subs were positioning themselves to submerge for attack.

But then, just before we were ready to submerge, another smoke contact was sighted to the north: convoy number 3. We had two convoys in sight. The new convoy, coming south from Japan, was undoubtedly loaded. Convoy number 2, headed north, was probably empty, or at least not carrying war supplies or troops. By voice radio, the commodore directed *Shark* and *Pilotfish* to move north and attack convoy number 3 and to keep us advised of position, course, and speed. *Pintado* would continue against convoy number 2.

Just before sunset we submerged 28,000 yards ahead of our convoy. The moon was brilliant. On the surface we had determined that their course was 320 degrees true, speed still eight knots. Shortly after *Pintado* submerged, the convoy was obscured by a rainsquall. When next sighted they had zigged radically to their left. The closest we could get was 8,500 yards, much too far for a shot.

Three hours later, distanced from the likelihood of being sighted in the near daylight of the brilliant moon, *Pintado* surfaced and started another end around. Within minutes, however, a trailing escort detected us, and with another escort started after us. *Pintado* turned to show her stern and outran them, but by this time we were well northwest of our area. All we were getting out of the exercise was loss of sleep, less fuel, and a trip to Japan, for which we certainly were not prepared.

A short consultation with the commodore resulted in the decision to join *Shark* and *Pilotfish* against convoy number 3, so at midnight *Pintado* set course to southeast, at full speed, to catch up with the other Blasters.

4 June   A radio message from *Shark* at 0600 gave her position plus that of number 3 convoy, consisting of eight ships on course 160 t, speed nine knots. Half an hour later we sighted one of our submarines and commenced closing her. It was *Pilotfish*, with whom we set up a scouting line to search toward *Shark*'s reported position.

At 1015 *Pilotfish* reported a smoke contact to her west. Our plot showed the contact to be convoy number 3. At 1130 we sighted the smoke and commenced tracking it. By radio the commodore confirmed that all three Blasters were in contact with convoy number 3. Then he directed *Pilotfish* to take a position fifteen miles ahead of the convoy, *Shark* fifteen miles on their starboard bow, and *Pintado* fifteen miles on their port bow. *Pilotfish* was to submerge for attack about 1400, and *Shark* and *Pintado* at 1430.

We saw *Pilotfish* dive on time. Thirty minutes later, with the tops of some of the convoy ships just visible by high periscope, *Pintado* submerged to commence her approach.* After we had maneuvered for almost two hours it was apparent that unless the convoy changed course radically, we would not get into a position to attack. Twenty minutes later we heard three loud explosions and watched the convoy turn away from us to head southwest. (Later we learned that *Shark* had made an attack at that time.)

We heard the first of fifty-two depth charges as we maintained a course that we hoped would result in a chance for us to attack, should *Pilotfish* drive the convoy our way. The hope did not materialize.

Late in the afternoon *Pintado* surfaced to commence another end around. The convoy was heading directly for Saipan.

5 June   Just after midnight *Pintado* was in position ahead of convoy number 3 and submerged, simultaneously calling the crew to battle stations and rigging for depth charge. The moon was bright, with clear skies and good conditions for a night periscope attack. One *Chidori*-class escort was leading, patrolling across the projected path of the convoy. He was pinging most of the time, stopping to listen every few minutes. Several times sonar thought the escort was getting echoes off *Pintado,* and reverberations of his sonar pings could be heard bouncing back and forth, yet the *Chidori* seemed in doubt of any contact.

At the point of making a final setup for firing, *Pintado* suddenly became heavy and sank to eighty feet; the change in ballast when the torpedo tube outer doors were opened was not adequately compensated for by the diving officer. The skipper didn't want to pump to adjust trim or to speed up, for fear the *Chidori* would be alerted by the noise. Everybody in the conning tower was using body English to try to pull the boat back up to periscope depth.

Cautiously adding turns to the screws, a few at a time, Robbie agoniz-

---

*On the surface, in smooth seas, we could raise the periscope to search beyond the bridge's horizon. That search procedure was termed "using the high periscope," or "by high periscope."

ingly worked us back to seventy feet. It was still not enough; sixty-two feet was necessary to use the periscope effectively.

Sonar, meantime, picked up heavy screws ahead, and heard pinging from three more escorts on the starboard and port bow. The deep-draft freighters were getting closer and closer, with sound bearings all around the dial. We were in excellent position to fire on sound information, but the skipper was concerned that we were too close to the escorts; so we crept away from a perfect opportunity to fire on sound data, directly beneath the enemy convoy.

The *Chidori* took two long check pings and speeded up. *Pintado* went to 400 feet and waited for depth charges as the convoy passed right over us. The escorts obviously thought that *Pintado* was one of their own ships, and they dropped no depth charges. So we waited for the convoy to move on and give us room to surface.

At 0215 *Pintado* surfaced to commence another end around, circling to the north and then east. The convoy was to the southeast at 24,000 yards. Twenty minutes later we made contact with another convoy of four ships, convoy number 4, to the northeast at 15,000 yards. The commodore directed *Pintado* to continue going after convoy number 3, and *Shark* and *Pilotfish* to go after convoy number 4.

I spent the night in the conning tower, wrapped in a blanket and sleeping as best I could on the steel deck, prepared to urge that we go after our targets. We had missed a great opportunity to attack on sound information when we were directly under the convoy, and I didn't want that to happen again. If there was a next time, at least I might be more persuasive.

Pintado's end around continued all day. We started from a position astern of the convoy and circled completely around them to gain position for attack, always staying far enough away to avoid detection, and continually alert for aircraft. We did dive for a few minutes on several occasions when patrol planes were spotted in the distance, but none came after us.

In position to attack just before midnight, *Pintado* submerged for a periscope attack on the five remaining ships of convoy number 3. Two ships were in a center column, two in the starboard column, and one in the port column. Escorts were stationed around the convoy, but we were never able to count them. They were hidden behind bigger ships, some on the far side of the convoy, and we were never quite sure just how many there were.

6 June At 0020, with moonlight almost like day, we went to battle stations and commenced our final approach. The plan was to go to a position between the port column and the center column and fire at the leading ship in the center column, so that ships in the starboard column would overlap the center column target and might be hit by any fish that failed to hit the center column target.

At 0044 the skipper turned the boat to bring the stern tubes to bear. The convoy zigged toward *Pintado* about fifteen degrees, reducing the firing range to much less than the TDC calculation. Ed hastily corrected his computer, calculated a new solution, and checked the gyro angles in the torpedoes.

At 0053 the skipper fired a spread of four Mk-18 fish from the stern tubes at overlapping targets *London Maru* and *Tatuharu Maru* at a very favorable range of 700 yards; but the convoy zigged again just as the fish left the tubes. All missed *London Maru*, but four loud explosions were heard with times corresponding to hits in *Tatuharu Maru* leading the starboard column. The last ship in the center column passed close aboard between *Pintado* and the starboard column, preventing any periscope observation of actual hits. A YP-type (patrol boat) escort headed directly for *Pintado*. We went deep and rigged for depth charge, but no countermeasures were taken against us.

At 0203 *Pintado* surfaced and commenced another end around. By 0800 we had attained position ahead of the convoy and were tracking the ships to check the accuracy of our TDC solution, waiting for the convoy to move closer. At 0855 a Mavis-type airplane was seen heading directly for us, so we dove to 200 feet and settled to a normal approach course at standard speed, using the pinging of the escorts for tracking purposes.

The Mavis didn't drop any depth charges, so we came up to periscope depth and saw that the convoy had made a course change that left *Pintado* seven miles off their track. We went back to 200 feet to make speed and close the distance. A short time later, at periscope depth, we observed the Mavis circling the convoy, so we returned to 200 feet and continued closing at standard speed. Another look at 1028 showed the Mavis still circling, so *Pintado* went deep again.

Our high-speed maneuvering while submerged was draining a lot of power from the battery, and the air temperature in the boat was very high. During another look thirty minutes later, with sonar reporting loud screw noises, we didn't see the Mavis around, but the leading *Chidori* escort, far in advance of the convoy, was passing only 700 yards away.

Pintado's screws turning at high speed were making so much noise that our sonar hadn't detected the change in convoy course. Immediately we went to battle stations and readied all torpedo tubes.

Astonished that our periscope was not sighted, the skipper commented that he could see many people along the rail of the *Chidori,* in uniform, as if manning the rail. At first he thought they were lookouts for submarine periscopes; but if so, they failed to detect *Pintado*. Then, on closer examination, he realized that the Japanese destroyer was packed with troops, probably survivors from a transport sunk by one of our Blasters.

There were four ships remaining in the convoy: two in the center column and one each in the port and starboard columns. *Tatuharu* was missing; our four fish had sunk him. We selected *London Maru,* lead ship in the center column, as our next target. The starboard column ship, *Gosyu Maru,* was lined up bow to stern with *London Maru*. A single ping by sonar gave the range to the *London* as 800 yards.

At 1113 the skipper fired a spread of six fish from the bow tubes at the overlapping ships, and we heard six explosions. The periscope dipped under momentarily due to water taken into the forward torpedo room bilges (This was not unexpected. It was a normal function of the poppet valves when fish were fired, to prevent a telltale bubble of torpedo ejection air rising to the surface.)

A few seconds later *Pintado* was back at periscope depth, and the skipper saw the *London* burning furiously, broken in two, bow and stern projecting up in the air as he went down. *Gosyu* was stern down, deep in the water, listing forty degrees to port, and enveloped in flames.

In deference to Mavis and the seven escorts that we had by now counted, *Pintado* went to 450 feet and rigged for depth charge. The wait was not long. Four minutes after we had fired torpedoes the first of fifty depth charges went off. Five of the escorts surrounded *Pintado,* taking turns running over us and dropping charges as we evaded, changing course and speed as the escorts speeded up on a charge-dropping run.

At 1210 six of the closest charges went off over the after torpedo room. Paint chips and pieces of cork insulation flew around. The gyro compass alarm went off, indicating that the gyro was disturbed on its gimbals. The high-pressure air connection to the separator in the after torpedo room broke, but the air was promptly cut off at the valve. The damages were not nearly as extensive and shocking as those on *Sculpin*'s two threatening experiences.

Captain Blair, sitting at his command post in the wardroom, was shaken up by a file cabinet door that dropped on his head. He was so startled that he threw his feet up under the wardroom table and badly sprained and bruised an ankle, so that he could barely hobble around the boat. (Rumors immediately went through the boat that he would get the Purple Heart for his injury.)

By late afternoon things had quieted down, repairs were completed, and *Pintado* came to periscope depth for a look around. We saw the tops of two freighters and several escorts milling around about 12,000 yards away, in the area of the sinkings. I suggested going in for another attack, but neither the commodore nor the skipper was receptive to the idea. All afternoon we watched the activities of the remaining ships from a distance, hearing other very strong explosions. Finally, just before sundown, the two remaining ships and seven escorts got under way, again heading for Saipan. At sunset we surfaced to commence another end around.

As we pulled away we could see a large fire in the direction of the sinkings, and at midevening we saw flares in that direction as we continued our end around. I felt very strongly that we should have been more aggressive about going after the convoy remnants as they were milling around, apparently picking up survivors. It would be worth the risk because every soldier in the convoy who got past us would be going on to Saipan to be part of the resistance to our marines when they went ashore. Again I slept on the deck of the conning tower, keeping my eye on the end around to be sure that no changes were made in *Pintado*'s actions without my being able at least to give my views. Chick frequently changed his mind, changed orders, and didn't keep me informed. I would find that courses, speeds, and intentions were altered without my knowing about it. He acknowledged the tendency but still had a bias toward running the ship as if he were navigator and executive officer as well as skipper.

7 June   At 0505 we were in position to commence another approach. Thirty minutes later *Pintado* submerged, but the convoy made an extreme course change and we were unable to attain an attack position. A Mavis search plane was again circling the convoy. My disappointment at not being more aggressive the day before was commented on by the skipper as he reconsidered that missed opportunity.

In any event, our time had run out. The expected landings on Saipan were to begin soon. ComSubPac didn't want us to be near there because Allied forces might mistake Blair's Blasters for Japanese submarines. So at 0945 *Pintado* surfaced to head west and clear the area at full speed. As we cruised west we passed through the scene of the last attack. For one and a half hours we were in water littered with debris and oil drums. The OOD was kept busy steering *Pintado* around the largest pieces of flotsam.

Messages were keeping the radio shack on its toes. ComSubPac directed *Tunny* to join the Blasters, and the commodore radioed rendezvous instructions to *Shark*, *Pilotfish*, and *Tunny*. Late in the afternoon *Pintado* changed course to the northwest to head for the meeting place, 200 miles away.

8 June   We sighted *Bowfin* at daybreak, eight miles to the southwest. We were expecting to see her; earlier messages from ComSubPac had alerted us. During visual signals with *Bowfin* the signalmen had a problem with call signs, getting our S-387 sign confused with her S-287. Each signalman thought the other was mistaken. In midafternoon we met *Shark*, *Pilotfish*, and *Tunny*, exchanged information by visual signals, then closed to bullhorn range and talked to each and afterward sent written messages by line-throwing gun. *Shark* had expended all her fish, so at sunset she departed for Midway.

ComSubPac ordered the Blasters to patrol an area in the South China Sea northwest of Luzon. We set a westerly course, the boats twenty-five miles apart, running on the surface at night and submerged in the daytime.

9–13 June   We were recovering from the exertions of the previous week, and these were routine days. Everyone was occupied with maintenance, repairs, routine watch-standing chores, and resting. I was finding that my time was so taken up with the jobs of executive officer and navigator that I didn't have time for the reading that I had enjoyed in *Sculpin*.

What a difference there was in the equipment on *Pintado* compared with *Sculpin*'s first six patrols! The SJ radar made a tremendous difference in tracking and attacking enemy ships, picking them up even when we couldn't see them—in rainstorms, at extreme ranges, or in fog banks. The SJ was invaluable for navigation. *Pintado*'s sonar was far superior to *Sculpin*'s, too. Our Mk-18 electric torpedoes were quiet and left no wake, so enemy ships had less chance to hear or sight the incoming fish and turn to avoid being hit, as they could do with *Sculpin*'s steam-turbine-driven Mk-14 fish. *Pintado* had six torpedo tubes forward, contrasted with only four for *Sculpin*, and all twenty-four torpedoes were carried in the torpedo rooms. No more snaking fish out of deck storage and man-handling them across the deck at night. *Pintado* could go to 450 feet to evade attacking destroyers. And the vapor compression water stills made enough water so we could bathe frequently.

14 June   In midafternoon we sighted Balintang Island to the west, twenty miles away. Near sunset *Pintado* commenced passage through Luzon Strait's Balintang Channel, eight miles north of the island. Simultaneously we made radar contact with the Batan and Babuyan groups of islands, forty miles away. During my last time in that area, on *Sculpin*'s first patrol, we had no radar. So, all navigation was by visual means. When visibility was limited, navigation could be very inaccurate. I remembered my earlier dead-reckoning navigation, and how inaccurate it could be.

15–16 June   *Pintado* was in the patrol area just after midnight of the fifteenth, and at daybreak we could see mountains on Luzon to the southeast, fifty miles away.

While the days were quieter, training courses, advancement in rating, and submarine qualification were getting attention again. During midevening ComSubPac instructed the commodore to stay east of 120° E due to the possibility of impending fleet action. Instructions were relayed to *Pilotfish* and *Tunny*.

Moving east through Luzon Strait on 16 June, during the midafternoon we sighted Batan and Itabayat islands to the east and the north, respectively. *Pintado* was experiencing a three-knot set to the north, so the skipper decided to go between Batan and Itabayat instead of using Balintang Channel. At 1915 we passed eight miles to the south of Itabayat. During the midevening ComSubPac instructed the Blasters to set up a patrol in the vicinity of latitude 22° N, longitude 136° E. We relayed instructions by radar signals to *Tunny* and *Pilotfish*, then set course to the east at fourteen knots.

17–22 June   On 17 and 18 June *Pintado* was en route to the new patrol assignment. We arrived there after midnight on the nineteenth. At 0530 we contacted *Tunny* and *Pilotfish* by visual signals and gave them their instructions; the Blasters were on an east-west line, centered on the 22° N, 136° E spot, thirty-five miles apart, patrolling back and forth, east and west, on the surface, looking for enemy ships. Nothing was seen during four very quiet days.

At midafternoon on the twenty-second we received instructions from

ComSubPac to terminate the wolfpack. *Pintado* was instructed to head for Majuro Island for refit. Our chart showed Majuro, a new name to most of us, in the Marshall Islands chain. The commodore released *Tunny* and *Pilotfish* to carry out their individual orders, and *Pintado* set course to the southeast for Majuro, some 2,650 miles away, at the fuel-conserving speed of fourteen knots. Our fuel was low because we had used so much on high-speed end arounds off Saipan. *Pilotfish* was also going to Majuro, but apparently she had more fuel than we did, because she soon disappeared over the horizon at seventeen knots.

23–30 June   Days rolled by; the time of day, the date, and the day of the week had lost all significance. Sometimes I would go for a couple of days before realizing that I needed some sleep. The excitement had been intense for everyone on *Pintado* during the wolfpack operations off Saipan. Now everyone could relax. I joined in chess and acey-deucey contests to determine the ship's champion. In the second round I managed to beat Fergie Ferguson in chess and Ray Emerson in acey-deucey, but I didn't make the finals. The welfare and recreation fund donated a $20 prize for each of the contests, and for a cribbage tournament, too, which I didn't enter.

My beard was flourishing, about at the stage it was in 1943 when *Sculpin* arrived in San Francisco for her major overhaul. Jerry Mitchell and I were the only officers with beards, and I won our competition hands down. Many of the crew also had beards.

Chick and Yeoman John Flynn were burning the midnight oil working on the patrol report. He and the commodore huddled often over what was being written. I expected to be asked to help, if only with the proofreading, but he was quite remote, which struck me as unusual. Meanwhile Robbie took over the navigation duties so I could concentrate on getting ready for refit, push the education programs, and have our paperwork up to snuff for Majuro. As a result of our school activities, there were twenty-seven new submarine qualifications and twenty advancements in rating, all the way from seaman/fireman to chief petty officer.

The *Pintado* team was shaping up. A little action certainly had done wonders for us. Chief of the Boat Red Hill was very dependable, put up with little nonsense, and was on top of every problem. My right-hand man in navigation, Chief Quartermaster Ray Emerson, was superb. Morale was high. The boat was in excellent condition. Habitability was good, primarily because we spent so much time on the surface during the patrol. Gerry's broken foot and the commodore's bruised and sprained ankle were the only casualties. Ken Tibbetts, GM3/c, was the champion lookout and claimed $30 for the planes and ships he had sighted during the patrol. Officers were not eligible to compete in the contest. I sensed that Chick had markedly changed posture and was staying out of the executive officer's functions, which made my work much easier. It could have been that he was busy writing the patrol report with the commodore, but I overheard him on several occasions tell officers to see Mendy over a decision that he previously would have made.

We passed through the Marshall Islands, several of whose atolls were reported to have Jap troops on them. They had been bypassed by the Allied movements toward Japan. We stayed well out of gun range.

Robbie plumbed *Pintado*'s fuel tanks and reported that we were nearing empty, so we cut our speed down to a bare ten knots. It would be most embarrassing to have to call Majuro for a towboat. However, another gauging of fuel tanks, and a second check to make certain, showed an error in the first calculation. Relieved at having a little more diesel than was first reported, we put on three engines. Even so, *Pintado* was still far below the ComSubPac required safety rule of a 10-percent reserve.*

The four expectant fathers in the wardroom, including myself, were eager to get to port for letters, progress reports, and arrival announcements.

The night of the thirtieth, expecting to arrive in Majuro in the morning, Chick and I were standing on the cigarette deck talking over the patrol. He put his arm around my shoulders and told me how much he appreciated my backing him up, how we wouldn't have had such a successful run had it not been for my help, adding that he expected me to get my orders to command soon.

1 **July**   We met the pilot boat off the entrance, proceeded into Majuro lagoon at 0900, and moored alongside sub tender *Bushnell*. The plans were for *Pintado* to be refitted by a relief crew from Submarine Division 141 (SubDiv 141). Everyone would leave the boat for two weeks in a rest camp. The boat was in excellent material condition, requiring little except routine inspections, preventive maintenance, and normal upkeep work. Commodore "Chief" Blair said good-bye, leaving the boat on crutches to catch a plane for Hawaii. We had enjoyed having him as our shipmate on *Pintado*'s first, very successful, war patrol.

---

*We had only 1,950 gallons when we arrived at Majuro, barely enough to wet the sides and bottoms of the fuel tanks.

After the skipper submitted his patrol report, I finally got my chance to read a copy. We fired sixteen torpedoes and got sixteen hits. What a difference from the poor torpedo performance earlier in the war! The electrically driven fish, slower but with much less noise and no steam wake, were far more effective. ComSubDiv 141's endorsement to the skipper's patrol report remarked that with sixteen hits from sixteen fired, we may have set a record.

Patrol Summary

Number of men on board	72
Number qualified, start patrol	28
Number qualified, end patrol	55
Number unqualified making first patrol	43
Number advanced in rating	15

Nautical miles covered:

Pearl Harbor to Midway		1,578
Midway to area		2,350
In area		5,887
Area to Majuro		2,650
	Total	12,465

Fuel used: 138,345 gallons (11.1 gal./mi.)

Duration:

Pearl Harbor to Midway		4 days
Midway to area		7 days
In area		24 days (8 days submerged)
Area to Majuro		9 days
	Total	44 days

Torpedoes fired: 16

Sinkings:

1 *Tarayasu Maru*		10,254 tons
1 unidentified		5,000 tons
1 *Tatuharu Maru*		6,335 tons
1 *London Maru*		7,191 tons
1 *Gosyu Maru*		8,469 tons
	Total	37,249 tons

ComSubPac, with his intelligence network, cut the sinkings down to four ships totaling 31,000 tons, with the *Tatuharu Maru*, 6,300 tons, assessed as damaged but probably sunk.*

At this time an awards criteria was in effect in the submarine force by which Chick Clarey would get the Navy Cross, and I, for a second time, the Silver Star. My first award of the Silver Star came as a result of Lu Chappell's recommendation.

Refit in Majuro

1–23 July   Submarine activities at Majuro were centered on Myrna Island, one of the ring of islands that surrounded the lagoon. Sub tender *Bushnell* was moored near Myrna, as was floating dry dock ARD-18. Transportation to and from Myrna was by regularly scheduled navy launches. We had been alongside *Bushnell* only a few minutes when a relief crew came aboard to take over and our crew was whisked off to the rest camp for two weeks. A few officers and petty officers were scheduled to return to the boat each day to help the relief crew with their work.

Myrna Island was not very big, and it was set up exclusively for submarine people. Palm and coconut trees covered the island, and fine beaches and coral reefs surrounded it. Quonset huts were scattered among the coconut trees as housing for submarine crews. The sub skippers had their own captains' hut. Enlisted men's huts were about a hundred yards away from the officers' huts. There was also a recreation hut with a bar, a mess hall, and an administration section for the camp commander and his staff. The huts were modified for the tropics, with open, screened sides to allow the trade winds to blow through. A cooling breeze seemed always to be blowing. There were no mosquitoes, flies, or other bothersome insects.

The camp commander, Commander Mitchell, was quite conscientious in scheduling recreational activities to make his guests comfortable. Planned activities kept everyone occupied; there was swimming and shell hunting, exploring along the reef and in the lagoon, volleyball, horseshoe pitching, softball games, boat trips to the other islands around the atoll, fishing expeditions in the lagoon, picnics, steak fries, beer parties, and even sailing. I was the only one who used the star-class sailboat during

---

*Months later, when we saw him in Pearl Harbor, Admiral Lockwood commented that the Blasters eliminated one division of Japanese troops from the fighting on Saipan.

the time *Pintado* was there. After only a few hours Robbie Robinson and Doug Morse suggested to the commander that our hut should have the name La Concha after the hotel we stayed at in Key West. In no time that name was over the entrance.

Several other subs were in for refit, but we spent a major part of our time competing at horseshoes, volleyball, softball, and bridge with the *Pilotfish* officers and crew, friends from Portsmouth days, who were housed next door. The "Grand Championship" softball game between *Pintado* and *Pilotfish* took place on the fourteenth. It was a lively game followed by perfectly broiled steaks and a picnic spread, thanks again to Commander Mitchell. *Pintado*'s win was welcome vengeance for *Pilotfish* winning the beer in Panama.

Randy Moore, '38, a fellow Texan; Skip Giffen, '38; and John Hess all came through on their way to command assignments.

One day Jerry Mitchell and I took the launch to the air station and caught a ride in an amphibious reconnaissance plane. Later I overheard some of our crew talking about how they had gone to the airfield and gotten a ride in a bomber that had dropped bombs on Jap positions on one of the neighboring islands. There were bullet holes in the plane when they returned to Majuro, they boasted. I put a stop to that, announcing that there would be no more such flights by anyone from *Pintado*. The last thing we needed was to have some of our crew shot down while on a bombing raid.

During a swimming party, Electrician's Mate Fred Powers swam offshore and pulled a drowning shipmate, MoMM Joe Bennett, out of the water. I went to see Joe in the sick bay on the tender as soon as I heard about the incident. He was recovering from shock and too much salt water in his lungs but would be fine in a day or so. The skipper asked me to write a letter recommending Fred for the U.S. Navy and Marine Corps Life-Saving Medal.

On the fifteenth I selected replacements from the manpower pool for twelve men that we decided were not making it on *Pintado*. Besides the replacements, I managed to add five men over allowance; so the sailing list consisted of seventy-six men. *Pintado* had bunks for only seventy-one men. A few would be hot bunking, sharing a bunk with someone with different duty hours.

After the transfers were all arranged, a shy young seaman 1/c came to the island and timidly asked if he could transfer to *Pintado*. He was all slicked up, with cleanest uniform, shined shoes, and fresh haircut, to make a good impression. I asked his name. "Lewis," he said. I remembered that Seaman 1/c John Lewis was one of the names I had selected from the list in the personnel office. When I showed him his name on my roster, he was a very happy sailor. John aspired to become a stew burner.

Our money machine for welfare and recreation came to an abrupt end when some busybody on the staff reported the slot machine and the commodore ordered it off the boat. It had served its purpose well, and we had a nice bankroll to tide us over, so regretfully we deep-sixed it.

The fun and games came to an end on the sixteenth, when everyone moved back aboard ship and began operating as a shipboard team. The relief crew had done a fine job of maintenance and repair, and the boat had been dry-docked so that the bottom could be inspected and minor repairs made there.

On the eighteenth we held captain's inspection. The skipper went through the boat with a fine-tooth comb. Then there was personnel inspection on deck. Afterward Commodore G. E. Peterson, '24, presented Submarine Combat pins to the crew. Everything went off as smoothly as could be expected from a group with almost no military training, whose salutes would never have been accepted in boot camp. One seaman, awestruck and from sheer fright (he had never been that close to someone of such high rank), forgot to salute the commodore when he got his pin. A fireman started to go back into ranks, then remembered that he should salute, so he quickly whirled around with a sheepish look and made his comical salute. Chuckles could be heard up and down the ranks. The commodore had an amused twinkle in his eye as he watched the awkward young crewmen doing their best.

On the twentieth *Seawolf* (Al Bontier, exec on *Sculpin*'s seventh patrol) came in for a stopover on the way to Australia. We wondered why he was commanding *Seawolf*; when I left *Sculpin* he was supposed to go to *Razorback*. I went back to the rest camp and had dinner with Al, and we talked so long that I almost missed the last boat out to *Bushnell*. I hesitated to ask about the *Razorback* to *Seawolf* switch, assuming that he would tell me if he wanted me to know. (Later, I learned that he *did* go to *Razorback*, then experienced a mishap on the East Coast of the United States; as a result, he eventually became captain of *Seawolf*.)

Lieutenant Commander Bill Lawrence, '34, a classmate of the skipper, reported to make his prospective commanding officer (PCO) run with *Pintado*. That meant we again had ten officers crowding the wardroom.

More and more Chick was accepting the fact that I was his exec and he was the captain. He stayed out of micromanaging the ship's work, letting me worry about that, and took on the role of setting policy and being the captain. It was making my job much easier.

While offshore on the twenty-second we challenged a submarine crossing our training area. It was *Seawolf,* heading south toward Australia. I signaled a message of best wishes and good luck to Al Bontier.*

Three days of training and torpedo practice in an operating area off Majuro ended our refit. *Pintado* was ready for her second patrol.

---

*It was the last time I ever saw him. In October 1944 *Seawolf* was tragically lost when she was sunk by friendly forces near Mindanao, Philippines, while on a special mission from Australia.

Pintado's Second Patrol

(24 July–14 September 1944)

24 July At 0530 *Pintado* was under way from alongside *Bushnell,* and we headed out of Majuro Lagoon. *PC 583* escorted us to the southern limit of the northern submarine safety lane. While under escort we made a trim dive to 450 feet, checked all systems, checked for leaks, and found everything working well.

Pintado was carrying a mixed load of twenty-four fish: Mk-18 electrics and Mk-23 steam.

Pollack passed at 1012, going to Majuro for refit. We signaled an exchange of best wishes and good luck. *PC 583* left *Pintado* to escort *Pollack* to the atoll, and we set course through the northern safety lane for latitude 29°30′ N, longitude 150°00′ E, where we were to meet *Croaker* on 30 July. *Croaker,* John Lee, '30, was to deliver our Operation Order (OpOrd) from ComSubPac.

25–30 July Running on the surface, *Pintado* made daily training dives, conducting drills, fire control problems, and various schools as a regular routine. As always, training was a high priority. We had made a few personnel changes at Majuro, and we had confidence in our good crew, but we always wanted to be better. Twenty-eight men were not yet qualified in submarines, and thirteen of them were making their first war patrol. As an insurance policy, we were five men over allowance. None of the commodore's bureaucracy appeared to notice the over-allowance status, or they said nothing if they did. I felt a sense of having put something over on the staff.

Doc Denningham and Yeoman John Flynn came up with a proposal to put out a ship's newspaper. The skipper enthusiastically approved the project. During previous times at sea, and during the first patrol, Doc and John had collaborated in making up humorous leaflets, cartoons, and stories. MoMM Harry O. (Pappy) Echols was another enthusiastic conributor. (Pappy appeared much older than most of our young sailors because of his balding pate; therefore the nickname.) Their paper would carry news from the wire services, sports news, social commentary, politics, cartoons, and their own added shipboard gossip. Doc had a great sense of humor and a gift of gab, and the paper was eagerly anticipated, with everyone wondering who would be the subject of an article or caricature.

The *Bushnell* technicians had recommended a procedure for operating the air conditioning that made living conditions better. One aspect of the improvement was a new small air conditioning unit which they installed in the forward torpedo room, making that compartment much more livable. In fact, with the new arrangement it was actually cool enough for sleepers to need a light blanket when on the surface in the tropical waters of Majuro.

Bill Lawrence slipped right into the watch routine just as Pete Galantin had done on his PCO run with *Sculpin,* and he was a welcome addition to the OOD complement, especially since Gerry Pettibone was taking a long time to qualify for top watch. Bill had a nervous temperament and was prone to nightmares. Several times we were jolted out of our bunks in the middle of the night by an unearthly scream that ended one of his dreams.

This would be essentially a single submarine patrol rather than a wolfpack patrol, so the skipper started off with either himself or me being awake at all times. With the PCO on the regular watch list and my coaching Gerry to stand OOD watch, one or the other of us was on the bridge or in the conning tower most of the time anyway. Gerry's broken foot was well enough by now for him to clear the bridge, so he was assisting Doug as OOD.

My daily schedule during surface running was about as follows: I was up at 0400 for star sights and navigation work, usually completed by 0430. The skipper, who had been up since just before midnight, turned in, and I kept an eye on things. He usually got up about 1000, and I relaxed a bit or worked on one of my projects. We had a cold lunch and then held school from 1300 to 1400. I got a couple of hours in my bunk before supper at 1730. After supper I took my evening star sights and worked out the ship's position, then I made my customary walk through the boat or stayed on the bridge until 0030, when the skipper relieved me and I could go below to sleep until 0400. There was always something for me to be doing.

30 July   At midafternoon *Croaker* was at the meeting place, right on time. *Pintado* went alongside in a mirror-calm sea to receive ComSubPac's

OpOrd, hand delivered. We were alongside just long enough to get the OpOrd, then both *Croaker* and *Pintado* headed west on their separate ways to the patrol area.

Pintado's orders were to go to the East China Sea (Tung Hai) and the Yellow Sea (Huang Hai), north of latitude 30° N, with China to the west, Japan to the east, and Korea to the north, in waters much more restricted and always much shallower than any we had been in before. *Croaker* and *Pintado* would be in the same area and would coordinate activities by radio. At the end of the patrol *Pintado* would go to Pearl Harbor for refit.

31 July   A radio intelligence message informed us that a Jap convoy was due to pass through latitude 29°30′ N, longitude 141°30′ E, on 1 August. *Croaker* and *Pintado* headed for the spot.

1 August   Shortly after midnight *Croaker* and *Pintado* were on location, twenty miles apart, waiting. We made a deep dive for trim and to check the water temperature, for use in possible evasion from depth charges, then came back to the surface.

At daybreak the bridge watch reported four columns of smoke to the southeast. *Pintado* opened the range to southwest, heading for a rainsquall in which to hide. According to the ComSubPac message, the convoy would be on a southwesterly course.

When the tops of ships came into sight, we put four engines on the line for flank speed and commenced an end around to get ahead of the convoy.

Only a few minutes on the way a lookout sighted a Betty patrol aircraft just as the SD radar reported an aircraft contact four miles away. The plane was coming in fast, so *Pintado* submerged, going to 200 feet to evade. Nineteen small explosions were counted. After thirty minutes we moved up to periscope depth. All was clear, so we surfaced to continue our end around. At the same time, breaking radio silence as directed, we sent a contact report to ComSubPac. Radio couldn't reach anyone to receipt for the contact report. Then the pesky Betty was sighted again, coming in from the southwest at four miles, so *Pintado* submerged. No depth bombs were heard that time.

Two similar episodes before noon convinced the skipper that we were getting nowhere with that air patrol around the convoy, so we gave up and stayed down for four hours. Back on the surface our contact report of the convoy cleared immediately through radio NPM, and we headed for our patrol area.

In late afternoon *Gato* came into sight to the west, moving south. We

signaled them our information about the convoy and continued toward
our patrol area. As we finished talking to *Gato* we sighted *Croaker* moving
toward the East China Sea.

Right at dark the SJ radar picked up Sofu Gan (Lot's Wife) rock, a
sheer pinnacle that rises from the depths about 360 miles almost due
south of Tokyo. Radar's report that Sofu Gan was 12 miles to the northwest confirmed my star fix position on the chart.

2–3 August   On 2 August the black gang converted number 4 fuel ballast
tank to a main ballast tank because all fuel had been used from that tank.
Pintado made two dives to wash the little remaining fuel from the tank,
continuing west toward our patrol area.

On 3 August, while we were using the high periscope, a patrol boat
was sighted in midmorning about twelve miles to the northwest. *Pintado*
turned south for a short time to avoid him. Then, an hour before sunset,
Akuseki Jima was sighted to the west, along with other islands of the
Tokara Gunto, the chain of Japanese islands that separate the North Pacific Ocean from the East China Sea. The islands were too far away for
radar to get a good range for me.

At sunset, again through the high periscope, that bothersome patrol
boat was sighted to the north, so we went to flank speed, hoping to make
our way south of Akuseki and on into the Tung Hai without interference.

At 2230 Akuseki was passed abeam to starboard at eleven miles. *Pintado* moved into the Tung Hai and set a northerly course toward Nagasaki.
Half an hour later we picked up Gaja Shima Light, which was showing
normal characteristics. The Japanese evidently left the light in operation
to aid their shipping. I appreciated the courtesy.

4 August   Shortly after midnight *Pintado* crossed latitude 30° N and was
in her patrol area, still moving north toward Nagasaki. We sighted a
patrol boat just as we entered the area, but we avoided detection. Two
hours later the patrol boat was again sighted and avoided. The area was
beginning to give a very busy appearance.

I mentally thanked the lighthouse keeper of Kusakaki Shima Light for
assisting me with my navigation by also having his light burning as *Pintado* continued north toward Nagasaki. We were among the islands of
the Nansei Shoto, so I was very attentive to just where *Pintado* was traveling. The SJ radar, used sparingly in order not to give away our presence,
also was helpful.

At daylight *Pintado* submerged 140 miles south of Nagasaki. Minutes before noon a light cruiser, thought to be of the *Natori* or possibly the *Kuma* class, was seen coming from the direction of Nagasaki with a float-plane screening him. He was making high speed and was about 14 miles away. We watched him by coming up to fifty feet depth to raise the periscope high above water. Twenty minutes later he turned and disappeared eastward, toward Kuchinoyerabu Shima. We made plans to be off that anchorage the next morning at daylight, anticipating that the cruiser was training in those waters and we might have him as a target.

Late in the afternoon a small freighter of about 500 tons came by. We tracked him, got an excellent setup, and moved into firing position, but didn't fire for fear of revealing our presence, which might spoil any possibility of getting a shot at the cruiser.

Surfacing at dark, *Pintado* moved toward the Kuchinoyerabu anchorage, described in the *Coast Pilot*, which we thought the cruiser might be using.

5 August   *Pintado* submerged just before dawn seven miles west of Kuchinoyerabu, waiting for the cruiser to venture out. Nothing developed. As the day wore on, we moved in closer, and from three miles out we saw no ships in the bay. When we surfaced for the night we moved north toward Bono Misaki, on the southwest tip of the major Japanese island of Kyushu, planning to spend the next day there.

The moon was brilliant. The skipper commented that the lookouts would have to be dark adapted before going below so they wouldn't fall down the hatch. At midnight *Pintado* was fifteen miles west of Bono Misaki point.

6 August   At 0128 sonar reported very faint pinging on 17.5 kilocycles (kc), bearing northeast. Ten minutes later we sighted smoke to northeast at 17,000 yards and commenced tracking. Although the moon was very bright, the horizon was slightly hazy. We used the SJ radar intermittently, avoiding land and being careful not to alert the convoy should they have radar detection equipment. We saw no indication that any land stations or the convoy were using radar. We counted eleven pips on the radar screen and saw eight merchant ships and two escorts from the bridge. Some of the escorts were quite small and might not show up very sharply on the SJ screen or be visible from the bridge.

We maneuvered for an attack position ahead of the convoy during the two hours after the sighting. The convoy tracked on a southwesterly course at a speed of eight knots.

Pintado submerged at 0322, 11,000 yards directly ahead of the convoy's projected track. The convoy was not zigzagging. We went to 200 feet to check the water temperature and found that it was isothermal to that depth, meaning that there was no place to hide down to 200 feet. There might be a break down deeper, but we would have to look for that later.

Our experience during the first patrol, and talks with other skippers at Myrna Island, finally convinced our skipper that the best technique for penetrating the escort screen while submerged was to go in from directly ahead of the formation, keeping *Pintado*'s bow pointed at the nearest escort insofar as that was possible in order to present a minimum target to the enemy's echo-ranging sonar. (Previously, expressing fear of detection, he had firmly rejected the idea of approaching a convoy from directly ahead, favoring an approach from the beam.)

Back at periscope depth, we continued boring in on the approach. An escort destroyer of the *Asashio* class was tracked from 2,400 yards until he passed us at 1,550 yards. He was weaving back and forth ahead of the convoy, pinging energetically. The convoy was in three columns, with two ships in the port column and three each in the center and starboard columns.

Two hours and forty minutes after first sighting the convoy the skipper fired a spread of six Mk-23 fish from the bow tubes at two overlapping freighters in the center and port columns. The range to the nearer target was 1,500 yards. The freighters were identified as *Nagoya Maru* and *Sinano Maru* classes, of about 6,000 tons each. While turning *Pintado* to bring the stern tubes to bear on other ships in the convoy, the skipper saw four hits in the target ships. Excitedly he told us that the stern of one ship had broken off and the second ship had burst into flames. Both were sinking as more explosions were heard.

The *Asashio* destroyer turned to head toward *Pintado,* and a PC boat (antisubmarine patrol craft) was closing fast, pinging on short scale, at zero angle on the bow. The ships in the convoy were scattering in all directions, so *Pintado* went deep. Sound reported loud hissing and popping noises as the targets sank. One last look by the skipper before the periscope went under showed that both targets had disappeared.

Below 220 feet the bathythermograph showed a beautiful eighteen-degree temperature gradient, which made evasion easy. The escorts dropped sixteen depth charges, but all were some distance away. As *Pintado* pulled clear we could hear more depth charges exploding. They were working over a false contact.

At daybreak, when we were back at periscope depth, only the destroyer and a PC were in sight, about 9,000 yards away, still working on their false contact, so *Pintado* continued to pull away, heading west in the direction of Uzi Gunto. Forty minutes later we could no longer see them, but we heard depth charges for another twenty minutes.

Pintado had been rigged for depth charge for more than two hours, with ventilation shut down and everything quiet to keep from making any more noise than was absolutely necessary. The atmosphere in the boat was humid and hot. I was soaked with sweat and had been on my feet for over twenty-four hours, so the skipper told me to get some rest.

I took off all my clothes and collapsed in my bunk with a fan directed full on me. Just as I dozed off I was jarred awake by the noise of a torpedo engine starting, running hot in the forward torpedo room. From earlier *Sculpin* experience I knew instantly that someone reloading tubes had accidentally tripped a torpedo starting lever. Fumes, smoke, and confusion immediately filled the torpedo room and officers' country.

I bounded out of my bunk—with no time for the formality of clothes—raced to the control room, slammed and dogged shut the door and vent flappers, and thus confined the smoke, fumes, and pressure to the forward part of the boat.

By that time the skipper had come down from the conning tower, excitedly asking what had happened. I explained what was going on. The men in the torpedo room telephoned control to report that they had stopped the torpedo engine. They also reported having trouble breathing. Pressure had built up, and the fumes were making breathing difficult. There was more than a hint of hysteria in the voices.

In order to vent the pressure out of the torpedo room and clear the fumes from the forward part of the boat, we decided to surface so that someone could go forward on the main deck, open the escape trunk hatches to the forward torpedo room, and release the pressure. Then, with all doors locked open from the torpedo room to an engine room, a main engine would be started to pull air through to remove the fumes.

To avoid trying to explain to someone what we were doing, and how and why we were doing it, I said that I should be the one to go on deck and open the escape trunk hatches as soon as we were on the surface. The skipper agreed. He had just made a periscope sweep and all was clear. There was a light fog or haze above us that would provide some protection from aircraft.

I still hadn't had any opportunity to get clothes, which were in the sealed-off officers' country. Events were moving much too quickly for such formality. *Pintado* surfaced, and I climbed down from the bridge to the deck and went forward to the escape trunk, carrying a sledgehammer to open the upper and lower hatches. The dogs on the upper hatch opened easily, and I swung it open. Then I hung down, my body inside the escape trunk, feet and legs on deck, to gingerly tap the dogs on the lower hatch, listening to the hiss of pressure being released from the torpedo room.

The men in the torpedo room decided to help me. From their viewpoint I was taking too long to get the hatch open, and they were understandably anxious. So impulsively they rotated the dogs open well before the pressure was equalized. The air pressure slammed the lower hatch up, and I was ejected from the escape trunk like a pea from a peashooter.

I landed on my right side, still hanging onto the sledgehammer. The bridge watch couldn't help laughing at the scene: the exec flat on deck in his birthday suit, firmly gripping a sledgehammer, having just been blown out of the escape trunk.*

The diesel engines pulled clean air into the boat in a few minutes. Then *Pintado* submerged to spend the rest of the day under. The quiet day allowed the crew to recover from the excitement of the night, and at nightfall we moved to patrol southwest of Koshiki Shima Light, about forty miles almost due west of Sasebo, Japan, in the southern approaches to Tsushima Strait.

7 August   The day was quiet off Koshiki Shima. I recalled studying the Russo-Japanese war and the battle at Tsushima in which the Japanese fleet decisively defeated the Russian fleet, never dreaming that someday I would be fighting a war in those same waters. Finding a history book in the library, we talked in the wardroom about the Battle of Tsushima Strait. As a result of yesterday's mishap, my muscles were very stiff and sore and there were black-and-blue bruises from my right ear to my right ankle.

That night *Pintado* proceeded to latitude 32° N, longitude 129°10′ E, and met *Croaker* for a previously arranged conference to work out plans for future activities. Both *Croaker* and *Pintado* were scheduled for lifeguard duty on 10 August at locations south of Korea. When U.S. bombing raids took place, submarines were stationed off the Japanese coast so that personnel from downed or damaged planes could be rescued.

Our two submarines lay only a few yards apart in a flat calm sea, using

---

*To this day, *Pintado* shipmates say that I am the only one who ever mooned the bridge and got away with it.

flashing lights and power megaphones, as we made plans for our activities when the lifeguard duty was concluded. We decided that both boats would make a run north in the shallow waters of the Yellow Sea (Huang Hai) toward Port Arthur. *Croaker* would take the waters on a route nearest the coast of Korea, and *Pintado* would take the waters farther offshore, near the China coast. During our meeting John Lee told us that they sank a light cruiser on the seventh. We thought that it was probably the one we had seen on 4 August.

8 August   Just after midnight *Croaker* went north of Danjo Gunto to work toward her lifeguard station. *Pintado* moved south of Danjo Gunto to work the Shanghai–empire traffic lanes while moving toward her lifeguard station on latitude 35° N, south of Mara To Light on the large island (Saishu To) south of the Korean mainland.

Pintado submerged at daybreak, still moving toward the lifeguard station. The weather was bad, with very rough seas. We were glad to be underwater where things were calm. During the day we heard a number of rumbling, explosionlike noises that we thought might be caused by an earthquake or undersea volcanos.

9 August   Shortly after midnight the SJ radar reported strong signals from the northeast. Radar followed the interference as it shifted slowly around to the west. We evaluated the signals as those of a patrol boat making an antisub sweep ahead of a convoy, and soon after we submerged at daybreak five columns of smoke were sighted to the northwest, distance about fourteen miles. The smoke was on the direct line between Shanghai and Shimonoseki, moving toward Japan. Twenty minutes later we saw the tops of seven ships. They were too far away for *Pintado* to make a submerged approach, and too close for us to surface to make an end around run to get into an attack position. So we ran away from the convoy at standard speed for a time in order to open the range so we could safely come to the surface.

Pintado surfaced at 0707 and spent most of the early morning trying to work around to a position ahead of the convoy against four escorts, two of them modern destroyers, one a *Chidori* escort, and the fourth a *Maru*-type escort.

Air patrols drove us down from time to time, and there was one floating mine to dodge. We would stay down for a short time, then pop to the surface to continue the end around. The water wasn't nearly as deep as we would have liked. The navigation chart showed an average depth of fifty fathoms. A one-time check with the fathometer registered all of sixty fathoms (360 feet).

By midmorning, with another thirty minutes estimated before we would be ahead of the convoy, an airplane came in and we submerged again. The skipper decided to try to close while submerged, so we put on standard speed. At 1130 we were 6,000 yards from the convoy, boring in, feeling that we had a chance to reach a firing position, when the *Chidori*, at 4,000 yards, locked onto us with a solid sonar contact. Our sonar could tell that he was getting a good echo, and he came directly on, driving us deep. He camped over us for a while but dropped no depth charges. Doug Morse, the diving officer, found a thermal layer at 165 feet, which threw him off.

Coming to periscope depth at 1245, we watched the *Chidori* return to the convoy, which was disappearing to the northeast. At that time all we could see was smoke. The skipper decided to give up and spend the rest of the day submerged, watching for another convoy.

At sundown *Pintado* surfaced to move to lifeguard station off Mara To.

10 August   We were on station before daylight, on the surface, waiting to pick up any downed aviators. At 1000, after waiting for six hours and receiving no radio information concerning an air strike, we submerged for the remainder of the day. Before sundown we surfaced to patrol in the vicinity of the lifeguard station while waiting for radio directions from ComSubPac.

11 August   *Pintado* spent the day submerged on lifeguard station, still waiting for that message from ComSubPac. Back on the surface before sundown we received word that we were released from lifeguard duty. We were pleased that none of our boys had been shot down, or at least they didn't come down near us.

12–14 August   Conducting a daytime submerged patrol along latitude 33° N *Pintado* moved west to longitude 123°10' E, from where we headed north through the Yellow Sea toward Port Arthur. *Croaker* was also moving north, off the coast of Korea.

Before dawn on 14 August radar reported a solid contact at 20,000 yards. We cranked up flank speed to chase the contact. After thirty minutes of tracking the contact turned out to be a very heavy rainsquall.

15–19 August   *Pintado* submerged for the day before dawn on the fifteenth. Robbie, then diving officer, found a temperature gradient right at periscope depth, and he managed to balance for four hours without using the propellers, pumping water occasionally to trim the boat. Balancing the boat can be compared with flying a balloon in air at a constant altitude. If the submarine can be balanced with water influences so that the boat stays at a particular depth with no headway, there is no need to use the propellers or the bow and stern planes to control the depth. All depth control is accomplished by trimming the boat—pumping water from one variable tank to another, or from and to the sea.

Robbie bet the skipper that he could accomplish the balancing act, and they engaged in a good-natured argument over the skipper's accusation that Robbie fudged shamefully in his interpretation of the rules for the wager while the control room watch looked on in amusement.

Radio instructions came from ComSubPac after we surfaced at sundown, and an hour later Gerry had the message decoded and checked. We were told to go back to our spot off Mara To and be there during the daylight hours of the twentieth. Our plans to see what was happening off Port Arthur were shelved. Using Shantung Promontory as a point of departure, we headed south, planning to patrol along the way and have more time to chase any contacts that we might make.

The move south—submerged during daylight, on the surface at night—was uneventful except for occasional sightings of fishing sampans along the way. At sundown on the nineteenth, when *Pintado* surfaced for the night, we were only a few miles from station and ready, with radio circuits manned in anticipation of messages.

An hour after sunset a message from ComSubPac asked for a weather report and also told us that the air strike would be delayed; *Pintado* was to stand by. Breaking radio silence, we sent the weather report, then we changed course to the southeast at flank speed to move away from the position of the transmission, just in case the Japs had zeroed in on our radio and sent patrols out to look for us.

20 August   Two hours before sunrise we received a message saying that the air strike was not going to be delayed; it was scheduled for 1700 and we were to stand by. At daybreak *Pintado* submerged to close the lifeguard spot. In view of the radio transmissions during the previous night, we thought that staying on the surface wasn't a good idea.

During midmorning sonar reported pinging to the west, and two minutes later a trawler-type antisubmarine boat was sighted about five miles away in the direction of the pinging. Then two pingers were sorted out. Each boat would take a turn, pinging a few minutes, then listening for a few minutes. *Pintado* moved away, watching, on the hunch that the pingers might be making a sweep ahead of a convoy. Sure enough, in the early afternoon we sighted two columns of smoke to the northwest, approximately twenty miles away. The smoke tracked as on a westerly course at a speed of ten knots. As we continued to track the smoke, holding our lifeguard assignment, we twice saw an air escort circling over the smoke.

We were eager to be dismissed from lifeguard duty so we could go after the convoy. *Pintado* came up to fifty feet to expose the vertical antenna and pick up any voice radio information on the U.S. air strike. The B-29 raid was in progress, and our radiomen listened to voice conversations among the B-29s concerning the very smoke we were watching, giving the location and composition: ten ships and three escorting destroyers. There was no information on any downed planes.*

Based on the B-29 reports of our convoy, which radio copied solid from the vertical antenna, we decided that the air strike was over and *Pintado*'s services were no longer needed. So near sundown we surfaced and started after the convoy at maximum speed, running a modified retiring search curve toward the west. Although the convoy was about seventy to eighty miles ahead of *Pintado,* we might be able to catch it shortly after sunrise. But at midevening our radio copied a message that a second wave of B-29s was scheduled to come in at midnight. *Pintado* gave up the chase and headed back to lifeguard station at fifteen knots. That was a heartbreaker; our first good contact in eleven days, and we had to give it up.

Back on lifeguard at midnight, we heard nothing about the air strike. *Pintado* waited.

21 August   After midnight Doug Morse, the OOD, sighted a phosphorescent streak abeam to starboard, headed toward *Pintado*. He backed emergency and turned hard left to avoid what appeared to be a torpedo. At the same time the skipper saw two streaks pass up the port side. "Whatever they were, they looked more like torpedoes than any fish we've seen, and they had about a fifteen-knot advantage on *Pintado*," he said. Swallowing their hearts back to normal position, they resumed course and speed to take a submerged station at dawn on the traffic route between Shimonoseki and Saishu To.

The rest of the day was uneventful except for infrequent sightings of patrol planes and patrol boats. *Pintado* surfaced at sunset.

*Later radio reports indicated that five planes were lost. None came down near *Pintado*.

During the evening a radio message gave notice of a convoy crossing our area. *Pintado* set course to the southwest at full speed to intercept the convoy. The report said that the convoy was a large one, moving north through the Tung Hai, destination Japan. The convoy positions, route, and speed provided by ComSubPac worked out that at full speed, on the surface, *Pintado* would be in the convoy's 1830 position at 1330, 22 August, giving us time to get there long before air and surface patrols could spot us. We could then make out the convoy formation, locate the escorts, and solve their course and speed for a submerged attack during daylight. Then we hoped to be able to surface after a reasonable time and make an end around run for a night surface attack on the remainder of the convoy. The nights were moonless and very dark, favoring night surface action.

22 August We carried out the plan, with no aircraft or patrol boats interfering with *Pintado*'s surface run to her appointment, and on schedule we submerged on the convoy's estimated 1830 position. The sea was flat calm. Three hours later we sighted smoke to the southwest, an estimated eighteen miles away. We commenced our approach; a short time later we heard pinging in the direction of the smoke.

During the next fifty minutes of tracking, the convoy was seen to be in three columns. In the center column was the *Tonan Maru*, a whale factory that had been converted into one of the world's largest tankers, followed by a large transport; the port column consisted of three large tankers of the *San Diego Maru* or *Sunosaki Maru* types, with two cargo ships of an unidentified class following. In the starboard column were four modern medium-sized cargo ships, also unidentified. The columns were about 2,000 yards apart, and all ships were heavily loaded. Three additional columns of smoke were visible astern of the first formation. Five escorts were spaced around the front and sides of the formation. The leading escort was a *Chidori*, patrolling back and forth across the front of the formation. The convoy was zigzagging on base course 030 t at seven and a half knots.

At sunset *Pintado* went to battle stations. Range to the *Tonan* was 10,000 yards; to the *Chidori*, 7,500 yards. A sounding of only thirty-five fathoms of water prompted us to rig in one of the sound heads as a precautionary measure. The two sound heads were vital parts of the sonar systems that projected beneath the ship's keel and could be retracted into the boat. The sensitive heads picked up sound waves in the water and were somewhat comparable to a radar's antenna. If we hit the bottom during evasion, we would have at least one sound head safely rigged in. The sea was oily calm, so the skipper planned to fire less detectable Mk-18 torpedoes.

Pintado used thirty minutes to work into position to pass between the center column and the starboard column, planning to fire stern tubes at the *Tonan*, then fire bow tubes at the ships in the starboard column. Fish that missed the primary target might hit the tankers in the port column.

Several times during the convoy's movement toward us the *Chidori* presented a zero angle on the bow and tested his pinger in our direction in a disturbing manner. He didn't change speed, however, and moved on in his search cycle. At 1842, with the periscope at low power because of the short range, the skipper described the *Chidori* crossing our bow only seventy-five yards away. *Pintado* then began swinging left for her final (firing) course.

At 1853 the skipper fired a spread of four Mk-18 fish from the stern tubes at the whale factory from a range of 1,200 yards, and immediately put on full left rudder to bring the bow tubes to bear on ships in the starboard column.

The skipper saw two hits in *Tonan Maru*. The explosions were heard and reported throughout the boat. He described the hits as amidships and forward and saw the target burst into flames just aft of his bridge and amidships. The two fires soon blended into one huge cloud of fire and smoke that enveloped the whole ship.

As soon as the whale factory was hit, the ships of the starboard column turned away, ruining the plan to fire bow tubes at them. The skipper kept left full rudder on, bringing the boat through almost a full circle, as he decided to fire more fish at the burning whale factory, which had slowed to seven knots, and overlapping ships in the port column. Any stray fish could go on to hit one of the large tankers in the port column.

Eight minutes after the stern tube shot *Pintado* fired a spread of six Mk-23 fish from the bow tubes at the whale factory, overlapping two tankers beyond in the port column, using a range of 2,000 yards and speed of seven knots. Two of the fish ran erratically, causing great alarm and anxiety as one circled over *Pintado*. The circler was heard passing first over the engine rooms, next over the after torpedo room. The other erratic fish ran out in the wrong direction. (Later analysis indicated that had they not been erratic, both would have hit the whale factory.)

Two minutes later there were two almost simultaneous explosions, one in the leading tanker, port column. The tanker following was hidden behind the burning whale factory, but time and distance were correct for a hit on it. The leading tanker burst into flames over his whole length, like an ignited kerosene-soaked log. The whale factory was burning briskly from bow to stern, and it was impossible to see where the sixth fish had hit. The night was becoming quite dark, and a heavy pall of black smoke filled the sky. Before we could reload the tubes it would be too dark for another submerged attack.

While the skipper was excitedly describing the scene on the surface, sonar reported pinging and light screws on several bearings in the direction of the burning ships, getting louder. So *Pintado* went down to 180 feet and hovered near the bottom to avoid being detected. Sound next reported three energetic pingers, and screws all around us. Keeping the pingers on both sides abaft the beam, we moved to the southeast at two-thirds speed. No depth charges were dropped and none of the escorts picked us up. We came to the conclusion that the hits in the center column, and a few minutes later in the port column, confused the escorts as to our most probable location. They concentrated their search in the wrong place as *Pintado* crept away from them.

Three tremendous explosions were heard during the evasion, followed ten seconds later by a fourth of equal intensity. They were loud and prolonged with a persistent water swish through our superstructure, indicating, we thought, unusually powerful blasts.

Coming to periscope depth at 2050, some 14,000 yards from the scene of the attack, we saw an incredible spectacle. Two burning ships were in sight, billowing smoke and flames hundreds of feet into the air. The glow of another huge fire could also be seen beyond the two in the foreground. Two pingers were silhouetted against the fires, circling the burning ships.

The crew was secured from depth charge quarters and all hands were invited to come to the conning tower to have a look at the fires through the periscope.

After all spectators desiring a look had been accommodated, *Pintado* came up to forty-five feet to check the SJ radar scope for interference. There was none. A sweep with the SJ showed nothing anywhere near us. *Pintado* surfaced at 2234 and steered various courses to skirt the fires at a distance. As we changed location we could see three enormous fires raging, separated by 5,000–6,000 yards, adding to the conviction that we had in fact hit that third tanker. A pall of dense black smoke covered 80 percent of the sky. *Pintado* lingered, watching and hoping for another opportunity to sink a ship.*

---

*An interesting aspect of the sinking of the *Tonan Maru* was that Chick Clarey had been

23 August   Satisfied, after five hours of raging fires, that those three ships were goners, at midnight *Pintado* set course to northeast at full speed in search of the rest of the convoy. Just after we got under way we heard another large explosion, and more flames shot into the sky.

At 0330 we were in the convoy's estimated 0300 position, but nothing was seen or picked up on radar, so we continued on toward the convoy's estimated 1100 position.

At 0600 *Pintado* submerged in the convoy's estimated 1100 position and waited until midafternoon without seeing any ships.

Shortly after we surfaced, we sighted a floating mine and sank it with 20-mm gunfire. Then we continued to look for the convoy on a retiring search curve to westward. As sunset neared with no sign of our convoy, we reversed the search to the east and north, planning to be at the convoy's estimated 0500, 24 August, position, east of Saishu To.

24–31 August   On 24 August at 0428 *Pintado* submerged in position as planned. Wind and sea were increasing from the northeast. Several times during the day we broached and had great difficulty getting back underwater. The seas were mountainous. A periscope attack would have been impossible, and torpedoes wouldn't hold depth at a setting above thirty feet. When we surfaced after sunset we set course for the open sea south of Saishu To to wait until the weather abated, giving up any thought of finding the convoy.

At daybreak on 25 August it took eight minutes to submerge to periscope depth because of the heavy weather. The sea was so rough that we continued to run at 100 feet all day, taking a very cautious periscope look once each hour. After sunset *Pintado* surfaced in continuing high seas and headed for a position between Fukae Shima and Danjo Gunto, hoping for a lee there, about 80 miles south of Nagasaki and 110 miles south of Sasebo. A midevening message from ComSubPac told *Pintado* to stand by for possible lifeguard duty about 30 August. The location of the lifeguard station would be sent later.

On the twenty-sixth *Pintado* spent a quiet day seventy-five miles southeast of Saishu To, again running deep because of the weather. When we surfaced after sunset the weather had improved considerably. We moved to patrol again between Fukae Shima and Danjo Gunto.

---

exec of the *Amberjack* when they sank that ship in Kavieng Harbor on 10 October 1942. The Japanese had raised the ship and towed it to Japan, where it was repaired and converted into a tanker. A distinguishing characteristic of the tanker was that it had two large stacks athwartship rather than the conventional in-line stacks found on most ships. It was the largest Japanese merchant ship sunk during World War II.

On the twenty-seventh, while we were submerged during daylight, we saw Betty patrol aircraft. At night on the surface SJ radar made contact with low-flying planes as *Pintado* patrolled the Tung Hai side of Tokara Gunto, using the SJ radar only infrequently and the SD radar not at all. There was no doubt in our minds that the Japanese could detect our radar.

The twenty-eighth was a quiet day spent off Uzi Gunto. No further word came in about lifeguard duty. We planned to move near Danjo Gunto, centrally located in our area, to be able to go easily to wherever *Pintado*'s lifeguard services might be needed.

Off Danjo Gunto on 29 August *Pintado* spent another quiet day. We made plans for a day off Nagasaki on the thirtieth, since indications from the radio messages were that Nagasaki would be the target for B-29 bombers, but all was quiet off Nagasaki and no word came concerning air strikes.

Anticipating the end of the patrol, we spent another quiet day on the thirty-first, off Danjo Gunto, edging toward the departure point for terminating the patrol on 1 September.

An interesting feature of this patrol area in shallow waters had been the large negative temperature gradients, which frequently enabled the diving officer to balance *Pintado* for long periods. An interesting feature for the navigator was the numerous islands, which could be pinpointed with the SJ radar, giving perfect position fixes.

1 September At 0330 *Pintado* crossed the patrol boundary at 30° N latitude, planning for a submerged patrol south of Gaja Shima during the day, and to be in position to transit the strait south of Akuseki Jima early in the evening and be in the Pacific Ocean for surface running on 2 September.

Before submerging we could see the glow of an active volcano on Sufanose Jima, about thirty miles east of us. After sundown *Pintado* surfaced to proceed in accordance with our OpOrd, and set course 090 t for Pearl Harbor, heading for the barn at eighteen knots.

2–4 September These were surface-cruising days, but, being so close to Japan, we had to be doubly careful of aircraft patrols. Each day we had extra lookouts on the bridge. And each day we submerged for a time when a patrol was seen in the distance. None of them dropped any bombs, although several turned toward us in a threatening manner.

On 3 September Sofu Gan, the navigator's friend—that rock intrigued me—was reported by radar at thirty miles to the northeast, giving me a perfect point of departure.

Summary patrol results were radioed to ComSubPac, along with our ETA at Midway as daybreak on the tenth. That would be the second tenth of September for *Pintado*. We would cross the international date line on the first tenth, then set the calendar back one day.

The periscope shears of a U.S. submarine were sighted in midafternoon on the fourth at an estimated range of ten miles. The shears disappeared almost immediately, as if she had seen a patrol plane and submerged. Later, a plane did cause *Pintado* to submerge for a time. When we surfaced after half an hour, we hoped that we wouldn't be bothered any more by the enemy and could stay on the surface until we got home.

5–10 September   During the transit, as on all previous patrols, concentration was on getting qualifications completed and advancement in rating examinations finished. There were the usual lists of repairs to be made and spare parts and supplies to be loaded in Pearl Harbor.

Doug and Jerry settled in to sharpen their navigation skills so I could do more at getting ready for the repair period, bring our paperwork up to snuff, and generally take care of administration. We were passing through a lot of open ocean, so the navigation was not as critical as it would have been if we were working our way through islands, channels, shallow waters, and shoals.

With four of us in the wardroom whose wives were expecting babies (Robbie Robinson, Gerry Pettibone, Ed Frese, and myself), there was more than enough talk and anticipation.* Robbie had been doing more than his share of talking, so Gerry Pettibone and Bonny Bonjour decided to provide him with a message like the one he so eagerly asked the radiomen about every few hours. They made up a message that appeared quite genuine and slipped it into the regular radio schedule at a time when it was Robbie's turn to decode. (All the officers except the skipper and I took regular turns at decoding the radio traffic.)

Robbie waked me at midnight with the "news." The message read: LT ROBINSON OF PINTADO IS TO BE CONGRATULATED ON THE BIRTH OF TWIN GIRLS X THIS IS THE FIRST SUCH FEAT IN THE SUBMARINE FORCE THIS YEAR X MOTHER AND DAUGHTERS DOING FINE X. Robbie was excited. He had names, color of hair and eyes, everything down to lining up

---

*In fact there were actually five of us. Doug Morse was a sly one and never hinted that Margaret was pregnant. Only later did we find out that they also had a new arrival.

high-school dates for them. We had to let him know that it was a joke, so we faked another message, which Robbie would again receive on his turn for decoding: COMMANDER SUBMARINE FORCE FEELS HELPLESS BUT PASSES ON THE DOPE TO PINTADO THAT LT ROBINSON HIT THE JACKPOT WITH LATEST SCORE TWO BOYS AND ONE GIRL INSTEAD OF SCORE PREVIOUSLY SENT X SORRY X.

Robbie still didn't catch on, but after reading the messages a few times, and thinking and listening to sly wardroom comments and suggestions, he finally realized that it was all a joke. Wardroom humor could sometimes be cruel.

Second 10 September   *Pintado* arrived off Midway at daybreak, entered the harbor, and commenced taking on water and fuel. Departure time was set for midafternoon, with ETA at Pearl Harbor on the fourteenth.

The skipper, Bill Lawrence, and I had lunch with Commodores Mike Fenno, '25, and Lew Parks, '25, in the flag mess. It was so good to eat fresh fruit, fresh vegetables, lettuce, and tomatoes, although the absence of fresh milk was disappointing. The commodores gave us an update of the submarine war and made us all feel very good about what was being accomplished.

While bustling around getting things done in the limited time at Midway, I saw Freeland Carde, exec of *Pilotfish;* my longtime *Sculpin* exec and friend Charlie Henderson, now captain of *Bluefish;* Jack Cunningham, chief engineer of *Pilotfish;* and classmates Paul Loustaunau and Benny Germashausen. Butch Robbins, '34, CO of *Sterlet,* told me that Paul Schratz was somewhere on Midway, but I was so busy that I didn't get to see him.

The sub staff in Pearl Harbor had anticipated *Pintado*'s Midway arrival and had many bags of mail waiting there for us, official as well as personal, to read on the way to Pearl.

Pintado departed on schedule, heading east for Oahu in company with *Pilotfish* and *Bluefish.*

11–13 September   On the downhill run to Pearl, one item of concentration was to clean the boat thoroughly and have her spick and span. We knew that we would have plenty of high-powered visitors as soon as we tied up, but we also wanted to turn a very clean ship over to the relief crew so they would be obligated to keep things relatively clean and have them that way when we returned from the rest camp.

The skipper and Yeoman Flynn were busily polishing up the skipper's report of *Pintado*'s second patrol. Chick asked Bill Lawrence to pitch in and help. The details of the report had to be gathered from each department of the ship.

On 12 September I was skeptical when Robbie woke me at midnight with a message from ComSubPac which said: CONGRATULATIONS ARE IN ORDER FOR LCDR MENDENHALL X HIS SON WAS BORN THE SEVENTH X MOTHER AND SON ARE FINE X. Skepticism vanished when a flashing light messages of congratulations came over from *Pilotfish*, signed Freeland Carde and from Charlie Henderson on *Bluefish*. I got out boxes of cigars to pass around.

On the evening of the thirteenth the skipper and I were taking the air on the cigarette deck, talking over the patrol. We both had been noticing the radio messages with orders to officers, seeing several of my sub school and academy classmates ordered to command, among them classmates who had gone to sub school long after I did. He told me how much he appreciated my backing him up and that he expected that I would be moved to command during the refit period, but he really wanted me to make at least one more patrol with him, saying that he couldn't do without me. The compliments were appreciated, but I would have much preferred a command.

14 September   *Pintado* steamed triumphantly through the Pearl Harbor channel with a broom lashed to the top of the periscope shears, streaming a halyard of tiny Japanese flags, one for each ship sunk on patrols 1 and 2.

A pierful of friends, led by Admiral Lockwood and a band playing martial music, greeted us as we moored at the sub base. Lu Chappell was among the welcoming group, and was I glad to see him! Besides praise for our patrol results and congratulations for the recent births of children, the skipper's promotion to commander was announced, Jerry Mitchell made lieutenant (jg), and Harold Brantner was promoted from machinist to ensign.

The skipper submitted his report of *Pintado*'s second patrol, and at last I got to read a copy.

On her first two patrols *Pintado* was credited with sinking nine ships for a total of 77,300 tons, and damaging one ship of 6,300 tons.

The results of the second patrol, according to SubPac's awards criteria, meant that the skipper would be awarded the Navy Cross for the second time, and I would get the Silver Star for the third time.

Patrol Summary

Number of men on board	76
Number qualified, start patrol	48
Number qualified, end patrol	59
Number unqualified making first patrol	13
Number advanced in rating	3

Nautical miles covered:

Majuro to area		3,591
In area		4,255
Area to Pearl Harbor		4,930
	Total	12,776

Fuel used: 124,340 gallons (9.7 gal./mi.)

Duration:

Majuro to area		10 days
In area		29 days
Area to Pearl Harbor		14 days
	Total	53 days (submerged 28 days)

Endurance Factors:

Torpedoes remaining	8
Fuel remaining	9,860 gallons
Provisions remaining	20 days

Torpedoes fired: 16 (Six-foot depth settings were used on all torpedo attacks. The incendiary effects at that shallow setting were substantiated by the results.)

Sinkings:

1 transport, *Nagoya Maru* class	6,100	tons
1 transport, *Sinano Maru* class	6,300	tons
1 very large tanker, *Nissin (Tonan) Maru*	16,800	tons
1 large tanker, *Sunosaki Maru* class	9,800	tons
1 medium tanker, *San Diego Maru* class	7,300	tons
Total	46,300	tons

Refit in Pearl Harbor

14 September–9 October   A relief crew came aboard and took over the boat, and the officers and crew were immediately bussed to the submarine rest camp at the Royal Hawaiian Hotel. A few officers and men were scheduled to return to the boat each day to help the relief crew with their work. *Pintado* was in great condition, with only routine maintenance and minor repair items to be handled by the relief crew. A parade of friends dropped in for coffee and to give their applause.

One of the greeters I was particularly pleased to see was my cousin Lieutenant Elery Holland, USNR, from Beaumont, Texas. He was administrative assistant to the captain of the navy yard. We were together frequently during the refit and got together with our mutual cousin from Beaumont, Major Norman Kopke, whom I had seen just before *Pintado* left on her first patrol.

George Murray joined us at the Royal, determined to go out on the third patrol and prove that he had his seasickness problem whipped. Everyone enjoyed two weeks of sun and fun at Waikiki Beach. I took the opportunity to see my Hawaiian friends, played tennis every day, and swam frequently. There were social activities and dances, too. Almost daily I pressed one or another of the *Pintado* officers into playing tennis or going on some other excursion. They joked that they had to hide from me in order to get some rest.

We got back to the boat on the twenty-ninth with enough coral scratches, bruises, and sunburn from beach games and surfboard riding to keep Doc from getting rusty. The crew turned to, checking equipment, loading, and preparing to leave on patrol on 9 October. A new radar-detecting instrument, APR, was installed.

Shortly after we were all back aboard ship, the skipper and Jerry Mitchell went on deck with their new insignia and were promptly tossed overboard. They had completely forgotten that they were candidates for a dunking. Unfortunately, when Chick hit the water his class ring came off and was lost. Divers from the sub base searched but failed to find it.

On 2 October Commodore Joe Grenfell, '26, came aboard to formally present Submarine Combat pins to each officer and crew member. The skipper was pinned with his first Navy Cross, I got my second Silver Star, and the other officers and crew got their medals and commendations. The awards for our first patrol had caught up with us.

Don Irvine, a classmate of the skipper's, reported to make his PCO run with us. That made eleven officers in the wardroom; we would be crowded. I had hoped to make a patrol with just our own officers, but that seemed not to be in the cards. Then, at the last minute, Doug Morse was detached with orders to go to the sub base at New London, bringing the count of officers back to ten. It was difficult to see that valued shipmate taken away. We would all miss Doug's quiet, competent ways and steady, reliable hand.

Refresher training included three days of under-way work during which Lu Chappell was with us to check on *Pintado*'s readiness for patrol. He told me in confidence that my name was at the top of Admiral Lockwood's list of those who were in line to get command. The admiral had interviewed Lu to inquire about my readiness, and he remembered me well from his cruise on *Sculpin* and from our time together in Fremantle and Albany.

Pintado's Third Patrol

(9 October 1944–1 January 1945)

9 October   At 1320 *Pintado* was under way to commence operations as Task Group 17.16 (TG 17.16). We were heading for Saipan in company with *Atule* (Jack Maurer, '35) and *Jallao* (Joe Icenhower, '36) as a coordinated attack group. The skipper was the group commander. The name given to the group was Clarey's Crushers. The group was escorted by a PC until dark, then traveled the submarine safety lane toward Saipan, well north of Midway. At Saipan we were to fill the fuel and water tanks and get voyage repairs before going on to our patrol area.

For the first time *Pintado* was carrying twenty-four electric Mk-18 torpedoes; and we were eager to try out our new APR.

The Crushers' patrol area, code name Convoy College, was in Luzon Strait between Luzon and Formosa, extending into the South China Sea toward China, and also extending a short distance eastward beyond Luzon Strait. The patrol area was divided into rectangles, checkerboard style, in which boats could operate adjacent to each other, sharing information about contacts and coordinating attacks on enemy shipping. The squares were given the names of various universities in the United States: Yale, Harvard, Colgate, Princeton, and so on. In preparation for the patrol the captains and execs of the boats had met in Pearl Harbor to go over communications procedures and tactics.

After dark the skipper and I were on the cigarette deck talking over plans for the patrol. He told me that Admiral Lockwood wanted to take me off *Pintado* in preparation for my getting a command, but he had convinced him that he had to have me as exec for one more patrol. That set me back on my heels, particularly after Lu Chappell's remarks concerning the admiral's plans. I was simply speechless. Fortunately the night was quite dark and Chick couldn't see the disappointment on my face when I quickly excused myself to go below and do some paperwork.

10–20 October   En route to Saipan the Crushers conducted daily wolfpack-type communications drills, training dives, tracking drills, fire control problems, and school of the boat. Each boat, in rotation, acted as the target for one day, while the other two boats tracked it and made surface and submerged approaches.

Training and schools were again stressed. Of the seventy-eight men in the crew, thirty were unqualified and fifteen were on their first patrol, so there was the challenge to get as many as possible through qualification, training, and examinations.

A great deal of interesting information was in the official mail that arrived while we were in Pearl. Much of that material had been obtained from Japanese prisoners from Saipan, Guam, or Palau. There were also excerpts of translations from captured secret Japanese documents. All was encouraging and led me to be even more optimistic that the war would be over before too many more months.

I kept thinking about Chick's volunteering that he had convinced the admiral that he had to have me for one more patrol. There was nothing that I could do about it; the two Navy Crosses that we had earned for him carried too much weight. I had to put it out of my mind and do my job as best I could. My hope was that we would end the patrol in Pearl Harbor and I would at least get my command before the war was over.

Pintado skipped 14 October, the day we crossed the international date line, and set the calendar ahead from the thirteenth to the fifteenth.

A radio message on the eighteenth told of a daughter born to Dorothy Frese, Ed's wife. No news had been received of the fourth baby due, Gerry's expected child. So far I was the only one with a son.

The pile of official mail kept us busy. Instructions, information, orders, changes in instructions, and personnel matters all had to be digested and acted on. The bureaucrats had a latch on those fighting the war. My days were filled with the usual tasks: navigation, drills, school, and exec's work keeping tabs on what was going on throughout the ship.

The ship's welfare fund checked out in good shape. There was a balance of $800 when we got in from the second patrol. By the time we left on the third patrol we had spent it down to $150. The biggest expense was the ship's party at the Royal Hawaiian just before we went back to the boat. Softball equipment and volleyballs were another sizable expense.

At 1100 on the eighteenth, SD radar picked up an aircraft at twenty-four miles and made IFF identification as friendly, but *Atule* and *Jallao* signaled that they were submerging, not taking any chances, we guessed.

Just before leaving Pearl we had received a gift of four boxes containing 100 phonograph records, which were played over the ship's loudspeaker system. There were also a 16-mm movie projector, several feature movies, some Disney cartoons, and training films, all greatly appreciated. Another addition was a new ice cream freezer that made a gallon in only a few minutes. Volunteers were always on hand to operate the freezer.

Having George Murray back with us was great. He was so stable and dependable, and it wouldn't take him long to become qualified. He took over from me the conduct of Sunday church services. After all, he was a divinity student turned submarine warrior. So far we had been experiencing only mild weather. George was hoping for some rougher going to test himself and to try out the medication that the doctors sent with him, just in case.

During the refit a minor change of shipboard duties took place: George Murray became assistant engineer and Brant Brantner replaced Doug Morse as first lieutenant.

On the nineteenth the Crushers entered the Saipan eastern safety lane.

On the twentieth I was catching up with recreational reading: the *New Yorker* magazine. An article caught my eye concerning strange place names in the United States. There was Winnie, Texas, where I had lived for the first eleven years of my life. While we were at the sub base a seaman named James Saunders had come by to see me. He had learned from mutual friends in Winnie that I was on board *Pintado*. We enjoyed talking about Winnie.

Radio news on the twentieth was full of the Allied landings at Leyte in the Philippines. The shortwave radio programs must have been intended for the Filipinos, with statements like: "MacArthur is fulfilling his solemn pledge, 'I shall return.'" It all sounded good, pointing toward an end to the war.

After lunch I went to the bridge for some fresh air. It wouldn't be long before we would be submerged during the daytime. Rain was threatening, then it began to come down in torrents. I took off my clothes down to skivvy shorts and enjoyed a good soaking. The tropical downpour felt good. I could hear the static electricity crackling on the radio antennas and in the periscope shears.

PCO Don Irvine settled quietly into his niche, taking turns as OOD, helping with decoding messages, watching the skipper as he managed his ship, and taking a part with the conning tower team during torpedo fire control activities.

21 October   After midnight, approaching Saipan, we passed Sarigan Island abeam to starboard, eleven miles away. At 0440 SJ radar made contact with our escort, *PGM-9;* we exchanged recognition signals and set course for the Saipan entrance at four-engine speed. Jap submarines might be waiting for a target, and we hoped that high speed would help *Pintado* evade them. At 1000 we passed through the submarine nets at Tanapag Harbor entrance, and twenty-five minutes later we were moored alongside sub tender *Fulton*.

Alongside *Fulton*, *Pintado* received every courtesy and service from ComSubRon 8 and the tender. We topped off with 39,350 gallons of fuel. Experts from the tender helped with minor repairs to the sonar equipment and to one hydraulic system. Conferences were held with the skippers of *Atule* and *Jallao* to complete plans for our work in Convoy College.

No mail was waiting for us at Saipan. There were many things of a higher priority than mail for a passing boat.

We thought that the security of the island must be well in hand, but were told that many nights fifteen to twenty Japs were killed or rounded up in the hills. We were allowed to go ashore in groups to very restricted areas, and then were required to carry weapons, ready to fire. We were warned to be constantly alert, to stay away from certain places, and to keep a special watch on deck at night to look for Jap swimmers who might try to get aboard on suicide missions. One of the seaplanes had been blown up by a swimmer a few nights before we came in. The swimmer tossed a grenade into the plane and was himself killed in the explosion.

The skipper went to lunch with the commodore and made arrangements for a staff car to take a few of us on a sightseeing trip. Adventurous crew members proposed that they take a couple of machine guns and go to the beach for a picnic, but that project was stopped in its tracks.

The lines were hardly secured alongside *Fulton* when I was surrounded by a dozen men from the local sub refit and repair organization wanting to know if we could take them with us when we left. Apparently they didn't like conditions on Saipan. The attitude was entirely different from Sub Base Pearl, where the entrenched staff was happy to stay comfortably in place. Unfortunately for the relief crewmen, we were far over allowance anyway, as a cushion against anticipated orders to transfer veteran qualified men to new construction or other urgent duty when we got in from patrol.

A great deal of activity was visible from our vantage point in the harbor. There were fifteen, twenty, even forty planes in the air at one time, every hour of the day. Earth-moving equipment was operating around the clock, building roads, completing a giant airport and other installations.

Bonny and I got a jeep and driver from the *Fulton* pool, and he drove us to the large plateau on top of the mountains where an airfield had been constructed for B-29s. I had never seen such huge earth-moving machines. From a distance they were like giant ants, busily adding airfield facilities around parked planes.

The villages were in shambles, beaten to a pulp by bombing and shelling from the navy guns. Some work was in progress to restore conditions to normal after all the devastation. The more I saw of the mud and dust, the more I was convinced that on board ship was the best place to be. We heard firsthand stories from marines. They had gruesome tales.

I was invited to dinner in the wardroom of the *Fulton* by a shipmate from my *Mississippi* days. Lieutenant Earl Ferrell was an electrician's mate in those days; now he was the assistant repair officer, and the repair officer was Lieutenant Commander Jim Flannigan, whom I first met on Midway. After a dinner of breaded veal cutlets, we went to see the movie being shown on deck. The movie was a stinker, but it was interrupted by a rainstorm just as I was going to sleep, which allowed me to go home early gracefully. I had been on my feet much of the night before, piloting *Pintado* into Saipan.

22–27 October   At 0927 the Crushers were under way, proceeding out of Tanapag Harbor and setting a westerly course in the safety lane toward Convoy College. The route would take us along latitude 20° N, through Balintang Channel, between Luzon and Formosa.

During a midafternoon trim dive number 2 auxiliary tank leaked in 5,500 pounds of water in twenty minutes. That leakage hadn't occurred during dives on the way to Saipan. Back on the surface, Eric Bailey's repair team found that the gasket on the manhole cover to that tank was faulty. The ocean was quite calm, so *Pintado* stopped to lie to and permit repairmen on deck to fix the leak. The manhole cover was removed, a new gasket was installed, and tests showed that the leakage was stopped. Elapsed time for the repairs was thirty-five minutes.

While we were running on the surface at night, either the skipper or I was on the bridge all night long. At the sub base at Pearl we had a bench installed on the after rail of the cigarette deck, and it came in mighty handy for those night duties. It was a place to sit, think, make plans, and even catch a nap once in a while.

One night I remembered that at home in Anahuac, Texas, it was the time of year for duck and goose hunting. When I was at home I helped to keep the refrigerator stocked with game and fish. We were approaching Thanksgiving, and in Texas on that holiday we would probably be eating shrimp or crab cocktail, roast goose with rice, giblet gravy, oyster dressing, sweet potatoes, broccoli, or cauliflower. Just thinking about it made me hungry.

Twice during the day on the twenty-third we saw friendly planes, exchanged signals with them, and went on our way. On the twenty-fourth *Atule* reported sighting an enemy submarine periscope, which she avoided. Then *Jallao* reported seeing a periscope. The contacts were within fifteen minutes of each other and too far apart to have been the same sub.

At 0815 on the twenty-fifth we received instructions from ComSubPac to form a scouting line along the safety lane between longitudes 128° E and 129° E to be on the lookout for possible enemy cripples from the naval battle in progress off the east coast of the Philippines, south of our position.* As soon as the message was decoded *Pintado* went to flank speed, continuing west, and instructed *Jallao* and *Atule* to take positions twenty miles to east and west of 128°30′ E. *Pintado* would be the pivot at 128°30′ E.

Shortly after noon ComSubPac modified his orders, moving the center position one degree to the west; so we kept on west at flank speed and reached that position near sunset.

Just after sunset a radio message from the wolfpack to the south of us, Roach's Raiders (named for their commander, Beetle Roach, '32), said that they were in contact with enemy navy ships, giving the position and speed of the contact. *Pintado* promptly set course at twenty knots to intercept the Raiders' contact. The other Crushers would, by preagreement, also head for the Raiders' contact.

At 2022 *Jallao* radioed that she was in contact with and tracking an unidentified ship, and after another forty-five minutes she reported her position and that the contact was on course 030 t, speed fourteen knots. *Pintado* adjusted course to intercept, still at twenty knots. We were squeezing every possible horsepower from our four diesel engines.

Three minutes after the *Jallao* report, *Pintado* made radar contact with a single ship to southwest at a range of 21,000 yards and sent a contact report to *Atule* and *Jallao*. Tracking showed that our contact was zigzagging between courses 000 and 035 t, at thirteen knots. We advised the Crushers of our tracking results.

After maneuvering for another thirty minutes our SJ radar picked up

*This was the Battle of Leyte Gulf, characterized by Clay Blair in his book *Silent Victory* as the greatest naval engagement in the history of the world. U.S. admirals Halsey and Kincaid defeated the Japanese forces commanded by admirals Kurita, Nishimura, Ozawa, and Shima.

Jallao ahead of the enemy, and we exchanged information by shielded light signals, giving her our solution of enemy course and speed. Running ahead of the enemy, at 2200 the skipper directed *Jallao* to attack, advising her that we would go in after she completed her attack.

From the larger than usual size of the pip on the radar screen and what we could see of the target in the moonlight, we thought it was a battleship. The skipper's plan was to continue tracking the target, staying on the surface while *Jallao* attacked, and be ready to shift position as necessary for our attack should *Jallao* not sink the target or should the target zig away. At the same time we were coaching *Atule* into position so she could attack after *Pintado*.

These were tense minutes. At 2230 we could see the target at 16,000 yards. Clouds temporarily shadowed the moon, then cleared away. In the moonlight we identified our target as a light cruiser. He had two widely separated masts and large, prominent stacks. We continued to run ahead of the cruiser, ready for our turn to attack should that be necessary.

At 2308 *Pintado* headed directly toward the target, prepared to attack right after *Jallao*. Then we heard three tremendous explosions spaced ten seconds apart. The target was at 15,000 yards. We could see a slight puff of smoke as radar reported that the target's pip became fuzzy, then disappeared from the screen. The starboard lookout reported that he saw a searchlight beam for a few seconds, pointing downward in the smoke. A few minutes later there was one more explosion. *Pintado* increased speed to flank and stood toward the last bearing of the target for twenty minutes. Nothing was sighted or picked up on radar. The cruiser had disappeared.*

As midnight approached we contacted *Jallao* by keying the sonar and advised her that she should surface. She came up just before midnight and, with signal lamps, we exchanged information about her attack. *Atule* was on the surface 7,500 yards to the northeast and moved in to join the conversation. Everyone was elated over *Jallao*'s success.

At 0005 on 26 October the Crushers formed a scouting line, east-to-west, searching to the north for other ships moving north from the battle. Most of the remainder of the night was spent reading radio reports, plotting intercepts, and looking for remnants of the Japanese fleet. At 0200 we sent ComSubPac a report of *Jallao*'s success. At 0330 the last position of enemy forces came in from ComSubPac as we continued searching to

---

*The ship was later identified as the light cruiser *Tama,* retreating toward Japan from our naval victory in the Battle of Leyte Gulf. Joe Icenhower, on his first attack of the war, had sunk an enemy cruiser.

the north as far as latitude 24° N in order to cover all possible escape routes of enemy ships toward Japan.

At 1100 the Crushers reversed course, moving back to the south and continuing the search. During the day we heard contact reports from *Silversides* and *Trigger* on the wolfpack radio circuit, but their contacts were too far to the northwest for us to pursue. Finally, in midafternoon ComSubPac instructed the Crushers to terminate the search and proceed on to Convoy College, so we set course for Luzon Strait.

At 0427, 27 October, *Pintado* crossed the eastern boundary of Convoy College, moving toward Luzon Strait's Balintang Channel. During midafternoon we sighted Batan Island to northwest. Radar gave a range of twenty-five miles as *Pintado* continued toward Balintang Channel. Shortly after sighting Batan, the starboard lookout saw a periscope near the starboard beam at about 800 yards. Don Irvine, OOD, rang up flank speed and turned away to avoid possible torpedoes as the skipper and I made an emergency run to the bridge to see what was going on. Don was understandably tense as he explained what had happened.

Returning to a westerly course, *Pintado* submerged twelve miles east of Balintang Island to approach the channel underwater and make the run through the channel on the surface after dark.

We surfaced at sundown, and forty-five minutes later passed Balintang Island to port at eight miles, continuing west. We would commence patrol in our square at midnight.

28 October   Before sunrise *Pintado* submerged in her square thirty-six miles west of Balintang Island. Boats were rotated in the squares of Convoy College on a calendar schedule. Roach's Raiders were in nearby squares. The other Raiders were *Halibut* (Pete Galantin, who made his PCO cruise with us in *Sculpin*) and *Tuna* (Steve Steffanides, my sub school classmate).

Each day we were expected to be in our square on the checkerboard and report any contacts to the other Crusher boats. *Pintado*'s skipper, Crusher group commander, would coordinate group attacks. During the first five minutes of each hour the boats were to come to fifty feet and listen on the SD antenna for possible radio messages from our group or from other wolfpacks. The day was uneventful, and after sunset we all surfaced and set course for the next day's square.

The movie projector that we got in Pearl was getting extensive use. We had exchanged movies in Saipan. The crew enjoyed some of the movies so much that they were shown over and over. Sometimes the projector was set up in the wardroom and movies were shown right there.

29 October We submerged before sunrise twelve miles northwest of Cape Bojeador Light, on the northwest point of Luzon. All was quiet until 1103, when the tops of a destroyer were seen to southwest at about twelve miles. Tracking showed a speed of sixteen knots, heading for the Babuyan Channel, zigzagging thirty degrees right and left of a course of due east. At 1105 we went to battle stations, but by 1143 it was apparent that we couldn't get close enough for an attack. Our closest approach was 8,000 yards.

We continued toward Luzon's Cape Bojeador, hoping that the destroyer would return or that he was an advance screen for other shipping. By noon the destroyer was no longer in sight, and we saw nothing more until midafternoon, when an Emily flying boat was observed headed south toward Manila.

After sunset we surfaced to set course for the next day's square. The new area was out of sight of any land.

My interest was aroused by a bulletin from the Bureau of Personnel, asking for applications from officers of my academy class to go to the postgraduate school at Annapolis to study ordnance engineering. The course would last for one and a half to two and a half years.

That bulletin, my conviction that the submarine war was rapidly drawing to an end, and my diminishing expectation of getting a command caused me to think very seriously about sending in an application. One of my career aims, developed over the years since graduation, was to go to graduate school to take the ordnance engineering course. It seemed to me to be good training for my future. The school wouldn't start until July 1945, and, the way the war was progressing, by then submarine action would be pretty well over. I might still be able to squeeze in a short command and go to school afterward.

When I let my thoughts be known, the skipper was negative, doubting that Admiral Lockwood would let me go. Chick was not much of a believer in technical schools and postgraduate training. He was not at all encouraging. His remark was, "They can't teach you anything that will be of professional help."

30 October *Pintado* submerged before sunrise in her square of the day. Just after noon two twin-engine bombers were seen flying north. The day was quiet but the weather was kicking up—the seas were getting very rough and the wind was increasing. After sunset we surfaced and set course for the next day's square, fighting huge waves and gale-force winds.

31 October By daybreak, when *Pintado* submerged, the weather was even worse. It was miserable all day submerged, trying to keep decent depth for a periscope watch, exposing the SD antenna once each hour. When we surfaced at sunset the weather continued overcast, gloomy, and raining. Seas were very rough. George was getting along fine; he wasn't sick at all and complained that he had a bottle of seasickness pills that he hadn't needed to use. The seas had bounced the boat around even at 150 feet, usually a depth where things smoothed out.

1 November By 0105 the seas had calmed some, then a report came from *Jallao* that she had a radar contact 26,000 yards from her position. *Jallao*'s contact was on course 120 t, speed fifteen knots; but at the same time we made a contact in the other direction at 28,450 yards and began tracking that. Several times previously we had made false contacts on heavy rainstorms, but we set out in pursuit anyway. After fifteen minutes our contact was evaluated as false, so we turned to follow up on *Jallao*'s contact. The weather was a factor to contend with. Waves were Force 5 from the northwest, and an end around on a fifteen-knot target would be very difficult. Nevertheless we kept plugging away.

At 0225 we made radar contact with *Jallao* at 7,450 yards and changed to an easterly course to try to get ahead of her contact. At 0304 additional information from *Jallao* indicated that we were sixteen miles south of her contact. We were heading directly into the pounding sea and continuously taking green water over the bridge. The best speed we could make was fourteen and a half knots, and that was very uncomfortable. By 0351 we decided that our position was hopeless in that heavy weather, so we set course for our next station and at daybreak submerged for the day, happy to be underwater where it was calm.

The weather had moderated when *Pintado* surfaced after sunset. The bridge watch soon reported possible smoke to the northwest. We came to a northwesterly course to investigate at seventeen knots. An hour later the smoke was not confirmed, so we slowed and set course for the next station.

2 November At daylight we submerged for another quiet day.

I had a brilliant home-handyman idea for displaying my personal snapshots in the three-man bunkroom. I talked Eric Bailey, the auxiliaryman, out of a piece of Plexiglas, cut it to size, drilled holes in the corners, and mounted it on my locker. The plastic was only the size of a sheet of legal paper, but I could slip a few snapshots behind it and have them to look at whenever I wanted instead of always having to pull things out of the locker. That started a trend, and in a short time other shipmates followed the exec's example. Eric complained that we were depleting his stock of Plexiglas.

At sundown *Pintado* surfaced to move on to the next square in the checkerboard. Thirty minutes later SJ radar signals were picked up, and we exchanged recognition signals with *Atule*.

Then, in midevening, we received a message from ComSubPac giving the route of a Jap naval force moving through the western edge of Convoy College, so *Pintado* set course 161 t at twenty knots to intercept them. When we radioed *Atule* and *Jallao* they replied that they had received ComSubPac's message and, anticipating our signal, were already moving that way at twenty knots.

3 **November**   Several times during the previous evening strong signals were detected at 176 mc (megacycle) on the APR, indicating aircraft nearby, and at midnight we received a very weak signal from *Jallao* telling us that she had been forced down by an aircraft using 176-mc radar.

At 0600 we were in position ahead of the anticipated Jap force on the track provided by ComSubPac, and at 0625 we submerged for the day. Nothing was seen.

At midafternoon we surfaced in daylight in order to copy any late radio traffic from ComSubPac concerning the message of the night before; and forty-five minutes later a contact report was relayed by ComSubPac from China-based planes concerning a Jap force of one aircraft carrier, one heavy cruiser or battleship, and three destroyers, located southwest of *Pintado*.

A search plan was initiated, with *Atule* and *Jallao* joining *Pintado* on a scouting line, searching to the southwest at eighteen knots. After sundown we radioed ComSubPac to tell him of our action and to point out our position. We were far out of our patrol area, eighty miles southwest of Convoy College.

Moonrise was just after sundown, almost a full moon. Twenty minutes later we made radar contact with a very large ship north of us at a range of 17,500 yards. We had been using the SJ radar sparingly in order not to give away our presence.

A few minutes later, with the horizon clearing as the moon rose higher, we could see the largest enemy ship that any of us had ever seen: a *Shokaku*-class carrier.

Pintado put on twenty knots and turned south to stay ahead of the carrier while tracking him. After a few more minutes of tracking we radioed a contact report to our group but got a receipt only from *Atule*.

At 2106 we went to battle stations, and at 2107 we sent our solution of the enemy course and speed to *Atule,* but we were still unable to raise *Jallao*. Ten minutes later we again sent *Atule* the enemy's position, base course 180 t, speed twenty-one knots, and informed her that we were going to submerge and attack.

The carrier was zigzagging, on six-minute legs, forty degrees to the right and left of his base course, which permitted us to stay ahead of him on our steady course at emergency flank speed.

The moon was quite bright, and the carrier was plainly visible, as were the masts of two ships, one on either side of him. Target zigs could be seen from the bridge, and the radar operator could tell a zig by the pip resolution on the A-scope. Radar could see no evidence from the enemy force that they had radar in operation, but there was SJ interference from the northeast, east of the target group.*

We submerged after another five minutes of tracking, anticipating the next enemy zig. The range had closed to 15,500 yards. The skipper planned to reach a position between the carrier and the port screen destroyer, then fire six fish at the carrier from the bow tubes, at the same time setting up the Mk-VIII angle solver to fire four fish from the stern tubes at the port screen. It was an ambitious plan, but with the TDC checking beautifully, it seemed quite reasonable.

Sonar reported pinging from the direction of the target, but we knew that their speed was too high for them to operate their sound gear effectively. Nevertheless we rigged for depth charge. The bright moon made the targets visible by periscope as if it were daylight. The TDC solution was such that all Ed Frese had to do was enter the zigs at the predicted times and verify them by periscope, and the solution tracked perfectly.

At 2140 *Shokaku* could be seen to have one destroyer screening on each beam and a light cruiser astern. The port destroyer was of the *Terutsuki* class. Seven minutes later it was apparent that we couldn't quite make the skipper's desired position inside the screen, so at 2147 *Pintado* fired at the carrier from a position outside the screen. This was a spread of six Mk-18 fish from the bow tubes, with a run of 2,200 yards.

*Later, we learned that the interference was from *Jallao*, who, unknown to us, was trailing the enemy force.

Just as the fish were fired, the port screen destroyer lined up abreast the center of the carrier. Our periscope dipped under immediately after firing because of the large amount of water taken through the forward poppets, and none of the hits could be observed, but four very loud explosions were heard and felt in *Pintado*.

Back at periscope depth eight minutes later, the skipper could see that the destroyer had shielded the carrier from being hit, and he described the destroyer being rocked by another explosion, forward, completely obscuring the carrier from view. An immense cloud of smoke, fire, more brilliant explosions, and tracers rose in the moonlight. Two minutes later the destroyer's stern projected up in the air at an angle of thirty degrees, rudder and propellers exposed, as he headed for the bottom of the South China Sea. A few seconds later his depth charges blew up with a tremendous explosion that jolted *Pintado*.

The carrier and cruiser made an emergency turn to starboard, heading directly away from us. The carrier appeared to be listing to port, or so we hoped, but he soon straightened up, so the skipper may have seen him recovering from his emergency turn to starboard. Still, we were unconvinced that all four explosions were from fish hitting the destroyer.

Two remaining destroyers commenced an attack on a contact at some distance from us, during which they dropped forty depth charges. *Pintado* remained at periscope depth, reloading torpedoes, in hope of getting a shot at one of them; but just before midnight their last depth charge went off and they departed to rejoin their formation before we could close in. I liked our more aggressive attitude.

4 November Right at midnight *Pintado* surfaced and exchanged calls with *Atule* by SJ radar. At 0100 a report of the attack was sent to ComSubPac. At 0145 our radio copied a contact report on the FOX schedule which *Jallao* had sent the previous evening. She was attempting to tell us that she was in contact and following the enemy formation, trying to lead us to her contact. She reported that her radio hadn't been working properly during the hours when we both were stalking the enemy formation.

As *Pintado* was returning to Convoy College on the surface after sunrise, the lookouts sighted *Atule* to the northeast ten miles away. By 1000 we were close enough to exchange visual signals. While sending visual signals she announced on the voice radio that she was diving from an airplane. The sky was perfectly clear, and no plane was in sight, nor did radar have any contact, so we didn't dive, keeping on toward station on the surface. At noon *Atule* was sighted well astern of *Pintado,* and we made no further attempt to communicate by visual signals.

During the late afternoon the engineers converted number 4 fuel ballast tank to a main ballast tank.

In the light of day, we plotted the attack on the carrier force and analyzed our information to determine, if possible, where and on which ships the hits had been made. Four hits in the destroyer seemed very unlikely, particularly since visual evidence indicated that the destroyer was hit forward, with his stern remaining practically intact. It was our conviction that at least one, and possibly two, of the fish hit the carrier. Two solutions were possible based on the timing of the explosions and other data: two hits in the carrier and two in the destroyer, or one hit in the carrier and three in the destroyer.*

5–12 November   Days became monotonous—surfacing after sundown, submerging before sunup—as the Crushers rotated to their assigned squares of the Convoy College checkerboard, watching and waiting for enemy movements. We saw no enemy ships.

The weather was generally bad and heavily overcast. Getting star sights to fix our position was impossible, and we were too far from land for a radar fix. Several times we surfaced during the day when the sun came out briefly so I could take sun lines. The evening of the twelfth I got the first good fix in four days and found that we were thirty miles south of our DR position, outside the patrol area.

After sunset on the twelfth we received *Gunnel*'s contact report of a *Yamato*-class battleship and a *Tone*-class cruiser coming north at eighteen knots, position reported as latitude 21°00′ N, longitude 118°42′ E. The skipper formed the Crushers on a scouting line to intercept, moving to the southwest, estimating that the enemy ships were headed for Bako in the Pescadores, or to Takao.

13 November   At 0312 we received a contact report from *Jallao* saying that she had a contact fifteen miles ahead of *Pintado*'s position, so we added speed to close the contact.

During the hour between 0300 and 0400 *Pintado* was queried by radio from ComSubGroup 17.12 concerning a report of a damaged submarine. Evidently they had copied a message on the radio circuit from a submarine

---

*On the basis of intelligence information *Pintado* was later credited with one, possibly two, hits on the *Shokaku*-class carrier.

that they couldn't identify, and they wanted to check the Crushers to see if one of our group might be in trouble. We reported that all three Crushers were okay.

At 0415 we asked *Jallao* for an update on her contact. She reported that she was still stalking the enemy formation on course 040 t, at speed sixteen knots. She asked if we were in contact, evidently holding off her attack until we were. We replied that we did not hold her contact. That was our last communication from *Jallao* for twelve hours.

At 0549 we heard several explosions, and from that decided that *Jallao* had finally attacked.* At 0551 radar made intermittent contact to northeast, range 37,000 yards. *Pintado* changed course to close but made no further radar contact after five minutes. Then, at 0612, we received *Atule*'s position, course, and speed, and information that she had made no contacts. At 0710 *Atule* informed us that she was diving from an airplane. Just before noon *Atule* reported that for a time she had had contact with a *Tahio*-class carrier escorted by one heavy cruiser and one destroyer on a northerly course, speed twenty, but they had gotten away. Finally, at 1225 we abandoned any further search and headed for our assigned station.

Sun lines during the morning indicated that we were about eighteen miles from our DR position. The foul weather for the past five days had worked to our disadvantage. Our doubtful position made it almost impossible to find a particular spot in the ocean. We made no contact with *Gunnel*'s battleship force. *Gunnel*'s position was probably as incorrect as ours was. *Atule* must have stumbled onto another group of ships to the west of our area that were headed toward Bako, Formosa.

An hour after sundown the APR began receiving signals on the 150-mc band. This continued all night and was diagnosed as coming from night search planes over the area. *Pintado* moved to the next day's square in the Bashi Channel, north of Luzon.

14 November   Before sunrise we submerged for the day in Bashi Channel. All day long we saw search planes over the area. Surfacing during daylight would have been very dangerous. At 1213 we heard three distant explosions. Twenty minutes later there were three more. Then, after another twenty minutes, sonar picked up pinging, followed by eight distant explosions and then more pinging. Action was obviously taking place in the area adjacent to *Pintado*.

---

*She later reported that she fired six fish at a *Takao*-class cruiser about 0549.

At 1253 the tops of a large, four-goal cargo ship were sighted to the south, along with the tops of two more cargo ships. Five minutes later *Pintado* came up to shallow depth, then broached, in order to get a better look. The four-poster was a type similar to *Atutsan Maru*. The convoy was too far out of our reach to attempt to close. Several types of planes were screening the convoy.

The closest we got to the ships was about twelve miles. Course of the convoy was northwest toward Takao, speed ten knots. We couldn't close them submerged, and the air cover prevented surfacing for an end around or even to get off a radio contact report.

Later in the afternoon sonar heard pinging, and immediately afterward the tops of a destroyer were sighted about ten miles behind the convoy, too far away for *Pintado* to attack. By dusk the convoy would be well up the west coast of Formosa. *Pintado* had expended a lot of precious oil chasing warships. It was our first opportunity to attack a convoy, and we couldn't get in. The air cover was the heaviest that we had ever seen over any convoy. It appeared that the Japanese were employing a distant air-screen covering twenty to thirty miles ahead and on both bows of the convoy, an inner air screen covering the immediate waters through which the convoy would pass, then a screen astern and on the quarter to prevent end arounds.

After sundown SJ radar picked up interference to the southwest. We attempted to exchange recognition signals but received no intelligible reply. Then, at 2000, radar was finally able to read the signals. They were coming from *Halibut*. Pete Galantin asked us to please close in, but with caution because his steering was damaged. *Pintado* cranked on flank speed and moved in. Radar contact was made at 12,000 yards as we continued closing.

From the distance of a few yards we talked with Pete for an hour, using the signal light and power megaphone. *Halibut* had been gravely damaged in the depth charging we heard earlier in the day. Her radio was out of commission and the interior of the boat was in shambles; and Pete asked us to transmit the damage information to ComSubPac. Further, he asked *Pintado* to stand by *Halibut* as she headed for Saipan, until their radio was repaired.

The skipper replied that we would be glad to accompany her and be of any assistance possible. *Halibut* soon made temporary repairs enabling her to steer a relatively steady course, so together we headed east toward Saipan at fifteen knots.*

* *Halibut*'s ordeal is described in detail by her wartime skipper, Admiral I. J. Galantin,

With all the excitement nearby, it was near midnight before *Pintado* got a message off to *Atule* and *Jallao* informing them of our intention to accompany *Halibut* toward Saipan and directing *Atule* to take command of the wolfpack until our return.

Then *Pintado* sent a message to ComSubPac concerning *Halibut*'s condition and our action in accompanying her toward Saipan.

15 November   *Halibut* submerged for a trim dive at 0545. Underwater for only a few minutes, she surfaced to report that she could dive, should it be imperative.

Pintado also made a trim dive at 0558, quickly surfacing to continue toward Saipan. At 1100 orders were received from ComSubPac to accompany *Halibut* all the way to Saipan. Since *Halibut*'s radios weren't functioning, we relayed ComSubPac's message to Pete with the signal light.

During the midday period we sighted *Pampanito, Besugo,* and *Searaven,* all heading for patrol in Luzon Strait. Another unidentified U.S. submarine was sighted, too far away to challenge, but from the silhouette we knew she was a friend. The waters were swarming with U.S. submarines.

16–18 November   During the trip to Saipan we were on the surface continually, holding field days, getting everything shined up to have a very clean ship and conduct captain's inspection while in port. There was also the usual paperwork, training, maintenance, repairs, and other routine work going on. I regularly exchanged position reports with Guy Gugliotta, '38, exec of *Halibut,* checking our navigation.

The quiet period gave us an opportunity to hold two court-martials: one for a torpedoman who went to sleep on watch, the other for an electrician's mate who lied to an officer. The torpedoman was reduced in rating from second class to third class and fined $40. The electrician had lied on three occasions and admitted it at the trial, so he lost his rating and was reduced to fireman first class. The exec had a busy week cracking down on a few people who thought that they could relax and let things go to pot now that we were out of the war zone.

19–25 November   At 0610 on 19 November *PC 1126* met *Halibut* and *Pintado* to escort them to Saipan, and at 1134 *Pintado* moored starboard side to sub tender *Fulton. Halibut* then moored alongside us.

---

in *Take Her Deep: A Submarine against Japan in World War II* (Chapel Hill, N.C.: Algonquin Books, 1987).

Reports on *Halibut* were that she was too gravely damaged to be repaired at Saipan. She would go to Pearl Harbor for more expert inspection and a decision as to how, or even if, she could be repaired.

During the stay in Tanapag Harbor the tender assisted our crew in cleaning both evaporators, repairing the main hydraulic system, which had been pounding severely while charging the accumulator, repairing a bad hydraulic leak in the port sound head, and renewing the muffler on number 1 main engine. The torpedomen loaded six Mk-18 torpedoes, and the engineers topped off the tanks with diesel fuel and lube. Departure date was set for 23 November.

I found a number of friends on the tender, among them classmate Paul Schratz. Frustrated over his experiences in the submarine war, Paul was waiting for an assignment on some submarine, any good submarine.* We got together for meals a few times in the tender's wardroom and to see movies on her deck. He found a sympathetic ear.

The navy was operating recreation clubs ashore, one for enlisted men and one for officers, where they could buy drinks and relax over games of liar's dice and acey-deucey, tell tall tales, or read.

In the Navy Club bar one afternoon we saw Lieutenant Henry Fonda with officers from one of the surface ships. Robbie, after a few drinks made him bold, went over to shake hands with his "old pal, Henry." Fonda gave him the cold shoulder, and Robbie got considerable ribbing over the incident.

I took the day off on the twenty-first to tour the island, in a station wagon this time, with a group of our officers. There were many B-29 bombers at the air base. We drove to one and were permitted to go aboard. They were huge planes.

Aircraft were in the air over Saipan constantly. From the air base on top of the plateau we could see the nearby island of Tinian, where there was another B-29 base, and from which there was another swarm of planes landing and taking off.

We also went through a prisoner-of-war camp. The prisoners tried to hide from us and we didn't want to stay long, pitying their plight.

We felt much more pity for the pathetic natives. Those poor people, homes completely leveled, were living in hovels made by propping a few pieces of cardboard or sheet iron on stakes. Their conditions were terrible. We were told that housing facilities were being constructed but didn't see them. That would make things better. I sympathized with the impover-

---

*He eventually went to be Jack Maurer's exec in *Atule*.

ished women most of all, with children to take care of. They appeared
cheerful enough, but they had no privacy, so they washed their clothes
and themselves standing naked by a few water wells, and went about their
tasks with tattered rags wrapped around them. Many families had small
gardens to tend. Youngsters stood in groups, seemingly all day long,
watching the hundreds of U.S. Army, Navy and Marine vehicles of various
types that churned the muddy roads into a quagmire.

We drove around the island for three hours, sightseeing, looking at the
devastated villages, and viewing our army and marine encampments.
There was no doubt about the mass of Allied military power on Saipan.
The scenery, as we drove through the hills, was attractive. We drove under
one natural bridge, but we watched the roadsides carefully because we
were told that there were still Japs hiding out in some of the caves.

Half of our crew went to a beach for a beer and steak cookout on the
twenty-second. They returned with a small piglet, calling it "Saipan Charlie," and wanted to keep it as a mascot. They were promptly sent ashore
to release the pig.

Spearfish came alongside to moor, and in the process hit *Pintado*'s port
propeller. Divers found two bent blades. That meant we would have to
go into the floating dry dock for a new screw. We had to wait our turn.
Other boats were in line ahead of *Pintado,* and our turn wouldn't be until
the twenty-fifth, so I made arrangements for trucks to take more of the
crew on sightseeing trips and another picnic–beach party.

An interesting feature of military life at Saipan was the army and navy
nurses. Commodores and staff officers were busily squiring the nurses
around to dinner or the movies, and reportedly engaging in liaisons in
staterooms on the tender and other navy ships. The army nurses were
eager to get invitations to meals, where the food was much more palatable
than in the camps on shore. Gossip had it that a little trading was going
on.

Before noon on 25 November *Pintado* entered ARD 25 to have the
damaged propeller replaced. Since we were in dry dock anyway, it seemed
only appropriate to take advantage of the opportunity to scrape and paint
Pintado's bottom. That just might let us squeeze an added fraction of a
knot out of the engines when we really needed speed.

Previously the task of scraping and painting had been done by a civilian
crew or some other labor force. This time, on the front line, that job
became an all-hands enterprise with our own crew, just as once happened
on *Sculpin.* Everyone took part—cooks, radiomen, radar technicians, en-

ginemen, torpedomen, firemen, seamen, and quartermasters, with officers leading the way. Without exception, everyone had to go over the side to clean the ship's bottom. When that news was broadcast, the howls were immediate.

It took some prodding to convince the officers and crew that we really meant it. Very few in *Pintado* had ever done that kind of dirty manual labor, the officers in particular. Such grimy work—scraping, wire brushing, and cleaning the sides and bottom—was a little below the dignity of many. There was some grumbling and hanging back, and some disappeared, only to be sought out and brought back to the job. We finally convinced everyone that we meant business. The skipper, meanwhile, was involved in a long conference on board *Fulton,* so he missed the fun.

Everyone rode floats rigged along the sides of the sub as the water was pumped out of the dock—scraping, wire brushing, and cleaning—until the floats reached the well deck of the dry dock. We finished just before midnight, and tools were put away and secured. Tired and very dirty, everyone was ready to clean up for a little sleep during what remained of the night. Repair crew painters went right to work applying anticorrosive, antifouling, and bottom paint with their special painting equipment.

While we were in dry dock, inspection of the starboard screw revealed a crack, so both screws were changed. The underwater sound heads, the fathometer, and the torpedo tube outer doors were checked and found to be in good condition. *Pintado*'s torpedo tube doors were not causing the headaches that *Sculpin*'s had.

26–30 November   *Pintado* left Tanapag Harbor directly from undocking in midafternoon, was outside the entrance thirty minutes later, and set course through the western submarine safety lane, speeding back to Convoy College.

Caiman was with us as we were escorted by *PC 1126* until dark. *Caiman* was going to another patrol area, so we lost contact during the night as we continued west.

The talk in the crew's mess and the wardroom was of our experiences on Saipan and of stories we had heard from the crews of other submarines refitting in Tanapag Harbor, *Halibut* in particular.

An hour after sunset on 30 November *Pintado* completed transit of Balintang Channel, headed for our square in Convoy College. During our absence, *Atule* and *Jallao* completed their patrols, so Clarey's Crushers no longer existed.

1–11 **December**   *Pintado* submerged at 0552 on 1 December. We were on the Takao–Cape Bojeador traffic route while continuing toward the square that we were to cover, reassuming our place in the rotation schedule.

For the next eleven days the weather was terrible. The sea was so rough that about all anyone could do was hang on. When not on watch, the only place for any rest was in a bunk. George held up very well and had no trouble with seasickness. Under the rough weather conditions no one felt very energetic.

One rough night John Lewis relieved the helm, as one station of the watch rotation, carrying a bucket. He set the bucket down on the port side of the wheel. The skipper was in the back of the conning tower by the TDC, wearing red goggles for night adaptation before going to the bridge. "What's that bucket for, Lewis?" he asked.

John replied immediately, "Well, I thought somebody might get seasick, Cap'n."

"And just who might get seasick?" asked the skipper.

John responded, "Well, Cap'n, it could be me!"

Under the prevailing weather conditions I managed to get poor sun sights and star sights on only three occasions, and each fix placed us far from where my DR said we should be. I didn't trust either my DR or the fixes. *Pintado*'s exact position was anybody's coin toss.

Once, when there was a break in the clouds at 0200, I took sights that placed us sixty miles from where DR said we were. My knowledge of star locations and constellations paid off, and with Emerson's preselection of stars, I could identify them through the infrequent holes in the heavy cloud cover; but there never seemed to be enough holes to get a decent fix. Running fixes were the rule, and those were not at all satisfactory.

Waves frequently swept across the bridge, dumping barrels of water down the conning tower hatch and on down into the control room. Heavy spray continually drenched the bridge, and rainstorms never seemed to end. Even submerged at 100 feet the boat rolled heavily. Attempting to work in those weather conditions was very discouraging.

I was thinking and talking more about asking for postgraduate school —not because of the weather but because I thought the education would be helpful in my navy career. I felt that graduate work certainly wouldn't do any harm, and it certainly would be good for the future to have the school behind me.

There was also my intuition that the work of submarines in the Pacific war would end in a few more months. The Japs would be bottled up, and our subs wouldn't have much in the way of targets. I would have liked to end my Pacific war service with a command assignment, but I thought it unlikely. Then, too, I didn't want to be caught up in demobilization. So I would be better off to go on to graduate school.

After graduate school I could go back to submarines, or possibly to surface ships. I needed to broaden my background by getting varied ship experience and command in surface ships.

On 11 December I composed a letter to Chief of Naval Personnel, applying for the ordnance engineering graduate course at the postgraduate school at Annapolis. This would give the skipper plenty of time to prepare his endorsement before we reached port.

12 December　We had been in heavy weather, with no fix for twelve days. At sunset the APR reported a very strong contact at 152 mc, a Jap aircraft frequency. It was the first spark of a contact for so long that the word went through the boat like wildfire. We could feel the enthusiasm.

Forty minutes later the exhaust of an airplane was sighted, but SD radar had no contact. *Pintado* submerged to allow the plane time to go away. If aircraft were flying in that weather, there must be activity nearby. Submerged for thirty minutes, *Pintado* surfaced, and APR promptly reported another contact at 152 mc. Nothing was seen.

Two anxious hours passed as we anticipated possible air attack, then at 2135 the SJ radar reported contact with three ships to the north at 8,800 yards. From the range at which they were picked up we guessed that they were not the largest of ships. They weren't seen from the bridge.

The sea continued very rough, with long, deep swells, and the night was quite dark, with the horizon obscured by extremely black clouds. The SJ was sweeping intermittently in order not to give the search planes too much signal to home in on. *Pintado* turned south to keep position ahead of the ships and to track them.

For the next hour and twenty minutes the convoy was tracked by radar and TDC as on course 220 t at a speed of nine knots.

At 2258 we went to battle stations, continuing to stalk the ships. The radar scope showed that the targets were close together, the two leading ships only about 200 yards apart, with one slightly in the lead and to port of the other. The third ship was about 600 yards on the port quarter of the leading ship.

At battle stations for twenty minutes, *Pintado* maneuvered for an attack, then the convoy increased speed to fourteen knots and commenced zigzagging between 190 and 250 t. The aircraft must have alerted them

after picking up our radar signals. The skipper adjusted *Pintado*'s maneuvers to accommodate the convoy's action.

The attack plan was to fire six bow tubes at the two leading ships from
about 2,000 yards, and then swing to fire the stern tubes at the third
ship. *Pintado* would take a position from which the fish would run approximately across the sea, which was Force 5, from 020 t. The running
depth of all starboard tube fish was set at six feet, all port tube fish at
ten feet.

Ten minutes before midnight *Pintado* steadied on course 310 t, stopped,
and waited for the convoy to move closer. The range was 3,000 yards to
the nearest ship. The ships were then sighted for the first time. The range
closed to 2,700 yards. The two larger ships were in the lead, and one
medium-sized ship followed, but because of the height of the waves and
the poor visibility they couldn't be identified. When *Pintado* was in the
trough of a wave, we could see nothing but black water topped with angry
white crests. On the crest of a wave the target ships might be in a trough
or hidden by spray. It was a wild night.

TBT (target bearing transmitter) bearings from the bridge were not
reliable because *Pintado* was rolling and pitching heavily, with saltwater
and spray breaking over the bridge. So firing would be done with radar
information only, after the TDC generated the desired bearings. The sea
and the visibility conditions in which we were operating meant that there
was little possibility that they would ever see us maneuvering into position
on the surface.

At 2355 the skipper commenced firing a spread of six fish from the
bow tubes at the two leading ships, with the nearest at a run of 2,400
yards. Problems with the forward gyro regulator and the forward angle
solver made it necessary to match gyros by hand and wait for a solution
light. Those problems, along with the fact that the boat was rolling over
twenty degrees and we were trying to fire when nearly on an even keel,
made for irregular firing intervals.

When the last fish was fired, at three minutes before midnight, the
skipper immediately ordered, "Right full rudder! All ahead full!" turning
into the sea for a stern tube shot at the third ship. Solid water came flying
over the bridge, and all hands were again soaked as the boat took a terrific
nose dive into a wave.

At 2358 we saw and heard the first of three tremendous explosions:
one hit in the leading ship and two in the second ship.

On seeing the explosions, the third ship turned to his left, away from
the explosions but toward *Pintado*. The range closed to 1,760 yards as

our next target continued his swing to an easterly course. The after TBT was put to use, and tracking commenced to get his new course and to clock any changes in speed. The new target settled on 080 t, pulling away from us, still at fourteen knots. We continued tracking, maneuvering for position to fire.

13 December   At 0003 the skipper commenced firing a spread of four fish from the stern tubes at the third ship, with the range opened to 2,300 yards. No hits were seen from the bridge, but below decks a number of explosions were heard and felt from either the first or the second attack.

At 0008 a tremendous explosion shook *Pintado*. From the bridge it appeared that a magazine or ammunition storage had blown up in one of the first ships hit. Flames and skyrockets shot high into the air. One of the first two targets disappeared from the radar screen. In the typhoon weather, identification of the ships was impossible.

For fifteen minutes a number of explosions pounded our ears, like a Fourth of July celebration, as we watched from our bridge. At 0017, with the range 5,100 yards and radar tracking him, the second ship of the first attack exploded, momentarily lighting up the whole sky. The radar pip reached saturation and abruptly disappeared.

While we watched the fireworks our last target had moved to the southeast. Range increased to 14,000 yards. *Pintado* set out in pursuit. Our fish may have damaged him but he had settled on a southerly course and was zigzagging wildly, still able to make a speed of fourteen knots.

With the heavy seas running, the job of reloading torpedo tubes had to be done with caution. If a torpedo shifted or came loose, a torpedoman could be killed or very badly injured. The skipper cautioned me to send Ed Frese to the torpedo room to supervise the reloading. I went, too, to be doubly cautious.

At 0225, having succeeded in making an end around, *Pintado* was in good position and again went to battle stations. During the end around we passed the target at a range of only 4,300 yards but couldn't see him in the towering waves. We had to rely completely on SJ radar.

Not knowing why our torpedoes seemed to miss on the previous attack, and because our perception was that the target wasn't a large one, the skipper set three fish to run six feet deep and three to run three feet deep. The plan was to catch the target on his base course so that the fish would be running across the waves, not through them.

At 0251 the skipper began firing a spread of six fish from the forward tubes, with a run of 2,200 yards. The three fish set to run at three feet broached, one turning to the right and two turning to the left. With three fish running wild, *Pintado* turned at flank speed to get out of the possible path of our own torpedoes circling back toward us. During the confusion of the next few minutes we were unable to follow the target. One explosion was heard below decks, while we above were ducking waves, torpedoes, and a school of fish, several of which were found on the bridge after the engagement.

At 0256 *Pintado* slowed to use the sound gear and listen for torpedo noises from the erratic fish. When none were picked up, everybody breathed more easily, and their heartbeats slowed down to normal. In the meantime the target had slowed to a speed of three knots. We followed and tracked him for the next ninety minutes, reloading the forward torpedo room's last four fish and making plans for another attack.

At 0417 *Pintado* was in position to commence another approach from the starboard side of the target, planning to close in and fire at a range of 1,000 yards. He had slowed to only three knots. As *Pintado* closed in, with seas and spray flying, the target must have sighted the commotion. He turned 180 degrees, headed north, then turned again to the southeast and attempted a burst of speed. It was too dark and the seas were too rough to even think of manning our deck gun.

We were deciding on *Pintado*'s next course of action when, at 0440, there was another tremendous explosion in the direction where our target was last seen on the radar. The whole sky lit up for a few seconds. Radar lost contact. *Pintado* immediately put on speed and stood toward the scene of the explosion, but we were unable to pick up the target again. An odor of charred wood similar to the odor around the prison camps on Saipan permeated the atmosphere. Nothing more was seen, although we searched for over an hour, until daylight.

The two larger ships of the convoy had exploded in a manner similar to the last ship. There was a delay following the torpedo hits while the cargo, whatever it was, smoldered internally and then suddenly ignited and blew up. At no time were we able to see enough of the ships to make an estimate of their type: masts, goal posts, type of bow and stern, and other features weren't distinguishable, although the bulk and length could be compared. Their sustained speed of fourteen knots in the prevailing heavy seas indicated that they were either fairly large ships or naval vessels. The last target was tracked by radar at 14,000 yards for a short time. (Radar technicians later found that the SJ radar had not been at maximum sensitivity during the engagement, leading to the conclusion that our targets were much larger than we first thought.)

Pintado had experienced rough weather for almost three weeks. Having to hold on and brace all the time was very tiresome. One of the lookouts was almost washed off the bridge by an unusually big wave. Sections of the deck and superstructure were wrenched loose and were banging about, and some were lost overboard. The constant rough weather was a new and tiring experience for everybody.

Before sunrise *Pintado* submerged for the day and everyone took a well-deserved rest. We surfaced in midafternoon so I could get a sun line, then stayed on the surface, hoping for a star fix at dusk. The weather was improving—the seas had smoothed some and the wind was not quite so strong.

14 December   *Pintado* submerged at sunrise to spend a quiet day, still recovering from the continuous rough weather of the previous week and from the action of the day before. At dusk we surfaced and I got my first star fix in fourteen days. My navigation wasn't far off because I had been able to make fairly good estimates of our position from radar ranges to the mountains of Formosa.

With confirmation of *Pintado*'s position, we headed for the Bashi Channel, leaving Convoy College to head east toward home, as directed in our OpOrd.

15 December   At 0240 *Pintado* was through Bashi Channel, having just passed Y'ami Island to starboard at fifteen miles. At 0300 a radio report was sent to ComSubPac giving the results of the patrol. Then at 0821 a Jake-type aircraft was sighted about five miles away headed right for us, so we submerged to 200 feet. He may have been vectored to our position from our radio transmissions. No depth charges were dropped, and we surfaced eight minutes later to continue east on the surface at flank speed. We wanted to get away from air searches as rapidly as possible.

At 1030 we received ComSubPac's message telling *Pintado* to head slowly for a position west of Cape Bojeador, Luzon, until we received instructions concerning the possibility of refitting in Fremantle. So we reversed course and headed west, back through Bashi Channel, anticipating that a refit at Fremantle meant we would go south through the South China Sea, the Dutch East Indies, and the Indian Ocean.

16 December   By midnight we were through Bashi Channel, again in the South China Sea, and moving south. At 0730 we received ComSubPac's message directing *Pintado* to go to Saipan for fuel, then to Brisbane for refit. We guessed that the submarine command was having problems keeping all their submarines busy.

We were closer to Balintang Channel, so we went that way to again exit the South China Sea, and set course for Saipan.

The weather turned bad once more. We were plowing through heavy seas and high winds, unable to make more than ten knots under the conditions.

In midafternoon a Pete aircraft was sighted to the south at a distance of three miles. *Pintado* submerged to 150 feet. He dropped one bomb fairly close, but we suffered no damage. The diving section did a great job in getting the boat submerged so rapidly under the adverse conditions. The plane was spotted by the sky lookout against stormy cloud formations, and he didn't hesitate to make his sighting known. The Japanese were flying in all kinds of weather. After that experience the skipper decided to remain submerged until dark.

At dark we surfaced to continue toward Balintang Channel.

During the previous patrols I had told the officers and crew many stories of the retreat from Manila, refit in Java, and experiences in Australia, and I had voiced hope that *Pintado* would go there sometime. The skipper wasn't at all enthusiastic about the prospect. When we got our orders to go to Brisbane for overhaul, he remarked that he hoped I was happy. I knew he wasn't.

17 December   At 0400 *Pintado* was again out of Luzon Strait, heading east for Saipan. We passed Balintang Island at eight miles on our starboard beam.

At 0755 an APR contact on 152 mc decided the skipper to submerge for a trim dive and to avoid possible detection. We surfaced at 0850 to continue east on the surface.

At 0949 the SD radar reported a contact at ten miles, so we submerged again for an hour and a half. Back on the surface at sunset we were out of Convoy College.

18–21 December   No aircraft bothered *Pintado* during the run to Saipan, so we were able to stay on the surface all the way. The weather was pleasant, and everyone enjoyed the change. The boat was dirty from the continuous bad weather in the patrol area, so a concerted cleanup campaign was under way. We expected visitors as soon as we arrived, and we wanted the boat to make a good appearance.

Robbie overheard the skipper and me talking about my application for graduate school. That started him talking about applying. I didn't see any application from Robbie, however.

22–23 December   This time *Pintado* was met by *Wintle (DE-25)* at the eastern end of the submarine safety lane, escorted to Tanapag Harbor, and by midafternoon was moored starboard side to *Kete,* in the nest alongside *Fulton.* No liberty was granted to anyone. We expected to leave as soon as possible the next day.

Just as we moored we received a note saying that we should assemble the crew for a presentation of awards by Vice Admiral John H. Hoover, '07. The decorations for *Pintado*'s earlier patrols were catching up with us.

The admiral pinned the skipper with the Navy Cross. I got the Silver Star, as did Ed Frese, Gerry Pettibone, and Chief of the Boat Red Hill. Gunner's Mate Emiel Sullivan got the Bronze Star. Fred Powers got his Navy and Marine Corps Medal for rescuing Joe Bennett from drowning at Majuro. Letters of commendation were awarded to Ben Sisti, George Morris, Aubrey Sanders, and Eric Bailey.

Don Irvine made the rounds of the boat, bidding everyone good-bye as he departed to await orders for his command. He had a quiet, pleasant personality and we had enjoyed having him as a shipmate. He participated in wardroom discussions, joined in our pranks, played acey-deucey, and helped with duties and work wherever he could be of assistance.

Late afternoon on the twenty-third, my twenty-eighth birthday, *Pintado* was under way for Brisbane, minor repairs completed, topped off with fuel, and with a few items for the cooks to make meals more palatable. *Wintle* escorted us as far as latitude 10° N, longitude 147°11′ E, as we headed south toward the submarine safety lane.

After dinner, for dessert, Steward John Singleton surprised me with a giant birthday cake. He had teamed up with Stew Burner Tim Dineen to bake it. After the officers had their dessert, the remainder went to the crew's mess for the watch standers.

24 December–1 January 1945   An hour past noon of the twenty-fourth our escort reversed course to return to Saipan. *Pintado*'s cooks were busily preparing a magnificent Christmas dinner from supplies that Jerry Mitchell had been able to scrounge from the tender at Saipan.

The twenty-fifth was like almost any other day for men who had been away from home as long as *Pintado*'s had been. George Murray organized a very nice Christmas service in the crew's mess from 1000 to 1100.

There was a surprisingly good turnout. Robbie, Ed, and Brant helped with the service. We sang every Christmas song we could think of and said a few prayers. George gave an inspirational talk. The microphone was there, so everything was broadcast throughout the boat. The men on watch appreciated that. The skipper later complimented us, so we must have done justice to the occasion.

George and Robbie gloated over the presents that their families had sent them ahead of time so they would have them on Christmas. The rest of us weren't that well organized, nor had our families realized that we would be away from the mailman for so long.

Everyone was excited in anticipation of crossing the equator. That would happen on the twenty-sixth. Only seventeen of the ship's complement had been across that line, so we shellbacks were telling the polliwogs about the dread things they would experience and making plans to initiate them.

On Christmas Day *Pintado* passed to operational control of Commander Task Group 71.9 (CTG 71.9) in Brisbane, and we radioed a request for an escort to accompany us while passing Manus Island. There was quite a concentration of Allied navy ships in that vicinity, and we didn't want *Pintado* to be mistaken for an enemy.

Pintado crossed the equator at longitude 148°15′ E on the twenty-sixth. The time was 0357, so only the watch and the navigator were up to note the time of crossing.

At sunrise we sighted the light carrier *Hoggatt Bay*, with two DE escorts, to the southeast at fifteen miles and exchanged recognition signals and call signs. A short time later our destroyer escort, *DE-635*, moved in, exchanged signals, and joined *Pintado* to accompany us as we passed Manus. We were never close enough to see the island.

Pintado's crossing-the-equator ceremonies were quite a show. Surprisingly, Brant, our old-time navy man, had never been across. He was on the bridge in dress uniform, carrying a long glass and watching to see that no seagulls soiled our decks. Ed was there in a full suit of long underwear with a bucket and swab, keeping the decks clean. We had Jerry decked out in a mess jacket, cook's hat, and apron—nothing else—and he was kept busy running between the galley, pantry, and bridge, bringing coffee and sandwiches. He would stagger up the ladder to the bridge with many cups of coffee, then the recipient of the coffee would take one sip and toss the coffee over the side with a "too hot," or a "too sweet," or a "too cold," and order him to bring a good cup.

Robbie was racing around the engine rooms wearing nothing but a jock strap and rain hat, shining valves. Bonny was in the galley with binoculars, looking for smoke. Gerry, in a complete set of long underwear and another of rainclothes, was sweating in the radio shack, listening on radio headphones. We really gave them a merry runaround. Everyone had a good time.

Then, for the initiation, I was the Royal Judge, so I put on a wing collar and bow tie, a pair of swimming trunks, dark sunglasses, a black beret, and a pair of boots. We dressed Red Hill up as King Neptune with some unraveled rope as hair, a fancy white robe that appeared from somewhere, and a makeshift crown. The Queen wore an outfit of women's underwear that was found in a bale of cleaning rags. She looked quite curvy, with balls of twine in the bra. Among King Neptune's court were the Royal Navigator, the Chaplain, the Doctor, the Baby, and the Chief of Police, all dressed in their own imaginative creations.

Each polliwog was required to appear before the Royal Judge and plead, on his knees, his innocence of some goofy infraction. I would assign a sentence. The Royal Barber, with a large paintbrush, might start working the polliwog over with heavy grease, paint, syrup, and various evil-smelling liquids. Polliwogs were blindfolded when the Royal Doctor moved in to look at their teeth, squirt bitter liquid in their mouths, and feed them a piece of cake made with soap powder, garlic, salt, and other awful-tasting things.

The initiation was a workout for both the shellbacks and the polliwogs. Everyone had a great time unwinding and laughing at the antics. A run on the showers took place when everything was over, and no one had a problem sleeping that night.

At sunset our escort departed, and *Pintado* headed toward Vitiaz Strait to go east around the eastern extremity of New Guinea.

The beautiful Southern Cross and Scorpio were rising higher and higher in the southern sky as we moved south, a nightly reminder that *Pintado* was getting nearer and nearer to Australia. The North Star had long since disappeared below the horizon.

While proceeding through Vitiaz Strait we sighted numerous merchantmen, tugs, and aircraft. At one time a sizable convoy passed, headed north. *Pintado* was in the submarine safety lane, and they recognized that we were friendly.

Later, following the convoy, a lone Liberty ship came into view. We had the ship in sight for over two hours before they suddenly became suspicious and fired six rounds at us with their deck gun. We turned away, flashing recognition signals, then resumed our course and continued on our way. About forty-five minutes later, after we were well past, they opened fire again, at a range of 13,340 yards, lobbing ten more rounds in our direction. We were glad that they were poor shots. Later, radio heard a contact report from that ship saying that we were a probable enemy sub; his communications were much better than his gunnery.

The shipboard submarine routine when returning for refit was following the usual pattern: cleaning up the boat, preparing work lists for the refit, holding school, examining for qualifications, and routine paperwork. The skipper was polishing off his patrol report, keeping the yeoman and the department heads busy with his requests for data to go into the report. I had given up volunteering my services to help with writing or proofreading patrol reports.

One problem facing us was that of finding a new chief of the boat before leaving on the next patrol. Red Hill had been complaining of headaches. He had trouble sleeping, and I saw an obvious nervousness in his attitude and his actions. He had lost noticeable weight. Doc Denningham was of the opinion that Red needed a long rest. Everybody, including Red, was of a mind that he should be rotated in Brisbane.

Replacing Red Hill would be difficult. He was a fine leading chief. He was a tough, wiry, redheaded, six-foot-two, no-nonsense, dedicated submariner who got results.

Jerry Mitchell was navigating so I could spend more time with administration. I kept an eye on his work, particularly when we were passing near the many islands along the way. The skipper kept checking, asking how Jerry was doing, looking at our charts and projected positions.

One evening an albatross sailed around the boat for a while, then perched on the radar antenna just as it got dark. He was spending the night. The word went through the boat in a hurry. Most of the crew, it seemed, went to the conning tower to ask for permission to come to the bridge to look at the bird. He was on the revolving antenna (a wonder he didn't get dizzy), head tucked under his wing, sound asleep, and he slept there the night through. He was still there at dawn when we made a trim dive, and that was his rude awakening.

The skipper added his endorsement to my request for postgraduate school. The letter was routed through Submarine Division 202, where I knew that my friend Lew Parks would give me a good endorsement.

According to the awards criteria for submarine war patrols, I knew that I would, as a matter of course, be awarded another Silver Star for the third patrol. I already had three of them. From reading the radio messages and the official mail, we knew that several of my contemporaries had been awarded the Navy Cross. Their work and experiences were little different from mine. And Chief Blair, we heard, was awarded the Navy Cross for being with us, for the ride, on the first patrol. Chick's contention that my work had contributed greatly to his being awarded two Navy Crosses, and another a cinch for this patrol, seemed to me an opportunity to see if his actions would follow his words—an opportunity for him to demonstrate the sincerity of his statements about how invaluable my contributions had been to *Pintado*'s successes and to compensate in a way for his preventing me from getting command after the second patrol.

I reminded the skipper that I already had three Silver Stars and asked him to recommend one of the other officers for the Silver Star, thus distributing the medals around more widely among our shipmates.*

I still hoped to get a command after this patrol. Several sub school classmates—contemporaries—were already commanding their own subs, according to radio messages and the official mail. I was reminded of this regularly during the patrol when we were operating next to *Tuna,* with Steve Steffanides as her captain. I thought often of the skipper confiding in me at the start of the patrol that Admiral Lockwood had wanted to move me to a command, but that he had convinced him that he had to have me for one more patrol. Then there was Lu Chappell's revelation of what he knew about SubPac's command plans and his surprise that I was again going out as exec of *Pintado.*

Now, with *Pintado* going to Australia and a different submarine leadership, the picture changed. My standing with Admiral Lockwood would carry little weight in the southwest Pacific. Even so I continued to hope that the command would come through. Graduate school was not scheduled to begin until late next summer, so there was still time for a short command.

On the evening before reaching Brisbane, the skipper and I were on the cigarette deck reviewing the patrol. He repeated what I had heard near the end of the first two patrols, telling me how much he appreciated me backing him up, that he couldn't have done without me, and that he fully expected me to be detached for command almost immediately. I couldn't help thinking, "I've heard that old song before."

---

*When we reached Fremantle I finally saw his recommendations for awards. In spite of his many statements of gratitude and respect for my support, he had recommended me for the lower-ranking Bronze Star. I felt as if I were caught in a trap.

Patrol Summary

Number of enlisted men on board	78	
Number qualified, start patrol	48	
Number qualified, end patrol	54	
Number unqualified making first patrol	15	
Number advanced in rating	11	

Nautical miles covered:

Pearl to Saipan		3,600
Saipan to area, twice		3,600
In area		3,600
Area to Saipan, twice		3,400
Saipan to Brisbane		3,400
	Total	17,600

Fuel used: 191,000 gallons (10.8 gal./mi.)

Duration:

En route to Saipan		20 days
In area		36 days
En route to base		18 days
In Saipan		9 days
	Total	83 days (submerged 30 days)

Endurance factors:

Torpedoes remaining		8
Fuel remaining	43,000	gallons
Provisions remaining	20	days

Torpedoes fired: 22

Sinkings:

1 destroyer, *Terutsuki* class		3,300 tons (attack #1)
1 large supply ship		7,500 tons (attack #2)
1 medium supply ship		4,000 tons (attack #2)
1 large supply ship		7,500 tons (attack #4)
	Total	21,300 tons

Damaged, one carrier   28,000 tons

1 **January 1945**   Colundra Head Light was sighted at 0328. Jerry Mitchell was the OOD, and in navy tradition wrote the first watch of the new year in rhyme.

Pintado picked up a pilot at the entrance to Moreton Bay, crossed the bay, and entered the river. At 1000 we were moored alongside the dock at New Farm Wharf. January first was *Pintado*'s first birthday.

A crowd of commodores, staff officers, and other well-wishers were on the wharf to greet us as we tied up. After a period of greetings the usual arrival conferences began.

Later, I got to read a copy of the skipper's patrol report:

> The performance of duty of all officers and men was of the highest order, and in keeping with the high standards of the submarine force. It is particularly desired to commend the lookouts for their untiring efforts and cheerfulness in spite of thirty days of rough, wet, and very disagreeable weather. They were continually soaked through to the skin in spite of foul-weather clothing.

Refit in Brisbane

1–15 **January**   There had been a remarkable change in submarine refit procedure since I was in Brisbane in 1943. Things were now done Pearl Harbor style. As soon as we were tied up at the dock a relief crew came aboard and *Pintado*'s crew left for the rest camp on the coast at Southport, about an hour's drive from Brisbane.

At *Pintado*'s personnel planning conference we were informed that we were required to transfer two officers and eighteen men for rotation purposes. The two officers selected for rotation were Gerry and Brant, our salty old navy veteran. Three new officers would be reporting: Lieutenant Herb Thornton, Lieutenant (jg) Bob Walker, and Ensign John Lennon, all reserves.

Later, the skipper met with the commodore and was told that I would probably move up to command *Pintado* after the fourth patrol, with Herb becoming executive officer. Herb ranked with the academy class of '41.

One problem after another needed attention at the sub base, consuming time until late afternoon of the second, when George Murray and I at last reached Southport and checked in to share a room at our hotel, the Surfer's Paradise.

Surfer's Paradise was the hotel for officers; another resort hotel for the enlisted men was only a few hundred feet down the beach. Except for the absence of crowds, the atmosphere could be compared to Waikiki in Hawaii. The beach seemed to be endless. It was a quarter mile wide and practically deserted. The surf was amazing. There was plenty of foliage, with lush trees and tropical plantings, all backed by forested green hills. The army also had hotels along the beach where they rotated their people from frontline activities to give them a break, rest, and recreation.

At each of the rest hotels there were Red Cross girls as activities directors. They were good-humored and energetic girls, in the twenty-five- to thirty-year-old range, and were outdoorsy, athletic types. Our hostess was Ellen Rosenburg, and our athletic director was Joan Smith. The two of them did a great job of organizing beach parties, tennis, volleyball, picnics, softball games, horseback riding, bike riding, and evening dances, with an attractive group of Australian girls.

Almost everyone joined enthusiastically in the activities; there was something of interest for all. Several days I went to Brisbane to check something or other on *Pintado* and to see Australian friends who thought I had deserted them to become a beach boy.

At breakfast on Sunday the seventh I saw a familiar face at the table next to mine. It was Johnny Williams, '40, an aviator who had just come in and was waiting for orders. He had been shot down in the Philippines area, spent six weeks with guerrillas, and was then rescued by one of our subs. He looked well and seemed none the worse for his experiences.

On the tenth I received a very pleasant surprise. Major Louis Pietzsch, U.S. Army, a friend of many years from Beaumont, Texas, who was returning to the United States after two years in India, discovered me at Surfer's. He was staying at the army hotel just down the beach, and we were together constantly until he left on a troop transport on the eighteenth.

Pintado was the last occupant of the navy rest camp. It was closing down for lack of business. The army and navy establishments were slowly pulling out of the Brisbane area, moving closer to the war zone. Except for *Pintado* the port was deserted, so we had the best of everything.

16–26 January   Everyone moved back to Brisbane to take possession of *Pintado* on the sixteenth and get ready for the next patrol.

Classmate Hank Lloyd wrote from Annapolis, having heard that I had applied to go to graduate school. He said that housing was hard to find and that many hours of study went with the schooling. Ann's letters reported that our son was doing all the things that a six-month-old boy was expected to do, and his mother and grandmother were lavishing attention on him. Doug Morse wrote that he was settled in at Sub Base New London, enjoying his work, and that Margaret had had a baby girl. That made four girls and my lone boy in our wardroom group.

Herb Thornton was given the job of making all arrangements for a gala ship's party to be held the night of the nineteenth and was busily getting everything in place, anticipating *Pintado*'s departure on schedule. The party went off with a bang, and the crew got a big kick over an impromptu prank involving my beard being butchered. Someone, I never was able to pinpoint just who, planned it in advance. In midparty I was surrounded by a number of our crew who, on signal, grabbed and held me while one of the dates, who just happened to have a pair of scissors, cut ragged slashes in my beard. The next morning I removed the remains of the beard.

Under-way training was first scheduled for 17–19 January but was delayed until 23–25 January because there were no surface ship targets for us to work with. The navy had moved north toward Japan. Everything went off well. *Pintado* was way above par. Only a few odd jobs, loading minor stores, and topping off with fuel remained to be accomplished before heading out on patrol. The unplanned extra days in port were causing some boredom.

Australian hospitality was more evident every day in the number of men who overstayed their liberty or went AWOL for a few days. When someone missed muster or was AWOL he was restricted to the boat, and the restricted list kept growing.

Pintado's Fourth Patrol

(27 January 1945–20 March 1945)

27 January   There seemed to be some confusion in the high command as to just what *Pintado* would do on her fourth patrol. We were standing by all day long, with the skipper bouncing back and forth between the boat and the offices on shore. The war had moved far north, and opportunities for sinking Jap ships had diminished significantly. It was obvious that the upper echelons were puzzling over just what *Pintado*'s mission would be, and messages were no doubt ricocheting around the Pacific.

In preparing for the fourth patrol wholesale changes were made in officer responsibilities: Herb Thornton relieved Jerry Mitchell as commissary officer; Robbie Robinson and Ed Frese swapped jobs, with Robbie heading ordnance and Ed taking over as chief engineer; George Murray took over as first lieutenant; Jerry Mitchell became assistant engineer; Bonny Bonjour took on communications; Bob Walker was radar officer; and John Lennon was assistant gunnery officer. The skipper, Robbie, and I were the only Regular Navy officers; the other seven officers were reserves.

During the day the crew loafed through their routine, polishing off ship's work, ready to leave, with Australian friends coming to the dock to say good-bye. One of my friend Chris Christopherson's ice cream trucks delivered four five-gallon drums of ice cream as a gift to the ship. Then Chris came to say a last good-bye.

Finally the skipper was told to be prepared to get under way at 2200 and proceed to Darwin to report to Task Group 71.1, where we would receive our orders. During *Pintado*'s trip to Darwin the problem of our mission would be hashed out, written orders would be delivered, and we would top off there with fuel.

The 2,875-nautical-mile route would take us east of the Great Barrier Reef, then west through Torres Strait, between Australia and New Guinea, and on to Darwin on the north coast of Australia.

On the bell at 2200, as we waited with maneuvering watch on station and engines running, a pilot came aboard to take us downriver and across Moreton Bay to the South Pacific.

28 January–5 February, En Route to Darwin   At 0126 the pilot got off at Colundra Head and northerly courses were set up the submarine safety lane toward New Guinea. At 0554 *Pintado* exchanged recognition signals with HMS *Howe,* stationed on our side of a task force of Allied cruisers, destroyers, and an air screen that passed us going north. At 0920 we made a trim dive, and surfaced after an hour and a half spent checking systems.

At 2155 *Pintado* exchanged recognition signals by SJ radar with S-47. She was bound for Brisbane.

George was trying his hand at navigation on the run to Darwin, while I tackled the piles of official mail, reports, and other administrative jobs that had stacked up while we were in port. Schools were the perennial challenge, with thirty-two unqualified men to train and advancements in rating to stress. Daily drills, fire control problems, and training dives, morning and afternoon, became the routine.

The weather was absolutely beautiful, in marked contrast to what we had battled our way through only a couple of months before in Luzon Strait. The moon and stars were very bright in the clear, cool air, and sunrises and sunsets were unusually colorful. During the daytime giant albatrosses sailed gracefully around us. Flying fish skimmed the surface as they hurried away from the giant steel fish rushing through their waters.

On 31 January *Pintado* rounded the northeast corner of Australia and headed west through the Coral Sea toward Torres Strait. That narrow passage between Australia and New Guinea was quite shallow and restricted, with many small islands and shoals. Several of the islands were named for days of the week, one of them the historically famous Thursday Island. A pilot was mandatory to negotiate the shallow and winding Prince of Wales Channel.

Back at the sub base in Brisbane, when I had been selecting personnel replacements for the men we were rotating, I was very careful in looking over the records, attempting to get only the ones who looked like top potential. The skipper was particularly insistent that I get an extra steward, but the personnel officer said that was impossible. However, the day before we left I just happened to be outside the division commander's office when I heard the flag personnel officer ask if they could use a couple of stewards. I immediately put in my two cents, and we got the extra steward the skipper wanted.

Getting that steward proved to be fortunate, because one of the other stewards came down with gonorrhea. We would have to transfer him for treatment when we got to Darwin. He was loudly proclaiming his objections to being left in Darwin, but there was no way out of it. It was our first case of venereal disease since leaving Panama almost one year ago.

Pintado continued west through the Gulf of Papua. After sunup on 2 February Bramble Cay was sighted and we began the transit of Bligh Entrance to the Great Northwest Channel. The Cape York extremity of Australia was only about 80 miles from New Guinea, and the shallow portion of Torres Strait was about 160 miles in length, with depths less than ninety feet. No one would have dreamed of making that passage a few months earlier when the Japs were on New Guinea.

At midmorning an Australian pilot, Captain Helm, boarded off Stephens Island and guided us through Prince of Wales Channel. The historical significance of the names Bligh, Wednesday, Thursday, and Friday islands was embellished by Captain Helm's commentary as we maneuvered through the channel. He had been a master of ships in the South Pacific islands and was very familiar with that area. During the Guadalcanal battles he commanded a ship that delivered ammunition to our marines.

The channel brought us very close to one island where we could see the natives riding surfboards in the surf. More were standing on shore watching *Pintado* go by, and others were sailing boats and fishing in the lee of the island. Captain Helm said that the islands were quite fertile, and their gardens grew many excellent vegetables and fruits. Some of the islands were uninhabited, he said. This prompted Ed Frese, who was OOD at the time, to join me in making plans to acquire one of those islands, on which we would settle down in regal splendor when the war ended.

By midafternoon the transit of Prince of Wales Channel was completed. We dropped the pilot off at Goods Island and continued west through the Arafura Sea toward Darwin.

On 4 February we got the news that General MacArthur's forces had taken Manila. We speculated that before long the submarine command would move from Fremantle back to the Philippines.

George was getting a nice variety of navigating experience. We were scheduled to enter Darwin through Clarence Channel Strait very early in the morning on the fifth, and I took part of his evening watch on the fourth so he could get some sleep and be ready for a call at 0500.

Everyone in the wardroom was enjoying the fact that, for the first time,

Pintado didn't have a PCO or other extra officer with us on the patrol: just our own family.

George and I were called at 0500 to be ready for the rendezvous with our escort. At daybreak *Pintado* fell in with *ML 813* to escort us through Clarence Channel and on to Darwin. The escort didn't establish identification. The fact that we were there on time and in the correct location must have been enough for them. Much later, after we passed through the submarine net, as a sort of afterthought they asked us our ship's name.

At the harbor entrance CTG 71.5 and Pilot MacArthur, RANR, climbed aboard from a motorboat to direct us to our berth alongside USS *Coucal*. Thirty minutes later *Pintado* was moored port side to *Coucal* and immediately commenced fueling.

The skipper and I had lunch with Commander Olsen, the local navy outpost commander. He had many amusing and interesting stories to tell about Darwin. It was backwater country. The rainy season was on, muggy and uncomfortably hot. There were several thousand army troops, a small navy detachment, and an Army Air Corps group. What a hot, unpleasant, insect-infested hole to be stuck in! Our steward was not at all happy over being put ashore there, but the commander told us that he would be airlifted soon to the hospital in Fremantle.

The skipper reported *Pintado* to CTG 71 for duty, and by midafternoon fueling was completed. We were ready for sea. Departure was scheduled for the next day, but our operation order hadn't arrived from Fremantle.

The postal clerk went to the local post office and found, to his surprise, that there was mail for *Pintado*. In the mail was a Christmas card from my *Mississippi* shipmate, former Aviation Cadet, now Lieutenant Commander H. E. Robinson. He was back in the States, at Corpus Christi, after a tour in the Pacific with Black Cat flying boats. A note from Hank Lloyd invited Ann and me to stay with him and his wife, Monty, until we could find a place to live in Annapolis. Through the grapevine, Hank knew that I was slated to go to graduate school that far in advance, although I didn't have any official word. Hank had always had the reputation of knowing what was going on before anyone else.

6–8 February   At midmorning on the sixth our CTF 71 operation order was delivered, and four hours later *Pintado* was under way for patrol. We completed transit of the swept channel and set course to pass just east of Timor Island.*

---

*Later, I was told that my friend Ole Jensen was a prisoner on Timor. The story was

Pintado's route would take her through the Banda Sea, the Java Sea, Karimata Strait (between Sumatra and Borneo), and on to a patrol area in the South China Sea between Saigon and Singapore.

The route ensured that the navigator would be very busy for the next week plotting progress, checking positions, and setting courses to pass through the deepest channels along the meandering 900-mile way through those confined, island and reef dotted, sometimes very shallow, waters. The last 2,475 nautical miles to the patrol area would be a challenge.

One of the tasks assigned *Pintado* on the patrol was to use the APR continuously and record any evidence of radar in the territories we passed.

Pintado cruised on the surface en route to the patrol area at fuel-conserving speeds, daily conducting schools, fire control problems, drills, and training dives when the water was deep enough. We were comfortable in feeling that the Japs were pushed to the north and would not be a danger to us until we got to the South China Sea.

Northbound in the Timor Sea on the seventh, well before sunset, we sighted the islands of Timor and Leti. Radar had made contact with them some time earlier and assisted navigation of the passage between them. There was no APR indication of radar from Timor or from any of the Sermata Islands. At sunset *Pintado* commenced passage between Timor and Leti, and three hours later we entered the Banda Sea.

8–14 February   Westbound at fifteen knots in the Banda Sea. On the eighth, just after daylight, SD radar reported an aircraft contact at five miles, so we submerged for almost an hour to avoid any possibility of being detected. Crossing the southern end of Makassar Strait, I used the peaks of Celebes and Borneo, seventy-five to ninety miles away, to fix our position as we moved into the Java Sea.

The Java Sea and Karimata Strait along our track varied in depth from fifteen to twenty-five fathoms until we were north of Karimata Strait on the twelfth. Those shallow waters were cause for concern. The Japs had planted mines in such tempting places. We were all keeping our fingers crossed and moving along at seventeen knots to get to the South China Sea as soon as we could.

Many native sailboats were sighted along this portion of the route, causing concern that they just might be disguised patrol boats. The lookouts were constantly reminded to be extremely alert.

---

that he was captured by the Japs near Manila, escaped from prison, worked his way south by boat with other escaped prisoners, was captured again and imprisoned on Timor, and died of mistreatment before he could be repatriated.

Near sunset on the tenth George Murray was OOD and reported sighting a periscope to starboard at about 2,000 yards. The skipper and I made emergency appearances on the bridge when George turned away and went to emergency flank speed. Immediately after that incident we sent a radio report of the contact, in the aircraft code, to Radio Coonawarra (Australia) and received an immediate receipt.

Approaching Karimata Strait on the eleventh, we put four engines on line and went to full speed to get through that treacherous piece of water that was much too shallow for comfort, and just might be mined. The hours were tense. The sad news of the loss of *Barbel* in the shallow waters of Balabac Strait didn't reduce our anxiety. My good friend Condé Raguet—sub school classmate, fellow renter of a house on Diamond Head, and best man in my wedding—was skipper of *Barbel*. Those were terrible losses. But we had to push on.

Before midnight *Pintado* completed transit of Karimata Strait and headed north in the South China Sea. Tensions went down, but only slightly. We were still in relatively shallow water. Our APR showed no evidence of radar on Karimata Island.

During the midwatch on the twelfth, the SJ radar reported a ship contact to north at 9,600 yards. From our radio notices we knew that a Dutch submarine was due to be in that position. The contact tracked as moving toward Karimata, as expected, at twelve knots, and we didn't investigate further.

Near noon the bridge reported sighting what proved to be the first of numerous native sailboats. At first we maneuvered to avoid being seen, but when more and more boats were sighted, it became apparent that we would be seen regardless of what we did. We might as well have been in Singapore Harbor. So we resumed our northerly course and ignored them.

On the thirteenth, as we moved northward to pass between the Anambar Islands and the Natuna Islands, the weather changed to give us very poor visibility with a great deal of rain. At 0426 sight contact was made, in a driving rainstorm, on a native boat about 500 yards on our port bow. Ed Frese, OOD, promptly turned to avoid being sighted, and the bridge almost immediately lost sight of him. Radar had difficulty tracking him and lost him at 4,000 yards. Radar then began to pick up numerous contacts at ranges from 800 yards to 3,500 yards. None were ever sighted. Just before daylight radar reported no contacts, and we left the fishing fleet astern in the rain.

Away from any land or islands, and finally in deeper water, *Pintado* continued north in the South China Sea on the fourteenth. The patrol area across the Saigon–Singapore shipping lane was almost in sight. A radio message from CTF 71 instructed *Pintado* to take the area to the south of our original area. *Hawkbill* would join us later in a coordinated patrol. After midnight *Pintado* entered her area and commenced a surface patrol.

The water depth in the patrol area varied from fifteen fathoms approaching the coast off Saigon to thirty-five fathoms nearer Singapore, not nearly the depth we felt comfortable operating in.

15 February–12 March

Pintado spent an unproductive patrol offshore along the Singapore–Saigon line and along the Malay–Lower Siam coast, on the surface most of the time. Frequent patrol planes caused us to submerge for short periods, and most of the time the SD radar gave no warning. We were fully dependent on the eyeballs of extra lookouts, but clouds gave the planes some advantage, and we had little confidence in the SD radar.

During the morning of 18 February we passed through an area of several square miles that was littered with flotsam. Numerous bodies of Japanese soldiers were seen among the debris. All were clothed in greenish khaki uniforms. We passed several close aboard, and we saw that they were in an advanced state of decomposition.

Reading between the lines of the official messages, we came to believe that Admiral Fife was moving the submarine command (CTF 71) to Subic Bay, Philippines. Then, on the nineteenth, the news of the Iwo Jima landings came in.

Nearing noon on the nineteenth a four-horned mine was sighted. The 20-mm gun crew took delight in getting to go topside for the fresh air and the exhilaration of sinking the mine. Afterward the weather closed in, with continual heavy rain every time we approached closer than twenty miles to the coast. We never did sight land, although we were within fifteen miles of it and I fixed our position with the radar several times.

Midmorning on the twentieth, south of Cape Kamao, a Dinah-type twin-engine patrol plane was sighted to the east at about six miles. The SD radar didn't pick him up. We submerged immediately when the plane turned toward *Pintado*. After forty minutes we surfaced to head eastward in hope that the plane was accompanying a convoy.

Two hours later what appeared to be the same plane came out of the clouds from the south about three miles away. Again the SD radar gave no warning. The plane was heading directly for us, so we made an emergency dive, turning toward him after we passed 60 feet. The skipper watched through the periscope until it went underwater. As *Pintado* passed 130 feet, two very close depth charges, astern, jarred the ship, causing some damage. The men in the after torpedo room were most affected and wasted no time in letting the control room know that they were very concerned. Robbie and I went back to calm their fears.

Just after the charges went off, the port propeller shaft began to squeal, and we knew we had a serious problem there. When we checked other damage we had a list that included five torpedo gyro spindles bent, would not retract; port prop revolution counter jarred off; stern plane indicator out of commission; several fuses blown; light bulbs shattered; and some closed valves, port side, partially opened.

Any possible convoy was now aware of our presence and would be routed around us, so we stayed submerged to repair damages. After four hours of recovery work *Pintado* surfaced to continue moving to the southwest and get away from that location.

Early in the morning of the twenty-first, Robbie reported that all torpedo tubes were back in commission. Every spare spindle had been used, plus a deformed one that was straightened manually.

Later, submerged to duck another air patrol, we conducted a more complete investigation of the shaft squeal. The noise started and stopped unpredictably, with maximum intensity at about 38 rpm, giving a noise frequency of about 14.8 kc. As the shaft was speeded up, the noise frequency decreased, passing out of the range of the JK sonar at about 50 rpm; it couldn't be heard on the JP sonar. A down angle on the boat intensified the squeal.

The port reduction gears were inspected, and at various speeds and depths the engineers tried to pin the noise down with a stethoscope. We finally concluded that the source of the noise was in the port strut bearing. Since the noise, though very loud at slow speeds, disappeared at about 50 rpm, the skipper decided to remain on patrol, planning to use only the starboard shaft at low speeds, and both shafts above 50 rpm on an approach or evasion.

Just after sunset on the twenty-first we received instructions from CTG 71 for lifeguard duty north of Singapore in connection with an air strike to take place on 24 February.

At noon on the twenty-second, *Pintado* moved to meet *Hawkbill* at a point given in radio orders from CTF-71. *Hawkbill* was sighted at the rendezvous before sundown. Recognition signals were exchanged and we closed in. One hour later the exec of *Hawkbill*, classmate Fred Tucker, came aboard by rubber boat for a conference concerning a coordinated patrol to be conducted by *Pintado* and *Hawkbill*. After an hour of going over plans, Fred went back to his ship.

By midevening the coordinated patrol was in motion to westward, moving toward the coast, with *Hawkbill* on a line twenty miles east of *Pintado*. The patrol continued, except for one day of unproductive lifeguard on the twenty-fourth, back and forth, until the twenty-sixth. No contacts resulted. Then *Hawkbill* departed for Subic Bay to reload and refuel.

At 0400 on the twenty-eighth, *Pintado* was again on lifeguard at latitude 4° N, longitude 104°20′ E, north of Singapore. Before noon a biplane similar to Pete was sighted three miles to the northeast, headed for *Pintado*. We submerged. There was no SD radar contact. We were considering tossing that equipment overboard for all the good it was doing. We fully expected to receive some depth bombs, but none came. Either his release gear failed or else he was out of depth bombs.

Pintado remained submerged for two hours, then surfaced to continue on lifeguard. By midafternoon, having heard nothing concerning the air strike, the skipper decided that our services were no longer required, so *Pintado* commenced a surface sweep across the familiar shipping lane. The patrol was getting to be a monotonous grind.

At sunset instructions were received concerning lifeguard services for an air strike on Singapore on 2 March.

At midmorning on 1 March *Sealion* was sighted, passing well east of us on a northwesterly course. Recognition calls by SJ radar established identity as she continued on. Then at noon *Sealion* reappeared northwest of us moving on a southerly course. We wondered what was going on, so we attempted to communicate with her but got no response. Eventually she called on the wolfpack frequency but sent no message.

From her actions we felt certain that *Sealion* had made contact with something. Then, forty-five minutes after first sighting *Sealion,* our lookouts reported smoke to the north. That explained the puzzling activities of *Sealion*.

Pintado commenced tracking the smoke. After thirty minutes we had the smoke on a steady course of 190 t and submerged twelve miles directly ahead of the contact. Before *Pintado* went down, the bridge watch saw *Sealion* submerge about eight miles west of us.

By that time we had concluded that our contact was a hospital ship about which we had been alerted in messages earlier in the week. There was no air cover, the ship was on a steady course, we saw no indication of surface escort, and only one column of smoke was seen.

Two hours after sighting smoke, I made a series of still and moving pictures of the hospital ship as he passed about 3,000 yards to the west, heading south at twelve knots. We could find no hospital ship in our recognition manuals similar to that one, but he was properly marked. The skipper estimated his tonnage was 4,000 tons.

We surfaced during midafternoon to continue our surface patrol. Nothing more was seen or heard from *Sealion* as we moved toward our lifeguard station for the next day.

Pintado was on lifeguard station before sunrise. At midmorning SD radar reported a contact at four miles, so we submerged; just as we were going down, a Pete plane was seen through the periscope to the northwest. No bombs were dropped. As we prepared to surface after one hour under, the periscope watch picked up a Mavis flying boat to the southwest about eight miles away. He was headed toward Singapore.

The sightings caused another hour's delay before *Pintado* surfaced to continue lifeguard. At midafternoon the SD radar reported a contact at eight miles, so we submerged again, staying down for two more hours before coming to the surface. An hour after sunset, having heard nothing concerning the air strike, the skipper decided that we weren't needed here, so *Pintado* headed northwestward toward Pulo Tenggol.

A submerged patrol twenty miles north of Pulo Tenggol on 3 March was unproductive. When we surfaced after sunset we were informed by CTF 71 that *Caiman* would join us for a coordinated patrol starting on the evening of 4 March and ending on 9 March, with the skipper to be OTC (officer in tactical command).

After sunset on 4 March we surfaced to rendezvous with *Caiman*. Forty-five minutes later we exchanged calls and closed her to exchange information by line-throwing gun and megaphone. The exchange was completed in an hour, and we took position seventy miles east of the Redang Islands with *Caiman* on a line thirty miles west of *Pintado*.

At midmorning on the seventh a message from CTF 71 sent *Pintado* on a search to the northeast at full power to look for a possible convoy. *Caiman* was instructed to proceed immediately on an intercept course.

Shortly after noon we sighted smoke to the southeast. We commenced tracking, sending contact reports to *Caiman* and to *Pampanito,* whose area we were about to enter. An hour later, having determined that the contact was on a northeasterly course at twelve knots, the information was sent by radio to our submarine friends.

At almost the same time we received a message from *Sealion* placing her position about twenty-five miles north of the contact. After running for eighteen minutes *Pintado* was in position fifteen miles ahead of the contact and radioed *Caiman* that we were submerging to attack.

There was, however, a suspicious lack of air cover, no sign of surface escort, only one column of smoke, and no pinging, reminding us of our previous experience with the hospital ship. Sure enough, during an hour of observation the ship was identified as the same hospital ship we had seen on 1 March.

Pintado pulled clear at standard speed in order to surface and notify *Caiman* and *Pampanito* that our contact was a hospital ship. Well before sunset, having lost sight of the hospital ship, we surfaced and sent our message. *Pampanito* came back to ask us if we were going to trail the ship and observe her after dark. We replied in the negative. *Pampanito* had been driven down by planes and was suspicious of the hospital ship.

During the evening *Pintado* sent a message to CTF 71 informing him of our lack of contacts and telling him of the squeal in our port shaft. Our refit would need to be scheduled where a dry dock was available.

During the night of 8 March we received instructions to lifeguard off Singapore on the tenth. This time we were to be at latitude 1°40' N, longitude 105° E. My chart showed that would put *Pintado* just outside the channel entrance, and only about seventy miles from the city of Singapore, in water only twenty fathoms deep.

At noon on 9 March *Pintado* set course for lifeguard and a few minutes later received instructions from CTF 71 to proceed to Fremantle on completion of the lifeguard on the tenth. *Caiman* left for other duty, and at sunset *Pintado* was out of her area, moving toward the lifeguard station.

A strong APR signal at 165 mc was picked up during midevening, believed to be a radar station on Mangkai Island in the Anambar group twenty miles southeast of us. The contact remained quite strong until suddenly, just before midnight, the operator shut his set off.

While en route to lifeguard station we received notice that the air strike on Singapore had been delayed because of bad weather, but that the strike would hit Kuala Lumpur instead. *Pintado* was directed to remain on lifeguard station until further notice. We were on station at daylight on 10 March to conduct a surface patrol.

After sunrise *Sea Robin* was sighted to the east. We closed and exchanged visual signals. She then departed northward. That location was becoming like Grand Central Station, what with so many U.S. submarines hanging around and no Jap ships to sink.

Midafternoon, the eleventh, a sail was sighted to southwest, so out of boredom the skipper decided to investigate. *Pintado* went to battle stations surface, manning the deck gun and the 20-mm guns.

The sailboat was crewed by three very friendly natives who had more than enough fishing gear all over their deck to establish that they really were only fishermen. We had hoisted our colors prior to closing the sailboat, and as we came alongside, the fishermen pointed to the colors and cheered. We gave them some rice, cigarettes, and matches, took a series of pictures of the boat, and resumed our patrol.

Just before sunset *Pintado* received information that the air strike on Singapore would take place at 1000 on the twelfth. We were directed to proceed to Fremantle after dark on 12 March. On the way we were to conduct a reconnaissance of the anchorages around Great Masalembo Island in the Java Sea.

On the surface at our lifeguard station we heard nothing concerning any services needed of *Pintado*. We were glad not to be needed, although inactivity was more and more tiresome. Then at sunset we headed for Fremantle, by way of Karimata Strait, the Java Sea, Lombok Strait, and the Indian Ocean.

On patrol station and in lifeguard duty *Pintado* had traveled 4,100 nautical miles. Our trip to Fremantle would add another 3,125 miles before the end of the patrol.

13 March   Approaching Karimata Strait from the northwest, before noon, we sighted the peaks on Seroetoe Island and Karimata Island by high periscope fifty miles away. An hour later *Pintado* submerged to enter those shallow waters undetected. After sunset we surfaced twelve miles west of Seroetoe Island and commenced transit of Karimata at best speed on three engines, giving us seventeen knots in the calm sea.

During the evening we made SJ radar contact with a craft at 6,050 yards. In the moonlight we could see that it was a submarine. Her radar was of a frequency that identified her as either British or Dutch, and although we had received no information that we should expect a friendly sub there, they seemed to consider us friendly. We didn't want to use our light to challenge, and her radar couldn't respond to our SJ signals. What to do? We turned our stern to her as she continued her course and speed toward the South China Sea. There was no doubt that they could see us and that they had continuous radar contact with *Pintado*. It was a most uncomfortable situation, in the narrowest and shallowest part of the strait. Later that night, interpreting the radio traffic, we decided that our sub contact was probably HMS *Telemachus*.

14 March   *Pintado* completed transit of Karimata as day broke and set an easterly course through the Java Sea, continuing the three-engine speed to get out of the constrained waters as quickly as possible. Midafternoon brought an aircraft of the Pete type to the north at about five miles, so we submerged. As we were going down the SD radar reported the contact. After forty-five minutes we surfaced to continue the run eastward.

Great Masalembo Island was picked up near midnight, 45,500 yards to the east. *Pintado* moved in to investigate the anchorage reported there.

15 March At midnight the SJ radar reported interference similar to radar transmissions coming from the direction of Great Masalembo. We cruised around the island, six miles offshore, investigating its western, southern, and eastern sides in rough weather and heavy rainstorms, and closed the anchorage near Raas Village to 7,250 yards.

Visually we could see nothing beyond a few hundred yards because of the heavy rain. Frequent lightning flashes spoiled all dark adaptation. We saw no evidence of any ships on our radar.

After three hours of probing, the SJ radar reported contact with a small vessel at 4,750 yards. Strong radar interference came from that direction. Then, another contact of about the same characteristics was picked up at 10,000 yards, and we were running east at high speed to avoid what we thought might be antisubmarine patrol boats. The water was only fifteen fathoms deep, and we didn't want to submerge unless that was our only way to avoid them.

At 0310 the skipper decided that we had spent enough time at Great Masalembo. Patrol boats were roaming around, and the weather wasn't favorable for visual observation. We didn't want to wait for improved weather, so he directed me to set course for Lombok Strait, continuing at three-engine speed, planning to go through during the next night.

The midafternoon bridge lookouts sighted the mountains on Lombok sixty-five miles to the south; then, a few minutes later, Bali Peak was seen to the right of Lombok at seventy-five miles. *Pintado* was speeding south to pass between them.

The high periscope then sighted a mast to the southwest that looked like the mast of a patrol boat, possibly a Jap patrol out of Lombok Strait. *Pintado* submerged to investigate, but after two hours the boat was identified as a native sailboat, so we surfaced to continue toward the strait and entered it just after dark.

16 March Our passage through Lombok Strait was completed after midnight. Robbie set course for Fremantle. He was practicing his hand at navigation on this leg of our journey. The lights on both Bali and Lombok were inviting. Relaxing on the cigarette deck, the skipper and I talked of visiting Bali sometime in the future.

There was no Japanese opposition to our passage and no APR evidence of radar in the vicinity of the strait, so much of the patrol was spent on the surface; it was almost like peacetime maneuvers. The patrol had been very disappointing. We saw no enemy ships to attack, which added more weight to my decision to go to graduate school; submarine involvement in the war was becoming less and less productive.

My final combat patrol was about to end. I had come through the war safely, but so many friends had been lost. I recalled with sadness those *Sculpin* shipmates; some, we heard, were in Japanese prison camps. Who were the survivors? Then there was Condé Raguet, best man in my wedding. I tried to keep them out of my thoughts with anticipation of new experiences in graduate school and being with my wife and son, away from the grim realities of war.

Pintado remained on the surface, moving south at fifteen knots, and during the evening sent an arrival message to CTF 71, stating a desire to meet the escort off Fremantle at 0600 on 20 March.

17–19 March   En route from Lombok Strait to Fremantle we sighted several U.S. submarines in the distance and experienced SJ radar interference from others too far away to be sighted. Those waters were also alive with U.S. submarines.

I was again able to have flying fish for breakfast. We were in smooth seas with beautiful weather. The crew enjoyed going to the cigarette deck for relaxation, to talk, and to smoke. There was the welcome feeling of tension released, with danger less threatening.

The usual lists of repairs, supplies, spare parts, and other preparations for going into refit were being readied. Speculation centered on what decision would be made by the higher-ups regarding *Pintado*'s squeaky port shaft. The skipper was polishing up his patrol report to be able to deliver it as we tied up in Fremantle. We knew that he would be relieved of command and expected, from indications in the radio traffic, that I would also be leaving the boat after we got to port. Chick's relief, a radio message told us, would be my friend and academy classmate Monty McCormick, and I eagerly looked forward to seeing him. I couldn't help a feeling of envy, because for a time I had been led to believe that I might get command of *Pintado* after her fourth patrol. Here I was completing the fourth as exec, and Monty was getting the command.

During the course of the eleven war patrols I had made, there was one unusual distinction which we talked about in the wardroom: I had circumnavigated the continent of Australia. How many other submariners, or other U.S. Navy men, for that matter, could say the same? Nine of my patrols received the Submarine Combat pin, six in *Sculpin* and three in *Pintado*.

20 March   The escort met *Pintado* on time and we proceeded into port. Activities were almost like peacetime in Pearl Harbor. We were moored at 0800 and ready to turn the boat over to a relief crew.

A gold-braided greeting party welcomed us with cases of fresh fruit and tubs of ice cream. Among the greeters was classmate Paul Glenn, who reported aboard as relief crew commander. We had repair matters to discuss and personal experiences to talk over.

In his patrol report the skipper made the following remarks:

> The performance of duty of the officers and men was of the highest order. In spite of the lack of contacts with the enemy, morale was excellent and everyone was on his toes, hoping for a chance to meet the enemy.

The Submarine Division 301 relief crew took over the boat, classmate Paul Glenn was relief captain, and the ship's company went to the rest camp at the Ocean Beach Hotel. Chick and I were both put up at the captains' rest home, Birdwood, in a pleasant residential section of Perth. I was classed as a prospective commanding officer by the local submarine authorities. There still was no official word about my graduate school orders.

The hostess and general manager of Birdwood was a personable young Australian woman named Gwen Plaistow. She was ready to play tennis, picnic, go swimming, ride horses, arrange parties, and generally assist in all recreational activities, participating enthusiastically in whatever was undertaken.

21 March–3 April   Back at the sub base on the twenty-first, cleaning up final paperwork and getting ready to leave the ship, I was notified that Jake Plummer, '40, would relieve me. Chick's relief was confirmed to be Monty McCormick. The ceremony was set for 1000 on 4 April. The crew would be brought back to the ship for the formalities of the change of command.

Jake came aboard to see me, look over the boat, learn what he could, and to invite me to dinner at his home. He had married an Australian woman.

Patrol Summary

Number of enlisted men on board	79
Number qualified, start patrol	47
Number qualified, end patrol	63
Number unqualified making first patrol	9
Number advanced in rating	12

Nautical miles covered:

Brisbane to Darwin		2,875 miles
Darwin to area		2,475 miles
In area		4,100 miles
Area to Fremantle		3,125 miles
	Total	12,575 miles

Fuel used: 145,427 gallons (11.6 gal./mi.)

Duration:

Brisbane to Darwin		9 days
In Darwin		1 day
Darwin to area		8 days
In area		27 days
Lifeguard		5 days
Submerged		3 days
Area to Fremantle		8 days
	Total	53 days

Birdwood days were filled with mostly outdoor activity: tennis, swimming at the beach, picnics, horseback riding, and enjoying the great weather.

Herb did us proud with a ship's farewell party. I was overwhelmed by the outpouring of brotherhood and heartfelt camaraderie. The crew had taken up a collection and presented Chick with a beautiful silver cocktail set. I was given an elegant silver tea set on a large silver tray, engraved: "Presented to Lt. Comdr. Mendenhall, from a grateful crew, 1945." The party didn't break up until 0200, with tears in the eyes of many, including mine, when we left the ballroom.

On 1 April Chick and I hosted a dinner at Birdwood for the *Pintado* officers. Gwen Plaistow planned and executed everything handsomely: thick, tender steaks, and chocolate soufflé for dessert, washed down with many glasses of Australian champagne. Toasts went around and around the table, and special toasts were made to the Marines whose invasion of Okinawa was just announced on the radio.

On 3 April, while waiting for paperwork to be done at the sub base, I learned that my friend Royal Navy Commander Tony Miers was stationed in Fremantle. I telephoned him, went to see him in his office, and we had a long talk during lunch at the officers' club. We met for lunch several times and I had dinner in his home and met his Australian wife.

4 April   The change-of-command ceremony went off smoothly with Commodore S. P. Moseley, '25, officiating. A crowd of staff officers and other interested officers and civilians watched. I was especially pleased to see my longtime Aussie friend Bob Watson and Tony Miers among those observing, as was Marge Plummer, Jake's wife.

After much handshaking and many good-byes, Chick and I left the ship. So ended a complex phase of my life. I couldn't say that I was not pleased to see the end of the epoch with Chick. He had his ego, could be temperamental, secretive, and hard for me to understand; and he had a sharp tongue, lashing out at inconsequential things. Frequently I had found myself defending other officers and crewmen that he had found fault with, but I had learned to overlook, be thick skinned, and compromise. On the other hand, I had a deep attachment to my ship and to my shipmates. We had been through much together. My eternal optimism, ingrained respect for the Navy and my ship, and deference to authority pulled me through.

I went immediately to ComSubDiv 301 and reported for temporary duty as a relief captain, and was advised that my first job would be as refit captain of *Blackfin,* due to arrive on 9 April. My sub school classmate Bill Kitch, '38, was captain of *Blackfin.* Another friend, Johnny Haines, '38, was PCOing with Bill.

From Fremantle to California (5 April–7 May 1945)

5–24 April   The commodore advised me to take it easy until *Blackfin* came in for refit, so I involved myself in recreation and social activity: tennis, picnics, beach parties, horseback riding, and frequently seeing Bob and Olive Watson. Tom Dabney, '36, captain of *Guitarro,* Norm Gage, '35, and Gwen Plaistow were continually promoting some activity with our Australian friends.

I volunteered to take Blish Hills, '33, and Chick to the airport to catch their plane east on the seventh. The plane was scheduled to leave at 0600, so I borrowed an alarm clock from Gwen and set it for 0430. A couple of subs had gotten in from patrol and would be having a big arrival celebration, added to the fact that Blish and Chick were going home. It was a noisy night at Birdwood: plenty of wine, women, and song.

Waking Blish and Chick was difficult. They had gotten to bed at 0400. I had arranged transportation to pick us up but it failed to arrive, so I got on the telephone. We finally reached the airport with only fifteen minutes to spare, and I poured them on the plane, anticipating that I would be catching that plane in a few weeks.

Blackfin came in as scheduled on the ninth, I relieved Bill Kitch as commanding officer, and the relief crew went to work. The regular crew was scheduled to come back to the ship on the twenty-fifth. The ship was in good shape, so there wasn't much to accomplish except routine maintenance. On that same day my orders to graduate school arrived in the *Pintado* mail: I was to be released when my current duty was completed and proceed home and report to the Submarine Administrative Office at Mare Island, California. After temporary duty at Mare Island I would go on to Annapolis and report to the graduate school on 30 July.

I took the orders to headquarters and began negotiations to see when I could break away. The commodore assured me that I would be released as soon as the *Blackfin* refit was completed. News about my orders traveled all over the base in short order, and I was congratulated at every turn. Brooks Harrell, '32, said, "You are a mighty lucky man." At dinner Harry Dodge, '30, said, "All those not jealous of Mendy hold up your right hand." Not a hand went up. I felt more and more fortunate.

Pintado's departure was set for 15 April. I had lunch on board several times with Paul Glenn to answer questions and help him with problems. The decision concerning the future of *Pintado* was that she would go to Pearl Harbor for more expert inspections and a ruling as to what would be done to correct the squeal in the port shaft.

News of President Roosevelt's death on the fourteenth had a heavy impact on the Australians. He seemed to be even more revered in Australia than in the United States. Australian and U.S. colors were at half-mast everywhere in Perth and Fremantle.

The good news came from Germany. The war was about over there. Military effort could now be concentrated on defeating Japan.

While working on *Blackfin* I was surprised to be told that Paul Glenn had permanently relieved Monty McCormick of his *Pintado* command.

The official rationalization was that Paul was more on top of the squealing shaft problem and would be the better one to take the boat back for repair. Monty was to get a combat-ready command.

On the fifteenth I was on board to shake hands with my *Pintado* ship-mates, wish them luck, and later watch them depart. My eyes were wet as they threw off the lines and headed out the channel.*

On the nineteenth the local navy people were in a state of shock. Monty McCormick had been killed in an airplane crash while on his way to another assignment. I felt badly that we had both been so occupied with our personal activities that I hadn't seen much of him. Funeral services were held on the twenty-first, with burial in the Karrakatta Cemetery. I felt a deep commitment to be there, not only because of our personal friendship, but also because I thought I was the only '39 classmate in the area.

On the twenty-second, after verifying work progress on *Blackfin*, I convinced the division commander that the refit was going so well that he could cut one day off it. The regular crew wasn't too happy over that news, and Bill jokingly threatened to cut my ears off. So, the regular crew came back on the twenty-fourth instead of the twenty-fifth, and I was detached.

On the twenty-fifth Bob Watson drove me to the airport to catch the plane heading for home. A commercial flight took me to Melbourne, where I spent the night, then the next day I took another commercial flight to Brisbane. In Brisbane I was told that there was a waiting list of several days for a military flight east to Hawaii. That gave me the opportunity to say good-bye to friends in Brisbane.

30 April–7 May   On the thirtieth I left on a military DC-3—bucket seats, no heat, parachutes strapped on—hitching my way across the Pacific.

One officer passenger, a navy lieutenant whose name I didn't remember, barely made the plane; he sat next to me, saying that he had been farewell partying all night. He dozed off, then waked to complain of a terrible headache. There was no aspirin on the plane. Later, when the plane made a scheduled fuel stop of twenty minutes at Townsville, Australia, the lieutenant made a fast trip to operations, returning with aspirin. As we flew on toward Milne Bay, New Guinea, where we were to make another

Pintado made two more lifeguard patrols off Japan. She was decommissioned 6 March 1946 and was finally struck from the Naval Vessel Register 1 March 1967, having served twenty-three years and two months.

short stop, he decided to take a nap on the pile of mailbags in front of us.

A couple of hours later, when I got up to walk around and give my cramped muscles a stretch, I noticed that the lieutenant appeared very quiet and his face was gray. One of the passengers was a navy doctor, so I asked him to look at the lieutenant. The doctor announced that the man was dead. Our pilot came back to assess the situation, and when we arrived at Milne Bay a military ambulance was waiting to remove the body.

From Milne Bay we flew on to Los Negros, Manus Island. There I was informed that I might have to wait for several days, as there was a big backlog of passengers ahead of me. On 1 May I did some sightseeing around the island in a borrowed jeep. That night I met several flight crews at the officers' club. The pilot of a flying boat scheduled to leave for Hawaii the next morning asked me if I would mind flying as a member of his crew. I jumped at the proposal.

We left the next day, stopped at Johnston Island to refuel, and arrived at Kaneohe, Oahu, on 2 May (west longitude) at 1600. Several times during the flight I piloted the plane for an hour or so from the co-pilot's seat.

At the Naval District transportation office I was told that there was a long waiting list for transportation to the West Coast, so I settled in at the sub base BOQ and made the rounds of friends on the base and in Honolulu.* On the sixth my wait was over and I left on a navy passenger plane, arriving at the Naval Air Station, Alameda, California, at 0800 on 7 May 1945.

I had begun my wartime submarine service in Manila Bay on 8 December 1941 as an ensign. It ended three and a half years later on the West Coast as a lieutenant commander. From being the most junior officer on board I had progressed up the ladder to the position of waiting for an opening to command a submarine. But the war was essentially over as far as submarines were concerned, and I was moving on to new challenges.

---

*During the wait, news was released that *Lagarto* was overdue and presumed lost. My distant cousin, Bill Mendenhall, '42, was serving in that submarine. Another tragic loss. Bill was one of the top men in his class. I had stopped to see him at the Naval Academy after I had finished sub school and was on my way to *Sculpin,* and he later told me that my enthusiasm for submarines was the reason he went into that specialty. Thus I felt both responsible and dejected at the news.

APPENDIX I

Roster of the *Sculpin*

	Rate	Patrols
Alderman, Merle E.	TM2	1, 2, 3, 4, 5, 6
Allen, John N.	LT	8, 9
Alvis, Frank R.	LTJG	4, 5, 6, 7, 8
Anctil, Alphonse J.	F1	6, 7
* Anderson, Edward N.	SC2	7, 8, 9
Anderson, Robert H.	SC2	1, 2, 3, 4, 5, 6
Apostol, Eugenio	OC1	5, 6, 7, 8, 9
Arnath, Eugene	S2	8, 9
Arthur, Lewis D.	TM3	1, 2
Austin, Ralph S.	MoMM2	6, 7, 8
#Bachofer, Paul A.	CMM	1, 2, 3, 4, 5, 6, 7
Baglien, J. W.	RM3	9
* Baker, Cecil E.	F1	8, 9
* Baker, Joseph N., Jr.	F1	8, 9
#Baldwin, Ernest S.	CMM	1, 2, 3, 4, 5, 6, 7
Barrera, M.	CK1	9
Bartlett, George F.	F1	4, 5, 6
Beidleman, E. M., Jr.	RT2	9
Bentsen, F. G.	S2	9
Berkley, Harold P.	FC2	5
Berry, Warren R.	TM1	7, 8, 9
Best, Dan Otto	MM2	1, 2, 3, 4, 5
Blum, Arthur G.	EM3	7, 8, 9
Bontier, A. M.	LT	7
Boos, Guy H.	TM1	1, 2, 3, 4, 5, 6
Bosse, Joseph E. R.	S1	8, 9
Boyd, Cleo L. C.	Matt1	1, 2, 3, 4
Brannum, B. C.	F1	9
Brennan, Thomas H.	EM3	4

*Recovered from Japanese prison camps
#Plank-owner

	Rate	Patrols
* Brown, George E., Jr.	LT	5, 6, 7, 8, 9
Brown, Thomas V.	S2	7, 8, 9
Brzezinski, Stanley C.	AS	4, 5, 6
Bur, George A.	S2	1, 2
Carlson, Lloyd E.	S1	1
Carawan, Ottis, Jr.	MoMM1	1, 2, 3, 4, 5, 6, 7
Carter, R. W.	S2	9
#Caserio, Joseph E.	CGM	1, 2, 3, 4, 5, 6, 7
Chappell, Lucius H.	CDR	1, 2, 3, 4, 5, 6, 7, 8
Cheney, George R., Jr.	MoMM2	1, 2, 3, 4, 5, 6
Clements, Kenneth B.	MoMM2	4, 5, 6, 7, 8, 9
Coleman, Charles S.	MoMM1	6, 7, 8, 9
Connaway, Frederick	CDR	9
Connors, Jack T.	EM1	1, 2, 3, 4, 5, 6, 7, 8
* Cooper, Billie M.	QM2	8, 9
Coulter, Alvin W.	QM3	5, 6, 7
Coward, Robert M.	EM1	7
Cox, George H.	S2	4, 5, 6
Cox, Gordon C.	S2	1, 2
Creighton, Adolph R.	S2	4, 5, 6, 7
Cromwell, J. P.	CAPT	9
Crown, Robert P.	SM3	4, 5, 6
Dawes, Arthur P.	CTM	4, 5, 6
Daylong, James E.	MoMM2	4, 5, 6, 7, 8, 9
#DeArmond, Chesley A.	CMoMM	1, 2, 3, 4, 5, 6, 7
Defrees, Joseph R.	LT	7, 8, 9
DeLisle, Maurice S.	MM3	8, 9
DeMonge, Robert L.	TM1	1, 2, 3, 4, 5, 6, 7, 8
Dickerson, Arthur W.	F1	1, 2, 3, 4
Diederich, D. L.	EM3	9
Dolan, Philip	TM3	3, 4, 5, 6
Donaldson, John W.	CTM	1, 2, 3, 4, 5, 6, 7
Dovey, Henry N.	RT2	7, 8
Dowell, William E.	TM1	1, 2, 3
#Dowen, Norman H.	CEM	1, 2, 3
#Durdle, George F.	MM1	1
#Dyboski, Frank J.	CEM	1, 2, 3, 4, 5, 6
Elliott, Henry L.	MM3	4, 5, 6, 7, 8, 9
Embury, G. R.	LTJG	7, 8, 9

*Recovered from Japanese prison camps
#Plank-owner

	Rate	Patrols
Emmons, William E.	SC2	5, 6
* Eskildsen, L. A.	RM3	9
Fedchin, Alexis, Jr.	S1	7
Ferguson, Joe C.	RM1	8
Ferkovich, Leroy S.	EM3	1, 2, 3, 4, 5, 6
Fiedler, W. M.	ENS	9
Fishley, William N.	S2	7
Freitag, Charles F., Jr.	FC3	5
Gabrunas, Philip J.	CMoMM	1, 2, 3, 4, 5, 6, 7, 8, 9
Galantin, I. J.	LCDR	7
Gamel, J. W.	ENS	9
Gardella, Silvio J.	FC3	6, 7
Goldsmith, Charles	ENS	9
Goorabian, G.	S1	9
* Gorman, M. T.	S1	9
Grant, Howard P.	S2	1, 2, 3
Guillot, Alexander B.	F1	8, 9
Gunnett, Clayton E.	F3	1
Hager, Raymond K.	F2	1, 2, 3, 4, 5, 6
Harper, James Q.	TM3	1, 2, 3, 4, 5, 6, 7, 8, 9
Harrison, James R.	F3	5, 6, 7
* Haverland, William H.	CMoMM	6, 7, 8, 9
Hemphill, Richard E.	CMM	1, 2, 3, 4, 5, 6, 7, 8, 9
Henderson, Charles M.	LT	1, 2, 3, 4, 5, 6
Hess, John B.	LT	2, 3
Hlavacek, Joseph F.	F1	1, 2
Holland, Erwin R.	MoMM1	2, 3, 4, 5, 6, 7, 8, 9
Hollenbach, John J.	MM1	2, 3, 4, 5, 6, 7
Hughes, Duncan G.	CCStd	1, 2, 3, 4, 5, 6
Ingles, William	TM3	3, 4, 5
Jay, Arthur L.	QM1	1, 2, 3, 4
* Johnson, Gordon E.	MoMM1	7, 8, 9
Jones, Henry B.	MM2	3
Kanocz, Steve	EM3	5, 6, 7, 8, 9
* Keller, E. K. F.	S2	9
Kennon, J. B., Jr.	SC3	9
Koza, Rudolph S.	S2	5, 6
Laman, Harold D.	MoMM2	2, 3, 4, 5, 6, 7, 8, 9
Langley, William S.	Y1	1, 2, 3

*Recovered from Japanese prison camps

	Rate	Patrols
#LaRose, Joseph, Jr.	MM1	1, 2
Larson, Leonard P.	TM3	1, 2, 3, 4, 5, 6
Lawton, C. J.	F1	9
Lebow, J. T.	RM2	5, 6, 7
Lee, Hubert E.	EM2	8
Lennox, William R.	LT	1
Lipthrott, William H.	F1	4, 5
Logan, William J.	RM1	1, 2, 3, 4, 5, 6, 7
Ludwig, John K.	RM2	1
Maguire, Stanley W.	EM2	7, 8, 9
Mancuso, Carl J.	S2	7
Mann, Bobby	TM2	8
Marcus, Grover W.	RM3	7, 8, 9
Martin, Merlin G.	FC3	8, 9
Matthews, Clair T.	S1	1, 2, 3, 4
McAfee, Harold	MM1	7
McCartney, James W.	S1	7, 8, 9
McTavish, J. F.	S1	9
Mendenhall, Corwin G.	LT	1, 2, 3, 4, 5, 6, 7
* Milbourn, Harry S., Jr.	MM3	5, 6, 7, 8, 9
Miller, Charles E.	TM3	8, 9
Miller, Cleland D.	PhM1	1, 2, 3, 4, 5, 6
Mills, Emmett W.	LTJG	1, 2, 3, 4, 5, 6
Moore, Weldon E.	CSM	1, 2, 3, 4, 5, 6, 7, 8, 9
Moreton, Arnold F.	EM1	1, 2, 3, 4, 5, 6, 7, 8, 9
#Morley, John W.	TM2	1, 2, 3, 4, 5, 6
Morrilly, Robert M.	EM3	8, 9
* Murphy, P. L.	MM3	9
Murray, E. T.	SM3	9
* Murray, L. J.	MoMM1	9
Nelson, Jackson C.	F1	3
Newton, A. L.	Matt3	1, 2, 3, 4
O'Leary, Michael B.	MM1	1, 2, 3, 4
Olson, Ernest M.	TM3	1, 2, 3, 4, 5, 6, 7
Overton, John H.	MM1	4, 5
Parr, J.	RDM3	9
Partin, William H.	S1	7, 8, 9
#Pepersack, John J.	WE	1, 2, 3, 4, 5, 6

#Plank-owner
*Recovered from Japanese prison camps

	Rate	Patrols
* Peterson, J. G.	RM2	9
Peterson, Orville O.	S1	7
Pitser, Charles E.	TM2	7, 8, 9
#Powell, Richard	MM1	1, 2, 3, 4, 5, 6
Reese, Aaron W.	Y1	5, 6, 7, 8
Richmond, William S.	S2	8
* Ricketts, Edward F.	MoMM2	7, 8, 9
* Rocek, George	MoMM1	1, 2, 3, 4, 5, 6, 7, 8, 9
* Rourke, John P.	GM2	8, 9
Salava, F.	FC3	9
Sanchez, Cipriano	F2	8
Schnell, E. V.	TM3	9
Schroeder, D. E.	Y2	9
Seaman, Edward L.	S1	1, 2, 3, 4, 5, 6, 7
Shaw, Alvin	MM1	2, 3
Shirley, D. B.	SM3	7, 8, 9
Shong, Junior	S1	2, 3, 4, 5, 6
Smith, C. G., Jr.	ENS	9
Smith, Leroy H.	EM2	3, 4, 5, 6, 7, 8, 9
Stafford, Arnold O.	Y3	4
Suel, J. T.	S1	9
Surofchek, Peter J.	CRM	2, 3, 4, 5, 6
Swift, John B.	EM2	1, 2, 3, 4, 5, 6, 7, 8, 9
Tabbutt, David H.	S1	1, 2, 3, 4
Taylor, Clifford G.	RM3	7, 8, 9
Taylor, Everett L.	SC2	7, 8
Taylor, Odis S.	S1	1, 2, 3, 4
Taylor, R. H.	S1	9
* Thomas, Herbert J.	TM1	7, 8, 9
Thomas, William H.	QM1	1, 2, 3
Thompson, Clell W.	TM2	6, 7
Tigen, Bernard A.	CEM	7
* Todd, Paul A.	PhM1	7, 8, 9
* Toney, H. F.	TM3	9
Tulao, Carlos	St1	5, 6, 7, 8
# Turner, John H.	LT	1, 2, 3, 4, 5, 6
Ulmer, Julian A.	TM2	2, 3
Van Beest, Henry	S1	5, 6, 7, 8, 9
Vancil, William A., Jr.	EM3	1, 2, 3, 4, 5, 6

*Recovered from Japanese prison camps
#Plank-owner

	Rate	Patrols
Wagner, Earl A.	F3	5
Waidelich, Keith E.	SM2	1, 2, 3, 4, 5, 6, 7, 8
Warren, Ellis E.	EM2	1, 2, 3, 4, 5, 6, 7, 8, 9
Warren, J. W.	S1	3
Weade, Clairborne H.	CTM	7, 8, 9
Welsh, William H.	S1	8, 9
White, Duane J.	MoMM2	7, 8, 9
Williams, James H.	Y3	1, 2, 3, 4, 5, 6
Wooden, Louis E.	S1	7
Wright, E.	EM3	9
* Wyatt, Robert O.	GM2	1, 2, 3, 4, 5, 6, 7, 8, 9
Zimmerman, Elmer T.	EM1	1, 2, 3, 4, 5, 6
Zwally, William R.	SC2	1, 2, 3, 4

*Recovered from Japanese prison camps

APPENDIX II

Roster of the *Pintado*

	Rate	Patrols
Abeita, John	S1	3, 4
#Alexander, John	MoMM1	1, 2, 3, 4, 5
#Alfaro, Edward	MoMM3	1
#Alman, Harold L.	EM3	1, 2, 3, 4
Angus, Charles R.	MoMM2	6
#Archie, Stephen G.	CEM	1, 2
Arnold, James E.	RT2	4, 5, 6
Asselin, Raymond R.	SM2	4, 5, 6
#Bailey, Eric P.	CMoMM	1, 2, 3, 4, 5, 6
#Ballou, Walter W.	F1	1, 2
#Beeson, Leslie D.	RM1	
Bell, John H.	EM1	6
Bell, Robert H.	EM2	4, 5, 6
#Bennett, Joseph R., Jr.	MoMM2	1, 2, 3
Bergenson, Walter H.	MoMM2	6
Bettencourt, Duane R.	TM3	3, 4, 5
Blair, Leon N.	CAPT	1
Blue, Joseph	StM2	5, 6
Bond, Alva B., Jr.	F1	5, 6
Bonjour, Earnest F.	LTJG	1, 2, 3, 4, 5, 6
#Bower, Edward T.	LT	
Branen, Melvin R.	S1	3, 4, 5
#Brantner, Harold V.	CM	1, 2, 3
Brown, Raymond R.	SC3	2, 3
Budd, Romondt	CDR	6
Burchett, Homer	S1	3
#Burns, William W.	EM1	1, 2
Buseman, Robert P.	CPhM	6
Cali, Thomas R.	PhM1	
Casey, John	CTM	

#Plank-owner

	Rate	Patrols
Chavis, James J.	RM3	2, 3, 4
#Clarey, Bernard A.	CDR	1, 2, 3, 4
#Clarke, Morton A.	RT1	1, 2, 3, 4, 5
Cooke, Franklin E.	QM2	4, 5, 6
Coon, John W.	COX	1, 2, 3, 4, 5, 6
Courtney, John A.	Y2	5, 6
#Crosier, James T.	EM1	1, 2, 3
#Davis, Donald	MoMM1	
#Davis, Kenneth E.	MoMM2	1, 2, 3, 4, 5, 6
Davison, Nolan	F1	2, 3, 4, 5, 6
#Denningham, John S.	CPhM	1, 2, 3, 4
DeVey, Robert F.	F1	4, 5, 6
Dineen, Timothy J.	SC1	2, 3, 4, 5
Dings, Murton A.	QM2	1, 2, 3, 4, 5, 6
Divis, Ferdinand L.	RM3	1, 2, 3, 5, 6
#Dobrowolski, Sigmund J.	SC2	1, 2, 3, 4, 5, 6
Doherty, Daniel J.	S1	6
Drapalski, Louis C.	MoMM3	1, 2, 3, 4, 5, 6
#Earnest, Frank M.	QM1	1, 2, 3, 4, 5, 6
#Echols, Harry O.	CMoMM	1, 2, 3, 4
Edwards, Russell E.	TM1	1, 2, 3
Eksteen, Robert R.	S1	1, 2, 3
#Emerson, Raymond G.	CQM	1, 2, 3
#Farmer, Kelly C., Jr.	MoMM2	1, 2
#Ferguson, Victor L.	EM2	1, 2, 3
Fitch, Harry J.	MoMM3	4, 5
Flynn, John J.	Y1	1, 2, 3, 4
#Foley, James A.	MoMM2	1, 2
Foster, Billy G.	EM2	4, 5
#Frese, Edwin W.	LT	1, 2, 3, 4
Fulton, Howard T.	LT	6
Gallop, James B.	St3	4, 5, 6
Gann, Rufus R.	RM1	1, 2
#Gear, Robert M.	EM2	1, 2, 3
#Gervais, Edward A.	SC2	1
Girard, Edmond J.	CY	6
#Gordon, William O.	MoMM1	1, 2
Grewell, Arthur B.	CMoMM	1, 2, 3, 4, 5, 6
#Griffin, Eric L.	BM1	1, 2, 3
#Grimand, Adrien M.	TM3	1

#Plank-owner

	Rate	Patrols
#Guntrum, Edward J.	MoMM2	1, 2, 3, 4
#Gurske, Donald E.	MoMM2	1, 2, 3, 4, 5, 6
Haddix, Floyd E.	MoMM1	5, 6
Harper, James L.	S1	6
Hart, James S.	MoMM2	3, 4, 5
Hassenplug, Harrison F.	ENS	6
#Hatfield, Robert D.	FC3	1, 2, 3
Heikes, Parker E.	RT2	3
#Higgin, George	CTM	
Hill, John R.	CTM	1, 2, 3
Hoffman, Henry P.	EM1	
Hollick, Frederick	F2	3
Holloman, David K.	MoMM2	4, 5, 6
Horn, Charles E.	RT2	6
Hranitzky, Walter W.	RM1	5
#Humber, William A.	MoMM3	1, 2, 3, 4
Irvine, Donald G.	CDR	3
Ivan, Andrew	CTM	3
James, Kenneth	EM3	5
#Johnson, Isaac W.	StM2	
Kaden, Donald F.	MoMM1	5, 6
#Kaelker, Charles W.	EM1	1, 2, 3, 5, 6
#Kazma, Victor	EM3	1, 2, 3
Keemer, Guy C.	S1	6
Kelly, Donald J.	MoMM2	2, 3
Kinter, Elmer	EM1	
Knowlton, Frank	StM1	1, 2
Kramer, Edward E.	EM2	4, 5, 6
Kuhn, James H.	MoMM3	6
Kunkowski, Frank A.	RM3	5
Lahr, Marvin P.	FCS1	5, 6
Lakofka, Frank A.	TM3	2, 3, 4, 5, 6
Laux, James A.	F1	4, 5, 6
Lawrence, William H.	LCDR	2
LeBow, J. T.	RM1	6
Lennon, John J., Jr.	LTJG	4, 5, 6
Lewis, John F.	SC3	2, 3, 4, 5
Lewter, Freddie R.	S1	5, 6
Lozano, George	MoMM3	3, 4, 5, 6
#Lutack, George A.	RM3	

#Plank-owner

	Rate	Patrols
Lyons, Philip L.	TM3	2, 3, 4, 5, 6
Maguire, John R.	MoMM3	1, 2, 3
#Mandak, Paul	F1	1
Mann, Charles F.	F2	2, 3
#Manson, Robert T.	SC3	1
Maren, Martin S.	TM3	6
Mathews, Thomas W.	TM2	4, 5, 6
Matthews, John M., Jr.	TM2	2
May, Gabriel C.	S1	5, 6
McCallum, Clarence J.	GM3	2, 3, 4, 5, 6
McCarthy, Hadley N.	S1	5, 6
McNeilly, Robert E.	S1	5, 6
#Mendenhall, Corwin G.	LCDR	1, 2, 3, 4
Mills, Emmett W.	LT	6
Minor, George C.	F1	3, 4, 5, 6
Mitchell, Gerald E.	LT	1, 2, 3, 4, 5, 6
#Morris, George C.	CRM	1, 2, 3, 4
#Morse, Douglas T.	LT	1, 2
#Murray, George M.	LT	3, 4, 5, 6
Nelson, Fred	CTM	4, 5, 6
Newsum, Hemon E.	S1	5, 6
Noble, Russell C.	CSM	
Ondell, Earl W.	S1	3
Ontko, Daniel G.	PhM2	5, 6
#Pettibone, Gerry E.	LTJG	1, 2, 3
Peterson, Gordon V.	EM2	4, 5, 6
Phillips, Jack D.	S1	3
Peinkowski, Edmund W.	TM3	6
#Poole, Russell R.	RT3	1, 2, 3, 4, 5, 6
#Powers, Frederick W.	EM3	1, 2, 3, 4
#Prosser, Robert A.	TM1	1
Pugh, Harold E.	TM2	4, 5, 6
#Randolph, R. V.	GM2	
Reed, Frank C.	MoMM1	4, 5
#Reedy, James J.	RM1	1, 2, 3, 4, 5, 6
#Regiec, Walter	TM1	1, 2, 3, 4, 5, 6
Rehtmeyer, Robert T.	CMoMM	
Reynolds, Lewis J.	CEM	6
Ripley, Charles B.	EM3	5, 6
Ritter, Andrew J.	TM2	4, 5

#Plank-owner

	Rate	Patrols
#Robar, Melvin A.	MoMM1	1
Robinson, Edward W.	S1	2
Robinson, Samuel J.	LT	1, 2, 3, 4, 5, 6
Rock, Homer J.	MoMM3	2, 3, 4, 5, 6
#Russell, Howard C.	TM2	1
#Ryan, Joseph E.	CMoMM	1, 2
#Sanders, Aubrey J.	EM1	1, 2, 3, 4, 5
#Schnurr, Henry B.	TM1	1, 2
Scruggs, Willie H.	Ck1	3
Shaffer, Charles	MoMM1	
#Shanks, Glenn W.	QM3	1, 2, 3
#Sheehy, Richard M.	S1	1
Shelhammer, Charles W.	RM2	4, 5, 6
#Shorey, Burley V.	S1	1
#Shular, Howard E.	QM3	1
#Simpson, Jack W.	S2	
Simpson, James L.	StM1	4, 5, 6
#Singleton, John	StM1	1, 2, 3
#Sisti, Benjamin	MoMM1	1, 2, 3, 4
Smith, Clarence E.	TM2	1, 2, 3, 4, 5, 6
Smith, Edward P.	S1	5, 6
Smith, James R.	TME3	2, 3, 4, 5, 6
Smolewski, Mitchell J. J.	F1	6
Soderstrom, John T.	SC1	6
Spiess, Edward A.	F1	3, 4, 5, 6
Steck, Earl N., Jr.	TM2	3, 4, 5, 6
Stevenson, Richard L.	EM2	2, 3, 4, 5, 6
Stewart, James J.	EM3	5, 6
Stooke, Charles W., Jr.	S1	2, 3
Sullivan, Emiel L.	GM1	1, 2, 3, 4
#Thompson, William R.	TM3	1, 2, 3
Thornton, Herbert D.	LT	4, 5
#Tibbetts, Kenneth M.	GM2	1, 2, 3, 4, 5, 6
Velez, Lester J.	Bkr1	1, 2
Walker, Robert F.	LTJG	4, 5, 6
#Walters, Floyd E.	CEM	1, 2, 3, 4
#Warren, Robert K.	TM2	1, 2, 3
Weilminister, Frederick	F1	5, 6
#Weiss, Joseph M.	MoMM1	1, 2, 3
West, James D.	MoMM1	3, 4, 5, 6

#Plank-owner

	Rate	Patrols
Williams, Alexander W.	MoMM3	2, 3, 4, 5, 6
#Williams, Charles	MoMM3	1, 2, 3
Windsor, William P.	EM2	4, 5, 6
#Wood, Raymond R.	TM3	1, 2, 3
Woodard, Robert L.	F1	5, 6
Yersick, Paul A.	MoMM1	4, 5, 6
#Zeitlin, Sigmund P.	Y2	

#Plank-owner

APPENDIX III

The Last Engagement of the USS *Sculpin*

(As orally related by Lieutenant G. E. Brown, USNR)

On the night of 18 November we had tracked a large convoy for some eight hours—at dawn we dove and went in to make a submerged attack. Just as we were in position to shoot, the enemy (consisting of one freighter, five destroyers, and a light cruiser) either spotted us or zigged normally. At any rate, they turned directly on us and came over us. The captain ordered me to "take her down," thus using negative tank, which made noise. I believe this outfit heard the *Sculpin* or were alerted, for the whole convoy speeded up. However, they did not drop any depth charges at this time. We stayed deep for an hour, and at 0730 Captain Cromwell and Commander Connaway decided that because of the large escort this Maru was very important and we must go after it; therefore he ordered us to surface, which we did. However, we evidently did not take a good enough look, for the Japs had left a "sleeper" [a large flotilla leader destroyer] which was about 6,000 yards from us when we surfaced. We got the submarine down again by the time he came over to drop his first string. The damage received by the first depth charges was not unusual but disconcerting. An exhaust valve in the after engine room was ruptured and we started taking water aft. Several sea valves were jarred off their seats and could not be made tight.

After about an hour, at 0830, he came over again, this time directly over us, and dropped eighteen charges. The hands of the depth gauge fell off in front of my face. The pressure gauges near the diving station commenced flooding, and there was other minor damage about the ship. The weather conditions were perfect for a destroyer, sound and echo ranging highly effective. There was a straight line on the bathythermograph down to 300 feet; our evasion tactics were next to useless on that day.

At 0930 he came over again and dropped a string. This added more minor damage, but we still had the submarine under control, in spite of the large up angle (thirteen degrees or more) and much weight in the boat. By now it was taking 100 or 110 turns [of the propellers] to maintain depth. At this time we heard a rainsquall in the distance and headed for it. With the aid of this surface disturbance we shook the destroyer for over half an hour. At this time we decided to pump bilges and endeavor to regain diving trim. However, neither the drain nor the trim pump would take suction. Captain Connaway then had me relieved from diving station so that I could inspect and report damage throughout the boat. Upon inspection I found the after engine room flooded to such an extent that I believed it unwise to attempt to place a bubble in number 4 MBT [main ballast tank] (which would have aided the trim considerably) because the flow of water forward might short main motor leads. We decided to bail the water forward to another compartment until we could trim the ship without endangering main motors.

While we were rounding up a bucket brigade the temporary diving officer broached the ship. However, no one could be blamed for this as the depth gauge was stuck at 170 feet, and, as I mentioned before, the pressure gauges around the diving station were all flooded out. When we stuck our nose out, the destroyer saw us and came over again, dropping another string which tore our radio transmitter from the bulkhead and smashed the receiver, also smashing light bulbs and severely damaging outboard vents in both torpedo rooms. We momentarily lost depth control and were down more than 500 feet before regaining control. The steering mechanism had been damaged to such an extent that it was next to impossible for exhausted men to operate the wheel in hand power. At this time our evasion tactics were about at a standstill. The heat in the boat was terrific; having made a full power run the previous night, all the engine heat had been sealed in the boat with us. Having vented negative two or three times and having so many leaks, the pressure in the boat was over five inches. However, we decided to try and hold out for one more string, which we received at about 1230. At that time the forward and after torpedo rooms reported cracks around the torpedo tubes. The sound heads were driven up into the boat, shearing the holding-down clamps. Thus we were without "ears." It required 170 turns to maintain depth, the battery was about shot, and it was six hours till sundown, so Commander Connaway decided to surface and fight it out with the destroyer, and while the gun crew was engaging the destroyer the rest of the crew who wished could abandon ship.

Commander Connaway had been so calm, resourceful, and persevering during the five hours of severe depth charge that it was hard for the crew to realize that the situation was as serious as it was. Commander Connaway said that it was a heartbreaking decision to have to make, but that he realized that the Sculpin could not take another string of depth charges. Therefore, he felt he owed his crew, who had fought so well, the chance to abandon since the Sculpin was now completely shattered.

As he started up to the conning tower, he ordered me to make sure *Sculpin* was scuttled in case we lost the one-sided engagement with the destroyer. He still maintained his calm, collected, courageous manner, which inspired his crew to carry on gallantly in the face of overwhelming odds.

We surfaced about 1300; the gun crew led by Lieutenant "Joe" Defrees manned the gun and opened fire on the destroyer. Commander Connaway stood on the bridge conning the ship into the most favorable position. Lieutenant J. N. Allen was in the conning tower relaying the skipper's orders to the wheel. Lieutenant (jg) George Embury manned his radar in the conning tower and relayed fire control data to the gun.

There were at this time some men in the control room who asked what they might do. I ordered them to the torpedo room to make ready the tubes. I intended to fire a spread from the control room. However, the Japanese, with their superior fire control equipment, soon found the range and put two shells through the conning tower. These killed Lieutenant Allen and Lieutenant Embury as well as Commander Connaway on the bridge. Flying fragments also killed Lieutenant Defrees on the gun.

At this time, I considered it unwise to wait longer for scuttling operations because the next shell might damage the hydraulic system, thus making it impossible to operate the vents [to the ballast tanks].

I ordered Emergency Speed and when answered ordered Abandon Ship. I waited one minute by the clock before ordering Philip Joseph Gabrunas, CMoMM (who had gallantly elected to remain with me and man a station not normally his) to open the vents. Before ordering Gabrunas to open the vents, I informed Captain Cromwell, who was in the control room, of my intentions. He told me to go ahead, that he could not come with us for he was afraid the information he possessed might be injurious to his shipmates at sea if the Japanese made him reveal it by torture.

As I left the conning tower door, water was coming waist deep over the sill, and I am certain no one left the ship after me. I last saw Gabrunas coming up the conning tower hatch. He either became fouled in wreckage or was killed by machine-gun fire.

I collected the men in the water into one group. Those of us who were strong swimmers aided the wounded and weak swimmers.

The destroyer picked us up around 1500 and took us into Truk Atoll. There were forty-one survivors at this point (three officers and thirty-eight men). After ten days of alternate beating with clubs and questioning at Truk we were divided into two groups and embarked on two aircraft carriers for passage to Japan.

On December second the USS *Sailfish* sank one of the aircraft carriers, and as a result we lost two officers and eighteen men. George Rocek, MoMM1/c, was the sole American survivor. One officer and twenty men arrived at Ofuna, the secret intimidation and interrogation camp of the Japanese Navy.

It is also my opinion that the following named officers and men displayed outstanding valor and perseverance in the face of overwhelming odds.

Captain John Cromwell, USN, for refusing personal safety to protect his shipmates and countrymen still engaged in war and operating at sea.

Lieutenant John Nelson Allen, USN, for his courage, leadership, and devotion to duty.

Lieutenant Joseph Defrees, USN, for his courage, leadership, and devotion to duty. It was his gun crew that held the destroyer at bay during scuttling and abandoning ship.

Lieutenant (jg) George Embury, USNR, the radar officer, for outstanding courage and devotion to duty.

Ensign Max Fielder, USNR, who preferred death in his ship to capture.

Ensign Charles Goldsmith, USNR, Ensign Worth Gamel, USNR, Weldon E. Moore, CSM, USN, for their leadership, courage, and devotion to duty, both before and after capture. They were instrumental in saving many of those struggling in the water before being taken aboard the Japanese destroyer as well as a great comfort and aid to me during our trying days at Truk.

W. E. Moore, CSM, USN; H. J. Thomas, TM1/c, USN; W. R. Berry, TM1/c, USN; D. J. White, MoMM2/c, USN; R. O. Wyatt, GM2/c, USN; J. N. Baker, F1/c, USN; E. F. Ricketts, MoMM2/c, USN; H. S. Milbourn, Jr., F1/c, USN, who so gallantly manned the 3-inch gun in the face of such overwhelming odds, to keep the destroyer at bay while their shipmates abandoned and scuttled.

J. Q. Harper, TM3/c, USN; E. Arnath, S2/c, USN; Charles E. Pitser, SN3/c, USN; W. H. Partin, S1/c, USN; J. P. Rourke, GM2/c, USN; C. S. Coleman, MoMM1/c, USN; A. B. Guillot, F1/c, USN, who so gallantly manned the 20-mm and light machine guns in the face of such overwhelming odds, thus facilitating scuttling and abandoning operations.

P. J. Gabrunas, CMoMM, USN, for voluntarily manning an unassigned station and materially aiding in the scuttling of the *Sculpin*.

Undoubtedly there are others of this fine crew who carried more than their load during those difficult hours, however, it is impossible for one officer to observe the entire crew who behaved so splendidly.

Respectfully submitted,   / s / George Estabrook Brown, Jr.
                                                          Lieutenant, USNR